ENGAGE AND EVADE

Engage and Evade

HOW LATINO IMMIGRANT FAMILIES MANAGE SURVEILLANCE IN EVERYDAY LIFE

Asad L. Asad

PRINCETON UNIVERSITY PRESS

PRINCETON & OXFORD

Published by Princeton University Press
41 William Street, Princeton, New Jersey 08540
99 Banbury Road, Oxford OX2 6JX

press.princeton.edu

Library of Congress Cataloging-in-Publication Data

Names: Asad, Asad L., author.
Title: Engage and evade : how Latino immigrant families manage surveillance
    in everyday life / Asad L. Asad.
Description: Princeton : Princeton University Press, [2023] |
    Includes bibliographical references and index.
Identifiers: LCCN 2022037473 (print) | LCCN 2022037474 (ebook) |
    ISBN 9780691182285 (hardback) | ISBN 9780691249049 (ebook)
Subjects: LCSH: Emigration and immigration—Texas—Dallas County. |
    Hispanic Americans—Civil rights. | Noncitizens—Texas—Dallas County. |
    Immigrant families—Texas—Dallas County. | Surveillance detection—Texas—
    Dallas County. | BISAC: SOCIAL SCIENCE / Emigration & Immigration |
    POLITICAL SCIENCE / Public Policy / Immigration
Classification: LCC JV7100.D A73 2023 (print) | LCC JV7100.D (ebook) |
    DDC 305.868/07642811—dc23/eng/20221212
LC record available at https://lccn.loc.gov/2022037473
LC ebook record available at https://lccn.loc.gov/2022037474

British Library Cataloging-in-Publication Data is available

Editorial: Meagan Levinson and Erik Beranek
Production Editorial: Natalie Baan
Jacket Design: Katie Osborne
Production: Erin Suydam
Publicity: Kate Hensley and Kathryn Stevens
Copyeditor: Leah Caldwell

Jacket image: Janice and Nolan Braud / Alamy

This book has been composed in Miller

Printed on acid-free paper. ∞

Printed in the United States of America

10 9 8 7 6 5 4 3 2 1

For Baba and Mama, whose hopes have allowed us to live our dreams.

For Samer, whose dreams are now our hopes.

When you go through a hard period,
When everything seems to oppose you,
. . . When you feel you cannot even bear one more minute,
　　never give up!
Because it is the time and place that the course will divert!

—RUMI

CONTENTS

MY FATHER'S WALLET HOLDS a crisp piece of laminated paper. It is official-looking, off-white, and bordered by a muted green. The colors have faded slightly after more than five decades of travel, but the words on the astoundingly simple document are still clear:

THIS IS TO CERTIFY THAT
LUGMAN ASAD
HAS CLAIMED UNDER OATH TO BE
A CITIZEN OF THE U.S.
THROUGH OWN NATURALIZATION.

I discovered the document during my first year in graduate school, back in Milwaukee for Thanksgiving. My dad had left his wallet on the kitchen table. It bulged. I couldn't help but look. Credit cards, business cards, receipts—every crevice stuffed with life's usual tedium. And then this clear-edged slip of hard plastic. I was an immigration-scholar-in-training, and yet I was stumped. *Why does Baba carry around his naturalization card?*

I went to find Baba in the family room, where he was watching the evening edition of WISN12 local news. When I held the card up with a quizzical glance, he answered with a shrug: "I just feel better with it on me; it's proof that I belong in the country." Now even more curious, I dared to return to the kitchen to interrupt my mother—hard at work preparing a meal for twelve—about her own card.

"I can't believe he still has that!" She didn't look away from the lamb, onion, and rice mixture she had simmering on the stove. "I don't even know where mine is anymore."

My parents are both from the West Bank but came separately to the United States—Baba on a student visa in 1971 and Mama as a permanent resident (more commonly referred to as a green card holder) in 1968. Baba was in his first year of college at Wayne State University, struggling to keep up as much with coursework as with tuition payments. In November 1971, he took a weekend trip to nearby Milwaukee for a cousin's engagement party. He laid eyes on a young woman, petite in size but tall in charisma, and asked around about her. By April 1972, Baba and Mama had married and embarked on their new life together in Detroit.

When two people marry, the administrative and legal records that have cataloged their lives up until that point often change. Perhaps one partner updates their last name on their driver's license or passport. Or maybe both partners opt to file their taxes "jointly." For my parents, as is the case for many other immigrants, marriage also changed their relationship with the United States. Baba, who dropped out of college shortly after marrying Mama, would soon lose his student visa; he would have to either leave the country or overstay his visa and risk deportation. Now that they were married, though, Mama could sponsor Baba's application for permanent residence and preserve his right to remain—and their right to live together. Baba received his green card in the summer of 1972. "It was faster to get a green card back then," he explained. At around the same time, Mama was approaching her five-year anniversary of living in the country, one milestone marking her eligibility for citizenship. She began the process right away: "It was just the thing to do those days. Once you got to five years, you would submit the paperwork to naturalize, have your fingerprints taken, and then take your citizenship exam. After you passed, you went to court to swear in as an American citizen." She said she never worried about the process: "You only worry if you've ever been convicted of stealing, killing, or not obeying the law. None of that was on my record!" Baba went on to naturalize a few years later.

I already knew all these details, but Baba's naturalization card nonetheless continued to mystify me after I returned to Cambridge. I was used to confusion at that point in my life—after all, I was not just a graduate student but one who was studying the convoluted reality of the U.S. immigration system. I tried to shake the feeling. But I could not. My parents have been U.S. citizens for more than five decades. They hold U.S. passports, carry Wisconsin driver's licenses, and vote in almost every election. *Why would Baba—all but equal in the rights and privileges afforded to me and every other citizen born in the United States—carry his decades-old, and functionally useless, naturalization card? Was he really worried that he would be deported? And why didn't Mama, also a naturalized citizen, feel the same way?*

These questions lingered in my mind throughout graduate school. It was only years later that I started to figure out an answer. This answer came not from my own family in Milwaukee and their various circuitous routes from the Middle East. It instead came from a thousand miles south, from my research with dozens of families in Dallas, Texas. Someone in each of these families—usually a mother or a father, sometimes both, other times a grandparent—had traced their origins throughout Mexico and Central America. These families—some undocumented and others documented; some naturalized U.S. citizens and others citizens by birth; most a combination thereof—did not know my own. But their stories evinced a similarly complex relationship to home, not unlike the one I had found in my father's wallet. For both my own parents and these families in Texas, and perhaps all immigrants, life in the United States seemed a shifting balance between feeling included and feeling excluded, an ongoing search for reassurance that they and their family belong, now and always, in their adopted country.

It's not hard to see why immigrants might need this reassurance. Within this shifting balance, there is plenty of room to fall. For decades, our national conversation about immigration has been defined by dramatic extremes—especially when it comes to immigrants from Mexico and Central America.[1] Everyone from politicians to federal immigration officials to the media have insisted that these immigrants are either ruining the country or essential to its continued prosperity. And these extremes have been used to justify greater surveillance of all immigrants and their families.[2] On the one hand, immigrants are depicted as outsiders storming the country's borders. Since at least the mid-1980s, the United States has invested in uniformed personnel, military equipment, ever more advanced technologies, and fortified infrastructure to deter undocumented immigration.[3] These efforts mostly have been in vain: the number of undocumented immigrants has grown right alongside the country's investments in border security.[4] One reason for this is because, since 2007, an undocumented immigrant is more likely to have first entered the country on a visa (which they then have overstayed) than by sneaking across the border.[5] This, despite the federal government's growing reliance on technologies that collate extensive data from visa applications and track visa recipients' entries and exits.[6] The xenophobic diatribes about protecting our border get most of the attention, but this kind of unlawful entry is only part of the story (in fact, less than half of the story). Efforts to regulate the undocumented population have, in turn, shifted away from the border and into communities across the country.[7] Portions of the southern border remain absurdly fortified, but immigration surveillance is no longer a border-state occupation: Immigration and Customs Enforcement has a presence—physical or technological—in all fifty states. Today, the federal government invests far more money each year on immigration enforcement than it spends on its primary criminal law enforcement agencies (i.e., the FBI, DEA, Secret Service, U.S. Marshals, and ATF) combined.[8] This widened dragnet of immigration surveillance is a perpetual reminder to immigrants that they can be deported, from anywhere in the country, at a moment's notice.[9]

On the other hand, immigrants are depicted in very different circles as the most American of Americans, insiders whose dreams embody the United States' promise. Such a depiction is especially true of the "Dreamers," the group of more than four million undocumented immigrants who have lived in the United States since their youth and who would have qualified for a pathway to citizenship under the stalled Development, Relief, and Education for Alien Minors (DREAM) Act of 2001.[10] A fraction of Dreamers benefit from Deferred Action for Childhood Arrivals (DACA), an Obama administration initiative that grants temporary relief from deportation and work authorization.[11] But Dreamers pay a steep price for these temporary protections and privileges, outing themselves as undocumented to a federal government that has waxed and waned in its support for them over the years. Many almost paid the ultimate price when, in September 2017, the Trump administration moved to rescind DACA.[12] Having surrendered their personal information to the federal government, Dreamers worried that their years of societal contributions would not be enough to spare them or their families from being located, detained, and deported.[13] The U.S. Supreme Court eventually preserved DACA on an administrative technicality.[14] Since then, the Biden administration has moved to fortify DACA and signaled its intention to grant Dreamers (and other superlative immigrants) a pathway to citizenship; meanwhile, a federal judge has ruled that DACA is unlawful and has blocked new applications from being processed.[15] The political tug-of-war over DACA highlights why even the most "successful" of immigrants might view surveillance as menacing.

Lost in this rhetorical wrangling of outsiders and insiders is the great complexity of the experiences of immigrants themselves, the millions of people caught between these extreme characterizations. Whether recent arrivals or longtime residents, whether Dreamers or non-Dreamers, the 10.5 million undocumented immigrants living in the United States constitute an integral part of the country's social fabric.[16] Most have lived in the country for over ten years, making it all but inevitable that the surveillance they endure also reaches their loved ones who are U.S. citizens.[17] The statistics support this claim: one out of every thirty U.S. citizens lives with a relative who is undocumented. Among citizens who are children, this figure is one in eleven and, among citizen children who are Latino, it is one in seven.

Because immigration is such a recurring—and divisive—topic in the United States, it is easy to assume that we understand it, that we know what it means to live under the specter of surveillance.[18] Many of us, including scholars and journalists, assume that undocumented immigrants live on the run from the authorities, constantly fleeing to the margins of society, staying in the shadows and away from the eyes of the law. The authorities, in turn, seem like an omnipresent and amorphous threat that can pound on their door at any moment, a group whose singular goal is to identify and remove them. Life off the radar becomes the norm, and undocumented immigrants evade any institution that creates an official record of their clandestine life in the country. No bank or tax records. No police or court records. No dental or medical records. No school or work records. This evasion, which limits their ability to make a living and exacerbates the hardships they already face, is the only way to remain on the run. This perception aligns with a view typical in academic research: that surveillance is a tool of societal exclusion, a way of separating ostensibly dangerous people from the general public.[19]

It turns out this account is incomplete. The families I spoke with agreed with some aspects of this standard story but, to my surprise, rejected many others. They taught me that evading institutions that keep formal records is a luxury that most undocumented immigrants (especially those with children) cannot afford. Every day, they and their families interact with a varied cast of institutional authorities—from police officers to doctors, teachers to social workers. These interactions are fraught with necessity and consequence, hope and fear. Necessity, because immigrants know that a better future for themselves and their children depends on working with these powerful authorities; consequence, because each interaction exposes immigrants to these authorities' scrutiny. If the authorities judge an undocumented immigrant to be "immoral," or an undocumented parent to be "incompetent," then that person could be turned over to the police or their children removed from the home. And yet evading these institutions would do little to allay these authorities' concerns. Rather than settle into a life off the radar, the immigrant families I came to know did the opposite: they selectively engaged with these institutions and their formal records. Their main goal was simple: to get by so that, one day, their children might lead easier lives than their parents.

In many ways, the immigrants I came to know in Dallas are no different from my parents. All ventured to the United States hoping for something better, and they understood that their interactions with institutional authorities would be consequential to achieving that aim. And yet, the gulf between my parents' stories and the ones I found in Dallas are vast. Baba's naturalization card is something like a talisman, a good luck charm for someone who almost lost his student visa and worried about his potential deportation; Mama, with her "clean" record, can't remember where her card is. For those I worked with in Dallas, most of whom are undocumented, their engagement with institutions that keep records of their lives in this country is an essential element of both their present and their hoped-for future, tinged with worry and aspiration. They understood that a well-curated record of their interactions with institutional authorities could help them stave off punishment in the short term and, hopefully, achieve formal societal membership (via access to permanent residence) in the long term. Surveillance, they showed me, is as much about a fear of exclusion as it is a hope for inclusion.

Many of the forms of surveillance considered throughout the book are such a routine part of daily life that they do not always register in most people's consciousness as surveillance. As ordinary people leading what they saw as ordinary lives—not the Rhodes Scholars but the line cooks, not the doctors but the house cleaners—many of the immigrant families I came to know insisted that their individual stories didn't matter and that I wouldn't learn much from talking to them. They didn't see how their everyday concerns would be helpful or illuminating. Still, whenever I showed up on their doorstep over a five-year period, they showed me kindness and patience. They had every reason to turn me away but trusted me with their life stories. I am grateful that they did so.

Asad L. Asad
Palo Alto, CA

ENGAGE AND EVADE

Introduction

"I DON'T THINK I'm hiding in any shadows," Alma told me as she sat in front of a large window, framed by two neatly tied cream curtains.[1] I had asked the thirty-year-old undocumented immigrant from Mexico about the narrative so many of us take for granted: that undocumented immigrants fearful of detection live a life on the run, on the margins of society, where they can dodge the immigration officials who stand ready to deport them to their birth country.[2] Alma paused for several moments, thinking earnestly about the contours of her life in the country since she arrived in the mid-2000s. She turned her face to catch more sunlight before turning back and looking straight at me: "I'm comfortable with the sun being right there."

When I met Alma in 2013, it had been eight years since she and her three sisters journeyed eight hundred miles north from their hometown of Tampico, in the Tamaulipas state of Mexico, to reunite with their parents in Dallas, Texas. The sisters would risk crossing the border illegally because, two years prior, their parents had done the same; after such a prolonged separation, the family was ready to reunite. A *coyote* (a hired smuggler) would help them do so. The plan felt simple enough to Alma. Her younger sisters would enter the country using visas that belonged to same-aged cousins who resembled them, but Alma, the eldest cousin by several years, would have to cross on her own, through a remote region along the Mexico-U.S. border. "I never thought about any of this as illegal or wrong or dangerous," Alma insisted. "I was young and wanted to see my parents."[3] The trip would take three days. The danger of the desert's harrowing heat was second only to the immigration officials Alma feared would capture her and prolong her family's separation. The *coyote* eventually led Alma to a small boat that shuttled her across the Rio Grande. Awaiting her were her sisters. Together, they boarded a pick-up truck to Houston and, ultimately, to their parents in Dallas. Alma said she never saw immigration officials and, more important, immigration officials never saw her. There would be no record that she had entered the United States.

Alma may have eluded a record of her clandestine border crossing, but once inside the country, other kinds of records seemed to follow her everywhere. Her priority was to find a job to help with the family's expenses. As an undocumented immigrant, Alma lacked both a green card and access to a social security number, which meant she could not verify to potential employers that she was authorized to work in the United States.[4] She asked her parents where she might find *papeles chuecos*, or false identity documents (usually both a green card and social security card), that would help her job search. Her parents condemned that strategy, telling Alma that she needed to be more cautious. Possession of *papeles chuecos* is a crime; if police officers found Alma with them, she would likely face jail time and, possibly, deportation. They instead encouraged her to find work cleaning houses, for which employers don't usually require *papeles chuecos*.[5] But Alma, who had completed over a year of college in Mexico, had aspirations beyond housecleaning. Against her parents' wishes, she purchased a fraudulent green card that displayed her real name and photograph, as well as a social security card, and used them to apply for a job at a local fast-food restaurant.[6] Her parents, frustrated, implored Alma to apply for an Individual Tax Identification Number (ITIN), a nine-digit code for filing taxes that the Internal Revenue Service (IRS) issues to anyone ineligible for a social security number. Unlike the green card–social security card combination, an ITIN does not constitute work authorization. But, as Alma's parents explained to her, an ITIN could serve as a form of counterevidence to her *papeles chuecos*: by reporting her income to the IRS, Alma could demonstrate to the federal government that compliance with the law was foundational to her daily life as an undocumented immigrant.[7]

The records cataloging Alma's life extend much further than the workplace. Although she entered the country as a single and childless nineteen-year-old, by the time I met her, Alma had started her own family. Together with Carlos, also undocumented and from Mexico, Alma was the mother of two citizen children under the age of six. Caring for two young children—daunting for any parent—entails another set of challenges when both parents are undocumented.[8] The couple's combined pretax income was about $35,000, enough to cover the rent on their cramped one-bedroom apartment, to pay their utility bills, and to purchase the children's school supplies. Neither of their employers offered them employee benefits, and what little money they had left at the end of the month, enough for a family meal at the neighborhood Burger King, would not stretch to pay for private health insurance. Theirs was hardly a life of excess.

Still, Alma explained that public assistance helped them make ends meet despite the overlapping legal, material, and social hardships to her family's life. During both her pregnancies, Alma received support from the Special Supplemental Nutrition Program for Women, Infants, and Children. The program, commonly known as WIC, provides access to nutritious foods for pregnant people of any legal status and low-income families (including fathers) with children under five. Applying for WIC is itself a feat. Screening appointments are done in person with a government worker, requiring identification, proof of residence, and proof of income for all family members seeking the support, as well as a probe into the pregnant parent's health. In addition to WIC, Alma sought coverage during both pregnancies from the Children's Health Insurance Program (CHIP), which has its own cumbersome application procedures and requirements. Under what is known as the "unborn child option," pregnant parents of any legal status are eligible for up to twenty prenatal doctors' visits and support toward labor and delivery charges. Alma's children, once born, would continue to receive public health insurance, but Alma's coverage would lapse after two postnatal visits.

The abundance of the institutional encounters in Alma's life astounded me. Although she took care to avoid a record of her clandestine border crossing in 2005, her time in the country since then seemed to embrace formal records. Alma must have heard the surprise in my voice when I asked whether, given her legal status, it worried her to engage with the various institutions producing these records. She sat up straight, looked me in the eye, and shook her head: "No." First, Alma described her ITIN as one way to stand out as a moral person who just happens to be undocumented. Second, she emphasized that the public assistance she received on behalf of her citizen children was legally permissible, materially necessary, and socially prudent:

They [Texas Health and Human Services (HHS)] would have denied me benefits if I were applying for myself since I'm not from here. But the kids were born here, I applied for them, and they [HHS] said yes. Besides, with how little we make, we wouldn't be able to pay for food or doctors' visits for the kids. If the kids went hungry or missed a doctor's appointment, they might take the kids away from us and send us back to Mexico.

Alma believed that institutional authorities held people like her, undocumented immigrants who are also parents to citizen children, to expectations that sometimes conflicted. But she was confident that she could manage these dueling expectations every day to maintain her and her family's precarious position in the country. At the same time, Alma recognized that the records cataloging this institutional engagement might one day help her demonstrate to immigration officials that she deserves to become a permanent member of U.S. society:

> There was something a few years back that would have been like DACA [Deferred Action for Childhood Arrivals] but for the parents of kids who were born in the U.S. I don't even remember its name [DAPA, or Deferred Action for the Parents of U.S. Citizens or Lawful Permanent Residents].[9] I'm very bad at remembering things like that, but I remember what I would have needed to do to get it. We needed to gather proof that we had been in this country for a certain number of years, and proof of everything we've done since we've been here. Proof that we paid taxes. Proof that the kids were born here. Proof that the kids were in school. Proof of where we live. We also would have had to pay a fee. I have a bag with all these documents in the back [of the apartment] that would prove all this.

She paused as she considered whether she had any additional thoughts about engaging with the institutions that document her presence in the country as an undocumented immigrant. "If you're not doing illegal things—and we're not—then you should be OK."

———

This book examines whether and how undocumented immigrants with young children, immigrants like Alma, engage with the various institutions that surveil them as they enter and make a life in the United States. I pay close attention to how undocumented immigrants make sense of the different forms of institutional surveillance they engage with or evade, and how their efforts to manage surveillance are rooted in the overlapping legal, material, and social hardships that characterize their daily lives as undocumented immigrants raising U.S.-citizen children. I also consider if the records that undocumented immigrants do—or do not—accrue as they manage their institutional engagement matter for their short- and long-term prospects for societal membership. This account combines interviews I conducted with Latino immigrant families in Dallas County, Texas, ethnographic observations of immigration officials in Dallas Immigration Court, and my analyses of national survey data that measure where Latinos (immigrants and not, families and not) spend their time. Through these multiple vantage points, I reveal how surveillance is as much about the fear of societal exclusion as the hope for societal inclusion.

To understand how undocumented immigrants engage with the different institutions that monitor them, a growing literature takes theoretical inspiration from scholarship on surveillance and punishment more broadly.[10] A dominant account offers that people worried about punishment from state authorities like the police—such as those with outstanding arrest warrants—are less likely to engage with institutions, including hospitals, banks, the workplace, and schools, whose records can be used to track them.[11] Even when they might personally benefit from the resources of these so-called surveilling institutions, they view the authorities staffing them as capable of facilitating their transfer into police custody. As people with a sanctionable status, one that marks them as "wanted" by the state, their fear of arrest demands their institutional evasion. And, because policing is unequal by race and class in this country, surveillance exacerbates inequality through the threat of punishment: already subordinated people become further alienated from institutions that might otherwise improve their life chances and promote their societal inclusion.[12] Such consequences reach their children, too.[13] It's easy to see how this process might apply to undocumented immigrants, especially when politicians seem eager, and immigration officers able, to detain and deport hundreds of thousands of them each year.[14] But the most basic contours of Alma's story make clear that our typical understanding of surveillance is incomplete.

Surveillance is so endemic to modern life that many people do not realize that they leave breadcrumbs of their behaviors, interactions, and transactions with institutional authorities almost everywhere they go.[15] Each doctor's office visited or paycheck deposited or apartment lease signed or utility bill paid or report card received (and on and on) catalogs our routine engagement with surveilling institutions. The same goes for people with a sanctionable status, including undocumented immigrants like Alma. Many will live in the United States for a long time and, even if they do not want to, will accumulate a record of their engagement with surveilling institutions along the way.[16] Alma's story shows how undocumented immigrants manage surveillance by selectively engaging with, rather than altogether avoiding, the institutions that monitor them. This selective engagement is necessitated by hardship, which is both signaled by their legal status and compounded by its constraints.[17] As we know, Alma is one of 10.5 million undocumented immigrants in the country, most of whom are Latino.[18] Her legal status hints at the dangers she endured to enter the country undetected, the difficulties she encountered finding a job, and the material scarcity she and Carlos still face when providing for their family. But these hardships also seep into the decisions that she makes every day. Alma, like anyone, must meet the many demands that characterize her daily life. She must be a good person, a good worker, a good partner, a good mother, and so on. Sometimes her legal status dominates her preoccupations, especially when the associated risk of detention or deportation feels acute.[19] More often, though, the demands of daily life overlap or even conflict with those of her legal status, requiring that Alma venture far outside the proverbial shadows to engage with multiple kinds of institutions.[20] Managing surveillance, even as punishment remains a threat each day, emerges as a prudent strategy.

Undocumented immigrants' efforts reflect the double-edged nature of institutional surveillance in the United States.[21] Institutional surveillance can certainly threaten undocumented immigrants' societal exclusion, just as dominant accounts would suggest. But it can also maintain and even promote undocumented immigrants' societal inclusion in insidious ways. I learned that undocumented immigrants are aware of this twin dynamic and behave accordingly. They do so in a way that corresponds to the concept of role alignment: people worried about state punishment strive to harmonize their institutional engagement with the sometimes competing expectations they believe authorities in these spaces hold them to, given their multiple social roles and responsibilities.[22] As an undocumented immigrant, Alma worries that surveillance can facilitate her societal exclusion via deportation. Yet Alma is not just an undocumented immigrant; she is also a daughter, a partner, a parent, and a worker. These additional social roles entail responsibilities that can supersede, overlap with, or be sidelined by those her legal status imposes; they, in turn, facilitate a coercive form of societal inclusion via institutional engagement. Alma recognizes that the authorities she could have encountered while entering the United States, and those she has encountered throughout her life here, concern themselves with the hardships that inhere into each of her social roles. For example, as we will see in chapter 1, Alma did not believe that immigration officials would approve her for a visa at the time of her migration because she was a broke college student whose parents were living without authorization in the United States. Although Alma was able to avoid immigration officials on her way in, such avoidance is not always practical or advisable once settled in the country. As someone who lives and works without authorization in the United States, Alma expects that her ITIN can convey to the institutional authorities she is likely to encounter more regularly—such as police officers or employers or tax officials—her deference to and respect for the law. And, as an undocumented parent, Alma understands that other institutional authorities—like doctors, nurses, teachers, or social workers—monitor whether the hardships that weigh on her impact her citizen children. By pegging her institutional engagement to these different authorities' perceived expectations, which can shift over time and place, Alma receives not only necessary material resources (e.g., income and public assistance) to make ends meet but also important symbolic ones (e.g., records documenting her morality and good parenting) to avoid more coercive interventions from these same authorities. Role alignment occurs first and foremost in response to the correlated hardships that undocumented immigrants confront each day. This role alignment is, in turn, situated within a context of diffuse surveillance that threatens to punish them for these same hardships. Alma nonetheless hopes that the records of her institutional engagement can, in the long term, constitute proof for immigration officials that she deserves formal societal membership. Thus, undocumented immigrants' selective institutional engagement reveals how surveillance entails both punishment and reward, the stakes of which vary situationally for their societal exclusion and inclusion.

Before we go any further, I want to offer basic definitions of the loaded but consequential terms used throughout the book.[23] An immigrant is anyone born outside the United States to foreign-born parents. Immigrants are a diverse group, with various kinds of legal statuses. For this book, the divide between immigrants who are citizens and those who are noncitizens is crucial.[24] Immigrants who have acquired U.S. citizenship are known as naturalized citizens and are mostly immune to deportation.[25] Those who lack U.S. citizenship—whether someone who entered clandestinely yesterday or a decades-long green card holder—are called noncitizens. All noncitizens are vulnerable to deportation. Yet, some categories of noncitizens are more vulnerable than others: the "undocumented" are those who lack authorization or permission from the federal government to live in the country; the "documented" are those who hold a valid permit, visa, or green card from the federal government that allows or authorizes their presence. The undocumented are statistically more likely than the documented to experience a deportation. Still, the boundary between undocumented and documented is blurry. Some noncitizens hold a "semilegal" status such as Deferred Action for Childhood Arrivals or Temporary

Protected Status that is neither undocumented nor documented but may share characteristics of both.[26] The boundary between undocumented and documented is also porous. Someone may initially be undocumented but later become documented, and someone may initially be documented but later become undocumented.[27] Most immigrants I interviewed for this book live in mixed-status families in which at least two members of the household have different legal statuses.[28]

These legal status categories offer a lens through which to evaluate immigrants' engagement with surveilling institutions, an umbrella term that refers to institutions that keep formal records as a matter of law. I further distinguish between surveilling institutions that are *regulatory* (meaning they are concerned with the administration or enforcement of law, such as lower courts and immigration, police, and tax agencies) and *service oriented* (meaning they provide public goods, such as hospitals, schools, and public assistance).[29] Most people can frequent most of these institutions, but as we will see, these institutions' surveillance feels especially fraught for undocumented immigrants. For regulatory institutions, that feeling revolves around engagement that can promote or indict undocumented immigrants' morality as people living and working without permission in the country; for service institutions, that feeling revolves around engagement that can promote or indict both undocumented immigrants' morality as individuals and their capacity as parents to raise citizen children. Underlying these feelings are formal records, a phrase that itself belies their ordinariness. Records can include government documents (e.g., passports, visas, vehicle registrations), travel records (e.g., visas or plane tickets), medical records, financial records (e.g., bank statements or money order receipts), employment records (e.g., pay stubs, W-2 forms), school records (e.g., transcripts or report cards), residential records (e.g., rent receipts, utility bills), and military records, among others that catalog our behaviors, interactions, and transactions with surveilling institutions.

People construct meanings about surveillance in relation to their multiple social roles, "the parts played by individuals in . . . [an] interaction which makes up some sort of social whole," and their multiple responsibilities, "those [norm-dependent] behaviors characteristic of one or more persons in a context."[30] Most of the people profiled here are undocumented immigrants, a marker of structural forms of inequality that circumscribes many aspects of their routines.[31] Whatever their legal status, immigrants—like anyone—have multiple social roles that require that they juggle multiple responsibilities.[32] Someone's social roles can vary across time and space; everyone in this book is also a parent of a U.S. citizen child, with most becoming a parent years after their arrival. The stakes of fulfilling their myriad responsibilities can vary depending on their other social positions (e.g., country of origin, race, class, gender, etc.).[33] For example, the immigrants profiled in the book are Latino, a group disproportionately targeted for deportation.[34] Many come from Mexico, though some hail from Central America. Latino men who are undocumented are deported more than their Latina women counterparts.[35] The stories here thus represent some of the people most concerned about institutional surveillance.

Surveilling Immigrants

When scholars or journalists think about how the United States surveils and punishes its undocumented population today, we often jump back to the mid-1980s, a time when different laws and policies started to give rise to our current era of "mass deportation."[36] If deportation refers to a country's forced removal of undocumented immigrants, then mass deportation refers to the unprecedented scale of these actions. The statistics support this characterization. While about 1.5 million deportations occurred between 1900 and 1985, another 6.5 million occurred between 1986 and 2018; in other words, four times as many deportations occurred in roughly half the time.[37] With greater frequency in the 1980s, the federal government turned to deportation in an attempt to control the growing number of undocumented immigrants from Mexico and Central America in the country.[38] Deportation rates started climbing in the 1990s, proliferated throughout the 2000s, and peaked at a rate of 3,914 per 100,000 undocumented immigrants in 2013. As figure 1 shows, deportation rates have more or less stabilized near that peak since at least 2010.[39]

These jarring numbers sketch deportation in its most basic form. But, looking more closely, we see an even more complex portrait. The most important complexity is this: undocumented immigrants may be deported when apprehended at the border, or they can be deported after being apprehended inside the country. Since 2012, most deportations have been concentrated at the border. At the height of the Obama administration's deportation efforts in 2013, for example, the overall deportation rate was 3,914 for every 100,000 undocumented immigrants. In that same year, the border deportation rate was 2,705 for every 100,000 undocumented immigrants, and the interior rate was 1,209 per 100,000 undocumented immigrants.[40] Put differently, for every two deportations at the border, one occurred from within the United States. This same pattern holds today. From these numbers, we learn that deportations are a persistent

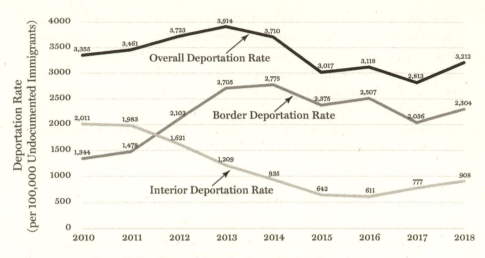

FIGURE 1. Overall, Border, and Interior Deportation Rate (per 100,000 Undocumented Immigrants), 2010–2018

and prevalent phenomenon. But these numbers also tell us that undocumented immigrants who settle in the country are less likely to experience a deportation than are those seeking to enter it. To be sure, two-thirds of undocumented adults have lived in the country for over ten years.[41] Deportation is the exception for undocumented immigrants inside the country, and deportability—the threat of deportation—is the norm.[42]

The statistical rarity of deportation, however, doesn't diminish the widespread impact of its possibility. As we have seen, the undocumented population numbered 10.5 million in 2018, or 3 percent of the U.S. population.[43] Undocumented immigrants are the most likely among noncitizens to experience a deportation, representing more than 80 percent of all deportations from the country.[44] But undocumented immigrants don't live in isolation from citizens.[45] About nine million citizens have family members who are undocumented immigrants, and though citizens are all but immune to deportation, they fear the havoc deportation can wreak on their family.[46] Almost twenty million people overall, citizens and undocumented immigrants alike—who make up 6 percent of the country's population—therefore have reason to fear the possibility of deportation.[47] This mass deportability informs these families' fears of surveillance in daily life—even those who have never, and may never, experience deportation.[48]

Although undocumented immigrants of all national backgrounds are deportable, enforcement is unequal. Mexicans and Central Americans make up 57 percent of all noncitizens in the United States but 65 percent

of all undocumented immigrants and more than 90 percent of all deportations.[49] This group's exposure to the possibility of deportation is also unri-
valed. Of the forty-three million Latinos living in the United States, about
fourteen million—or one in four Latinos—are noncitizens from Mexico
and Central America.[50] These noncitizens are split between permanent
residents (46 percent) and undocumented immigrants (56 percent). Simply put, there is no other group whose members' lives are so threatened by
the possibility of deportation.[51]

This era of mass deportability offers a starting point for examining how
undocumented immigrants make sense of a diffuse context of institutional
surveillance as they carve out a life for themselves in the United States.
Much of this surveillance carries with it a threat of punishment, a fundamental feature of undocumented immigrants' experiences entering and
settling in this country. Yet I want to round out this viewpoint by considering how punishment is one element of surveillance that exists alongside reward. This duality makes room for the contradictions that different
laws, regulations, and policies impose on undocumented immigrants each
day: as people who are not here and here; who are ineligible and eligible;
who are excluded and included; and so on.[52] It poses questions asking
how undocumented immigrants manage institutional surveillance as they
grapple with overlapping hardships, how they balance the threat of punishment emanating from this surveillance alongside its possible rewards,
and how they understand this surveillance to matter for their short- and
long-term societal membership.

A growing scholarship teaches us that undocumented immigrants are
both aware of institutional surveillance and attempt to avert (or avoid
or evade) it as an agentic strategy of self-preservation. But we know less
about whether, how, and why undocumented immigrants seek out institutional surveillance. When someone enters or lives in the United States
without permission, the federal government often defines that person
by what they are not: they are not U.S. citizens, they are not permanent
residents, they are not visa holders, and they are not supposed to be here.
Colloquially, these individuals are called undocumented immigrants,
a category that does not technically exist in the country's immigration
laws but that nonetheless circumscribes their lives.[53] This category has
powerful social meaning. Undocumented immigrants are depicted as on
the run from both immigration officers and other state authorities who
can turn them over to immigration officers—like the police.[54] Undocumented immigrants adopt several strategies to avoid this fate. They are
said to keep to themselves, seldom venturing out of their homes except for

absolute necessities.[55] When they do need to go out, they do so early in the day or late at night when they believe these authorities are less active.[56] At other times of day, they ask friends who are documented immigrants or U.S. citizens to drive them just in case one of these authorities pulls them over.[57] If these friends are not available, undocumented immigrants are careful to style their hair and clothing in a way that "looks American" to avoid attracting officers' attention while they drive without a license that many states deny them.[58] The insights emanating from these different accounts are as compelling as they are true. They nonetheless represent just one lens into the complex dynamics of surveillance and punishment.

This book offers a complementary account of how undocumented immigrants manage surveillance, one that views institutional engagement and evasion as twin strategies of self-preservation and as inevitable features of societal presence. Spotlighting the contradictions that define their daily lives, I examine how undocumented immigrants make sense of institutional surveillance considering the multiple social roles and responsibilities they hold across their journey to and time in the United States. I do not begin from the premise that avoiding surveillance is a preferred or even prudent strategy. Rather, I understand institutional surveillance as pervasive for all people, with higher stakes for some depending on the social roles that characterize their daily lives and the institutional and interactional contexts in which these social roles become more or less salient. Undocumented immigrants carry with them the opportunities and constraints that they recognize as intrinsic to their legal status, including those that delimit which types of institutional surveillance are to be pursued and which are to be avoided. But their responsibilities as undocumented immigrants do not always render those of other social roles obsolete. Like other populations worried about surveillance and punishment, undocumented immigrants sometimes see the responsibilities of their other social roles as superseding, overlapping with, or sidelined by those of their legal status.[59] I examine how these dynamics unfold in the context of undocumented immigrants' institutional engagement, interactions fraught with surveillance as authorities decide whether to punish them or offer them important material and symbolic resources. By paying attention to how undocumented immigrants manage this surveillance, we learn the sometimes surprising ways institutional engagement helps them avoid punishment in their daily lives—by meeting the perceived expectations of state authorities they encounter regularly—and its possible long-run implications for their formal societal membership. More broadly, we see how surveillance is as ubiquitous as it is inescapable, dangling the threat of societal exclusion alongside the promise of inclusion.

A dizzying array of laws, regulations, and policies have created the surveillance that undergirds our current era of mass deportability.[60] We will review many of them in great detail throughout the book. But the Illegal Immigration Reform and Immigrant Responsibility Act (IIRIRA) and the Personal Responsibility and Work Opportunity Reconciliation Act (PRWORA) are pivotal and bear mentioning here.[61] Both reflect long-time efforts from politicians, immigration officials, and the media to frame undocumented immigrants from Mexico and Central America as "criminal" for their legal status and as "public charges" (i.e., dependent on government assistance) for their limited use of public benefits.[62] IIRIRA laid the groundwork for multiple partnerships between immigration officers and local police to detain undocumented immigrants in their local communities nationwide; these efforts intensified following the terrorist attacks of September 11, 2001.[63] PRWORA, meanwhile, excluded undocumented and many documented immigrants—but not their citizen children—from federally funded cash and food assistance and health insurance except in the case of limited emergency health care.[64]

The consequences of these and other laws, regulations, and policies for how undocumented immigrants understand institutional surveillance are mixed. On the one hand, most scholars' conclusions have remained consistent since the earliest studies were published in the 1980s: undocumented immigrants, fearing that institutional surveillance will bring about their punishment, "avoid any kind of action which brings them into direct contact with public authorities."[65] Evidence supports this claim in a variety of institutions, particularly in times and in places where the threat of deportation is most salient.[66] A fear of institutional surveillance keeps some undocumented immigrants from calling the police.[67] It contributes to undocumented immigrants' unease at the workplace, where they believe they will be found out and punished for working with *papeles chuecos*.[68] It prevents many from seeking health care because they worry about receptionists, nurses, and doctors identifying them as undocumented.[69] And it discourages undocumented immigrants from applying for public assistance, "even when this means denying children the social, medical, and educational services they need," because they fear detection and deportation, as sociologists Cecilia Menjívar and Leisy Abrego show us.[70] In brief, undocumented immigrants' legal status becomes a "master status," a phrase used by sociologist Everett Hughes to indicate a characteristic that "tends to overpower, in most crucial situations, any other characteristics which might run counter to it."[71]

On the other hand, some scholars conclude that undocumented immigrants not only engage with these various institutions but also actively keep records of their engagement. Anthropologist Susan Bibler Coutin sees this dynamic as a form of agency that emerges from the vulnerabilities connoted by undocumented immigrants' legal status. In this line of work, institutional engagement offers undocumented immigrants a way of living a "double life," "carry[ing] out daily activities while considering how their lives look to an imagined external gaze."[72] Specifically, Coutin outlines how one Los Angeles-based nonprofit instructed their undocumented clients who were pursuing concrete legalization opportunities to "not only live their lives but also [to] produce a documentary record that they can submit to U.S. immigration authorities."[73] Anthropologists Sarah Horton and Josiah Heyman show how wide-ranging the records are that undocumented immigrants keep to meet requirements for these exceedingly rare legalization opportunities: identification cards (e.g., birth certificates, driver's licenses, or student IDs); medical records; and employment and financial records (e.g., check stubs, bank statements, or tax records).[74] These records establish undocumented immigrants' identity and family relationships; length of residence in the country; and how well their attitudes and behaviors align with immigration officials' expectations.[75] And, once an undocumented immigrant has submitted a legalization application and been approved for a green card, they continue to experience personal and social changes that distance them from anti-immigrant stereotypes.[76] Such changes are reflected in their institutional engagement, like having a legal (rather than religious) marriage, joining the military, or volunteering regularly, in ways not expected of most undocumented immigrants who lack immediate or long-term legalization prospects.[77]

I build on both sets of research to offer unique contributions to the study of how undocumented immigrants manage institutional surveillance in this era of mass deportability. First, I offer a coherent theoretical framework for reconciling undocumented immigrants' simultaneous engagement with and evasion of institutional surveillance. This framework pays attention to both the type of institutional surveillance encountered (e.g., regulatory or service) and the social roles and responsibilities that are most salient to someone in that context (e.g., as migrants, workers, or parents). Second, through analyses of in-depth interviews and national surveys, I consider how undocumented immigrants recruited from their residential environments (rather than immigrant-serving nonprofits) manage institutional surveillance out of prudence—rather than instrumentality, duplicity, or performativity, as other scholars have often characterized their strategies.[78] This mode of recruitment permits a direct examination of what institutional surveillance means to every-day undocumented immigrants: those going about daily life without a legalization opportunity on the horizon. Although immigration officials will want to see evidence of their eligibility if one emerges, many undoc-umented immigrants have passed decades without such an opportunity and may wait several years more before they ever encounter immigration officials.[79] By contrast, undocumented immigrants regularly encounter other institutional authorities—police officers, doctors, nurses, teachers, social workers, and so on—who threaten to punish them and their families for the overlapping legal, material, and social hardships that characterize their daily life. Finally, through the in-depth interviews and an ethnog-raphy of immigration court, I reveal whether and under what conditions undocumented immigrants' records of institutional engagement matter for their formal societal membership.

Managing Surveillance

Although institutional surveillance can feel like an abstract concept, it becomes more tractable if we distinguish between two broad types of institutional surveillance that undocumented immigrants must manage: immigration surveillance and everyday surveillance.[80] As we will see more fully momentarily, undocumented immigrants' efforts depend on the type of surveillance and the social roles and responsibilities most salient to them in that interactional context.

Many laws, regulations, and policies give rise to what we might call *immigration surveillance*; these exist at federal, state, and local levels of government to circumscribe the conditions under which immigrants may enter and remain in the country, as well as the opportunities and con-straints of their legal status.[81] Perhaps the federal ones are the most obvious, the presidential executive actions or the congressional bills or resolutions that dominate media coverage. Many of us are no doubt familiar with the executive actions that enacted DACA or that banned immigration from Muslim-majority countries. Some of us are probably less familiar with the Immigration and Nationality Act (INA), which lays out the key provi-sions of the contemporary immigration system. The INA, which Congress has amended several times since its passage in 1952, delineates the condi-tions under which an immigrant can enter the country and the conditions under which they can remain. Federal regulations, policies, and guidance specify how relevant executive agencies understand and implement a law, such as when U.S. Immigration and Customs Enforcement (ICE) explains that it tends to avoid enforcement actions in "sensitive locations" like schools and churches.[82] States have their own laws, regulations, and policies that delimit the opportunities and constraints of an immigrant's legal status, such as those that determine whether state police collaborate with immigration officers, whether undocumented immigrants may be issued a driver's license, or that outline immigrants' eligibility for public assistance. Counties and municipalities can enact immigration surveillance, too, so long as their laws, regulations, and policies do not contradict the state's.

Beyond immigration surveillance, there is a host of other laws, regulations, and policies that contour what we might call *everyday surveillance*. Though it parameterizes daily life for everyone in the country, regardless of legal status, everyday surveillance is often weightier for people like undocumented immigrants who grapple with overlapping forms of legal, material, and social hardship. We can think about the federal requirements that govern who can start a business, that mandate minimum workplace health and safety standards, that protect us from workplace discrimination, and that compel us to file income taxes. Or about the state requirements on similar topics that, sometimes, contradict those set by the federal government (e.g., marijuana use remains illegal under federal law but is legal in some states). States can also differ from one another in how they implement different federal requirements. For example, everyone in the country is entitled to a public education through high school, but states have wide latitude in determining what public education looks like. Counties and municipalities have their own laws, regulations, and policies, and these can cover a range of topics pertaining to local businesses, policing, municipal courts, behaviors (e.g., loitering), and, as we have seen throughout the COVID-19 pandemic, even wearing a face mask.

Categorization, the process of assigning people to two or more groups with differential rights and privileges, informs the stakes of both immigration surveillance and everyday surveillance. As sociologist Charles Tilly noted, paired categories—such as immigrant and nonimmigrant or undocumented and U.S. citizen—denote social groups with unequal access to the material and symbolic resources that societal institutions confer.[83] For example, nonimmigrants can serve as president of the United States but immigrants cannot, and U.S. citizens can secure driver's licenses that comply with federal standards but undocumented immigrants cannot. Yet no single category defines the totality of any one person's life or reflects the entirety of their institutional access.[84] To be sure, people may occupy multiple social groups that themselves imply situations of institutional exclusion based on one category and situations of inclusion based on others. These social groups, in turn, have their own social roles and responsibilities. Federal law denies undocumented immigrants work authorization, for instance, but does not prohibit them from working as independent contractors who are responsible for paying their own taxes, health insurance costs, and retirement benefits. Such inclusion is situational, allowed by the laws, regulations, and policies of particular institutions in a particular context and need not have benevolent origins. Rather, institutional inclusion can stem from more coercive processes that reflect tensions between a person's social groups and their associated social roles and responsibilities. Extending the previous example, undocumented immigrants may not be "breaking the law" by working as independent contractors, but this form of institutional inclusion can (and does) allow their employers to exploit them in the workplace.[85]

Perhaps no social role exposes how undocumented immigrants' multiple group memberships can at times entail their institutional exclusion and at times entail their inclusion better than parenthood. And, though it certainly matters for immigration surveillance (e.g., access to visas at the time of migration and green cards), parenthood's stakes are more apparent for everyday surveillance. Every state enshrines, in its legal code, parents' rights and responsibilities.[86] These rights and responsibilities apply to all parents, but their import for undocumented parents experiencing overlapping hardships is clear. In Texas, parents have a "duty of care, control, protection, and reasonable discipline of the child," which includes "providing the child with clothing, food, shelter, medical and dental care, and education" and "to hold or disburse funds for the benefit of the child."[87] Undocumented immigrants are themselves excluded from much public assistance and denied access to jobs that offer living or even minimum wages, not to mention employer-sponsored benefits. As a result, many experience food, health, and/or housing insecurity.[88] But, as forms of insecurity that contravene the responsibilities the state expects parents to fulfill on behalf of their children, they can lead to undesirable forms of state intervention—whether policing, a Child Protective Services investigation, the termination of parental rights, or even deportation.[89] In brief, undocumented immigrants may experience a coercive form of inclusion in some institutions as they attempt to prevent the effects of the hardships imposed on them from passing to their children.

Neither immigration surveillance nor everyday surveillance happens on its own. Rather, both occur in consequential moments of interaction with empowered institutional authorities who enforce government laws, regulations, and policies. Political scientist Michael Lipsky calls these authorities street-level bureaucrats.[90] And, given this current era of mass deportability, everyday surveillance tends to arise more regularly than immigration surveillance (though they certainly interrelate). For many people, most of these encounters can seem routine, such as a visit to the emergency room after falling off a bike, a meeting with someone in human resources to correct employment paperwork, or even walking by a police officer with crying children in tow. For undocumented immigrants, though, they reflect fraught moments of everyday surveillance. Most interactions do not result in punishment, but each gives institutional authorities an opportunity to evaluate how well undocumented immigrants square with the laws, regulations, or policies of the city or state or country they call home. Are they compliant with the law? Are they taking proper care of their children? Are they productive members of their communities? The answers to these questions are not decided in neutral or equitable ways; they vary by additional social positions such as race, class, and gender.[91] Whatever the answer, authorities catalog the result of the interaction in their institution's records, which live on and grow in subsequent interactions with the person. Records beget more records, and an extensive paper or digital trail forms.[92]

Surveillance is nonetheless mutual. Authorities surveil undocumented immigrants and, though relatively disempowered, undocumented immigrants surveil the laws, regulations, and policies that these authorities enforce. Aware that their attitudes, behaviors, and transactions are on full display in these encounters, undocumented immigrants recognize that mundane interactions can quickly become very meaningful—depending on where they are being watched, who is watching them, and what is at stake. An unpaid traffic ticket from last year can become cause for arrest if a police officer pulls them over for another infraction, for example, or last month's paystubs can demonstrate to a case worker that their children are eligible for public food assistance and allay a teacher's concerns of food insecurity at home. Undocumented immigrants understand that authorities lack the resources to evaluate them as whole people in any one interaction; they, therefore, strive to minimize negative interactions (that might lead authorities to mark them for investigation, arrest, or more) and maximize positive interactions (that might reassure authorities of their morality or good parenting), given the responsibilities of the social role on display in an interaction. These various interactions with institutional authorities generate formal records. Sometimes undocumented immigrants pursue these records because they believe themselves eligible for a concrete legalization opportunity, as existing research suggests.[93] But the records more often reflect everyday forms of surveillance that threaten to penalize undocumented immigrants for the overlapping hardships imposed on them and their families.

A focus on interactions, and the formal records they produce, is key to understanding whether, why, and with what consequences undocumented immigrants engage with the various institutions that surveil them as they enter and make a life in the United States. Scholarship on this topic is proliferating and, with it, seemingly incompatible conclusions about undocumented immigrants' institutional engagement. Much of this work examines differences between undocumented immigrants and U.S.-born citizens, using either quantitative or qualitative data, in a single interactional and institutional context. It shows that undocumented immigrants both trust and distrust the police, whom they call at similar rates to U.S. citizens.[94] Undocumented immigrants both regularly seek, and regularly avoid, medical care.[95] Their personal use of public assistance is lower than that of U.S.-born citizens, a reflection of undocumented immigrants' exclusion from many of these programs; still, that on behalf of their children approaches that of U.S.-born citizens.[96] These findings are all the more puzzling when considering rates of immigration enforcement across states and counties. Although we might expect undocumented immigrants to evade institutions that surveil them in places where immigration enforcement is most active or visible, they sometimes increase it.[97] All of this work provides important lenses into dynamics of surveillance and punishment. They nonetheless tend to see institutional engagement and evasion as all-or-nothing processes, complicating efforts to explain the mixed evidence of these dynamics that scholars observe in our empirical data.

Institutional surveillance matters, in different ways, for the undocumented immigrants I came to know as they made a life for themselves and their families in the United States. Their legal status represented a category that signaled one set of responsibilities governing their social role as immigrants, which was sometimes reflected in their institutional evasion. But, for the same reason, they sometimes saw institutional engagement as more prudent. At the same time, their parenthood represented another social role with a different set of responsibilities that often necessitated their institutional engagement, even when this conflicted with the perceived responsibilities of their legal status. They seldom explained their institutional engagement or evasion in relation to a legalization opportunity they were pursuing or would soon pursue; many had spent large fractions of their lives in the United States without authorization and did not expect that to change soon. Instead, they referred to their interactions with the institutional authorities they encountered as a necessary part of their ordinary routines—and how they believed those authorities expected them to behave, given their multiple social roles and responsibilities, even if they felt those behaviors would jeopardize their eligibility for a green card. Scholars studying policing and immigration enforcement have considered some of these dynamics among undocumented immigrants, but fewer have examined them as part of a larger constellation of institutional interactions that undocumented immigrants manage each day.[98] In many ways, it is impossible to understand one form of institutional engagement without reference to others. Making multiple forms of institutional engagement the focus of our study allows us to see more fully what is at stake for undocumented immigrants and their families as they interact with institutional authorities; how they weigh the perceived costs and benefits of institutional engagement alongside those of evasion; and how their multiple social roles and responsibilities factored into this calculation. Moreover, the consequences of this engagement or evasion—both outside and inside the context of legalization opportunities—become clearer.

We learn something different from Alma's story at the start of this chapter by examining her institutional interactions in light of her multiple social roles and responsibilities rather than her legal status alone. Specifically, it illuminates how interactions with diffuse forms of institutional surveillance are a feature of Alma's daily life. Alma exhibits a *selective engagement* with the institutions that surveil her, sometimes interacting with them and sometimes avoiding them depending on the type of institutional surveillance encountered and the social roles and responsibilities most salient in an encounter. Underlying this selective engagement are her understandings of what authorities in these spaces expect of her during these interactions; in other words, she aligns her institutional engagement or evasion with the responsibilities of the social role most relevant in a given interaction. Sometimes this alignment manifests as evasion. From the moment Alma understood she would leave Mexico, institutional interactions were a primary concern. Most salient were her possible interactions with regulatory institutions governing immigration surveillance. A smuggler would help Alma navigate the tumultuous journey into the United States, but a key question that Alma could not answer was whether immigration officers patrolling the border would capture her along the way. The answer to this question was important. If captured, she would almost certainly be deported—but likely not before her fingerprints were taken and stored in immigration databases. She would inevitably try to reenter the country, but if captured once more, she would likely not be deported right away; she might first face time in prison, because immigration officers would have a record of their prior interactions. Alma was risking not just being caught, but also what the record of her interactions with immigration officers would mean to future attempts to enter the country.[99]

Once inside the United States, though, Alma's efforts at role alignment more often reflected a selective set of interactions with institutional authorities than outright evasion. We see this in Alma's engagement with other regulatory institutions, especially those bearing on more everyday surveillance in the domains of policing, employment, and taxation. Despite her legal status and its associated vulnerabilities, Alma was not content to hide in the shadows as an undocumented immigrant newly settled in Dallas. She started searching for ways to lead what she saw as a full life—and prioritized institutional interactions that would allow her to do so in as lawful a manner as possible. Sometimes the constraints of her legal status got in her way, such as when Alma purchased *papeles chuecos* to land a job because the federal government denies undocumented immigrants work authorization. But, aware of the illegality of this purchase, Alma used her real name and other personal information to apply for an Individual Tax Identification Number from the IRS so that she could pay income tax. She also extoled her lack of negative police interactions, as evidenced by her "clean" criminal record. Alma described this balance of institutional interactions as a recipe for undocumented immigrants like her to make it through each day without experiencing punishment from the authorities they encounter regularly.

The stakes of this role alignment increase when the responsibilities of multiple social roles conflict; in other words, when one social role suggests avoiding institutional interactions but another suggests seeking them out.[100] Service institutions, in which authorities distribute public goods such as health care, education, and public assistance, exemplify this tension for undocumented parents because they are spaces where immigration surveillance and everyday surveillance interrelate. And, as with regulatory institutions, a selective engagement takes hold. Alma's legal status means that she is all but excluded from public health insurance. Her employer does not provide her insurance coverage, nor does her employer pay enough to allow her to afford private coverage. Yet her legal status did not disqualify her from the limited but important pre- and postnatal care and resources she received from CHIP and WIC during and after each of her two pregnancies. Her children continued to receive these services once her own coverage lapsed, enabling Alma to shepherd them to regular doctors' visits. Alma's oldest child is enrolled in public school, and she told me that she plans to do the same once her second reaches school age. For Alma, the overlapping hardships imposed by her legal status necessitated these various institutional interactions on behalf of her children. She didn't feel that she could or should avoid them either; doing so might have given institutional authorities a reason to intervene in her and her children's lives in potentially destabilizing ways.

Interactionist theory helps explain whether, how, and why undocumented immigrants worried about surveillance nonetheless engage with institutions that surveil them. According to interactionist theorists, people orient their behavior in relation to the expectations they believe other people have of them in a given interaction. But interactions often happen in a specific context, implying that the meanings someone assigns to their own actions, and their beliefs about how others interpret their actions, are situational.[101] As sociologist George Herbert Mead summarizes, a person "selects, checks, suspends, regroups, and transforms the meanings in light of the situation in which [they are] placed."[102] Social roles inform whether and how people seek out and experience interactions in a specific context, such as when a worker asks their employer for a raise on the basis of their performance or when a parent demands that a teacher offer their child accommodations for a missed assignment.[103] Often, though, more than one social role is relevant in a given interaction and situation, such as if that same worker is also an immigrant or if that same parent is a school board member. Sociologist Erving Goffman famously theorized that people who share a social role (e.g., as worker or parent or immigrant) do not experience the stakes of an interaction in similar ways; rather, within social roles, the stakes increase for people in social positions (e.g., race, class, gender, legal status) that society devalues.[104] For instance, the stakes are higher when a house cleaner asks for a raise than when a professor does. The stakes are even higher when women (rather than men) ask for a raise, and they are higher still for Black women (rather than White women), as intersectionality theory reminds us.[105] In other words, social roles unfold in interaction and in context to shape people's unequal access to resources.[106] For undocumented immigrants managing institutional surveillance, then, interactionist theory urges an investigation of whether, how, and why undocumented immigrants fulfill the responsibilities of their multiple social roles in different interactional contexts of surveillance. Such an approach brings us closer to a fuller understanding of their selective engagement with surveilling institutions.[107]

An emphasis on interactions in context uncovers the complex ways categorization relates to the institutional reproduction of inequality. To be sure, some categories may be so powerful that they come to represent a social role of their own and dominate all others in institutional interactions, as some criminologists studying surveillance and system avoidance have suggested. For example, even when a criminal record does not prevent someone from accessing an institution (e.g., a hospital or school), research shows that people with a criminal record fear interacting with institutional authorities.[108] A person's criminal record, their sanctionable status, becomes their orienting social role, underlying their institutional evasion because they expect authorities to punish them.[109] They reimagine seemingly mundane institutions, whether hospitals, banks, the workplace, or schools, as risky sites because law enforcement may use the records resulting from their interactions to track, arrest, and punish them. Such evasion occurs even when it entails material or symbolic costs for themselves or their loved ones.[110] Criminologists analyzing ethnographic data or in-depth interviews uncover the meanings of institutional evasion for people with a sanctionable status and those separately analyzing large-scale administrative or survey data show statistical support for this idea, on average, for particular types of institutional interactions (e.g., emergency room visits or having a checking account or formal employment or school enrollment).[111] But, in emphasizing interactions avoided, we learn less about the interactions that do occur and what they mean to the people who have them.

Surveillance entails elements of punishment and reward, meaning that both risk and gain are at stake, in ways that can make necessary people's institutional interactions despite—or because of—their fears of sanction. Michel Foucault argued that institutional surveillance was one way for governments to discipline the general public by normalizing the punishment of people who do not comply with its rules and the reward (or, at least, nonpunishment) of people who do.[112] Discipline operates both through direct interactions with authorities in surveilling institutions, such as when someone is a student in a teacher's classroom, and indirect ones, such as when someone's parenting skills are called into question through a teacher's observation of their child in the classroom. Every time authorities deem someone noncompliant with a rule, they can document that noncompliance in an ever-accumulating set of records. Compliance, too, can be recorded. Whether revealing compliance or noncompliance, these records are powerful; they allow authorities to both evaluate a single person and compare that person against the behavior of others they have interacted with. If authorities judge someone to meet their expectations, they can reward them materially (e.g., income or public assistance) or symbolically (e.g., a record of good parenting); otherwise, they can punish the person (or refer them to others for punishment).

This idea has been influential, particularly in studies of poverty governance. Research in this area teaches us that institutional authorities pervade the lives of low-income families and that they are disproportionately menacing to families of color.[113] Most of the families studied are U.S. citizens. Whether in their engagement with hospitals, schools, or welfare agencies, scholars describe how parents cannot evade institutional authorities but rather withhold information from them to guard against sanction, to maintain public assistance receipt, or both.[114] Sociologist Kelley Fong calls this "selective visibility," whereby low-income parents conceal personal details or behaviors as they interact with institutional authorities.[115] For example, a parent may not admit to food or housing insecurity, even if it means forgoing public assistance, lest a doctor or teacher refer them to Child Protective Services. There are nonetheless limitations to selective visibility, as sociologist Cayce Hughes uncovers in a study of low-income Black mothers living in public housing. He finds that concealment is not always feasible, particularly in contexts where institutional authorities are regularly present, routinely monitor a person's compliance with opaque rules, and constantly threaten to punish them.[116] In revealing that surveillance is unavoidable for some American families, this scholarship teaches us that institutional interactions can mean the difference between punishment and survival.

I complement these conclusions with several additional contributions to the literatures on surveillance and social control. First, I show how the exclusionary or inclusionary effects of institutional surveillance for people worried about punishment depend on their multiple social roles and responsibilities, which themselves vary situationally. Although people with criminal records often evade the institutions that surveil them, undocumented immigrants do not always behave similarly, as scholars of surveillance and system avoidance expect. Put simply: undocumented immigrants do not evade institutions wholesale; rather, they avoid specific institutional interactions. Such selective engagement is conditioned by the real or perceived responsibilities of undocumented immigrants' multiple social roles—as immigrants, as workers, as parents, as community members, and so on—that are themselves circumscribed in myriad laws, regulations, and policies that differ across institutional type (i.e., regulatory or service institutions). For example, police officers may actively search for someone with an outstanding arrest warrant, but such active pursuit is less typical in the case of policing and immigration enforcement, given policies at the federal, state, and/or local level that circumscribe them. Likewise, undocumented immigrants are excluded from many service institutions, especially those related to public assistance, but their citizen children are not. Undocumented immigrants, therefore, may at times evade and at times seek out institutional interactions, depending on the perceived benefits and costs of interaction in a given situation. In this way, their daily lives may more closely resemble those of other people grappling with overlapping hardships in contexts of diffuse surveillance— whether street vendors, unhoused people, or low-income parents—than people with criminal records retreating from public life as they flee from the police.[117]

Second, in taking seriously that surveillance entails elements of both punishment and reward, I demonstrate how institutional inclusion can itself reflect inequality, even absent evidence of higher rates of evasion among people worried about punishment. For scholars analyzing administrative or survey data, these unequal rates constitute evidence of system avoidance, as we have seen. But I argue that the absence of difference in such outcomes does not imply the absence of other forms of inequality; rather, it points to more insidious forms of inequality reproduced in institutional interactions that vary situationally.[118] In addition to sanctions, institutional authorities distribute important material and symbolic resources—including to people worried about punishment. Some undocumented immigrants like Alma work with *papeles chuecos*, for example, and seek to counterbalance that criminalized offense in the eyes of institutional authorities by paying income taxes through an Individual Tax Identification Number. Others secure public assistance on behalf of their citizen children because they worry that the overlapping legal, material, and social hardships that weigh on their families will lead their children's doctors or teachers to refer them to the police or Child Protective Services. In other words, their interactions align with the perceived expectations they believe powerful institutional authorities hold them to, given the responsibilities of their multiple social roles. These expectations are themselves rooted in inequalities built into the laws, regulations, and policies that deny undocumented immigrants the rights to work authorization and public assistance, among others. In that sense, they underpin a more coercive form of institutional inclusion: undocumented immigrants recognize that institutional authorities might punish them for the constraints of their legal status but value those whose constellation of institutional interactions shows them to be moral people, responsible taxpayers, hard workers, and doting parents. A focus on interactions, therefore, illuminates how the meanings of surveillance for institutional exclusion and inclusion are situational. Attention to these meanings will become more important as states and localities become increasingly differentiated by the character of immigration surveillance and everyday surveillance.

Data and Methods

This book is based primarily on interviews and ethnographic observations collected in Dallas County, Texas, in the summer months between June 2013 and August 2018, alongside original analyses of national survey data that bolster some of the key findings from the interviews. A detailed description of all aspects of data collection and analysis is available in the book's two appendices. Below, I summarize the research that informs this book and report on Dallas County as a site for studying how Latino immigrant families manage surveillance.

I interviewed and observed Latino immigrant families in the Dallas area. Most interviews were conducted in Spanish and took place in these families' homes, a reassuring sign that they trusted me enough to let me into their most intimate spaces. A handful of interviews took place in fast-food establishments, such as McDonald's or Burger King, largely to distract study participants' young children with ice cream, fries, and playrooms as we talked. The sixty adults who came to participate in the study represent twenty-eight Latino immigrant families. To enroll in the study, they had to identify as Latino and have young children in the household. Legal status was not a criterion for recruitment, but study participants included thirty-five undocumented immigrants, four semi-legal immigrants, twelve permanent residents, four naturalized citizens, and five U.S.-born citizens. Most of the immigrant adults were born in Mexico, though two came from El Salvador, two from Guatemala, and one from Honduras. Sixteen reported having experienced a deportation, usually as they entered the country; the other thirty-nine told me they had never been deported. The median year of arrival for immigrant study participants was 1996. The families lived throughout Dallas, in

White-, Black-, and Latino-majority neighborhoods whose residents have average incomes that range from low (<$25,000) to mid (between $25,000 and $75,000) to high (above $75,000); this ensures that the study's findings do not reflect dynamics unique to any one neighborhood type.

In-depth interviews are a powerful tool for showing how and why undocumented immigrants manage surveillance as they go about their ordinary routines. And conducting those interviews in a single place allows for a richer analysis of the local-level contexts that enable or constrain their institutional engagement.[119] It is nonetheless useful to know whether and how findings in Dallas manifest nationwide so that we—whether we are scholars, policymakers, activists, or interested people—can have productive conversations about patterns of surveillance and punishment outside Dallas.[120] To examine national patterns of institutional engagement among Latinos, I turned to the American Time Use Survey (ATUS), a long-running survey administered by the federal government that measures how people living in the United States spend their time on a typical day. Importantly for our purposes, the ATUS takes extra care to survey large numbers of Latino households with and without young children so that reliable estimates for these groups can be produced. I use these data in several ways. One is to contextualize some of the correlated hardships that burden Latino noncitizens relative to naturalized citizens (chapter 1). Another is to bolster the book's argument that Latino immigrants circumscribe their daily lives first and foremost in relation to regulatory, rather than service, institutions (chapter 2). Finally, I rely on the ATUS data to statistically evaluate a core idea that emerged from the in-depth interviews: that undocumented immigrants exhibit a selective engagement with institutions that surveil them, which varies based on their multiple social roles and responsibilities (chapter 3). I discuss only the substantive results of the survey analyses in the main text of the book; appendix B offers a full explication for interested readers.

A final source of data consists of ethnographic observations in Dallas Immigration Court. While interviews with families and statistical analyses offered me an astounding amount of information, I still wasn't sure if study participants' efforts to manage surveillance made a difference to immigration officials who make consequential decisions bearing on undocumented immigrants' formal societal membership. I gained leverage on this question in the summer months of 2015. As I continued to interview the families I had met in prior years, I started to observe Dallas Immigration Court—visiting the five courtrooms operating at that time. Over three months, I spent about fifteen hours per week sitting in court and interacting with courtroom interpreters, federal police and prosecutors, immigration attorneys, and five immigration judges. I did not formally interview any of these officials, though all allowed me the opportunity to ask them informal questions about my observations over the course of the ethnography.[121] These data helped me to round out the insights emerging from the in-depth interviews—confirming many of the core ideas on display throughout the book and refining several others.

Dallas County (hereafter, Dallas) offers several analytical payoffs to a study interested in how Latino immigrant families manage surveillance.[122] With a population of about 2.6 million, Dallas ranks in the top ten most populated counties nationwide and, behind Houston's Harris County, the second most populated county in Texas.[123] About 40 percent of Dallas residents are Latino, totaling 1.04 million people; more than 450,000 (about 44 percent) are immigrants. Among these immigrants, 51 percent are undocumented, 29 percent are permanent residents, and the remainder are naturalized citizens. This means that, among the Latino immigrants in Dallas, four out of five are vulnerable to deportation; of these, two out of three are undocumented. Most come from Mexico, with much of the remainder from Central America. Sixty-five percent of all Latino citizen children in the county—over 215,000 kids—live with either a parent or relative who is vulnerable to deportation. These present-day demographics reflect Dallas' status as an established destination for Mexican and, increasingly, Central American immigrants.

Like Arizona and California, Texas has received immigrants from Mexico and Central America for well over a century. But various changes to U.S. immigration law and policy beginning in the 1940s all but guaranteed a steady stream of undocumented immigration to these states.[124] By the 1980s, politicians, immigration officials, and the media stepped up their efforts to depict undocumented immigrants from Mexico and Central America as a danger to society.[125] The result was the 1986 Immigration Reform and Control Act (IRCA), which we will revisit in chapter 1. Among other changes, the act fortified the United States' southern border ostensibly to deter immigration. But it backfired. Rather than prevent people from entering the country, the added security simply dissuaded them from leaving. As a result, IRCA transformed what had been a circular flow of temporary labor immigrants in three states into a settled population of immigrants who, over time, went on to have families.[126] Dallas today exemplifies this history.

Dallas (and Texas more broadly) represents a site of "deportable inclusion," making it a revealing context to study institutional surveillance. Public health scholars Maria-Elena De Trinidad Young and Steven P. Wallace define sites of deportable inclusion as those where "[n]oncitizens are subject to enforcement and surveillance while possessing rights and protections in other areas of their lives."[127] In other words, federal, state, and local laws, regulations, and policies make deportation a very real threat for undocumented immigrants, but they also offer spaces for undocumented immigrants to access institutions that might improve their life chances. Reviewing these different laws, regulations, and policies can cause whiplash. Texas has participated in several programs that facilitate cooperation between immigration officers and state and local police, which we will explore in greater detail in chapter 2. But, over the course of research for this book, Dallas County Sheriff Lupe Valdez, and her successor Marian Brown, opposed this collaboration.[128] Texas led national efforts to undermine federal programs (i.e., DACA and DAPA) intended to shield some undocumented immigrants, including the parents of U.S. citizens, from deportation. Yet, as we will see in chapter 3, the state and Dallas County extend some rights and protections to these very groups in the domains of health, education, labor, and other sectors.[129] Accordingly, Dallas occupies a middle space with respect to the threat that undocumented immigrants may perceive from institutional surveillance. This threat is likely higher where state laws actively exclude them (e.g., Alabama, Georgia, Kansas, North Carolina, Pennsylvania, and Tennessee); comparable in places whose patchwork of laws is similar to Texas (e.g., Florida, Massachusetts, New York, Oklahoma, and Wisconsin); and lower in places that are more proactive in their inclusion of immigrants (e.g., California, Colorado, Illinois, Rhode Island, and Washington State). But variation exists within states, meaning that local context matters, too.[130] One county may have policies in place that exclude undocumented immigrants from daily life even as a neighboring county has inclusionary policies in place. Readers should understand the evidence here not as an account of how all Latino immigrant families manage surveillance nationwide but as an in-depth look into the complex ways institutional surveillance can matter to these families' daily lives and ordinary routines.

Preview

Throughout this book I present the stories of real people who are also undocumented immigrants and parents to citizen children. I explore whether, how, and why they engage with various institutions that surveil them as they attempt to meet the many demands of daily life.

Each chapter centers on a particular social role, as well as the institutions that the people I spoke with engaged or evaded to meet the responsibilities they associate with that role. Chapter 1 examines study participants as *prospective migrants*, focusing on the regulatory institutions governing immigration surveillance that they considered or encountered before they even set foot in the United States. For them, the path toward becoming a migrant was rooted in deprivation, a feeling of lacking or missing something at home, which motivated their desire to leave their lives behind in their country of origin and start anew. But what they lacked mattered for the type of migrant they would eventually become. To secure visas or other travel documents requires proofs of income or wealth, or of an immediate family member with permanent residence or citizenship, among other proofs. For the few with access to these resources, crossing with a visa felt routine; for the remainder, crossing without one was accepted as inevitable. How they migrated delimited the scope, quality, and consequence of their interactions with immigration surveillance on their journey into the country—and the stakes of managing the everyday surveillance that they would soon encounter.

The next two chapters examine study participants as *immigrants* who have established lives in the United States, but with slightly different emphases. Chapter 2 focuses on *immigrants as individuals*, who must learn to navigate the everyday forms of institutional surveillance they encounter as part of their ordinary routines. Many laws, regulations, and policies threaten undocumented immigrants' presence in the country— especially those concerned with policing, employment, and taxation. Yet, for the people I interviewed, the threats these regulatory institutions posed were not only identifiable but also controllable. Whether based on their own perceptions or experiences, or those of loved ones, they sought to manage their institutional interactions. This strategy entailed limiting negative, and maximizing positive, interactions with authorities in one or more regulatory institutions. For example, undocumented immigrants talked about moderating personal behaviors that they believe to be "criminal" or "suspicious" (such as driving with any alcohol in their system or spending time in neighborhoods that police racial minorities) to reduce the possibility of punitive police interactions, even as they called or visited police stations or courthouses to pay or contest fines and fees. They likewise used *papeles chuecos* to work without authorization but filed taxes using an ITIN, as we have seen. Undocumented immigrants felt that this institutional engagement offered them material and symbolic resources: materially, some of this engagement was necessary to meet the demands of daily life; symbolically, it helped them meet or exceed the expectations they believe authorities hold them to each day and, as a result, stave off the threat of punishment.

Whereas the previous chapter focuses on immigrants as individuals, chapter 3 considers their role as *immigrant parents* to children who are U.S. citizens. By design, all study participants are parents. They described parenthood as rewarding but risky, given their perceptions that it subjects them to forms of everyday surveillance that they had previously learned to minimize. This risk felt most acute in service institutions concerned with the provision of public goods, where they noted a tension between their social roles as undocumented immigrants on the one hand and as undocumented parents on the other. As individuals, many undocumented immigrants are excluded from most federally funded service institutions except in the case of emergency medical care and public schooling; the laws, regulations, and policies governing their engagement with state-funded service institutions depend on their state of residence. As parents, though, undocumented immigrants felt that they had no alternative but to seek out this engagement on behalf of their children to make ends meet. The result was a selective engagement with service institutions, with study participants circumscribing their personal engagement even as they became engaged on behalf of their children. Selective engagement with service institutions offered tangible material resources to otherwise constrained families. A record of this engagement also offered symbolic resources, showing the authorities they regularly interacted with as part of their children's schedules that they are good, competent parents who do not require more coercive forms of state intervention to support their children.

However they engage with institutional surveillance in daily life, the previous chapters suggest that this quotidian engagement prepares undocumented immigrants for a longer-term evaluation: one that allows them to demonstrate to immigration officials that they are deserving of permanent place in society. Chapter 4, therefore, examines study participants as *petitioning immigrants*. Most undocumented immigrants have lived in the United States for a decade or more without ever encountering immigration officials; the same was true of the undocumented immigrants I interviewed. Yet some did eventually become eligible to submit applications to immigration officials that would facilitate their permanent residence. Some were eligible for an affirmative petition, which they submitted to U.S. Citizenship and Immigration Services through an ostensibly non-adversarial process that nonetheless felt adversarial to them. As a petition they could opt into, they waited to apply until they could hire a lawyer whom they trusted to evaluate their records and confirm that it was wise to apply. Legalization did not cure these formerly undocumented immigrants' fears of societal exclusion; in some ways, they felt more exposed to immigration surveillance by virtue of their permanent residence. Others never became eligible for an affirmative petition. They instead became eligible for a defensive petition, meaning, despite their best efforts, they had been placed into removal proceedings. Although a successful defensive petition would mean the difference between permanent residence and deportation, undocumented immigrants often felt compelled to forgo an application because of structural and organizational features of immigration court that risked compounding the legal, material, and social hardships their families already faced. For the few who did apply, some of these same structural and organizational features emerged to complicate immigration officials' favorable evaluation of their applications. In brief, these findings suggest that the contexts in which undocumented immigrants present their formal records to immigration officials reflect distinct opportunities and constraints—outlined in myriad laws, regulations, and policies—that delimit the meanings of these records for their formal societal membership.

In the conclusion, I outline the implications of these various arguments for how we understand and respond to the effects of institutional surveillance on undocumented immigrants and their families. Surveillance is as much about the threat of exclusion as the hope for inclusion. Undocumented immigrants' engagement with the institutions that surveil them often emerges out of a need or desire to satisfy the responsibilities that correspond to their multiple, sometimes conflicting, social roles. But it can also occur to satisfy more coercive expectations, such as those they believe the institutional authorities they encounter regularly hold them to. As such, the threat of punishment, of exclusion, looms large over undocumented immigrants. No amount of symbolism accrued through the records documenting these interactions is likely to help them avoid this exclusion in the long run without meaningful government intervention.

I suggest immediate reforms to immigration surveillance and everyday surveillance that might ensure a more stable present in the country for undocumented immigrants and their families, and I point to more substantial, long-term changes as well. Whatever changes we adopt require a commitment to addressing the myriad ways that laws, regulations, and policies allow inequalities based on legal status to take hold and grow in our societal institutions.

CHAPTER ONE

Deprivation and Deportability

LONG BEFORE STARTING A life as an immigrant settled in the United States, someone must first decide whether to migrate—and, if so, how. Rarely is deciding to become a migrant simple or straightforward; it is fraught with weighty questions and answers that have different stakes. Should they even go? Should they travel with a visa, or should they cross the border without one? Is it too dangerous to travel without a visa? Would hiring a *coyote* to sneak them into the country help? Should they travel with identification? These questions are intense and emotional. And, yet, they all require prospective migrants to anticipate the opposite—how immigration officials enforce the emotionless laws, regulations, and policies that give rise to the different forms of immigration surveillance that determine whether they receive a visa, or not. Are caught at the border, or not. Detained, or not. Fingerprinted, or not. Jailed, or not. Deported, or not. This chapter illustrates how these forms of immigration surveillance—and how well migrants believe their personal circumstances align with the scope of the laws, regulations, and policies that immigration officials enforce—come to define both a person's decision to migrate to the United States and the meanings of their earliest interactions with institutional authorities once inside the country.

———

We sat at a glass dining table just off Elizabet's kitchen. It was late afternoon, and she needed to keep a watchful eye over the fragrant *caldo* simmering on the black stovetop. Though almost forty, she could have passed for twenty-five. The cross that dangled from her pink, beaded necklace rested on the "bebe" lettering stitched on her white tee. As I readied the audio recorder, Elizabet stared through the transparent tabletop to the calm colored tiles of the floor beneath. "Tell me the story of your life," I offered as a prompt to start the interview. She didn't hesitate. Her narration of the highlights was matter-of-fact: "Well, I was born in Mexico, and I came to the United States undocumented. All my family is here, except my parents."

Elizabet moved to Dallas seventeen years before we met, in 1998. Much of her journey—that she would migrate and that she would do so undocumented—now seemed inevitable to her. The youngest of fourteen children, Elizabet was born in the late seventies in a rural town near San Luis de la Paz, in the Guanajuato state of Mexico, to a grocery store manager and a homemaker. The family lived in a modest ranch-style home; four or five children shared each bedroom. In her childhood, Elizabet spent much of her time going to school and helping her mother with various household chores. She followed this routine until, at age fifteen, Elizabet was the only sibling left in Mexico; the rest had followed others in their community to find work in Dallas. According to Elizabet, her siblings took "a chance on a better life"; she wanted to do the same. Though all her siblings had traveled without a visa, Elizabet figured she could bypass an increasingly guarded and dangerous border by applying for a visa. With her mother's help, Elizabet applied for a tourist visa, noting on her application that she wished to visit her brothers and sisters. But immigration officials in the U.S. Consular Agency in nearby San Miguel de Allende denied her application. Reflecting on this outcome years later, Elizabet told me that she should have expected it; with more than a dozen siblings already living without authorization in the country, immigration officials likely figured that she planned to overstay her visa and settle in the United States. Elizabet would have to travel undocumented, just like her siblings.

The trip turned out to be even more complicated than Elizabet had anticipated, lasting just over a month. On her first attempt at crossing, Elizabet and her cousin, who accompanied her, hired a *coyote* to get them into the country on foot. The cousin fell ill along the way, and the pair flagged down officers patrolling the border so they could be sent home. On the second attempt, the pair's new *coyote* got them a few hundred yards across the U.S. border when another officer spotted them and returned them to Mexico. On her third attempt, her third *coyote* gave the pair fraudulent visas, and Elizabet and her cousin hopped on a bus bound for Houston. An officer clad in tactical gear boarded the bus shortly after it had entered the United States and, in scrutinizing the visas, discovered their fraudulence. The officer arranged for the cousins' deportation—but photographed and fingerprinted the pair first. On the final attempt, another *coyote* again gave them fraudulent visas. They tried their luck on a different bus to Houston and, this time, the officer who inspected their visas barely glanced at them. When the bus reached its destination, Elizabet realized that she was finally, truly, if not quite legally, in the United States.

Elizabet took a breath after narrating her journey. I asked whether, nearly twenty years later, she still thinks about any aspect of her trip. Her answer was almost immediate: "The first two times they caught me, they didn't take my photo or fingerprints; they just sent me back. But the third time, they took them both. The officer who did it even recognized me. 'You've been through here already, right?' 'Yes,' I told him, 'because I really want to cross. But they won't let me pass. I'm not going to do anything bad; I just want to work, to live.'" I asked Elizabet why the photographing and fingerprinting worry her. "If they catch me again, they're going to treat me like a criminal since they caught me crossing before. They'll put me in prison and kick me out, back to Mexico. But my only sin is that I came here looking for a better life."

———

Many discussions of the institutional forms of surveillance that characterize daily life as an undocumented immigrant begin inside the United States. This focus makes sense, given that most undocumented immigrants have lived in the United States for over a decade and worry about the laws, regulations, and policies that make their detection and deportation more likely. Elizabet's story nonetheless suggests that immigrants reckon with institutional surveillance before even leaving their country of origin. Thus, we must first look outside the United States to examine how immigrants understand and manage surveillance prior to their arrival.

No other regulatory institution defines the stakes of a person's migration to the United States quite like this country's immigration system. Its many laws, regulations, and policies establish who can enter the country and through what channels, as well as the costs of noncompliance. These laws, regulations, and policies, in turn, give rise to different forms of immigration surveillance; for people deciding whether to migrate, these can include visa applications and procedures, as well as border securitization, detention, and deportation. Migrants' interactions with these forms of institutional surveillance—whether they apply for a visa, whether they enter without authorization, whether they are detained at the border, whether they are fingerprinted, and so on—matter, as Elizabet's story illustrates, both upon entry and long after they have settled in the United States. They can place migrants "in the system," starting the first of a series of formal records that migrants understand as cataloging their presence in the country, demonstrating their compliance with the law, and bounding their eligibility for possible legalization opportunities in the future. In brief, whether and how migrants engage with authorities enforcing immigration surveillance on their way into the country can entail short- and long-term implications for their formal societal membership.

Who migrates to the United States, and why, is a selective process. To be sure, most Mexicans and Central Americans will never enter the United States, a reflection of people's capacity to choose to not migrate.[1] Those who do migrate are not the poorest or least educated in their hometowns but have, on average, low incomes and low levels of education by U.S. standards.[2] This reality is visible in the analyses of national data in appendix B. Table B.2 shows that, on average, foreign-born Latinos who live in the United States—whether citizens or noncitizens—are less likely than U.S.-born Latinos to complete higher levels of education, to be enrolled in school, and to have annual incomes over $50,000.[3] The material and social resources these individuals possess, however limited they may be, are nonetheless what enable them to migrate in the first place. And they can migrate for one or more reasons.[4] Some move in pursuit of greater income, seeking work in the United States that pays them more than similar work in their home country.[5] Others, motivated by wealth, migrate to diversify their assets.[6] Some move to reunite with family members who left for the United States before them.[7] And still others see material or social resources as secondary to other goals they have in migrating, such as finding a sense of adventure or an elusive feeling of safety.[8] What it means to migrate, and to become a migrant, can therefore refer to a broad range of motivations and experiences.

The motivations for becoming a migrant are many but, especially for Mexicans and Central Americans, the pathways to becoming a migrant who travels with authorization to the United States are few.[9] Elizabet's story teaches us that the same material and social resources predicting someone's migration are associated with that individual's legal status upon entry and, likely, their access to citizenship.[10] We see evidence of this latter dynamic in the analyses of national data presented in table B.3: among foreign-born Latinos, those who are women, who are not born in Mexico, who are longer-term residents of the United States, who are high school graduates or higher, who have higher household incomes, and who are employed are more likely to be naturalized citizens than noncitizens.[11] In other words, a migrant's access to material and/or social resources matters for their long-term access to visas that include a pathway to citizenship.[12]

Even when someone possesses sufficient material resources to apply for a visa, as in Elizabet's case, they may lack sufficient social resources to be approved for one (or vice versa). Others might have both resources but lack another—namely, time—required to endure the visa application process. For most of the people I met, unauthorized entry becomes inevitable against this backdrop. They scrape together whatever material resources they have and rely on the extensive social resources of people in their hometowns who previously have journeyed the same way. They are aware of, and accept, the myriad risks of immigration surveillance associated with entering the United States unauthorized. They hope to avoid capture by immigration officers, authorities who might photograph or fingerprint them before deporting them. Although everyone I talked with made it in eventually, having their data stored in the records of the immigration system raises the stakes they perceive of engaging with other surveilling institutions once inside the country.

This chapter examines how immigrants who have settled in the United States understand their motivations for having migrated to this country, and how they make sense of the different forms of immigration surveillance they encounter along their journey. I focus on the fifty-five study participants who are foreign born and who, therefore, long ago decided to become migrants.[13] My argument is that migrants' engagement with immigration surveillance on their way into the United States is selective, reflecting their understandings of whether and how their personal circumstances align with the perceived expectations of the immigration officials implementing or enforcing the various laws, regulations, and policies to which they are subject. These understandings inform migrants' mode of entry (e.g., as undocumented or documented) and the risks they perceive of interacting with immigration officials along the way. While migrants often assign different meanings to their different modes of entry, migrants entering with and without authorization sometimes report shared meanings. In these moments of similarity, we learn how migrants' earliest interactions with immigration surveillance reflect the deprivation that motivated their migration in the first place—and demand that they learn to manage the everyday surveillance that they will encounter once settled in the United States.

Deprivation and the Migration Decision

To understand how migrants' initial interactions with the immigration system reflect the hardships that motivate them to move to the United States, we must first understand what motivates people to migrate. Every immigrant I talked with, whether they ventured to the country with or without authorization, described deprivation as motivating their journey. When social scientists write about deprivation, we generally refer to poverty and its correlated conditions of disadvantage.[14] But deprivation need not align with conventional measures of poverty. It can instead, as I use it here, refer to a perceived lack of material, social, and/or psychological resources that limits a person's ability to promote their well-being.[15] A person can feel that they lack the income or wealth necessary to provide for themselves or their family members, even when their assets place them above the poverty line (material deprivation). Or perhaps they miss living near relatives or friends (social deprivation). In some cases, deprivation might look like a longing for adventure, a break from the monotonous routine of a daily life that no longer excites them, or safety, the sense that home is a sanctuary for self and family (psychological deprivation). These feelings may co-occur, such as when someone feels deprived of income or wealth based on visible signs of other immigrants' successes (e.g., a truck or home purchase) in their origin community (material and social deprivation).[16] Although deprivation has a subjective evaluation, it emerges from identifiable structural conditions: the most common include wage differentials between home and destination countries; economic uncertainty in one country or the other; growing economic and political interdependence between both countries brought by capitalism, colonialism, or globalization; and a history of migration between the two countries.[17]

The perceived lack of material, social, and/or psychological resources underlies study participants' decision to leave their home country for the United States. These forms of deprivation do not always align with the immigration system's eligibility criteria for visas, which, as we will see in the next section, explains why most in the study migrated without authorization. Some I talked with felt deprived of sufficient income in their home country, where they thought they made too little for work they believed paid substantially more in the United States. For others, deprivation emerged from broader and uncontrollable economic problems—like a recession, high inflation rates, or environmental issues—that left their families struggling to make ends meet. Still others decided to migrate when they felt deprived of their family members or friends, who left for the United States long before they considered going themselves. In some cases, deprivation manifested simply as a desire to venture north, even absent material need. And, for a handful of people, it was the danger that home represented—from drugs, gangs, or political violence—that motivated them to seek out safety in the United States.

A perceived lack of income or wealth was a primary motivation for migrating to the United States among most everyone I interviewed, regardless of their class standing in their home country. Forty of the fifty-five migrants I interviewed said they grew up poor, with minimal prospects for economic advancement in their home country. Of these, thirty did not make it through high school, nine graduated from high school, and just one graduated from college (and only after having moved to the United States). Humberto, a stout man in his early sixties with the energy of a young adult, is in the first group. He described his childhood in a rural farming village in the Durango state of Mexico as full of "hunger and necessity." School, an eight-mile walk away, was not an option for Humberto who, at the age of twelve, started working with his father planting and harvesting beans. "I didn't want to go to school," he emphasized. "I wanted to work so I could eat." They would sell what they could spare and use the rest as their main source of food. Hunger nonetheless continued to mark Humberto's adolescence. He found some work picking tomatoes in the neighboring state of Sinaloa, but the work paid too little to support himself, his parents, and his four brothers. "That is why me and my brothers fought to come to the United States." Humberto figured they would make more money for the same kind of work. "Dollars are worth more than pesos," he explained. By depriving themselves of their parents, whom they left behind, the brothers could provide for their whole family. The brothers have now spent more of their lives in the United States than Mexico.

Few who described material deprivation felt they had any option but to migrate. Esmeralda, petite and in her late twenties during our interview, was adamant that she had not wanted to leave her hometown in Michoacán, a state in the south-central part of Mexico. Though her family was poor, they got by with what little her father and brothers earned farming corn. Esmeralda and her mother, meanwhile, did what they could to sell tortillas and other homemade goods to their neighbors. "We survived over there because we all just kept working and working and working," Esmeralda reflected. When their father suddenly took ill, though, Esmeralda felt it necessary to not only recoup the lost household income but also to earn enough to help pay for her dad's medical care. Her brothers would leave for the United States in search of that income, and a nineteen-year-old Esmeralda would go with. "We all had the responsibility to help him."

Though nearly everyone mentioned some form of material deprivation, social deprivation was more salient for eleven of the fifteen migrants I interviewed who grew up working- or middle-class. None were the first in their families or communities to venture to the United States. As they observed more people leaving, the sense of loss, or of missing out, grew.[18] Alma, whose story opened the book, hadn't seen her parents in over two years and simply wanted her family reunited. Luisa, a reserved woman in her late fifties with a warm smile, never anticipated that she would live in the United States. She was content to raise her six children in San Luis Potosí, a city in central Mexico where her husband Pancho farmed his own land and tended to his livestock. When Mexico experienced a financial crisis in 1982 that left the *peso* devalued, though, Pancho set out in search of income in the United States and left Luisa alone with the children.[19] The family remained separated for about fourteen years before an opportunity emerged, as we'll see, that would allow Luisa and the children to reunite with Pancho. The social deprivation she and her children experienced was motivation enough for Luisa to venture to the United States: "Family comes first. We had a chance to be here together, and we took it."

Material and social deprivation often overlapped among working- or middle-class migrants in the study. In Elizabet's case, material deprivation prompted her search for "a better life," but she knew where to look for that life because of her siblings who migrated before her. Fernando, too, said he discovered that moving to the United States was an attractive option to combat material deprivation by noticing how well other households in his hometown fared after they sent someone to work there. A handsome thirty-something clad in a plaid shirt and crisp Dockers, Fernando said he was lucky to have survived his childhood in his rural village in the western state of Jalisco, Mexico. He started working at a young age, tending to corn, beans, and chilies to support his parents and five younger siblings. But the long hours he worked only seemed to help his family get by; others in his community seemed to be getting ahead. Fernando eventually realized that the families doing better than his all appeared to share one trait: they had someone working in the United States. "They would receive brand name clothes, or they would start building new houses," he explained. Fernando thus set his sights on doing the same, with the hope of overcoming both the material and social deprivation he and his family experienced.

For a handful of migrants I interviewed, neither material nor social deprivation was primary in their decisions to move to the United States. They instead described more psychological forms of deprivation, such as feeling deprived of adventure—or safety—in their daily lives. Some, especially those from middle-class families who left Mexico as young teenagers, tended to center their motivations on adventure. Rosario, whose fresh face belies her mid-thirties age, was just fourteen when she decided to head north. Her family owned one of the few auto repair shops in their village in Guanajuato, a state in the central part of Mexico, and Rosario recalled "always having enough food to eat, to dress well, and to live well." What led her to journey to the United States was a desire, in her words, for "something new" after a teenage romance gone awry. The young couple ended their relationship (she broke up with him), and Rosario was desperate to get out of her hometown. "Wherever you went, there he was," she remembered. "I couldn't stand seeing him anymore!" With just the slightest bit of dramatic flair, Rosario described the United States as a place where she could "start over, just like so many other people from my village had done." Her mother would accompany her on the trip, too, using it as an excuse to visit her brother-in-law whom she had not seen for over a decade. "To this day, my mother says it's my fault we left for the United States," Rosario chuckled as she reflected upon the circumstances that motivated her journey. "It was my life's adventure."

For others, especially those I spoke with from El Salvador, Guatemala, and Honduras, a lost sense of safety in their home countries motivated their departure.[20] For these individuals, migration represented their best chance for escaping political turmoil that threatened their lives or livelihoods. David, tall, with chiseled features, and in his mid-thirties, had no desire to leave either his well-do-to family or his Guatemalan hometown, along the border with El Salvador. He was enrolled in college, had a newborn daughter with his wife, Maite, and helped manage his family's bustling fruit export company. But drug traffickers were starting to infiltrate the life of the town; David's father worried that his son, then aged nineteen, would be dragged in: "There was a lot of drug trafficking in town at the time," David told me. "My father thought that I might be tempted to join those circles, which seemed to allow for a luxurious lifestyle. So, as a precaution, he sent me to the United States." Maite—three years older, a college graduate, and a schoolteacher—resisted joining him at first. But, after six years, Maite and her daughter missed David; it was time to reunite the family. As we'll see in chapter 4, David's father would, many years on, play a pivotal role in shaping the couple's interactions with the immigration system.

Some of the people I talked to experienced more direct threats to their lives. Ricardo, from a city in the northwestern part of Honduras, reflected fondly on his adolescence. He described his upbringing as "middle class." Though his father died young, his mother took over the family's rent-to-own furniture and appliance business and helped provide a stable home and good education for Ricardo and his siblings. This stability also allowed Ricardo to pursue his goal of playing professional soccer, and Ricardo told me that he had made it on to an elite junior league team by age fifteen—a harbinger of things to come. At around the same time, *maras* (gangs) had started to penetrate his hometown. They demanded weekly payments from his mother's business, threatening to burn it down if she refused. Ricardo said his mother complied with these demands for over a decade. But, when business slowed and she could not keep up with the weekly payments, the *maras* took her life. It was then that Ricardo decided to go to the United States, leaving his whole life behind in a quest for safety: "It was hard. When I decided to come here, it was because they destroyed our business. They destroyed our family. They killed our mother. They destroyed our lives."

Deprivation and Legal Status

Everyone I spoke with, whatever their personal characteristics or story, experienced one or more forms of deprivation in their home country. It is human to want to overcome the obstacles we encounter. Moving to the United States is how the migrants in this study hoped to reckon with these obstacles. If this seems like an extreme or sudden fix, consider solutions to life problems that many U.S. citizens may take for granted. They change jobs or careers when they feel bored, underpaid, or undervalued.[21] They change addresses when they are too far from, or too close to, their loved ones.[22] They change homes or neighborhoods when their current one makes them feel unsafe.[23] Given the longstanding movement of people from Mexico and Central America to this country, moving to the United States was one change available to the people in this study. For them, once they decided to migrate, the key question was how they would accomplish that task. Specifically, would they venture with authorization, or without? The answer largely depended on the deprivation that motivated their migration and how they saw that deprivation aligning with or diverging from their expectations of the visa application process.

Before I flesh out this argument, let's take a moment to consider the steps involved in applying for a visa. There are two visa types available to people who wish to enter the United States: "immigrant" and "non-immigrant" visas. The 1965 Immigration and Nationality Act (INA) lays the foundation of the federal government's current approach to allocating immigrant visas, so called because recipients become permanent residents and have a pathway to U.S. citizenship.[24] There are three broad categories of immigrant visas—some concerned with employment, others with family reunification, and others with humanitarian causes—that the country still uses and that is managed by the Department of State and U.S. Citizenship and Immigration Services (USCIS).[25] Employment-based visas are subject to numerical restrictions—currently, about 140,000 per year, with the principal applicant, their spouse, and any dependent children they may wish to bring with them each claiming their own visa—and privilege elite occupations (think academics, athletes, engineers, and executives).[26] There is an unlimited number of family reunification visas available for the spouses, unmarried minor children, or parents of U.S. citizens; in contrast, complex numerical restrictions determine how many visas are available each year for other relatives of U.S. citizens (adult children and siblings) and permanent residents (spouses and adult or minor children).[27] Humanitarian visas are those issued to refugees, which the INA defines as someone outside their birth country or country of habitual residence who "is unable or unwilling to return . . . because of persecution or a well-founded fear of persecution on account of race, religion, nationality, membership in a particular social group, or political opinion."[28] The number of refugees the United States accepts has fluctuated in recent years, zigzagging from 85,000 under the Obama administration to 18,000 during the Trump administration to 125,000 under the Biden administration.[29] Despite the importance of immigrant visas to the contemporary immigration system, almost no one I spoke with applied for one. There was little reason to do so for most study participants. Based on information gleaned over our interviews, I determined that none were likely to have been eligible for an employment-based visa at the time of their migration, that seven were eligible for (and did apply for and use) a family reunification visa, and just one—Ricardo—was likely eligible for a humanitarian visa (depending on the exact nature of his persecution).[30] This limited eligibility is a feature, not a bug, of the laws, regulations, and policies governing the visa application process that generally reward applicants with existing material and social resources.

"Nonimmigrant visas," so named because they generally permit only a finite stay in the country, are the second broad type of visa available to people who wish to enter the United States. Nonimmigrant visas are also governed by the INA and managed primarily by the Department of State. Unlike immigrant visa holders, most nonimmigrant visa holders will not acquire a green card or have a pathway to citizenship. Like immigrant visas, though, nonimmigrant visas privilege people with material and social resources. The Department of State manages about three dozen different categories of nonimmigrant visas, spanning purposes such as employment (e.g., au pairs, business visitors, or farmworkers), education (e.g., exchange professors or students, international students), and tourism.

Employment visas require sponsorship from a U.S.-based employer, who must go through their own application process with the Department of Labor and USCIS before a prospective worker submits their own visa application; in general, they remain valid for the length of the employment contract. Education visas require a person's admission to a school or program before the Department of State will receive their application; in general, they remain valid for the length of the course of study or program. Tourist visas do not list any prerequisites to an application but, as we'll see momentarily, these are baked into the process; these remain valid for up to ten years (with a maximum stay of 180 days per entry).[31] The application process varies depending on the type of visa someone applies for and what country they live in. In this study, no one I talked with considered applying for employment- or education-based nonimmigrant visas, usually because they didn't know a potential employer who would sponsor them or didn't complete enough schooling to qualify. Three study participants, all but one from Mexico, told me they used a tourist visa to migrate. Accordingly, we'll now review the application process they followed.

The Bureau of Consular Affairs, one of the many realms within the U.S. Department of State, receives applications for tourist visas, all of which must be submitted online these days. If that sounds simple enough, consider that, in Mexico, fewer than half of households have a computer, and slightly more than half have internet access.[32] (Compare these rates with the United States, where about 80 percent of households have both a computer and internet access.[33]) And the application itself is extensive; it collects personal data on where the applicant lives, where they're going, who they're traveling with, where they've traveled previously, who they're visiting, the names of any relatives who live in the United States, their educational and occupational background, and a battery of questions on "security" that include whether they've ever been involved in and/or skipped deportation hearings, helped someone enter the country unlawfully, or ever violated the terms of any previous visa they've held. After trudging through this application and paying a hefty fee (currently $160), the next step is to complete another online registration process and book an in-person interview with a consular officer. That interview takes place in whatever local agency or embassy or consulate of the Department of State that is closest to the applicant. (Mexico has about twenty-two such offices scattered throughout the country; Honduras has two; and El Salvador and Guatemala have one each, in their respective national capitals.[34]) It might occur anywhere from several days to several months from now, depending on the wait times at the office nearest them.[35] During the interview, consular officers verify the information the applicant provided and use the applicant's answers to evaluate their means and intentions to return to their home country once their visit to the United States is complete. For people of certain national backgrounds, including Mexicans and Central Americans, consular officers also take their photograph and fingerprints. Thereafter, the applicant will either receive an approval packet in the mail or a letter outlining why the officer rejected their application. Appeals, entailing their own cumbersome procedures, are possible.

If the process of applying for a tourist visa sounds like a challenge, that's because it is. This challenge is something that all prospective migrants face, to some degree, but it burdens those from Mexico and Central America in particular. And this challenge is not solely bureaucratic or logistical. Rather, I argue, this challenge represents its own self-fulfilling cycle of deprivation and deportability: the deprivation that motivates people in the study to migrate is the same basis on which they believe consular officers will reject their visa applications—all but compelling their entry without authorization.[36] If someone is a poor farmer whose application for an employment visa is rejected, they will likely assume that is because they are a poor farmer. I talked to fifty-five migrants; of these, forty-five first entered the country undocumented. All acknowledged that, as a legal matter, unauthorized entry is wrong. But they also qualified that acknowledgment, explaining that what divides those who enter with or without authorization is not respect for the law but rather the forms of deprivation they faced at home.[37] Everyone who entered undocumented told me they were aware of how to apply for a visa; two told me that they even submitted applications. Yet many felt the outcome of that review was foretold: those who didn't have access to the material and social resources privileged by the visa application process—specifically, income and wealth and a network of family members with legal status already in the United States—would not receive authorization to enter.[38] Simply put, if we accept that people migrate because they lack something, then we must recognize that, in many cases, what they lack is precisely what they need to migrate with authorization.

In all cases, the migrants I came to know disclosed their legal status to me without my asking directly. They usually brought up legal status in response to the first interview question—"tell me the story of your life"— much as Elizabet had done at the start of this chapter. Although I had expected that the subject would be sensitive or taboo, it turned out to be an important part of their life story. When people described the deprivation that motivated their migration, they also referred to that deprivation to explain their mode of entry. None of these accounts imply a causal relationship between the different forms of deprivation and access to visas.[39] Rather, they reveal how people make sense of their present conditions in relation to the opportunities and constraints they experienced in the past, given a particular social role.

Most migrants I met who said material deprivation motivated their move to the United States saw unauthorized entry as their only option. Humberto, the stout man from earlier, entered without authorization in the mid-seventies. He told me that he "never even thought about getting a visa back then." Cost was one reason why: "You needed money for a visa—you still do. . . . But I didn't have any money when I was growing up." Adriana, who was born in a rural community in the central highlands of Mexico's Guanajuato state, told me that most everyone in her hometown grows up in poverty. In this context, Adriana, now in her mid-forties, said there was "no need" to apply for a visa when she set out for the United States in 1994.

ASAD: What is the process to get a visa from Mexico to come here?
ADRIANA: Before you come to the United States, you fill out an application and they [the U.S. Department of State] ask if you have money in the bank, if you own animals like cattle or goats, or if you own land. They want to give the visa to people who want to visit family but who have a reason to go back to Mexico, or something like that.
ASAD: Is it hard to get a visa?
ADRIANA: Yes! Many people don't have any money or land. They're poor. We're poor. There are other people who do have these resources— money in the bank, land—and they can get a visa.
ASAD: And have you ever asked for a visa?
ADRIANA: A visa? No, there was no need to. I didn't have the means to get a visa—I didn't have money. So, I didn't apply.

Material deprivation helped Adriana explain both her decision to move to the United States and her decision to do so without a visa. She reasoned that the same deprivation motivating her journey would have been the basis on which immigration officials rejected any application she might have submitted, assuming she could have afforded it in the first place.

Eloisa, a composed woman in her mid-thirties, also explained her undocumented entry in relation to the material deprivation she experienced at home. She was born in Puebla, a state in southern Mexico, where she remembered growing up "with financial stability" as the daughter of an account executive for a petroleum company. When her dad lost his job after almost a decade with the company, he decided that the family should relocate to the United States in search of a new beginning. Eloisa told me that her parents applied for tourist visas for the whole family—but that a consular officer rejected their application shortly after their interview. An adolescent at the time, Eloisa never learned why they were denied but speculated that her dad's unemployment had something to do with it: "People who have money, or who have something to go back for, get visas. When my dad lost his job, he had nothing to go back for."

For most of the people I talked with who entered without authorization, it was not for a lack of awareness of how to get a visa. Whether they applied and were rejected, or didn't apply at all, they all had some indication of the information visa applications collect. Alma—from the introductory chapter—was very aware of how to apply for a tourist visa. She had done the research herself when her parents asked her to join them in the United States:

> The application asks for everything. How much do you earn? What is the status of your bank accounts? How long are you going to stay? How much money do you have to get over there [to the United States]? Is it enough to travel? How did you earn it? How much spending money are you going to bring with you? They find out everything. . . . Then, they ask if you have property. They think it's more likely that that you won't leave that behind to stay over here [in the United States]. Do you have a stable job [in Mexico]? They already think you are going to stay [in the United States] forever. They want to hear why you won't be staying.

But Alma, who was in her second year of college at the time, felt that these extensive requirements to prove "why you won't be staying" disadvantaged people like her. She was a young adult with limited income of her own and, as a result, she decided to forgo the application process entirely: "I saw all the requirements and knew I didn't have a shot." She also acknowledged that applying when she knew a rejection was likely would just prolong the two-year separation from her parents that she and her sisters had already lived through: "My parents also told me it would take too long and that I should just come join them. So, I did."

In addition to material deprivation, study participants referred to social deprivation to explain their migration without authorization. Most longed to reunite with relatives they had not seen in years. Although a category of visas exists that is ostensibly designed to address this form of social deprivation, few had the "right" kind of relative—namely, a parent, spouse, or adult child who is a U.S. citizen or permanent resident—who could sponsor them for a family reunification visa. The social deprivation they experienced from being apart from their relatives, therefore, also motivated their journey without authorization. Some, like Adriana from above, identified material deprivation alongside social deprivation to make sense of their undocumented entry. Adriana told me that, when she left Mexico, she lacked relatives who were U.S. citizens or permanent residents. But she riffed that, had she still lived in her hometown today, she might now be able to find an American husband at a nearby tourist resort who could sponsor her application: "A lot of Americans live down there now. Maybe I would have gotten lucky and married a *gringo* and had them arrange for me to migrate with papers."

Others, like Marina, exemplify this self-fulfilling cycle of deprivation and deportability. Marina, whose home city in the state of Veracruz borders the Gulf of Mexico, followed her parents to the United States in the mid-2000s—at fifteen years old. Marina's parents had traveled without authorization eight years prior. They hoped one of Marina's several aunts and uncles, who are permanent residents, would sponsor Marina for a family reunification visa. Marina and her parents were disappointed to learn that her aunts and uncles "couldn't help me because I was just their niece; I had to be their daughter. Or my parents or one of my siblings would have to sponsor me—but I didn't have anyone in my [immediate] family who could do that since they didn't have papers either." Marina, now in her mid-twenties with a knack for quiet self-reflection, said she hesitated to journey undocumented. But her dad assured her that "now was the time to cross," warning that it would be more difficult to do so as she transitioned into adulthood and had children of her own. "After a while," Marina concluded, "I realized he was right, and the best thing to do was to be in the United States with my family, even if it was like this, illegally, you know?" The social deprivation Marina felt by being separated from her parents, coupled with the social deprivation of lacking family members who could sponsor her for a family reunification visa, helped Marina make sense of her undocumented entry.

Entry with authorization was the exception. While most left their home countries deprived of the material and/or social resources useful for accessing a visa, as we have seen, ten people in the study did have this access. Two of these people described themselves as having had access to tourist visas because their families were socioeconomically advantaged and could demonstrate that they had a reason to return to their homeland. David, whose father decided to send him to the United States, entered with authorization because he already had a tourist visa: "My parents had gotten it for me a few years before I left," David remembered with a breezy smile. "Since we were well-off financially and had a good business, it wasn't hard to get." Araceli, from a state in north-central Mexico called Zacatecas, also told me that her family never struggled for money—her father managed a large farm that raised livestock—and that was likely why she had access to a tourist visa. The visa enabled a young Araceli and her mother to regularly travel to the United States, visiting her older siblings who lived across the border in El Paso, Texas. "Thank God I had that visa, so I didn't have to enter the country illegally," she said. "I came like I was on vacation at the age of fifteen. But I didn't leave after that."

Given that material deprivation motivated most study participants' migration, those who entered with authorization more commonly explained their access to visas in relation to their social resources. Specifically, eight people in this study—including seven from the same household—had a relative who sponsored them for a family reunification visa. Lucero, a seventy-plus-year-old woman from the south-central state of Michoacán in Mexico, was born to a Mexican father and an American mother. Her parents met as teenagers in her mother's hometown of Floresville, Texas, where Lucero's dad worked as an undocumented farmhand. They quickly fell in love, wed, and moved to Mexico—much to the chagrin of Lucero's maternal grandparents. Over the next several years, the couple had seven children, with Lucero the youngest of the bunch. Despite being born to a U.S. citizen, neither Lucero nor her siblings would automatically derive citizenship from their mother. U.S. law at the time meant that any citizen woman who married a foreign-born man would lose her citizenship; the same was not true of a citizen man who married a foreign-born woman.[40] Although the laws governing birthright citizenship changed several times over the next two decades, Lucero's mother would have limited recourse for sponsoring her children's citizenship; having married at age thirteen, she did not meet a requirement that she live in the United States for at least ten years preceding their birth, with at least five of those years occurring after the parent's fourteenth birthday.[41]

Things changed for Lucero, then aged seventeen, when her parents separated. Lucero's mother left Mexico to reunite with her birth family in Texas. There, she asked her parents to help legalize her children under the family reunification provisions of the recently passed 1965 Immigration and Nationality Act. But the family could afford to legalize only three of the seven children. "They started with the two oldest kids and me, the youngest in the family," Lucero explained. "That's all we could afford to do with the money we had." Their applications were approved, and, in 1969, Lucero and two of her siblings crossed into the United States as permanent residents. But the remainder of her siblings would be deprived of their mother—and the access to a family reunification visa she represented—shortly thereafter. "We were the first and the last ones to fix our status," Lucero told me. "The other siblings remained in Mexico and couldn't do anything to fix their papers because my mother fell ill and passed away."[42]

The one other example was Luisa, the warm but reserved woman from earlier, who was able to secure visas for herself and her six children through Pancho, her husband. Though she and her children would be deprived of Pancho for the better part of fourteen years, Luisa resisted his several invitations for them to join him without authorization. "I refused to come. If I were to have come, I would have had to bring all six of my children. How can you come here illegally with six children? It's too dangerous. I wasn't going to leave them in Mexico either." But, in 1986, Pancho was able to start the process of becoming a permanent resident, thanks to the Immigration Reform and Control Act (IRCA), which granted amnesty to some undocumented immigrants and allowed them to legalize.[43] "He fixed his own legal situation first, and then he arranged for us to follow him," Luisa explained. She emphasized that it was worth the wait: "It took [another ten] years, but in 1996, we came with papers that said we were allowed here."

Among a final category of immigrants in the study—those who left their origin countries because they felt deprived of safety—the most common feature of their stories was that time was of the essence. Time, or the lack thereof, was an explanation for whether they entered with authorization. David, with the breezy smile, did not enter undocumented because he already had a tourist visa. Ricardo, from Honduras, had no such visa—despite his family's access to material resources. And he emphasized that he didn't have time to apply for one following his mother's murder. In hindsight, Ricardo called his decision to journey undocumented "stupid," figuring that he could have secured one since he had previously entered the United States on a visa as a member of his soccer team. But his need to escape the *maras* weighed on him: "I was so desperate at that moment, and they were stepping on my toes, trying to catch me and take away what I had. When I learned that they had a plan to grab me, too, I left that instant."

Surveillance at the Border

The consequences of the deprivation that motivated study participants' migration, largely without authorization, took shape once these individuals set off on their journey to the United States. And, while it is one thing to journey with authorization and another thing entirely to do so without

authorization, these consequences do not always align neatly with someone's mode of entry. To be sure, entering with authorization entails fewer
risks—whether measured in terms of the risk of detention, deportation, or
even death—than entering without.[44] Everyone I talked with was aware
of these differing risks; it was hard *not* to be, given their connections to
people who had left for the United States before them. Yet, for the same
reason that they knew it would be dangerous to enter without authorization, they also knew that it could be done.[45] What their interactions
with immigration officials looked like on their way into the country would
ultimately color their short- and long-term relationship with the immigration system. Despite Elizabet and Alma both entering undocumented,
Elizabet's relationship with this system after four attempts and a round of
fingerprinting differs from Alma's after her single entry undetected.

We now consider how the migrants in the study understand the interactions they have, or don't have, with immigration officials on their way
into the United States. These understandings point to two truths about
migrating to the country. First, as an administrative matter, it is far easier
to enter the country without authorization than with it. Just ten of the
fifty-five migrants I interviewed reported an initial authorized entry, a feat
requiring hefty sums of money, the right social connections, and sometimes a yearslong application process with no guaranteed outcome. For
the remainder, their initial unauthorized entry also required hefty (and,
often, heftier) sums of money but usually occurred within a month of their
deciding to migrate.[46] Second, as a physical matter, it is far more dangerous to journey unauthorized than authorized. Whereas those who entered
without authorization recounted harrowing experiences—punctuated by
surveillance and experiences of immigration officers' racism and physical
or symbolic violence—those who entered with authorization recounted
seamless ones. Yet, no matter their mode of entry, everyone I talked with
characterized the immigration system as unfair, detrimental to the presence of Mexicans and Central Americans in the United States.[47] Immigration officials were seen as the enforcers of that unfairness. Such feelings
were most palpable among people who entered with authorization and
the thirteen people who were caught entering unauthorized. At the most
general level, these study participants understood that interactions with
immigration officials—and the formal records they could produce—would
reverberate beyond that single moment of entry and follow them for as
long as they lived in the country.

Every interview I conducted discussed whether and how migrants
interacted with immigration officials on their way into the United States.

I asked study participants to narrate, step by step, how they entered the country. The resulting stories were generally thorough but, on more than one occasion, study participants reminded me that the mind blocks out what it doesn't want to remember. Still, their stories coalesced around a central theme: being judicious about their interactions with immigration officers at the border. For those entering without authorization, this did not always mean evading immigration officers. In contrast, interaction with immigration officers was typical among those entering with authorization.

People in the study who entered the country without authorization often mentioned doing so via a remote part of the southern U.S. border. These remote areas connote both dangerous physical conditions and safety from surveillance, a longstanding tension that has become more fraught over time.[48] When Humberto, from above, first ventured to the United States as an undocumented immigrant in 1974, he told me that "it was hard to cross back then—but not as hard as it is now." At the time of his crossing, security at the border was a shadow of what it is today. Immigration officers guarded the border but, in practice, that was mostly a symbolic effort. The federal government tolerated, even accepted, clandestine crossings—so long as its officers didn't observe them directly—because these migrants were crucial to agricultural production in Arizona, California, and Texas.[49] But Humberto wouldn't chance it. He hired a *coyote* to lead him through the desert in the Nuevo León state of Mexico, across the Rio Grande, and into Laredo, Texas: "It was hard. We walked and walked and walked for four days until I got blisters under my feet. But I couldn't stop because then I'd either get caught or lost. I kept going until we finally crossed the river and made it into Texas."

In the years following Humberto's journey, new investments in border security pushed the undocumented to more remote areas to avoid immigration officers. Congress invested more money in enforcement operations at the border in 1986 and, four years later, funded the hiring of a thousand additional officers.[50] These investments were on display when Adriana, who riffed about marrying a *gringo* above, decided to cross without authorization in 1994. A friend who served as her *coyote* warned that they would have to venture through a less guarded part of the border. Adriana remembered that she felt scared but, given the deprivation she faced at home, she had no choice but to try: "I was risking my life to come. Everyone knows that they could die on the way." But the *coyote* reassured Adriana. "He told me that he knew the way and how to avoid their patrols." They walked through the hot desert near Piedras Negras, a city along the northeastern edge of the Coahuila state in Mexico, for one day, pausing frequently "to check to see if there was movement." They eventually made it to the Rio Grande, hiding in the area until they could traverse the river at nightfall to enter the country undetected.

Advances in surveillance technologies would further expand the reach of officers' patrols—and push the undocumented to more remote, and dangerous, entry areas.[51] The 1996 Illegal Immigration Reform and Immigrant Responsibility Act provided for the hiring of ten thousand immigration officers and the purchase of military equipment—including airplanes, helicopters, four-wheel drive vehicles, night-vision goggles, night-vision scopes, and sensor units—to support their surveilling.[52] Linda, a thirty-something woman with bright brown eyes, experienced the weight of these investments on her way into the United States. She told me that she left her small town in the Mexican state of Jalisco in 1999. Linda paid $2,000 to a *coyote*, who would escort her into the country through the Chihuahuan Desert near El Paso, Texas.[53] They walked in the dark of night toward the border when, seemingly out of nowhere, a patrol car descended on their location:

> The *coyote* screamed at us, "Bend down! A patrol car is coming." We bent down in a kind of ditch. We were lying down there, and the patrol car stopped above us. . . . The *coyote* kept telling us, "Shut up! Shut up! Don't say a word." And then he told us to start dragging ourselves until we left the patrol car behind. When we could stand up again, we started running for a while.

Their running brought them to a safehouse along the border, just across the way from El Paso. They waited there for several days until the *coyote* arranged for her transport to the city in the trailer of a semitruck. As they approached a border checkpoint, Linda started to feel "so scared that they'd find us." An immigration officer peered into the trailer's lone window. "There was another guy in the back with me praying while the officer checked the truck," Linda remembered. They stayed as quiet, and low, as possible to avoid detection. After what felt like an eternity, the *coyote* announced to them, "It's over now. You can relax. We made it."

To avoid interactions with immigration officers meant accepting the risk that unauthorized migration entailed for one's physical safety. Natalia, warm with a smiley disposition, told me that she left her hometown in the mountains of the Mexican state of Guerrero in 2002 to reunite with her husband in Dallas. "I was scared," she recalled. "I knew I would be risking a lot by coming here illegally." When I asked Natalia to explain what scared her about the journey, she immediately offered, "That *La Migra* [immigration officers] might catch us." Her fears were not unfounded. A year before

Natalia started on her way, the United States doubled down on border security in response to the terrorist attacks of September 11.[54] Natalia's fear of capture, in her mind, justified the many dangers she would confront as her *coyote* led their group of ten through the desert in the Nuevo León state of Mexico and into Laredo, Texas:

> You know the risks you're taking to avoid them [immigration officers]. We walked and walked and walked through that desert. After walking all night, we rested until midday and then started walking again. It was sad because I saw people every day who had died. We saw corpses. . . . There were some people who were coming with us, but they couldn't keep up. . . . Later on, if we didn't see someone who had been with us earlier on in the trip, we knew why. Because they couldn't walk anymore, or they were no longer interested in going. It wasn't a hard choice: walk, or don't walk. Do you want it, or not? . . . There's a lot of things that can happen crossing the way we did.

Others told me much the same thing. Although most reported they had not been caught on their way in, their experiences avoiding immigration officers at the border nonetheless teach them that institutional authorities can be detrimental to their presence in the United States.

Avoiding immigration officers was one strategy for entering the United States, but it was not always a preferred or viable strategy. Sometimes interactions with immigration officers were necessary—as a means or consequence of unauthorized entry, or as a requirement of entering with authorization. Such interactions were especially characteristic of the people in the study who entered the country between the late nineties and mid-aughts. And, for these people, the material and social resources they did or did not have were the most consistently consequential factors in shaping the outcome of those interactions.

Some people in the study who entered the country without authorization did not bypass immigration officers. Those with extended relatives who were U.S. citizens or permanent residents used their proximity to these individuals to facilitate their unauthorized entry.[55] We saw in the book's introduction how Alma's sisters entered using visas that belonged to the cousins they resembled. Rosario, whose breakup and adventurous spirit motivated her to leave Mexico, told me that she and her mother crossed into the United States similarly in 1996:

> My mother's brother-in-law is from the U.S. My mom called him and told him I wanted to come to the U.S. with her. He told her he'd cross

my mom using her sister's documents since they looked alike; one is two years younger than the other. And I would cross pretending to be his daughter, who was around my age.

"It was a bold plan," Rosario told me. (I agreed.) "I didn't think we'd be able to make it through." But when they presented their entry documents to the immigration officer, he waved them into the United States: "They took a quick look at our passports and welcomed us home." Rosario remembered feeling relieved: "I didn't have to suffer to get into this country. I have never known what it's meant to run from immigration officers. We crossed as if we were legal."

There are advantages to using another person's passport or visa to enter the country. Most notable are the reduced physical dangers that someone might otherwise encounter. But this strategy is also risky; if an officer suspects fraud, capture is all but guaranteed. This outcome was especially likely among those in the study who used visas that did not belong to relatives. For example, Elizabet was detained, fingerprinted, and photographed for presenting a fraudulent *coyote*-furnished visa to an immigration officer aboard a chartered bus. Fernando, with the Dockers from above, had a similar experience. When he left Mexico in 2003, a *coyote* provided him with another person's visa to enter the United States as if his trip were authorized. But, as Fernando explained, things didn't go as planned:

> The *coyote* gave me a visa for someone who looked like me and told me to pass through the border checkpoint with that. I was just about to pass through, but they [immigration officers] checked the visa thoroughly. "You are not him," they told me. And that was it. They took me into the office and took my fingerprints to confirm that I was not that person. So, I was caught and thrown back to Mexico.

After this interaction, Fernando's *coyote* changed strategies. "We needed to make sure I didn't get caught again," he told me. "If they caught me again, they would detain me for longer this time since they had already caught me once before." His *coyote* instead crossed him into the United States, without incident, through a remote region of the border near El Paso.

Others in the study told me they had been caught entering the country without authorization despite their best attempts to avoid capture. And, as with Fernando, it was common for them to try again until they were successful. This dynamic is not simply a result of the study design (although everyone I talked to did live in Dallas at the time of the interview). Rather, it was in large part the result of having risked so much—and come so far—to overcome their deprivation that they saw no other choice but to keep trying.[56] And, increasingly, they did so despite another round of congressional funding in 2004 for more immigration officers, more military equipment, and more detention centers.[57] This is the backdrop against which Marina, the young woman from above with the knack for self-reflection, left Mexico the following year:

> We left Puebla for Mexico City to catch a plane to the border to Hermosillo. From there, we tried to cross through Nogales [near Tucson, Arizona]. We were deported on our first attempt. It was very cold at night. I think the *coyote* tried to cross us at 2:00 a.m. It was very cold. There were a lot of rocks. When you slipped, you hurt yourself. I had lots of bruises for days. But [immigration officers] caught us, so all that effort had been in vain. We were already in the country too, but someone touched the fence and that's how the officers knew we were in the area. Supposedly, the fence has heat detection sensors.

Marina and the rest of the group were taken to a detention center, where an immigration officer took their fingerprints before putting them on a bus back to Mexico about five hours later. Despite this experience, Marina explained that she was determined to try again: "We didn't know what would happen, like whether we'd get caught again or die on the way, but we had to try. We were so close." The *coyote* crossed her into the country through Nogales, ensuring that no one touched the fence. And, a few days later, Marina was reunited with her parents in Dallas.

For the few people I talked to who had a valid visa, interactions with immigration officers at the border were a prerequisite to their entry. As we have seen, applying for a visa entails an extensive vetting process. Once approved, though, visa holders generally gain the privilege to enter the country with minimal added scrutiny at the border. It is perhaps for this reason that—without exception—those I talked to who entered with authorization described their journeys as "uneventful" when compared with what they could have been: full of danger and suffering. They viewed unauthorized entry as the normative experience for migrants from their countries—and benchmarked their own crossing against that experience. Some even expressed guilt about having had the opportunity to cross with authorization when so many of their peers could not.

Most of the people I met who traveled with authorization recounted difficulty in securing a visa. But, once secured, they noted their smooth passage into the United States. Lucero, whose late mother sponsored her application for permanent residence, implied that the most arduous part of her journey was the application for her green card:

> I didn't have the misfortune of coming here illegally because my mom was able to apply for my green card. But not without sacrifice. The process takes time, and the lawyers charge a lot of money—which we didn't have a lot of. My mom was able to sponsor me and my two oldest siblings [before she died].

The green card ensured that Lucero had an almost unremarkable journey into the country. As she explained: "When I came here, I didn't have to suffer like everyone else. I was set with the green card that my mom helped me get." Luisa, whose own green card application that her husband Pancho sponsored took more than a decade to be approved, told me that the wait "felt like a lifetime." But, in the end, the wait was worthwhile because it allowed Luisa and her six children to travel together to the border from the safety of a car. "We didn't have any problems at the border. But there's no way I could have crossed that border with my kids and without papers."

The routine entry that visas afforded sometimes came with the weight of guilt. Such feelings were especially common among the three study participants who entered with a tourist visa that they then overstayed.[58] The guilt centered on the reality that, even though they would become undocumented, they had avoided the dangers of an unauthorized crossing, which most of the undocumented people they knew had experienced. In some cases, this guilt manifested within families. David, whose father sent him to the United States on a tourist visa, had no trouble entering the country. But his wife and daughter, who endured years without David, did so in part because David needed time to earn enough money to fund the pair's safe passage. David knew the dangers that journeying from Guatemala would entail. "They would have had to walk for weeks, maybe months. I would have had to pay $4,000, and they would have suffered like everyone else. I didn't want them to go through that since I got here on a visa," David told me. He spent years working and saving money so that they could come on a plane with fraudulent Mexican visas for roughly double that price. As we have seen, this is a risky strategy but, in the end, both Maite and their daughter made it in.

In other cases, guilt emerged in relation to friends or community members who did not have the opportunity to enter with authorization. Araceli, whose tourist visa enabled her to enter the country like she was "on vacation," never ended up returning to Mexico. She instead stayed for the summer to help take care of her sister's children while her sister worked. As summer ended, Araceli moved with her sister to Dallas, where their brothers had relocated in pursuit of more lucrative construction jobs. Araceli asked to be sent home to Mexico, but her parents and siblings decided that she should stay in Dallas. "And that was that," Araceli reflected somberly. But she acknowledged the privilege of not having to "suffer the pain of crossing without documents," contrasting her story with that of a friend from her hometown of Zacatecas who disappeared on his way to the United States without authorization:

> A friend from my town was coming to Texas with a bunch of other people. He got tired, said he'd catch up, and the group left him behind. To this day, he has not been found. That young man who went missing had a cell phone with him during the trip, and he was texting his brother along the way. I talked to his brother, and the last message his brother received was while his brother was in the desert. It said: "I can't keep going." And his brother replied, "Go back home." But that was the last message he got from him. And to this day—it's been a year and a half—no one has heard from him.

Araceli's story about her missing friend is not exceptional, and it reveals how one piece of paper—a visa—can represent the difference between life and death. Since 1998, U.S. Border Patrol has identified more than 7,800 people who died attempting to enter the country without authorization; Border Angels, a nonprofit organization that aims to reduce the number of fatalities at the southern border, estimates the number of deaths to be more than 11,000.[59] "Most people make it, but some don't. We all know the risks of crossing without papers. He knew them, too," Araceli told me with sadness in her watery eyes.

Conclusion

When someone leaves their birth country for another, deprivation is a primary motivation. This feeling of lacking or missing something at home was shared by everyone, sometimes in ways that belied their or their family's access to material or social resources. And yet, whatever material or social resources they did have when deciding to migrate mattered for how they entered the United States and the scope of their interactions with immigration officials along the way. This chapter showed that migrants selectively engaged with the immigration system, given their expectations of how immigration officials would evaluate their personal circumstances around the time of migration.

The material, social, or psychological deprivation that motivated people's decisions to migrate emerged from broader structural conditions. Leaving for the United States was widely viewed as a pathway for overcoming material deprivation. The sources of this material deprivation varied. Sometimes it was a fact of life, as for those who worked from a young age to support their household's survival in their rural farming village that left them few opportunities for socioeconomic advancement. Other times it manifested only after a disruptive event—such as a family member's sudden illness or a nationwide economic, environmental, or political crisis—that strained household finances and demanded new sources of income. In some cases, social deprivation was a more salient motivation for migration than material deprivation. These people were seldom the first in their families to venture to the United States, and they often followed parents or partners whom they missed or who missed them. People, like Elizabet, also reported overlapping forms of material and social deprivation. And, in a few instances, deprivation was more psychological, manifesting as a lack of adventure or safety.

Deprivation was consequential both for people's decisions to migrate and whether they did so with authorization. Although the deprivation that people said motivated their migration often entailed a subjective evaluation, the material and social resources they had access to made all the difference in how they entered the country. The laws, regulations, and policies that establish eligibility criteria for visas privilege applicants with material and social resources—the same resources that immigrants knew they lacked when asked why they migrated. Most everyone, therefore, turned to entry without authorization. They thought their chances slim that consular officers would approve any visa application they submitted. On the one hand, many lacked crucial material resources that they recognized as important for demonstrating their means and intention to return home. On the other hand, many lacked social resources—such as U.S.-based employers or immediate family members who are U.S. citizens or permanent residents—necessary for sponsoring their visa applications. The few who entered with authorization tended to have these resources available to them. In some cases, particularly in situations when their lives or livelihoods were in danger, people with access to these resources entered the country without authorization because they felt they lacked another resource: the time to wait for a visa. Thus, the resources we have go a long way toward shaping the decisions we can make.

The dual decisions that people confronted—whether to migrate and, if so, how—had titanic ramifications for their lives. Everyone I met set off for the United States between 1974 and 2007, a period during which the federal government invested progressively more in immigration surveillance at the southern border. For those crossing without authorization, strategizing around this immigration surveillance was paramount. Most traversed remote and life-threatening parts of the border to avoid immigration officers. Others used fraudulent visas to bypass physical dangers but, in so doing, opened themselves up to immigration officers' scrutiny. Though most were not caught, some—like Elizabet—were. Here, too, having material resources (to pay for high-quality forgeries) and social resources (to use relatives' visas) resources made all the difference. Capture often entailed migrants' detention, as well as their photographing and fingerprinting, and represented the start of the formal records cataloging their engagement with surveilling institutions. For those entering with authorization, submitting their own records was a feature of the visa application process that ultimately allowed them to cross into the country with limited difficulty. For both groups, their interactions with, or attempts to avoid, immigration officers prior to their arrival set the stage for how they understood the everyday forms of institutional surveillance they would encounter once inside the country.

This chapter advances social science research on cross-border migration and inequality. Scholars have examined the material and social resources that predict whether people migrate or remain in their home country.[60] Their work tells us that income and wealth initiate these movements, that social networks sustain them, and that deprivation undergirds each of these processes.[61] But, because these resources are unevenly distributed within origin countries, who becomes a migrant—and when—tends to reflect these inequalities. The earliest people to leave one country for another are, on average, more privileged in terms of income, wealth, or social networks than those they leave behind.[62] Over time, the costs of migration fall, and more and more people who lack these privileges migrate, too.[63] In this way, migration becomes a more egalitarian, and unequal, process: those who want to migrate are increasingly able to do so, but they are less likely than those who left before them to have access to material and social resources that smooth their journey.[64] Perhaps this explains why everyone in the study described deprivation as motivating their migration.

Yet the deprivation that motivates migration is also associated with the hardships that beset immigrants once settled inside the United States.

Migrants' shared feelings of deprivation should not lead us to overlook the real differences in material and social resources they have access to when they migrate. Scholars are aware of these dynamics, which is why they account for them in statistical and ethnographic analyses that explain migration relative to nonmigration.[65] These inequalities nonetheless move with migrants as they cross national borders. As a growing body of research shows, what were once material and social inequalities in the origin country may take on new forms—here, inequalities in access to visas—in the destination country.[66] This chapter contributes to this literature by connecting the deprivation that motivated people's migration to their mode of entry. I showed how the material and social deprivation these individuals endured in Mexico or Central America helped them make sense of the legal status with which they entered the United States. In other words, legal status is both a reflection of the hardships that motivate cross-border migration and a mechanism by which these hardships are exacerbated following migration.

The material and social hardships that migrants face back home do not cease to matter once these people settle in the United States. They instead become compounded with others that come to characterize their daily lives in the country. For their part, these individuals do not accept these hardships as insurmountable. They come to establish routines that they believe will facilitate their long-term residence in the United States. And this dynamic is most evident in their selective engagement with the regulatory and service institutions that constitute everyday surveillance.

CHAPTER TWO

Deportable but Moral Immigrants

MIGRANTS BECOME STRATIFIED by legal status on their journeys into the United States. The material and social hardships that motivated them to leave their birth countries follow them across the border, subsumed under the banner of the legal status that constrains their daily life. Most I spoke with entered the country without authorization, avoiding multiple forms of immigration surveillance along the way. Such evasion would prove less possible, and less prudent, amid more laws, regulations, and policies that circumscribed their social role as undocumented immigrants living and working without permission in the country. Deciphering these laws, including what they meant for how they managed their engagement with more everyday surveillance (such as the police, hospitals, work, and school), became an urgent task. To be sure, engagement could mean the difference between their societal exclusion and inclusion, depending on the records accrued in the process. This chapter examines how undocumented immigrants manage their engagement with regulatory institutions concerned with policing, employment, and taxation. The undocumented selectively engage with these institutions. They strive to maximize their positive, and minimize negative, interactions to align with the expectations they believe that authorities in these spaces hold them to as undocumented immigrants worried about deportation.

———◆———

Evening had started to give way to night when I exited the East R. L. Thornton Freeway. I was on my way to visit Ricardo, who fled

Honduras in 2001 following the gang-related murder of his mother. He lived in a new apartment complex just down the road; the parking lot was freshly surfaced, surrounded by young elm trees. As I walked from my rental car, the air felt refreshingly light; the day's stifling, 102-degree heat had finally relented. I knocked on the door, and after two minutes, Ricardo opened it and welcomed me inside. He was wrapped in a blue bath towel, fresh from a shower after working outside on his construction site all day. "I had to wash the stink off of me," he said. We chatted quickly about interview logistics, deciding to talk over a late dinner at a nearby Chinese buffet. Ricardo disappeared into his bedroom to get dressed, emerging shortly thereafter in a muted yellow tee and dark green cargo shorts.

Nestled in a corner booth at the run-of-the-mill Chinese buffet, plates full, Ricardo and I got to talking. This was our second conversation in as many years. Knowing that he entered the country unauthorized, and continued to live here without authorization, I asked him whether he felt his legal status complicates any aspects of his daily life. Between bites of beef and broccoli, he sipped Coca-Cola from a frosted red cup. "When you don't have documents, you're always afraid," Ricardo reflected in no uncertain terms. "Anyone who doesn't have papers is afraid. We have to be careful." I prompted him to explain what, specifically, he had to fear. He responded, "You are afraid of the police stopping you because you've committed a crime and didn't know it." In Ricardo's mind, policing made salient his vulnerabilities as an undocumented immigrant.

Even as the vulnerabilities associated with his legal status weighed on the almost forty-year-old, Ricardo was quick to point out that they had not yet crushed him. Nor did he think they ever would. Ricardo told me that he has managed two decades in the country as an undocumented immigrant because he has a deep respect for the law. And, as evidence of that respect, he boasted about his lack of a criminal record—and his complete absence from the criminal-legal system. This respect, Ricardo believed, is what has allowed him to "live as normal as any American citizen." I had no sooner asked Ricardo to clarify what he meant by "normal" when a police car pulled into the restaurant's parking lot. Ricardo noticed it through the window next to our booth. He watched two police officers park and start walking toward the restaurant before answering:

> We can look out the window and see the police officers out there. You [Asad] are an American citizen and I'm undocumented. But I'm in the same position as you. If you are behaving properly, why would a police officer come to arrest you? And why would they come to arrest me if I'm

behaving properly? But if you are causing trouble and I'm still behaving properly, who will the officer arrest? You.

I took a bite of my orange chicken, thinking about Ricardo's recognition of the legal vulnerabilities that characterize his life and his belief that he can manage them. Perhaps sensing my thoughts, Ricardo emphasized: "It's up to you to decide how long you want to be here."

It was not enough for Ricardo to lack a criminal record as he managed these vulnerabilities each day; he also wanted to cultivate a record of his respect for the law. Ricardo was all too aware that the authorities he feared— namely, police and immigration officers—would not accept the absence of a criminal record as evidence of his morality. He felt that he had a higher bar to clear as a migrant who entered the country without authorization and as an undocumented immigrant who has resided in the country for almost two decades. By seeking out forms of engagement with other institutions relevant to his daily life, he hoped to overcome this hurdle. Ricardo saw the workplace as the right setting for this kind of selective engagement. On the one hand, his legal status did not authorize him to work. On the other hand, he had to work to support himself following the gang-related destruction of his family's business in Honduras. Reconciling these competing constraints was unavoidable for Ricardo.

I asked Ricardo how, given the confines of his legal status, he managed these dual tensions. Without missing a beat, he told me that he found a way to work legally: he is self-employed as an independent contractor. Ricardo explained that he applied for an Individual Tax Identification Number (ITIN), a nine-digit code issued for tax-processing purposes to anyone ineligible for a social security number, from the IRS. This number does not grant him work authorization, but it allows him to report, and pay taxes on, his earnings. In addition to the ITIN's pragmatic purposes, Ricardo saw it as evidencing to institutional authorities he encounters each day how he chooses to lead his life: "You show you want to work legally, and the ITIN is legal. I think it is an example for the [federal] government that, even though you're illegal, you pay your taxes. Some U.S. citizens don't even do that."

Managing the laws, regulations, and policies that circumscribe his daily life as an undocumented immigrant was not simply a way for Ricardo to avoid the societal exclusion wrought by deportation. Rather, Ricardo viewed his efforts to selectively engage with regulatory institutions as fundamental to all undocumented immigrants' societal inclusion. Nursing our respective bowls of vanilla ice cream near the end of our dinner, I asked Ricardo what he would tell a politician about undocumented immigrants like him if given the opportunity. He minced no words: "A lot of us come here to work or to help our family. We should be allowed to stay here and be granted a pathway to citizenship. But for those who come here to drink, to steal, to harm others? Why should they be given the opportunity to be here? Throw them back."

———————

To many Americans, the word "illegal" is among the first to spring to mind if someone mentions immigration from Mexico and Central America.[1] But the racialized and classed stereotypes it evokes can vary from one person to the next.[2] For some, the word might suggest an immigrant's mode of entry to the country, such as those described in chapter 1. For others, it might connote a particular "type" of immigrant—a young, unmarried man who is poor, uneducated, and in search of better employment opportunities, or the parents of four citizen children working endless hours in the corner bodega to make ends meet.[3] And, sometimes, the word might characterize a certain lifestyle, serving as a shorthand for life on the run from omnipresent immigration and police authorities.[4] The stereotypes of "illegality" imprinted into the minds of many Americans are, in short, numerous.[5] But, as Ricardo's story makes clear, immigrants internalize these stereotypes, too—and their decisions about whether and how to engage the institutions that surveil them every day inside the country both reinforce and challenge these stereotypes.[6]

A variety of surveilling institutions define immigrant life inside the United States. We categorized these institutions as either regulatory (concerned with the administration or enforcement of law) or service oriented (concerned with the provision of public goods) in the introductory chapter. These everyday institutions are not unique to immigrants; many U.S.-born citizens engage with the police, go to work, pay taxes, and take their kids to the doctor, school, and the welfare office every day. Yet the laws, regulations, and policies governing access to these institutions entail high stakes for the undocumented: many need the material and symbolic resources these institutions offer but worry about opening themselves up to surveillance from institutional authorities who might punish them because of the hardships that followed them into the country. At the same time, these institutions are endemic to daily life and, therefore, feel inevitable. Decisions about whether and how to engage these institutions can mean the difference between making ends meet or falling short, and between making it home safely or not at all.

This chapter is the first of two that considers whether and how undocumented immigrants engage with the institutions that surveil them as they go about their daily lives inside the United States. Although regulatory and service institutions can matter at the same time, and sometimes interrelate, most of us learn about the laws, regulations, and policies circumscribing our lives vis-à-vis regulatory ones.[7] Regulatory institutions define the boundaries for how we believe authorities expect us to lead our lives; in this country, this often means as individual, law-abiding citizens who take responsibility for our own behaviors. The immigrants I interviewed, most of whom entered as teenagers or young adults when they began living in the country without authorization, understood this expectation. And, given the overlapping hardships that characterize life as an undocumented immigrant, they sought to align their individual attitudes and behaviors with the expectations they believed authorities in regulatory institutions held them to. As we will see in this and the next chapter, these attitudes and behaviors were set long before study participants became parents—though parenthood factored into how they understood their engagement with service institutions. The analyses of national data in appendix B further support this point. Tables B.4, B.5, B.6, and B.8 show that Latinos' engagement with regulatory institutions varies by citizenship (especially for financial institutions) but not by parenthood. In contrast, both citizenship and parenthood matter for their engagement with service institutions.

Policing is the primary regulatory institution through which immigrants in the study made sense of all other forms of institutional engagement. It had to be. Unlike their experiences with immigration surveillance at the border, immigration officers felt less visible to them in Dallas; just four of the people I talked with recalled seeing immigration officers throughout their time in the county. (Aside from the downtown area, where Dallas Immigration Court is located, I noticed immigration officers on just two occasions as I drove around Dallas County over the course of the fieldwork for this book.[8]) But the perceived absence of immigration officers did not translate into an absence of deportation fears. These fears remained among the people I interviewed, but the fears were based on the belief that Dallas County and Texas police officers could funnel them into immigration officers' custody. Accordingly, the immigrants in the study all grounded their deportation fears in quotidian forms of policing (rather than in more exceptional, high-profile events, like raids, though these did happen).[9] The source of these fears varied, depending on either the records these individuals had accumulated from any prior interactions with immigration officers (i.e., those who had been deported previously or who entered with a visa) or the perceptions and experiences of social ties they had.

Near-universal fears gave way to a shared strategy for minimizing the perceived risk of deportation: selective engagement with regulatory institutions. This selective engagement took two forms.[10] The first is avoiding negative interactions with authorities in regulatory institutions—meaning, almost exclusively, state and local police officers. Although they recognized immigration and police officers as being in cahoots, few said they interacted with police officers in their daily lives. In the national survey data in appendix B, fewer than 1 percent of Latinos reported spending time interacting with government or civic institutions, police officers included, on a typical day; as above, Tables B.4, B.5, B.6 and B.8 show that this rate did not vary by citizenship. Perhaps because of these limited encounters, the people I interviewed seldom saw the police as an inevitable pathway to deportation. Instead, they learned from their own personal experiences, those of their social ties, or media reports that police officers were largely interested in punishing behaviors that racialized and classed stereotypes associated with Latino immigrants. By moderating their own personal behaviors, such as respecting traffic laws and limiting alcohol or drug use and choosing to live or spend time in certain neighborhoods, they believed that they could minimize the risk that quotidian forms of policing would bring about their deportation. Sometimes avoiding negative interactions meant accepting responsibility for paying traffic tickets that a police officer issued them; other times, it meant contesting these tickets when they felt an injustice had occurred. The second is amplifying positive interactions with authorities in regulatory institutions—especially those related to employment and taxation. Whereas avoiding negative interactions is thought to convey someone's lack of criminality, amplifying positive interactions is thought to convey someone's deference to and respect for the law.

This chapter focuses on how undocumented immigrants selectively engage with regulatory institutions once inside the United States. Where appropriate to corroborate some of their perceptions, I also share experiences of permanent residents and naturalized citizens. I argue that the meanings undocumented immigrants attach to their interactions, or lack thereof, with regulatory institutions highlight their capacity to conceive of, consent to, and contest state punishment in their daily lives. They make active efforts to minimize negative, and amplify positive, interactions to demonstrate their lack of criminality and abundance of morality to the institutional authorities they encounter regularly. Although most note that institutional authorities in their home countries would have expected similar kinds of interactions, they recognize these interactions' higher stakes in a country where they believe authorities view them with suspicion because of their legal status. Taken together, these interactions align with dominant societal conceptions about which immigrants "deserve" a place in the United States—and, in so doing, reify notions of who should be excluded through deportation and included through legalization. But, as we will see in chapter 4, these everyday efforts sometimes help, sometimes hurt, and sometimes don't matter to immigration officials making deportation or legalization decisions.

Deportability in Daily Life

It is perhaps unsurprising that most undocumented immigrants I interviewed told me that they fear deportation. In fact, these fears were common to both undocumented and documented immigrants, a reflection of their shared vulnerability to deportation.[11] Most disclosed these fears in response to questions about whether there were challenges they face in daily life that their citizen neighbors do not. What is remarkable, though, is that many undocumented and documented immigrants held these fears even when they reported never having seen—let alone encountered—immigration officers in Dallas. They instead recognized state and local police officers as key actors in immigration enforcement, with many asserting that immigration and police officers are either "the same" or "work together."[12] Unlike immigration officers, police officers were common; everyone reported having seen a police officer over the years, often while driving but sometimes in more mundane situations such as while dining in a restaurant. Though most police encounters do not result in arrest, they can. Informing these fears were their personal experiences while entering the country, with police officers seen as the authorities who would decide whether they would make it home each day or be deported and forced to traverse the country's dangerous southern border once again.

The character of these deportation fears makes sense, especially in the context of Dallas County, where all interview participants lived. It would be reasonable to assume that the United States' border is that dividing line on a map separating this country from Mexico and Canada. Though these dividing lines have their import, when it comes to immigration enforcement inside the United States, the border is best conceptualized as a zone that extends a hundred miles into and around the entire country; approximately two-thirds of the U.S. population lives in this zone.[13]

Within that zone, where cities such as San Francisco, Houston, and Boston fall, immigration officers have the authority to detain individuals they "reasonably suspect" are in violation of immigration law. Outside that zone, where cities such as Las Vegas, Dallas, and Nashville fall, these powers are more constrained. No one mentioned the border zone in our interviews, though many recognized that immigration officers were more visible closer to the United States' shared border with Mexico. The border zone, and Dallas' location outside it, helps us make sense of study participants' claims that they did not notice immigration officers.

Although immigration officers may be less present in localities outside the border zone, state and local police officers are everywhere. And, especially since the 1996 passage of the Illegal Immigration Reform and Immigrant Responsibility Act (IIRIRA), the federal government has enlisted state and local police to support immigration enforcement efforts inside the country.[14] IIRIRA first permitted this cooperation through its 287(g) program, which authorizes police officers to fulfill functions previously restricted to immigration officers—such as inquiring about someone's legal status, detaining an immigrant until an immigration officer takes them into custody, and even initiating the removal process.[15] No police department is required to participate in a 287(g) agreement, but this cooperation exploded following the terrorist attacks of September 11, 2001 and reached its peak in 2013.[16] Though Dallas County has never had a 287(g) agreement, neighboring Rockwall County and Tarrant County have since 2017.[17] Individual cities or police departments can enter into 287(g) agreements, too; Carrollton and Farmers Branch, on Dallas County's northwest edge, are examples.[18]

Over the years, other initiatives have complemented or supplanted the 287(g) agreements. Under both the Criminal Alien Program (CAP) and Secure Communities, state and local police have transferred people they suspect are deportable to immigration officers. CAP is the primary mechanism through which police turn immigrants over to immigration officers for deportation, accounting for between two-thirds and three-fourths of all interior removals between 2010 and 2015.[19] ICE publishes few details about counties or localities that participate in CAP; Irving, a city on the western side of Dallas County, is a known participant.[20] Still, despite CAP's wide dragnet, most people ICE encounters through CAP are neither arrested nor deported.[21] Secure Communities—which launched in 2008, activated in all Texas counties in 2010, and rolled out nationwide in 2013—accounted for a fraction of these deportations. The Priority Enforcement Program, with which the Obama administration replaced

Secure Communities between 2015 and 2017, was similar in design but, as the name suggests, prioritized noncitizens with certain criminal convictions and/or immigration violations.[22] The Trump administration reinstated Secure Communities in 2017, and the Biden administration discontinued it again in 2021.

As policing has expanded to facilitate immigration enforcement, the number of crimes that can trigger an immigrant's deportation has grown. In 1988, amid the United States' ongoing war on drugs, the Anti-Drug Abuse Act required the deportation of noncitizens convicted of "aggravated felonies."[23] These felonies included crimes as severe as the name implies, such as murder and drugs or firearms trafficking. In 1990, an amendment to the 1965 Immigration and Nationality Act eliminated federal judges' power to review immigration officials' decisions to deport noncitizens with criminal convictions.[24] The Violent Crime Control Act of 1994 expanded the list of aggravated felonies to include crimes such as theft, burglary, kidnapping for ransom, and child pornography. More directly relevant to immigrants, though, the law also included "alien smuggling" (e.g., serving as a *coyote*) and document fraud (e.g., using false social security cards) as deportable offenses. And, in 1996, IIRIRA and the Antiterrorism and Effective Death Penalty Act (AEDPA) expanded the list of deportable offenses even further to include any crime where the person is sentenced to at least one year in prison. Given parallel changes to the criminal-legal system that made use of mandatory minimum prison sentences, many low-level offenses—such as jumping a subway turnstile or carrying a small amount of recreational marijuana—could now result in deportation.[25]

Against this backdrop, undocumented and documented immigrants in the study almost universally saw state and local police as capable of instigating their deportation. All described everyday policing as a major source of surveillance that they feared. There were nonetheless some small differences in the content of these fears. For the few undocumented immigrants whom immigration officers fingerprinted or photographed at the border, these experiences were front-of-mind as they went about their routines. Recall Elizabet from chapter 1, who recounted being captured three times before finally entering the country. She identified the fingerprinting she endured nearly twenty years ago, and her resulting presence in immigration databases, as a lingering source of worry. I asked her whether she had ever seen immigration officers in Dallas. "Well, no, I've never seen them here," she acknowledged. "I only saw them at the border." She was nonetheless quick to clarify that she has seen police officers in Dallas: "And they can arrest you and take you to jail. Once they take you, you're off to immigration."

The real and perceived connection between immigration officers and police officers made deportation feel inevitable among undocumented immigrants who had been caught at the border. Eduardo, a forty-something-year-old with a sharp tongue who has lived in Dallas for two decades, noted: "I know that one day it's going to happen. God forbid, right? But it's happened to a lot of people, and no one is immune." His encounters with immigration officers at the border taught him as much. When Eduardo left Mexico, the year was 1995. He had no sooner crossed into the United States near McAllen, Texas, when U.S. Customs and Border Protection officers apprehended him. They detained him for two days, photographing and fingerprinting him before deporting him. Undeterred, Eduardo crossed successfully into the country the following day. Like Elizabet, Eduardo told me he had yet to see immigration officers over his years in Dallas. He emphasized, though, that seeing them is beside the point: "Here, police and immigration are the same. The police connect you to immigration." And, he reminded me, one encounter gone wrong with the police was all it would take for immigration officers to deport him: "You [Asad] are a citizen, and you know that it's not going to happen to you. But people like me, we don't have anything to protect us from going through that again." We will revisit Eduardo in chapter 4, where we will see how additional police encounters in his life resulted in another deportation.

Immigrants who entered with authorization described fears akin to undocumented immigrants who had been caught at the border, though the source of their fears was slightly different. Those who entered with authorization but went on to overstay their visas and become undocumented worried that the police would discover this violation and turn them over to immigration officers. When David left his native Guatemala to escape nascent gang activity in his hometown, he entered the United States with a tourist visa. "But, once you spend a few months living here," David reflected, "you lose the protections the visa gave you." He explained that, while he had never seen immigration officers in Dallas, "it's usually the police who stop you here. And they can turn you over to immigration." Araceli, who settled in Texas with her older siblings in the early nineties, put it more bluntly: "It doesn't matter if it's a police officer or someone from immigration. They will do the impossible to make things worse for us."

Those who entered as permanent residents likewise worried that everyday policing would lead to their deportation. Even though they had authorization to live and work in the country, they were concerned that police officers would arrest them for any small offense and facilitate their deportation. Lucero, whose mother helped her secure permanent residence prior to her passing, acknowledged that "the police cooperate with immigration." This cooperation, she explained, means that "[permanent] residents who do any small wrong can be deported." Although Lucero has since become a U.S. citizen, she remembered being vigilant as a green card holder: "If I had done anything wrong like hurting someone or stealing something, they would have deported me. I would have been quickly taken to the police station and sent to immigration. They don't want anyone bad here." Luisa, who waited over a decade for a green card so she and her six children could join Pancho in the United States, told me something similar. She saw immigration officers as "focused on those trying to enter the country," and police officers as "focused on preventing or solving crime in the country." But she also saw their functions as related: "I can be deported if I do something wrong or criminal. The police arrest you and turn you over to immigration, who can take your papers away from you and then deport you."

Though perhaps surprising, it makes sense that immigrants who entered with authorization would fear policing in ways similar to undocumented immigrants who had been caught at the border. Programs that facilitate cooperation between immigration and police officers, like CAP and Secure Communities, depend on criminal and immigration databases. When a police officer arrests someone as part of those programs, they run that person's name and/or fingerprints through these databases. Both immigrants who had been caught entering without authorization and those who entered with authorization are likely to have their information stored in these databases.[26] The records accrued on their way into the country, then, contributed to the heavy weight of policing on these individuals' psyche.

Everyday policing also weighed on immigrants who entered the country without authorization and undetected. For these immigrants, their personal experiences at the border mattered insofar as they reminded them of what was at stake if they encountered a police officer who turned them over to ICE. Many had endured dangerous border-crossing conditions to overcome the deprivation they felt in their home countries and, given this feat, did not want to endure these conditions again following an untimely deportation. Marco, a lanky man in his mid-forties with a salt-and-pepper beard, emphasized that he is "very careful about the police." He felt that police officers surveil Latino undocumented immigrants in particular: "The police see that we look Mexican and will try to get you for any small thing. That's what I'm scared of, that they could grab me any day and that's it. Some police officers let you go, but others don't."

That the police racially profile Latinos was a sentiment common to undocumented immigrants in the study, regardless of how they first entered the country. Texas prohibits the undocumented from holding a state-issued driver's license, in contrast to their permanent resident counterparts. This prohibition means that the commute to work (or school or the doctor's office) can itself represent a criminalized behavior. It was, therefore, typical for undocumented immigrants to identify—and report avoiding—spaces in or around Dallas County where they felt cooperation between police and immigration officers was most apparent and racialized. These spaces include those reviewed above, such as Tarrant County (home to cities such as Fort Worth and Arlington) and the cities of Carrollton, Farmers Branch, and Irving within Dallas County. Alma, from the introductory chapter, explained her belief that police behavior varies within Dallas County: "The police are not as strict here in [the city of] Dallas. They're stricter in Irving and Farmers Branch." Maritza, in her mid-thirties, sat with me in the sunroom of a Wendy's as she offered a similar assessment: "In places like Farmers Branch and in Arizona, you can't even go around walking because if they see that you're Latino, they stop you and ask to see your papers." She equated policing in Farmers Branch to policing in Arizona, a state that notoriously passed a law in 2010 that, among other provisions, would have required officers to determine someone's legal status during traffic stops or arrests if they suspected that the individual was undocumented. Critics warned that this provision allowed for racial profiling.[27] Maritza thought the same, an understanding that she saw widely reported on Spanish-language news channels. "The police get you and, when you're in jail, that's when they hand you over to immigration."

Avoiding Negative Interactions

Undocumented immigrants report a general urgency to manage their interactions with police officers in their daily lives, given the vulnerabilities of their legal status that render them fearful of deportation. One way this urgency manifests is through their attempts to avoid negative interactions with the police, who they understand as capable of turning them over to immigration officers. Avoidance largely entails immigrants' attempts to align their own attitudes and behaviors with the expectations they believe police officers hold them to as people worried about deportation. Still, undocumented immigrants recognize that these "weapons of the weak" might not be enough to resist negative interactions with menacing state authorities in their daily lives—especially given the racialized and classed inequalities they see as inherent to policing in the country.[28] When they do have a negative police interaction, they make concerted efforts to manage the records that accrue from that encounter, with the goal of minimizing the risk that they might be arrested, jailed, and, ultimately, deported as they go about daily life.

Such avoidance reflects immigrants' multiple forms of legal consciousness—the different ways that they understand the law as a nemesis to evade and as a game to engage.[29] These forms of legal consciousness are not ideational or idiosyncratic; rather, they reflect broader cultural orientations that emerge in part from this country's approach to immigration enforcement. What's more, these cultural orientations impact individual behavior. On the one hand, as we have seen, policing can be detrimental to immigrants' long-term presence in the country. Immigrants recognize that the police can cooperate with immigration officers to deport them for a range of offenses, including many low-level ones. This cultural orientation might, therefore, lead us to expect that immigrants worried about deportation should avoid the police entirely.

On the other hand, there is a certain predictability to police cooperation with immigration enforcement. Policing is the primary mechanism through which interior enforcement efforts occur, but different presidential administrations set their own priorities for who they target for deportation. For example, the Obama administration prioritized the deportation of immigrants with any criminal conviction beginning in 2009 and the deportation of immigrants with "serious" criminal convictions in 2011.[30] The Priority Enforcement Program, described above, furthered these and other priorities. The Trump administration cast a wider dragnet than the Obama administration, deporting similar numbers of immigrants with criminal convictions but increased numbers of immigrants without criminal convictions.[31] The Biden administration returned to priorities similar to the Obama administration.[32] Despite zigzagging changes in federal policy between the Obama, Trump, and Biden administrations, in Dallas County, Sheriff Lupe Valdez, and her successor Marian Brown, have continued to prioritize the deportation of immigrants with serious criminal convictions. The county does not have a formal sanctuary ordinance that prohibits police and immigration officers' collaboration but, in practice, it limits the type of collaborations that it permits.[33] Unlike the first cultural orientation, then, the second would suggest that immigrants need not avoid the police entirely—just particular types of interactions with police officers that seem especially likely to lead to deportation.

The undocumented immigrants I talked with described both orientations to policing, which informed their understandings of what constitutes a negative police interaction and how to manage any records they accrued. Ricardo, whose story opened this chapter, exemplifies this dual orientation. He linked his deportation fears to the policing he encountered as he went about his ordinary routines in Dallas. At the same time, he felt certain that he had the power to avoid negative interactions with the police, so long as he comported himself in a way that did not attract their ire. To paraphrase Ricardo's earlier statement, it was up to him—not police or immigration officers—to decide how long he would live here. And a key factor in this calculation was whether he could avoid negative interactions with police officers—by respecting traffic signals and not driving while intoxicated—that anyone might hope to avoid.[34]

Immigrants recounted several ways by which they came to hold these dual orientations. One is by leading their usual lifestyle. Most people, immigrants or not, hope to lead moral lives. This same broad ideal—morality—permeates both the immigration and criminal-legal systems in the United States. Accordingly, many of the immigrants I spoke with told me that they could live as they had been in their country of origin and all but avoid negative police interactions. In extoling his many virtues as a law-abiding individual who happens to be undocumented, Ricardo explained it this way: "Why would I come here to do all these things when I don't even do them in my home country? It's like if I went to your home and started jumping on your bed. This house is not mine. I must look after it and respect it. And, if I do, everything will go fine."

Such sentiments helped immigrants reconcile the tensions they felt in their attempts to lead moral lives as people who lacked authorization to reside in the country. Selena, in her mid-thirties and from a rural town in the Oaxaca state of Mexico, expressed her trepidation as follows: "Perhaps we're not respecting the laws because we're here illegally, but we're not doing it on purpose—we're doing it out of necessity." This necessity is borne out of the material and social deprivation that she and her husband, Samuel, experienced in Mexico. Selena nonetheless explained that the couple, who have resided in Dallas together since 2003, abide by a simple motto: "Whether here or in your own country, you must always follow the rules." Neither reported seeing immigration officers in Dallas for as long as they have lived there. Nor did they expect to see them. Continued respect for the law, Selena assured me, would help them avoid negative police interactions that might otherwise bring about their removal: "We're here each day being careful, making sure we do everything right to not be deported."

The perceptions and experiences of social ties also informed—and validated—immigrants' dual orientations about policing. Although Ricardo entered the United States with ideas about how to lead a moral life, his girlfriend (and now wife) Reina and his older brother Lorenzo reinforced his beliefs. Both settled in the country a few years before Ricardo, communicating their respective lays of the land to him. Lorenzo, who saw what happened to some of his own coworkers, taught Ricardo that "there are four things you cannot do in this country: steal; buy or sell alcohol and drugs; disrespect others; or be violent." Reina emphasized some of these same ideas, drawing on the example of her nephew who had been deported:

> He would go around drinking and getting into car accidents. He had unpaid tickets. The police pulled him over one day, checked him in their computer, and saw that he had been in trouble before. They passed him to immigration and sent him back to Mexico. You get tired of telling people that this isn't our country. What are you doing on the streets drinking and making a mess? You will be deported! But what can do you do?

Reina nonetheless concluded that Ricardo was unlikely to meet a similar fate, as Ricardo remembered: "She told me that I've always been an exemplary, well-mannered person, so I shouldn't have these problems."

Comparisons with the situations of relatives, friends, or coworkers who had been deported from within the United States were common. Marco, the lanky man from above, has lived in Dallas without authorization since the early nineties. In the decades since his entry, he told me, he has avoided negative police interactions by "focusing on work and taking care of my family." He felt that his strategy has served him well over the years—and he explained that he shares this same advice with more recent arrivals from his hometown of Ocampo, in the Guanajuato state of Mexico. But Marco lamented that his advice is not always heeded. He recalled the story of a friend who arrived in Dallas a few years after him. According to Marco, his friend would often drink and drive and, sometimes, abuse his wife. One day, a neighbor called the police to report a domestic disturbance at the friend's home, and, shortly thereafter, "he was in jail for three months before they deported him to Mexico." Marco told me that his friend, with his wife's forgiveness, had since returned to Dallas but faces up to two years in prison should he be arrested again because he reentered the country undocumented. For Marco, his friend's lifestyle was too risky: "I can't see him anymore. He drinks too much and gets crazy. And he won't change. He's lucky that he hasn't been caught, but they are going to get him eventually. And I can't be there when they do."

These comparisons were so informative to immigrants in the study that even those who had been deported at the border learned to temper their orientations to everyday policing. Marina, whom we met in the last chapter, beamed a bright smile when she told me that no one in her family had been deported since immigration officers caught her and her aunt entering the country more than ten years prior. I asked her what advice she would give to someone who hoped to evade capture for as long as she has. Without a moment's hesitation, she offered:

> You shouldn't behave crazily, going from one party to the next. I believe you should go to work and then go home. Many people like to go out clubbing. I don't share those notions. They go clubbing and then never come back. They shouldn't perpetuate that bad image of Latinos.

Marina explained her belief that this strategy has protected her family, invoking the story of a family friend whom the police arrested "because he was drunk. He had a few unpaid tickets and, once he was in jail, they gave him to immigration and deported him." Marina shrugged her shoulders, seemingly resigned to the fact of her family friend's deportation. "Just go to work, then go home," she reiterated.

Undocumented immigrants harbored an implicit, and often explicit, sentiment that people whom the police had apprehended and turned over to immigration officers got what was coming to them. This sentiment—palpable in Ricardo, Marco, and Marina's stories—struck me as harsh. But it exemplifies a pattern detected in interview after interview. Immigrants perhaps did not understand all details about the laws, regulations, and policies to which they were subject. They nonetheless understood a key punchline: negative police interactions were to be avoided and, as they saw it, such avoidance was well within their control. This belief informed their orientations to policing and, in turn, reproduced some of the same stereotypes that politicians, immigration officials, and the media use to justify greater restrictions on their lives. It also informed how some immigrants made sense of their rather extensive personal experiences with policing in daily life.

Our current era of mass criminalization means that, despite our best efforts, a police officer will almost inevitability issue many people a ticket for running a red light, not making a complete stop, driving with a broken taillight, or some other low-level infraction.[35] In Texas, these offenses are prosecuted as Class C misdemeanors, which result in fines of up to $500; as "fine-only" offenses, they usually result in arrest when someone has failed to pay the fine or has failed to appear in court.[36] A few undocumented immigrants in the study had extensive experience with these offenses. Adriana, who riffed about marrying a *gringo* in the previous chapter, rebuffed my questions asking whether she had reason to fear police interactions: "Why should I run away from the police? People who do that . . . have done something bad, like not paying their tickets." Her beliefs manifested despite having received upward of a dozen parking and speeding tickets over her more than twenty years in the country. "I pay them," she told me with pride in her voice. "In installments, but I pay them." For Adriana, these payments offer her a way to reframe or upend the meanings that might otherwise be associated with her extensive record of negative police interactions: "People who are scared of the police owe tickets, maybe, or they drive drunk or something. The officer puts the ticket in the computer when he gives it to you. And then it's up to you to go pay it. I went in [to the police department] and asked if I could pay in parts, and they told me yes. As long as you don't owe tickets, you don't have to worry."

This belief—that following the letter of the law, particularly after a negative police interaction, could prevent undocumented immigrants from being turned over to immigration officers—was common. And they learned it from either their own experiences with policing or those of their loved ones. Eloisa, who suspected in the last chapter that immigration officials denied her family's visa application due to her father's unemployment, admitted that she had been arrested for failing to pay several speeding tickets. "I had four tickets and lots of warnings," she admitted with a knowing smile. But Eloisa, who works as a house cleaner, simply could not afford to pay the tickets that her lead foot had brought her. The warnings ran out when a police officer pulled Eloisa over as she rushed to a client's home. "He looked me up in his computer and saw that I had unpaid tickets." The officer arrested Eloisa and held her in the local jail until her husband, Manuel, paid the $500 in tickets that she owed to Dallas Municipal Court. That experience taught Eloisa that it's OK to receive traffic citations, but that she should try to pay them as soon as possible so that "nothing else will happen." Gerardo, who spent over a decade in the country undocumented before becoming a permanent resident (thanks to his wife, Teresa, who is a naturalized citizen), learned a similar lesson when he was arrested for his own history of unpaid speeding tickets. "I was young and stupid," the Mexican national in his early thirties told me. "The police took me to jail because I hadn't paid my tickets, and they towed my car. I don't want to go through that again, so to this day, I pay any ticket I get right away." Taking personal responsibility for tickets accrued, they believed, would limit future negative police interactions.

Study participants often resented when their loved ones did not assume a similar level of personal responsibility. Rocío, undocumented and in her mid-twenties with long, wavy hair that she brushed throughout the interview, criticized her husband, Juan, also undocumented and of a similar age, for his history of unpaid speeding tickets that ultimately led to his arrest. For Rocío, her concern was not that Juan had received tickets but that he hadn't paid them and, thus, had given a police officer reason to arrest him: "I was like, 'You're stupid! Why didn't you pay them off? I told you to pay them off.'" The arrest was especially fraught given immigration officers' cooperation with local police. "If that wasn't an issue, I would have told him to do his time," Rocío said. In reflecting on the situation, Rocío emphasized that there are some rules that "apply to everybody" regardless of their legal status: "Just because you get into more trouble if you're not a citizen doesn't mean it's OK to drive recklessly if you're a citizen." For Rocío, compliance with those rules, and making amends for any infractions committed, are part of the deal for anyone in the country. She nonetheless recognized that the stakes of noncompliance aren't as high for U.S. citizens as they are for undocumented immigrants: "Some citizens, not all of them, but some don't care as much about paying tickets. If you're undocumented, you have to put a lot of thought into it and pay them off as soon as you can." The risks of not doing so, in the estimation of many in the study, are simply too high.

Norma, in her mid-thirties, from Mexico, and undocumented, took a deep breath before answering my question about whether her family had ever had police involvement. She then described how her husband, Pablo, had: "A police officer driving behind us ran our license plate while we were at a red light, and he saw my husband hadn't paid his tickets." The officer arrested Pablo—also in his mid-thirties, from Mexico, and undocumented—on the spot. Worried that police officers might turn Pablo over to immigration officers, Norma raced to gather hundreds of dollars from family members and friends to bail Pablo out the same day he was arrested. Pablo was scheduled to appear in Dallas Municipal Court to resolve his tickets, which worried him and Norma; a cousin had warned them that immigration officers might arrest Pablo at the courthouse (the courthouse's website suggests that no one will be arrested at court).[37] Whatever might happen, though, Norma felt it important for her husband to follow through with the appearance: "We decided he should go to court and leave it in God's hands. We didn't want them to think that we were bad people if he skipped court." Pablo ended up settling his tickets without incident. But, as Norma explained, the experience lingers with the couple: "When we get a ticket, we try to pay it as fast as we can so that everything will be OK."

Keeping in good with policing wasn't just about blind fealty to police officers issuing traffic citations. In a handful of cases, undocumented immigrants told me they challenged traffic citations that they felt were unjustified. Elizabet, whose story opened chapter 1, fears deportation just as much as anyone else I spoke with. But she explained that, when it comes to the police, she has learned to temper those fears over the years. Central to that temperament is the payment of traffic citations. "She who owes nothing, fears nothing," Elizabet declared during one of our conversations. She thus took exception one day when, on her way to the grocery store, she was pulled over for turning right on a red light without first stopping. Elizabet claimed that several cars had done the same before her; she attributed the ensuing traffic ticket to the officer's racism. She chastised the officer for the "injustice," telling him, "I'm going to go to court and tell them what you did to me." She hired a lawyer and, as her court date neared, the lawyer checked the status of Elizabet's ticket in the court's online system; the ticket wasn't there. Feeling unsettled—Elizabet didn't want the ticket, but she didn't want to miss the chance to pay it either—she flagged down a passing patrol car in her neighborhood to ask the officer about the status of her ticket. The officer told Elizabet that he could not find the ticket in his system, a sign that the original officer likely never submitted it. Elizabet was relieved: "It was a heavy burden taken off me because I never want to owe the police anything." Though she never had her day in traffic court, Elizabet's willingness to attend, alongside her willingness to approach a passing police officer to inquire about her ticket, highlights immigrants' efforts to manage not just their negative police interactions but also the records resulting from any such interactions.

Efforts to limit negative police interactions are one way that undocumented immigrants manage the institutional surveillance that they encounter each day. Such efforts are necessary (but insufficient) conditions of avoiding deportation; to be sure, study participants described many seemingly negative police interactions that did not result in their deportation. Some of this is likely about the federal enforcement priorities in effect at the time of the encounter, and some of this is likely about local policies that circumscribe police behavior. Still, the fact of prioritization lends credence to the widespread perception among study participants that limiting their own negative police interactions lowers the likelihood that a police officer will turn them over to ICE as they go about their daily lives. Although an important everyday strategy, limiting these negative interactions also has important long-term implications. As we will see in chapter 4, the records of these interactions can make all the difference, both if they are turned over to ICE and if a legalization opportunity emerges for which they are eligible.

Amplifying Positive Interactions

Evading negative police interactions was one way that undocumented immigrants managed the institutional surveillance they encountered as part of their ordinary routines. This evasion was a given for many, something they would have done in their home countries anyway. Less of a given, though, was what kinds of interactions with regulatory institutions they should prioritize. It was one thing to not engage in criminalized behaviors that few people seek out in the first place; it was another to engage in behaviors that demonstrate their efforts to live like any U.S. citizen might. In other words, they wanted to amplify their positive interactions with authorities in regulatory institutions, too. No setting exemplifies this tension in the lives of undocumented immigrants quite like the workplace. Although many undocumented immigrants in the study were motivated to move to this country in pursuit of income or wealth, the federal government all but prohibits them from working. To manage this tension, they actively sought interactions with authorities in employment and tax institutions. They hoped that these interactions would not only allow them to work in institutionally validated ways but also convince everyday and immigration authorities that they are as moral as any U.S. citizen.

Perhaps no number is more important to daily life in the United States than a social security number. This nine-digit code, which traces its roots to the Social Security Act of 1935 and was designed to be available to anyone who lived in the country, serves many purposes. It helps establish a person's work authorization.[38] It allows the federal government to track a worker's earnings across their lifetime and to deduct payroll taxes from their paycheck. It allows workers to report their incomes, and pay applicable taxes, to the IRS. It allows people to open bank accounts and to apply for credit cards, loans, and mortgages. It allows people to receive public supports from federal and state governments when times get tough. Yet, as sociologist Cybelle Fox has shown, the federal government barred undocumented immigrants from accessing a social security number starting in 1972—part of a larger punitive turn in how the country responded to a growing population of Latino undocumented immigrants.[39]

Today, undocumented immigrants without a social security number can pursue employment through one of three options. One is to work off the books. In this scenario, a worker is usually paid in cash, with neither the employer nor the employee reporting those earnings to the government or paying any associated taxes on those earnings. This option is risky for several reasons. Research shows that employers can exploit undocumented immigrants who work under the table—in the form of low or withheld pay; long hours; and few to no employee protections.[40] What's more, there may be immigration consequences to working off the books, either in the form of deportation or forgone legalization opportunities, given the limited paper trail cataloging this employment and any earnings or tax payments.[41] Few undocumented immigrants in this study reported working off the books. The four who did were seldom the primary breadwinner in the household and, instead, worked infrequently as house cleaners. Earnings rarely exceeded a couple hundred dollars a year.

A second option is that undocumented immigrants provide employers with fake identity documents that usually include a green card and a social security number, or what Alma called *papeles chuecos* in the introductory chapter. Sometimes information from these documents is made up, filled in on an application for a wage or salaried job. More commonly, false documents displaying one's real name are purchased, readily available in the neighborhood. *Papeles chuecos* proliferated following the 1986 Immigration and Reform Control Act (IRCA), which sanctioned employers who "knowingly" hired undocumented immigrants; employers could shield (and have shielded) themselves from these sanctions by claiming that they hadn't known the documents their employees submitted were fake.[42] In 2015, twenty-two states required at least some employers to confirm employees' social security numbers through E-Verify, a database administered by the Department of Homeland Security. Some states, such as Arizona and Tennessee, require most employers' participation in E-Verify; others, such as Colorado and Texas, require only public employers' participation.[43] Working with false identity documents carries many of the same risks as working off the books but, given the possibility of forged or stolen numbers on the documents, the immigration consequences can be more severe.[44] There are nonetheless important advantages to using *papeles chuecos*. Chief among them is that the undocumented are paid on the books and have payroll taxes deducted from their paychecks. If these individuals work under the same false social security number over an extended period, the IRS will have a record of their contributions to the country's tax base. The Social Security Administration estimates that 1.8 million undocumented immigrants used a false or stolen social security number in 2010.[45] These individuals' contributions are substantial: upward of $12 billion per year to Social Security and $3 billion per year to Medicare, two federal programs that remain solvent through the contribution of undocumented immigrants who are ineligible for their benefits.[46] Most of the undocumented in the study reported having purchased *papeles chuecos*.

A third option is the Individual Tax Identification Number (ITIN). The U.S. Department of the Treasury created the ITIN in 1996, in part the direct result of the federal government's decision to exclude the undocumented from social security numbers.[47] It is a nine-digit code that is available to anyone in the country who is ineligible for a social security number. It is used for tax processing, but, unlike a social security number, the ITIN does not help establish work authorization. To receive an ITIN, an individual need only apply to the IRS with at least two documents that prove one's age and identity.[48] About one million undocumented immigrants use the ITIN to file taxes each year after having worked using *papeles chuecos*.[49] Although the IRS does not issue fines to these filers or report them to immigration officers, we will see in chapter 4 an example of an undocumented immigrant in this situation who suffers many of the same immigration consequences as those who use only *papeles chuecos*. The ITIN can also be used independent of *papeles chuecos*, allowing undocumented immigrants to work as freelance contractors who report their income and pay taxes directly to the IRS.[50] And, unlike the alternatives, this arrangement entails only positive immigration consequences, something even the IRS has acknowledged.[51] The IRS estimates that, altogether, about 4.4 million people—many of whom are undocumented—file taxes each year using an ITIN.[52] Thirty-three undocumented immigrants in this study reported holding an ITIN, with twenty-two doing so alongside *papeles chuecos*.

If the above proved tough to follow, that is to be expected. It is widely acknowledged that immigration law is second in complexity only to tax law, with the exception that "there is no Turbo Tax for immigration law," as one immigration judge has quipped.[53] Yet, for undocumented immigrants in the study, navigating these various laws, regulations, and policies was unavoidable. It was a given that they would work—almost everyone was employed at some point during the study period—and, as a result, "break the law." The pretax income they earned, a median of $31,000 in 2015, nonetheless offered them a way to fend for themselves and their families despite both their legal status and the overlapping material and social hardships they endured. Whether they worked was as important a consideration as how they sought work. Some prioritized working off the books, or in jobs that didn't require them to provide a social security number, which helped them avoid the more serious crime of working with *papeles chuecos*. Others worked with *papeles chuecos*, viewing these documents as a crime of necessity that both employers and state authorities validated. In most cases, those who worked off the books or with *papeles chuecos* also filed taxes using an ITIN. Finally, a handful said they relied exclusively on their ITIN to work. Undergirding these beliefs was a desire to amplify positive—or at least minimize negative—interactions with state authorities. Thus, undocumented immigrants' engagement with and evasion of regulatory institutions are two sides of the same coin.

Elizabet, from above, told me that she works infrequently—but, when she does work, she does so off the books. Most of these jobs have been in housecleaning, but Elizabet riffed that she isn't picky: "So long as they tell me that they won't ask for *papeles chuecos*, then I'll do it. I don't care if the job is to mow grass!" It's not that Elizabet couldn't get *papeles chuecos* if she wanted to; many of her family members and friends in the neighborhood have them and can tell her where to buy them for a couple hundred dollars. Rather, she expressed concerns about what state authorities would think about her possession of these false documents: "Having them would make me a liar, and I don't want to lie to this country." She noted that this is a sentiment that her husband Pedro shares. Pedro, who entered the country without authorization from Mexico in 1992, uses an ITIN to work as a subcontractor with his friend's construction company. Pedro reports his $30,000 in earnings to the IRS each year. Elizabet underscored the couple's care to "not lie" as a key reason why immigration officers haven't come for her family:

> We haven't been bad. I imagine they would come if I was bad, or if my husband was bad, or if we were both criminals. . . . But we haven't done anything wrong. Our only crime is being here without papers. That's the only thing. Otherwise, we work. We go to church. We pay our taxes. I don't think they come grab people like us.

The reality is perhaps more complex than Elizabet assumes. When it comes to employment, it may be more that the U.S. economy depends on undocumented immigrants' labor every day and less that immigration officers are concerned about their morality. About eight million undocumented immigrants work nationwide, making up almost 5 percent of the country's labor force and 8 percent of Texas' labor force. These workers are concentrated in industries that rely on their labor, such as farming, construction, manufacturing, and service.[54] Elizabet is right in that prioritization during the Obama administration meant that few undocumented immigrants were arrested due to their employment relative to the Bush administration.[55] Yet the Obama administration did regularly audit the I-9 forms employers had on file for their employees; when irregularities were discovered, employers often fired their undocumented employees.[56] In addition to audits, the Trump administration raided worksites that employ large numbers of undocumented immigrants; the total number of immigrants arrested via a worksite raid was about 1,800 between February 2017 and December 2019.[57] (The start of the COVID-19 pandemic shortly thereafter transformed many undocumented immigrants into "essential workers," with raids taking a backseat to the federal government's need for undocumented labor.[58]) The Biden administration returned to Obama-era policies and practices.[59]

Yet the perception that working off the books is less risky than working with *papeles chuecos* was common among women in the study who were not the primary breadwinners in their household. Mónica, whose story we will learn more about in the book's conclusion, is married to a U.S.-born citizen named Ignacio. When I first met them, Ignacio worked as a support technician at a local public school and Mónica did not work regularly. Like Elizabet, Mónica knew where to find *papeles chuecos*, which she felt could help land her a job on the assembly line of a nearby factory. She nonetheless saw *papeles chuecos* as making her deportation more likely: "Eventually, somebody comes to realize that the documents you gave are not legal, and they send you back to Mexico. A lot of people have been sent back to Mexico through their jobs." Rather than work with *papeles chuecos*, Mónica fills in as a house cleaner for a few members of her church's congregation every so often. This mode of work, she assured me, allows her to make it through each day in a way that *papeles chuecos* would not:

> I don't have documents, and I don't like lying. . . . I don't have to lie to do my work. I came here to work and to earn money, but you have to respect the country that is not yours. Even if you know you're illegal. You have to try to be an honest person. To follow the rules. To respect the law more than anything.

As we will see in the concluding chapter, Mónica would feel validated for her intuition when she started the application process to become a permanent resident.

It was typical for undocumented immigrants in the study to refer to *papeles chuecos* as "lying," contrary to the expectations they believed state authorities held them to. But few saw themselves as having another alternative—especially if they lacked social ties who could facilitate their hiring without these documents or whose legal status granted them work authorization. Given this tension between the need to work and the need to respect the law, most relied on a combination of *papeles chuecos* and the ITIN. People who worked in wage or salaried jobs with established local franchises, think McDonald's or Motel 6, were especially likely to do so. Alma, whose story is described in the book's introduction, is one example.

Felicidad, a forty-year-old from Mexico who has lived in the United States without documents for almost half her life and works in the kitchen of a local food-and-games establishment, claimed that the *papeles chuecos*-ITIN combination is common among undocumented immigrants she knows. In response to my question about how undocumented immigrants find work, Felicidad told me that the first step is "to buy *papeles chuecos*."

> We have to ask around to see who sells *papeles chuecos*. They sell them for maybe $500 at most since they know we need them to work. They [the seller] take your pictures, make up a fingerprint [for the fake green card they give you with the social security card], an expiration date [for the fake green card], and then you start looking for a job. You carry that lie with you for as long as you work in this country.

That lie seemed to weigh on Felicidad. I followed up by asking her what it means to "lie" as an undocumented immigrant who is not authorized to work in the country. She played with the Tajín seasoning left on the dining room table from that afternoon's lunch. "We do it because we have to," Felicidad reflected. But she was quick to remind me that, while employed, it is imperative that undocumented immigrants hired with *papeles chuecos* apply for an ITIN and file their taxes under that number: "No, we can't work legally here since we're undocumented, but we can pay our taxes. The ITIN is a number they [the federal government] give you to show that you want to be here." For Felicidad, filing taxes under the ITIN offsets in the eyes of state authorities any criminal offense that she might have committed by using *papeles chuecos*.

Time and time again, the undocumented in the study noted how their ITIN could counterbalance their use of *papeles chuecos*. Maritza, who works a few hours a month as a house cleaner, told me that her husband works in an auto parts store. He landed the job with *papeles chuecos* but, as this couple sees it, the ITIN they use to file taxes each year makes up for any infraction associated with holding those documents: "Many people use *papeles chuecos* but pay taxes with their ITIN. The IRS gives us [the undocumented] the number for us to use so that we don't file using false or forged documents." Maritza reflected on this development, noting that she views it as a positive: "Here, when you come, you need to attach yourself to things in order to be here. If U.S. citizens pay taxes, then you also have to pay taxes, so I think it's good."

Common as it was, this perception surprised me. It seemed to me that working with *papeles chuecos*, and filing income taxes each year under an ITIN, was tantamount to leaving a trail of breadcrumbs that all but guaranteed a guilty verdict should they be brought to court. But, as it turns out, the *papeles chuecos*-ITIN combination is so common that the IRS has come to expect it—and has even updated its e-file system to enable these workers to submit their taxes online rather than on paper.[60] The update allows the undocumented to claim the wages they earned via their *papeles chuecos* under their ITIN. A "mismatch" results, usually because the filer's name doesn't match that of the holder of the social security number, and is flagged in the IRS database. High-ranking officials in the Social Security Administration concede that these filers are likely undocumented immigrants.[61] The IRS is prohibited by law from sharing information on filers' citizenship with other federal agencies except in extreme circumstances. Accordingly, many undocumented immigrants pay taxes in the hope of keeping in good with state authorities—even if a criminalized behavior brought them there to begin with.

A handful of study participants recognized the possibility that the *papeles chuecos*-ITIN combination might not be as positive an interaction with regulatory institutions as many hoped. For this subset of undocumented immigrants, usually those who completed at least high school and/or who came from well-to-do families, *papeles chuecos* were simply not an option. Ricardo, whose story opened the chapter, rejected that he would ever use *papeles chuecos*: "If a police officer finds me with *papeles chuecos*, it has a federal penalty. I don't need them. Why would I take something that I don't need if it will get me into trouble?" He instead outlined how he uses his ITIN to work as an independent contractor: "Wherever I go, I give my ITIN and I submit my [Honduran] passport. . . . I want to do things the right way." And he does so in expectation of institutional authorities' evaluations of him should he ever be arrested, which he learned about by watching his family members and friends' experiences with policing in the United States: "If I ever have my day in court, they will see that I have lived more correctly than any U.S. citizen."

Maite, the schoolteacher from Guatemala we met briefly, had similar impressions about her ITIN. She described how her experiences looking for work informed these perceptions. When she arrived in the country, Maite spent two years volunteering in her daughter's public school. Her goal, in her own words, was to "learn how things worked in the school district since the teaching process is very different here than in my own country." Once she felt like she had learned the ropes, Maite went to apply for a job with the school, much to the excitement of the principal. Just before she applied, though, the principal asked Maite about her legal status. Maite thought about telling the principal that she was a permanent resident and getting *papeles chuecos* to corroborate her story. But she decided against it: "I had to tell her the truth because you can't lie in that aspect, especially if you want to work in a school. It's a felony." The principal turned Maite away on the spot, encouraging her to return if she ever legalized.

This outcome shattered Maite, who "cried and cried and cried until I was tired. You want to give it your best, but if you don't have the little card that says you're legal here, then you can't do anything." Disappointed but undeterred, Maite decided to "start reading" to figure out what kind of job might allow her and her husband, David, to work without breaking the law. Through her online research, she discovered that the IRS expects all immigrants—even the undocumented—to report their earnings. Maite was horrified to realize that David had neglected to do so in the years since his arrival in 1999, and that she had neglected to do so since her own in 2006. She called the IRS to inquire about how to correct this oversight: "They explained it to me. But if I hadn't called, can you imagine? I would be like a blind person in this huge country." From this conversation, she learned how to apply for an ITIN and that she and David could use the ITIN to work as independent contractors. The couple now sells housewares door-to-door, taking care to report their earnings to the IRS each year. For Maite, taxes are an obligation for all people—especially the undocumented: "These are the laws of the country that has taken us in."

Aside from personal experiences, study participants learned from family members about the nuances of the laws governing their employment and taxation. Eloisa, with the lead foot from above, admitted to having purchased *papeles chuecos* early in her time in the country. She used those documents to work in different restaurants over the years but, ultimately, came to realize how "limiting" they were in a conversation with her father:

> Most undocumented immigrants want to work for people who own their own businesses so they can work without being asked for papers. Other than that, there's a lot of people who use *papeles chuecos*, but they lose their jobs when their bosses find out their numbers are fake. It's been a long time since I used *papeles chuecos*. I started working for myself for precisely that reason. I am a house cleaner, but landscapers also do it, and you don't need *papeles chuecos* for that. Just an ITIN.

Her father helped her apply for an ITIN. Eloisa uses that number to run her housecleaning business, whose logo adorns the side of her tan sedan that she drives around Dallas. For Eloisa, these efforts help her lead a life that she believes aligns with the expectations that state authorities would hold her to—both in Mexico and in the United States. "Even in Mexico," she explained, "you have to register your business and pay taxes. You always have to pay taxes."

Whether working off the books, using *papeles chuecos*, or with an ITIN, beliefs about amplifying positive interactions with employment and tax institutions become ingrained. I noticed this through conversations with study participants who had once lived and worked in the country without authorization but who, through one path or another, had managed to become permanent residents or U.S. citizens. Yajaira was one such case. She spent years as an undocumented immigrant before her husband, Javier, sponsored her for permanent residence. A green card holder by the time of our first interview, Yajaira told me that she works as a house cleaner on an informal and ad hoc basis; like others in the study, she accepts nominal payments in cash. Although she isn't the primary breadwinner in her household, and her hundreds of dollars in earnings hardly qualify as income to her, Yajaira explained that she is careful to report her income alongside her husband's each year: "We file our income tax return together, and I give them my social security number and income with my husband's."

Part of the reason she does so is to keep up her positive interactions with the IRS. There are numerous uses for someone's social security number, as we have seen. Given its importance to her daily life in the short and long term, Yajaira thinks of the number as a tool of surveillance that state authorities use to monitor her behavior as a permanent resident. That is why Yajaira told me she often declines to loan her social security number to several relatives and friends—despite her not using the number to pursue formal employment:

I have a sister-in-law in Oklahoma who asked my husband for my social security number. I said, "Nuh-uh!" They [immigration officials] told me [when they approved my green card], "You should never do that." . . . My husband even told me that. So, no, I won't give her my information, or my own sister, or my cousin, or the Holy Mother. . . . I don't give that information to anybody. . . . The IRS will figure out if I give it to someone else. How can I use my social security number in Texas and Oklahoma at the same time? . . . I don't lend it. I don't want someone to mess it up or mess me up with the government. No.

Borrowing a relative or friend's social security number is a common enough occurrence that there is even a term for it: identity loan,[62] as anthropologist Sarah B. Horton calls it. It is a criminal offense that can result in deportation, particularly when the federal government can demonstrate that an immigrant knew they were using someone else's number.[63] The stakes of protecting one's social security number are, thus, high. And, in Yajaira's case, they are high enough that she wouldn't loan hers to even the Virgin Mary.

Beyond the criminal-legal implications, using someone else's social security number might limit an undocumented immigrant's ability to prove to immigration officials that they are eligible to legalize. Teresa used *papeles chuecos* for years as an undocumented immigrant. Now a naturalized citizen with a social security number of her own, she said she fields many requests from family members and friends to borrow her number. She explained why, beyond the criminal-legal risk she would assume, she declines the request every time:

I won't consider doing it. I'd get caught. I stop them before they finish asking. I tell them that, if they decide to take an opportunity to become a [permanent] resident with my number, there's nothing that will prove that they have been in the country for a long time, and other things [eligibility criteria] like that. Most undocumented immigrants use *papeles chuecos*, and they [their employer] will take taxes off them. I think that's for the best. If you work at a job, always pay taxes. Try to do everything as legal as you can. Of course, you can do it all illegally because you're not legal here, but it'll help in the future if there is a way of you getting legalized here.

As with minimizing negative police interactions, then, amplifying positive interactions with authorities in employment and tax institutions is a matter of both staving off societal exclusion and promoting societal inclusion.

Conclusion

Of the different kinds of institutions endemic to daily life inside the United States, those concerned with the administration or enforcement of laws that govern individual behavior are perhaps the most important. These so-called regulatory institutions matter for most people, regardless of where they were born or their current legal status, because state authorities within them hold power over them—the power to monitor them and, should they decide to, the power to punish them. Yet surveillance and punishment are experienced unequally and, for some, a fact of life. In the case of undocumented immigrants who are also navigating material and social hardships, whether and how they engage or evade these institutions entails high stakes. The right interactions mean not just getting through the day but also holding out hope that they might eventually become a permanent member of society; the wrong ones mean game over.

To minimize negative interactions entails the avoidance of attitudes or behaviors in daily life that undocumented immigrants imagine state authorities frown upon. Here, the state authority they are most concerned with is the police, who they recognize as pervasive in their local communities and as collaborating with immigration officers to remove undocumented immigrants under certain conditions. Whether from personal experiences, those of their social ties, or media reports, the undocumented in the study extol the need for all people to moderate their personal behaviors to minimize negative police interactions. They nonetheless recognize the stakes of this moderation are higher for them as undocumented immigrants. Moderation entails simple acts like being mindful of how they drive, their alcohol and drug use, and where they spend their time. Inevitably, though, efforts to minimize negative police interactions fail; speeding, rolling through stop signs, and other routine traffic violations afflict even the most cautious people in this ongoing era of mass criminalization. When this happens, the undocumented stress that any ticket issued is a ticket to be paid or challenged: otherwise, an accumulation of unpaid or uncontested tickets provides police officers with a justification for an avoidable arrest. Accordingly, they believe that following an initial negative interaction through to its end minimizes the chance that they will be arrested and, ultimately, deported.

Amplifying positive interactions entails the complement—the abidance of attitudes or behaviors in daily life that undocumented immigrants imagine state authorities favor. The authorities who weigh most heavily in this setting are, in the short term, tax and employment officials and, in the long term, immigration officials. Positive interactions emerge, in part, from the catch-22 that the undocumented confront each day: most have "broken the law" to enter the country but, at the same time, want to demonstrate their respect for the law in a way that is legible to state authorities. That demonstration of respect, though, can itself mean admitting to a criminalized behavior. For example, most undocumented immigrants in the study work either under the table or with *papeles chuecos*, themselves actions that violate some of the laws that govern their daily lives. All in the study are aware of this infraction, and most strive to offset its commission by interacting with the IRS. Many apply for and use an ITIN to report and pay taxes on their income each year; a handful even become self-employed through the ITIN to ensure that they no longer need to "break the law" to work. Whatever their mode of work, undocumented immigrants express a shared respect for the law—a respect that they say they carried with them from their countries of origin and that they believe rivals or exceeds U.S. citizens'.

These efforts clarify why undocumented immigrants can at once fear and trust legal authorities, institutions, and processes. Scholarship on procedural justice teaches us that the quality of a person's experiences with legal authorities, more than the outcome of those experiences, predicts whether that individual sees their interactions with the authority as fair and legal institutions more generally as legitimate.[64] In the context of policing, less important is whether an individual receives a traffic ticket than whether they feel the interaction with the police officer that results in the ticket is respectful. Given the hyperpolicing of disadvantaged communities (e.g., by legal status, race, and/or class), though, scholarship on legal cynicism shows that disadvantaged people view legal authorities, institutions, and processes as illegitimate.[65] Sociologists Abigail L. Andrews, Angela S. García, Amada Armenta, Greg Prieto, and Rocío Rosales, in their respective studies of undocumented immigrants' attitudes toward policing, draw inspiration from this research.[66] Each connects undocumented immigrants' negative police interactions to their perceptions of policing as untrustworthy. My findings support some of these claims but also qualify them. Undocumented immigrants, including those who reported never having interacted with the police, fear policing. A cautious trust in the law nonetheless prevails. They recognize that the police can turn them over to immigration officers, but they see this as the exception that proves the rule. Policing is thought to be predictable in its scope and, as a result, no less manageable for them as undocumented immigrants than for any U.S. citizen. To paraphrase several study participants: people must respect the law in most countries, not just in the United States. This respect is neither an adaptation nor a performance; it enters the country with them and informs their understanding of how to minimize negative police interactions. Police interactions, of course, sometimes turn sour. But trust in legal authorities, institutions, and processes remains. Sociologist Monica C. Bell finds a similar dynamic in her study of low-income Black mothers, who are both cynical of the police and occasionally rely on them for help.[67] For Bell, attitudes toward policing reveal a larger cultural orientation about law and order. We uncover these attitudes when we examine the meanings that people attach to not just their avoidance of legal authorities, institutions, and processes but also their interactions.[68]

This chapter exports these insights about undocumented immigrants' fear and trust of legal authorities, institutions, and processes outside the context of policing as well. Although the literatures on procedural justice and legal cynicism are vast and diverse in the contexts they consider, their insights are seldom applied to the case of undocumented immigrants' engagement with employment and tax institutions.[69] These institutions are almost certainly more mundane than policing but arguably as consequential to undocumented immigrants' daily lives. Scholars and journalists alike often extol undocumented immigrants who pay taxes and other fees. These taxes and fees are unavoidable for most people, regardless of their legal status, and people take pride in paying them as "evidence that one is a responsible, contributing, and upstanding member of society, a person worthy of respect in the community and representation in the government."[70] Less remarked upon are undocumented immigrants' concerted efforts to seek out engagement with employment and tax institutions. Although they fear reprisal for working without authorization, they trust authorities in these spaces to recognize their attempts to offset this offense—for example, by applying for and using an ITIN to pay income taxes. In fact, many in the study see the ITIN as an olive branch that the federal government extends to undocumented immigrants to show that they are as moral as U.S. citizens.[71] When considered alongside the avoidance of negative police interactions, then, the amplification of these positive interactions with tax and employment authorities reveals how institutional engagement and evasion can represent two sides of the same coin for this group.

These insights refine our theoretical understandings of crime, law, and deviance; surveillance and system avoidance; and legal cynicism. Research on crime, law, and deviance is extensive. In particular, this scholarship shows that when legal authorities, institutions, and processes mark someone as deviating from societal norms—for example, by arresting them for the commission of certain criminalized acts like driving under the influence or petty theft—and punish them, that person is likely to change their behavior in ways unintended by the same.[72] Drawing inspiration from these insights, sociologists Alice Goffman and Sarah Brayne posit that reduced engagement with surveilling institutions is one such behavioral consequence. Both authors show that people who have been stopped by the police, arrested, convicted, or incarcerated are more likely to evade surveilling institutions when compared with people who have not had these experiences.[73] One reason why is the legal cynicism—the perception that law enforcement is "illegitimate, unresponsive, and ill equipped to ensure public safety"—that emerges following someone's negative police interactions. This cynicism generalizes toward other institutions that might place the person on the radar of other authorities, institutions, and processes that they might associate with government surveillance.

Less considered in these literatures is people's legal consciousness, or how they understand, experience, and act in relation to legal authorities, institutions, and processes.[74] To use a phrase coined by sociologists Patricia Ewick and Susan S. Silbey, people with negative police interactions certainly can evince an "against the law" legal consciousness.[75] They use their prior experiences with legal authorities to inform their understandings that authorities in surveilling institutions are dangerous and, thus, to be avoided. The perceptions and experiences of the undocumented immigrants in this study align with aspects of this narrative and diverge from others. They all recognize themselves as "marked" by their legal status; regardless of how they entered the country, they live and work in the country without the government's permission. And, to a certain degree, they see the legal authorities, institutions, and processes they encounter as part of their daily lives as dangerous, capable of shuttling them into deportation.

But undocumented immigrants also evince a "with the law" legal consciousness. They recognize legal authorities, institutions, and processes as allowing them "a set of permissible roles, transactions, and purposes" despite their legal status.[76] Both against the law and with the law, undocumented immigrants circumscribe their institutional engagement in ways they believe compatible with these roles, transactions, and purposes. In this way, the undocumented—and likely other populations worried about state punishment—do not avoid systems or institutions wholesale but rather particular interactions. And structural features of regulatory institutions can enable or constrain these interactional efforts. For example, in the context of policing, its predictability alongside the statistical rarity of interior efforts at immigration enforcement may encourage these individuals to interact with legal authorities, institutions, or processes that they might otherwise have good reason to fear and avoid. Likewise, in the context of employment and taxation, the ITIN offers an institutionalized pathway for undocumented immigrants to comply with crucial tax obligations even as they are denied work authorization. From the perspective of undocumented immigrants, these efforts have several payoffs: they allow them to distance themselves from racialized and classed stereotypes and bring them closer to whatever ideal of "American" they imagine institutional authorities want undocumented immigrants to display. Undocumented immigrants are not too far off in their impressions, as we have seen and will see more closely in chapter 4, but the structure of the immigration system means that even the most superlative of undocumented immigrants can one day be excluded from society.

CHAPTER THREE

Good Immigrants, or Good Parents?

UNDOCUMENTED IMMIGRANTS SELECTIVELY ENGAGE with regulatory institutions in ways they believe mesh with authorities' expectations of them as people living and working without permission in the United States. But legal status alone does not define undocumented immigrants' lives. Over time, they come to juggle multiple social roles and responsibilities that sometimes align, and sometimes conflict, with one another. Given the study's requirement that all households contain at least one young child, parenthood is the most relevant to the undocumented immigrants I met. The responsibilities they associate with being parents are in tension with those they associate with being undocumented. As undocumented immigrants, they endure overlapping forms of material and social hardship exacerbated by the constraints of their legal status; as parents, they worry about passing on these hardships to their children. Finding ways to counteract the effects of these hardships on their children while also respecting the laws, regulations, and policies that govern their lives as undocumented immigrants, therefore, emerges as a new challenge. This chapter examines this challenge in the context of undocumented parents navigating service institutions that distribute public goods (e.g., health care, education, and public assistance). Undocumented immigrants limit their own engagement with service institutions, even as they engage with these institutions on behalf of their children. This selective engagement has high stakes for their own and their families' societal inclusion and exclusion.

———

I was outside a veritable fortress. This building—a few minutes from downtown—stood out in this neighborhood of disinvested apartments. It was well guarded and maintained. On the other side of an iron gate were several potted plants lining a paved walkway and a small, manicured stretch of grass. A never-ending row of large windows punctured the otherwise impenetrable brick façade. I used the intercom to dial Samuel and Selena's unit, and, almost immediately, the curtains to a unit facing the street flung open. Two excited-looking children waved. One disappeared and, within a minute, emerged from the building to open the gate and accompany me inside. Samuel, handsome with olive skin, and Selena, whose flowing black hair accentuated her high cheekbones, were waiting for me at the marbled dining table just off their galley kitchen. Samuel had a cheery disposition, Selena a bit more reserved, but both were welcoming.

The couple's warm reception contrasted with the coldness of the material and social deprivation that they told me motivated their move to the United States. They grew up in neighboring rural towns in two different states in the southern part of Mexico—Samuel from Guerrero and Selena from Oaxaca. Their families depended on subsistence farming to get by; Samuel and Selena both left school at an early age to work to support their households. Neither had envisioned a life for themselves in the United States but, in the late nineties, more and more people from their hometowns were heading north. Their own journey soon seemed inevitable. Samuel left first, in 2002, finding work in a factory packing gum and cigarettes alongside his oldest brother who had arrived a few years before him. He saved what he could to pay for a *coyote* to escort Selena, who was carrying their first child, into the country safely. Selena miscarried before Samuel had saved enough, but by 2003, the couple had reunited in Dallas.

The deprivation that characterized their lives in Mexico followed them to the United States, albeit compounded by the constraints of their legal status. By the time I met the couple in 2013, they counted more than ten years living and working in the country without authorization. And, despite feeling caged in by their legal status, Samuel and Selena have tried to make a life for themselves. Samuel, who worked in a nearby mattress factory with his *papeles chuecos* when we met, earns about $14,000 a year. Selena, who used to clean houses in the area, is a stay-at-home mom to the couple's four children under the age of eight—all born in the United States. Finances were tight. "We don't have rich people's lives," Samuel acknowledged, "but we can buy what we need to survive."

Myriad service institutions have been pivotal to that survival. Two years after Selena's arrival in the country, sudden stomach pains sent her to a nearby emergency room. A nurse offered her a pregnancy test, and upon discovering that Selena was pregnant, encouraged her to sign up for Texas' Children's Health Insurance Program (CHIP) and Special Supplemental Nutrition Program for Women, Infants, and Children (WIC). CHIP's "unborn child option" affords pregnant people of any legal status twenty prenatal visits and support toward labor and delivery charges. Though Selena's coverage would lapse following two postnatal visits, the child's coverage would not. Similarly, WIC offered a pregnant Selena a monthly allowance to purchase healthy food, which her children would receive until age five. Selena said she hesitated to apply for this assistance; she didn't want to "burden the government." But, when a hospital social worker insisted they complete the applications, Selena relented. She and Samuel needed the help. What's more, Selena wanted to make sure the social worker saw the couple as good parents: "We wanted them to know that we were doing everything we can so our kids can do better than us." Selena reenrolled in CHIP and WIC for each subsequent pregnancy.

Engagement with service institutions proved invaluable a few years after the birth of the couple's third child, whom doctors diagnosed with a life-threatening cancer at just six years old. Treatment would not be easy; it required years' worth of chemotherapy and radiation. Initially, Samuel, Selena, and their four kids found themselves all but living at the hospital. It was hard for Samuel to work while he worried for his child, and it was hard for Selena to keep the kids quiet in a sterile hospital room by herself. A hospital social worker informed them that additional forms of public assistance might alleviate some of their burden. Things moved fast after that. The social worker contacted Samuel's employer to shorten his workday so that he and Selena could take turns being present for their kids. To offset the reduced income, the social worker helped the family apply for the Supplemental Nutrition Assistance Program (SNAP; colloquially, "food stamps"), which supplements poor families' food budgets, and Supplemental Security Income (SSI; colloquially, "disability"), which offers financial support to citizens with severe functional limitations. Finally, the social worker secured public housing for the family, where we conducted all four interviews between 2013 and 2018.

I asked the couple whether the hardships that characterized their daily life weighed on them as they received public goods from these various service institutions. Both quickly corrected me: the two of them received nothing—only their citizen children did. This distinction was important, as Samuel explained: "The government doesn't give help to those of us who are undocumented, just those who were born here." He went on to explain how receiving these public goods—here, health care and public assistance—was as much an immediate material necessity as a prudent long-term judgment. As undocumented immigrants raising citizen children, service institutions help them make ends meet despite the material and social hardships they face. Yet, for the same reasons, they worry about what *not* receiving these public goods would mean to the doctors, nurses, teachers, and social workers they encounter as part of their children's ordinary routines: "Imagine if something happens to the children because we couldn't afford to take care of them. We would be in a lot of trouble." Selena interjected, partly agreeing with Samuel and partly reminding him that they might still find themselves in trouble with immigration authorities one day for having secured these goods for their children: "A lot of undocumented immigrants do it and, so far, nothing has happened to them. But I don't know, to be honest. We have to be careful." Samuel countered, recalling what the hospital social worker had explained to them. If either faces deportation, "we can use the help we received for our children to help us stay here since the kids can't live here without us." Both are right in their own ways, as we'll see, revealing the short- and long-term tensions between their societal inclusion and exclusion that undocumented parents must navigate every day to get by.

———◆———

It is one thing for undocumented immigrants to endure compounding legal, material, and social hardships as they go about their own individual lives, but it is another thing entirely for these hardships to afflict their children.[1] Many have stories like Samuel and Selena's, venturing to this country as teenagers or young adults for a chance at something better than what they had in their birth countries. They knew that their lives here would not be luxurious; it's hard to luxuriate when policing and immigration enforcement feel like real threats each day, when only certain kinds of jobs are available to them, and when those jobs stifle their income potential. Still, in venturing to the United States without authorization, many accepted these hardships in the hopes of overcoming the deprivation that brought them here in the first place. Most I talked to weren't parents when they arrived in the country; that transition happened after they had lived here for a few years and carved out a new life for themselves. But parenthood carried with it a new set of challenges for undocumented immigrants. Like most parents, they wanted to provide for their children. The overlapping hardships of their legal status nonetheless posed complications to that goal in ways that threatened their caregiving. This tension between being a "good" immigrant and being a "good" parent would be reflected in their institutional engagement—including its meanings for their societal inclusion or exclusion.

Our focus in this chapter is on service institutions. Although we can name discrete categories of service institutions, categories such as "health care," "education," and "public assistance" encompass a broad range of institutions and authorities. Health care can refer to hospitals, a stand-alone medical office, urgent care, or a community health clinic, as well as all the doctors, nurses, social workers, and other staff within them. Education includes private, public, or charter schools and universities, as well as all the administrators, teachers, and other staff within them. And public assistance refers to various programs; the most important here are CHIP, WIC, SNAP, and SSI, as well as all the supervisors, caseworkers, and other staff within them. Perhaps more so than their regulatory counterparts, service institutions illuminate how undocumented immigrants manage their crisscrossing social roles and responsibilities as individuals vulnerable to deportation and as parents to young, U.S.-citizen children.[2] Several laws, regulations, and policies govern what undocumented immigrants' access to service institutions can look like; these vary (across institutions, time periods, and states) but, generally, noncitizens have less access than naturalized citizens (and, among noncitizens, the undocumented have less access than permanent residents), whose access ostensibly equals that of citizens born in the country.[3] We observe some of these differences in the national data analyzed in appendix B. In table B.4, which considers Latinos' engagement with service institutions on their own behalf, we see that Latino noncitizens have less engagement on a typical day than Latino naturalized citizens, who have less engagement than U.S.-born Latinos.

But many of the laws, regulations, and policies that circumscribe undocumented immigrants' personal access to service institutions do not apply to their children who are born in the United States. As with regulatory institutions, then, undocumented parents must seek out some interactions with service institutions and avoid others. The rub is that service institutions are common to most parents' daily lives, and it is impossible—if not inadvisable—to avoid interacting with the authorities who staff them as part of their children's routines.[4] This tension is magnified for parents navigating correlated hardships. We again see evidence of this dynamic in national data. Whereas table B.4 considers Latinos' engagement with service institutions as individuals, table B.6 adds time spent on behalf of one's children. Among Latino noncitizen parents, their engagement with service institutions quadruples when we account for their children. We still observe gaps between noncitizen and U.S.-born parents, but the differences are attributable to noncitizen parents' more limited personal engagements. What's more, and as shown in B.7, B.8, and B.9, gaps by parental citizenship generally disappear when accounting for demographic characteristics (e.g., income and educational attainment). In brief, Latino noncitizens, whether undocumented or permanent residents, align their engagement with service institutions with their multiple social roles and responsibilities.

This chapter examines how undocumented immigrants manage their engagement with the service institutions institutions they encounter in daily life. I also incorporate, where appropriate, the experiences of semi-legal immigrants or permanent residents to offer additional context. Whereas the previous chapters have presented the stories of undocumented immigrants as standalone individuals worried about deportation, this chapter expands that focus to include their social role as parents worried about their children's well-being. Both social roles matter—sometimes independently, sometimes interdependently, and sometimes successively—depending on the social context under consideration. A person's legal status is one signal of the correlated legal, material, and social hardships they experience in this country. These hardships manifest even without kids in the household. And, although many U.S. citizens can turn to service institutions when times are tough, the undocumented are generally prohibited from doing the same. The consequences of these hardships are several. One is that they interfere with undocumented parents' responsibilities to their children. When parents are denied legal, material, and social resources, their children suffer. Although the undocumented are willing to endure these hardships, they try their best to mitigate these hardships' impacts on their children. Service institutions offer them a way to do so. It's not hard to understand why: this is what any parent would do. But, beyond that simple truth, they recognize another: they are poor parents who must be wary of the unavoidable racialized and classed scrutiny of these authorities.[5] Aligning their institutional engagement with the perceived expectations of these authorities, therefore, emerges as a lifeline that offers not only real resources but also staves off referrals to more punitive regulatory bodies—namely, the police or Child Protective Services—who might otherwise threaten their families.[6] This engagement with service institutions on behalf of one's children can have long-term immigration consequences for the parents, too, pointing to the successive import of undocumented immigrants' multiple social roles and responsibilities for societal membership.

Compounding Hardships

The overlapping legal, material, and social hardships that undocumented immigrants experience have profound implications for their children. Though some of these hardships are unique to parents and others are unique to nonparents, many others simply characterize life as an undocumented immigrant. We saw in the previous chapter how undocumented immigrants selectively engage with regulatory institutions as they live and work in the country. They continue to experience legal, material, and social hardships despite these everyday efforts. In each interview, study participants shared with me their perceptions of and experiences with work, including whether they worked full time and how much they earned. I then took that information to calculate whether that person's family lived in poverty, according to federal poverty guidelines.[7] The result was not surprising, but it was jarring: half of the study families, all containing at least one undocumented parent, lived in poverty. With a handful of exceptions, the remainder were still "low income"—earning too much to be classified as living in poverty but not enough to do more than make ends meet each month. In both cases, the associated legal, material, and social hardships had real consequences for how these families lived and how they would understand their selective engagement with service institutions on behalf of their children.

It should come as no surprise by now that the federal government's decision in the 1970s to exclude undocumented immigrants from social security numbers underlies some of the overlapping hardships they experience. As we learned in the previous chapter, these nine-digit numbers help establish proof of an employee's authorization to work in the country, which they submit to their employer via U.S. Citizenship and Immigration Services' (USCIS) I-9 form. This form gathers information about the employee's legal status and work authorization. Accordingly, it confirms to an employer that the person they have hired possesses all usual workers' rights and protections and makes it more likely that an employer will pay an employee their due wages or salary.[8] A social security number also allows people to access jobs that are less hazardous to their physical well-being (think about the difference between laying a roof and cleaning a school, for example).[9] Should an employer engage in exploitative or otherwise questionable labor practices, having a social security number is associated with a greater likelihood of an employee reporting that employer to the U.S. Department of Labor (DOL).[10] All these things grant workers access to one important resource: money. Over time, they earn more money, are promoted at work, and/or find another job that better remunerates their accumulated work experience. These resources, in turn, facilitate a person's ability to "move up" in life, such as by buying a home or moving into a neighborhood that has low crime rates and high-quality public schools.[11]

For undocumented immigrants, working off the books, with *papeles chuecos*, or with an Individual Tax Identification Number (ITIN) rarely affords them these opportunities. And the hardships associated with their legal status are a primary reason why. Employers are required to keep an I-9 on file for each person on their payroll, retain the form for up to three years, and make the form available for inspection if requested by the DOL, the Department of Homeland Security (DHS), or the Department of Justice (DOJ). All this to say, when someone works without authorization, employers usually know.[12] And, given the employees' lack of work authorization, employers offer undocumented immigrants lower wages than they might otherwise get.[13] The same goes for contractors working with an ITIN (though they would fill out a W-9 form from the IRS that employers issue to independent contractors). Working unauthorized entails both lower pay and higher job instability, with employers regularly dismissing these employees.[14] Such dismissals are common in advance of inspections from DHS, DOL, or DOJ authorities, who have increasingly turned to worksite audits of employers' hiring practices as a tool of immigration enforcement.[15] The Obama administration came to rely on these audits, the Trump administration prioritized worksite raids that arrested employees, and the Biden administration reverted to Obama-era audits.[16] Moving up in life proves difficult against this backdrop.

Labor market statistics reflect these correlated hardships.[17] In Texas, about 1.6 million undocumented immigrants are of working age, and most come from Mexico or Central America. Many did not complete formal schooling: 54 percent did not graduate high school, and two-thirds of these did not make it past the eighth grade. A similar fraction reports speaking English "not well" or "not at all" (53 percent), with Spanish the top language spoken at home among this population (85 percent). Two-thirds of working-age undocumented immigrants in Texas are employed and, given the above, they tend to concentrate in blue collar occupations. These include construction (30 percent), food or entertainment services (15 percent), professional services (12 percent; e.g., landscaping, groundskeeping, and custodial work), manufacturing (8 percent), and others (8 percent). Almost two-thirds of undocumented immigrants statewide have family incomes that place them below or just above the poverty line.

No one I talked with needed to have these hardships explained to them, or what these hardships meant for their families. Many had experienced them firsthand over their years in the country. Most were employed full time, and many reported working overtime. They worked in laborious occupations like cleaning, cooking, construction, and manufacturing, but their yearly income seldom reflected this labor. The median annual pretax income of study households with at least one undocumented member was $31,000, with most describing their incomes as "low" or "insufficient" to make ends meet. But, in accounting for this figure, the undocumented explained how the correlated hardships they endured limited their opportunities for moving up. Few employers were willing to hire them, and those that did paid them low wages—if they paid them at all. They also faced job instability. There would be no way of moving up, they acknowledged, since these hardships kept their families struggling to get by.

In the United States, undocumented immigrants are concentrated in labor-intensive industries. Eduardo, with the sharp tongue from the previous chapter, put it like this: "We work in all kinds of jobs. If you've gone out to eat, or looked at construction sites, or inside the factories, or inside office buildings where cleaning is done, we're everywhere. No one else wants to do this work."[18] His insights are supported by the jobs that the undocumented immigrants in the study held, with each of the industries he mentioned well represented. For his part, Eduardo works as a line cook. Dorinda, his partner, works as a housekeeper in a hotel. They told me that they bring in about $32,000 every year, money that all but dissipates once they have paid payroll taxes, their monthly bills, and the rent on their crowded one-bedroom apartment they share with Dorinda's three children. But neither felt there was anything they could do to boost their income, given the hardships of their legal status that they say their employers take advantage of: "No one in this country pays us a lot. You can find work, but you're not going to earn as much as someone who is from here." Eduardo stopped for a minute and grimaced. "One coworker I have who was born here makes like $16 an hour," he said with a shrug. "That's the way it is everywhere." Were he authorized to work, he supposed he would be paid closer to that amount rather than the hourly minimum wage of $7.25 he reported. Instead, as he summarized, "we come here and give it our all. We struggle. We suffer. And we get no help from anyone."

Low pay is a fact of life for many undocumented immigrants. Alejandra, in her mid-thirties with big brown eyes and a bigger smile, works for a small party-planning business. With her forty-something-year-old husband Mauricio, the couple drives around Dallas setting up and taking down bouncy houses for children's birthday parties. This work is not only dangerous from the standpoint of their position as undocumented immigrants prohibited from accessing a driver's license in Texas, but the couple explained that it is also low-paying—they reported earning just $16,000 a year. Already minimal for two people, and even less for a family with two children, they have the added challenge of an income that varies widely. In the summer months, the days are long and the heat is sweltering. But those long days are essential to get them through Texas' cooler months— roughly December through March—when bouncy houses are less popular and their income plunges. Alejandra detailed how she and Mauricio stretch this limited income:

> We take advantage of good weather and save for when it turns bad so we can have money then. Suppose we have a lot of work one weekend. We decide to save this much and we'll spend this much on expenses. And if you don't spend all the money you budgeted for expenses by the end of the next week, then you save that. And, when the cold sets in, you use what you've saved. . . . Some people say I'm very cheap, but that's not being cheap—that's knowing how to save because when you don't have money where will you get it from? How will you live without money?

Despite their best efforts, Alejandra and Mauricio's modest income can only go so far to support their family of four. They have, on more than one occasion, looked for new jobs that are less physically taxing and that pay more. But, as Mauricio told me, "we haven't been able to find anything. We got this job through a friend, and there's no other work for us since we're undocumented. So, if not this, then what?" Leaving one job without another lined up, risky for many workers regardless of their legal status, can mean all the difference between making ends meet and going under for undocumented immigrants navigating overlapping hardships.

More than just poorly compensated, undocumented immigrants' jobs are also likely to be precarious. Few see today's job as guaranteed tomorrow. Some told me stories of employers who had let them go without notice or cause, and many more told me similar stories of family members or friends who had gone through the same. In each case, they described how the constraints of their legal status maintained or exacerbated their already precarious material and social situations. Samuel, whose story opened this chapter, changed jobs five times over the five years I interviewed him. He attributed this instability to his lack of work authorization as an undocumented immigrant: "You can get *papeles chuecos* like me, but you know they're not secure." When he lost his job at the mattress factory, it was in advance of a worksite visit from the DHS; his employer simply told anyone with *papeles chuecos* to leave and not come back. Similar visits plagued the other jobs Samuel found until, ultimately, he got his foot in the door at a bread factory. Samuel told me that he was upfront with the hiring manager about his legal status; the manager hired him anyway. "Who knows how long it will last," Samuel wondered with a tone of resignation. "But at least there's been work." He was grateful to have a job, even if his yearly income of $14,000 poses challenges for him and his family: "You have to be OK with what you have. But you do still dream of more, of not living day to day, you know?"

Aspirations for secure jobs were common, even among study participants who reported never losing their jobs due to a worksite audit; their perceived precarity emerged from stories of job instability they heard through the grapevine. Natalia, the woman with a warm and smiley disposition we met briefly in chapter 1, put it plainly when I asked about her work as a full-time seamstress: "When you don't have documents that allow you to get a steady job, you can't feel good and stable. . . . Everything is temporary." At the time of our interview in 2014, Natalia had worked at the same shop for more than two years, a job that the mother of two told me she enjoys because it allows her time to sit alone for several hours a day. She nonetheless expressed concerns that the $30,000 a year in pretax income she and her husband, also undocumented and from Mexico and who works at an auto parts manufacturer, bring in is not enough to support their family. But the couple doesn't take their income for granted, knowing that their loved ones have lost the jobs they had depended on to provide for their own families: "To this day, we haven't been affected, but it has happened to others who lose their job in the blink of an eye because they don't have documents. They lost their job because they don't have a social security number." Planning for the future, hard enough for anyone already, is that much more difficult when the job someone relies on for survival can disappear without notice.

Even when undocumented immigrants experience job stability, their legal status means that their employers may choose not to pay them—with limited perceived recourse for workers. Wage theft, or the lack of payment for services rendered, was something that everyone I talked with reported experiencing at least once. But it was especially common among undocumented immigrants who worked as independent contractors. Paco, a husky man in his late thirties, installs carpets for a living. His work is steady because he works exclusively with a larger company that contracts his services. The forty-plus hours he puts in each week are back-breaking, but he told me that his $33,000 a year in pretax income validates his efforts. Still, his wife, Esmeralda, petite and in her late twenties, didn't mince words when she chimed in about Paco's work: "[Employers] discriminate against the undocumented because we're undocumented, but they also want us to work for them because we're hard workers. Sometimes they take advantage of that, having us work but humiliating us by keeping our pay." She told me that has happened to Paco on several occasions, and that they feel there is little he can do in response. They have thought about filing reports with the DOL, which fields complaints about exploitative employer practices from workers regardless of legal status, but they thought better of it. To quote Esmeralda: "My husband tolerates a lot of humiliation so that they don't fire him." Looking for another job, let alone one that pays Paco as much as he earned at the time of our interview and that he depends on to support his family, felt as uncertain an option as appealing to state authorities for their help in adjudicating disputes with an employer.

To be sure, the overlapping legal, material, and social hardships that they face become apparent when undocumented immigrants consider escalating instances of wage theft to state authorities. Rafael, in his mid-thirties with burly arms and skinny legs, remembered one such occasion from May 2015—two months prior to our interview that summer. He uses an ITIN to work as a housepainter. Rafael secures contracts through a larger company that specializes in home remodeling; he pays the company for the contracts and, in turn, the contracting party pays Rafael for his work. Rafael is proud of the work he does, and he appreciates the opportunities the company grants him despite his legal status. But, every so often, Rafael lamented, a client refuses to pay him: "What makes you angry is the helplessness of not being able to do anything. It's not about the money; it's about the rage you feel. . . . I'm talking about $300. It's not much. But, for us, it's a lot." Rafael's anger got the best of him on this occasion, and he refused to leave the client's home until they paid him. The client threw Rafael's tools out of the house and threatened to call the police if he didn't leave.

Rafael was angry but knew he had to proceed cautiously. He texted his wife Araceli, from chapter 1, to update her about the situation. Araceli begged Rafael to leave at once: "I told him, 'Please, darling, please come home. Don't get into any trouble.'" Rafael heeded his wife's request, got in the car, and called her to vent as he started home. He drove for no more than five minutes before a police officer pulled him over; Rafael told Araceli what was happening and hung up the phone. As Araceli explained, "You can't imagine the twenty minutes of uncertainty I lived in." Her young daughter, noticing that her mother was upset, asked Araceli what was wrong. Araceli comforted her daughter but, on the inside, Araceli was spiraling:

> My nerves were killing me. Time went on and on. And he did not call me. And he still did not call me. What was happening? Maybe they already detained him. I imagined the worst had happened. When the phone finally rang, my daughter said, "It's Daddy." I picked up the phone, and it was like my soul came back to my body. And I asked him, "What happened?" He said, "This woman called the police on me."

The police officer heard Rafael's side of the story and, according to Rafael, sympathized with his experience. But the officer encouraged Rafael to take the client to court. "He told me, 'If you go to her house, she will have you arrested.' I told him I understood, and he let me go." Although Rafael made it home safely, he recognized just how easily things could have turned sour: "I could have gone to jail, and maybe then immigration would have taken me away. And maybe they would have gotten my wife, too. Maybe you would not be here doing this interview." Advocating for one's livelihood simply poses too risky an endeavor for some.

Given the overlapping hardships of their legal status, undocumented immigrants come across few opportunities to move up at work—whether moving up means a higher wage or salary, a promotion, or landing a job that best aligns with their accumulated work experiences. And, in the rare event that such an opportunity emerged, the constraints of their legal status reared themselves again to prevent these individuals from seizing it. Alma, from the introductory chapter, offers one example. Over the years I came to know her, she has told me how she excels at her work in a local fast-food franchise. The franchise's owner has appreciated her efforts, too, promoting Alma to lead the kitchen staff at a new restaurant location they opened in Dallas. Alma welcomed the promotion, though it did not include a wage increase: "I like my job, but it would be nice if my efforts were reflected in what they paid me."[19] Still, Alma trusted her boss and felt that they were setting her up for success within the local franchise. Her boss even pushed her to participate in a television commercial for the national chain. Alma told me that she "was very excited about the opportunity in the beginning." She had made it through two rounds of interviews with the production team when, suddenly, they asked her to submit an I-9. Alma, whose boss knows she works with *papeles chuecos* and does not participate in E-Verify, was dismayed. "I couldn't continue with the commercial anymore." The hardships that constituted her daily life as an undocumented immigrant got in her way.

It is possible to overcome these hardships, particularly if the federal government grants the undocumented a rare opportunity to transition to a semi-legal or otherwise documented status. When people who are undocumented gain work authorization, they can begin the process of moving up.[20] Marina, who in previous chapters we saw entered the country alongside her aunt, lived in Dallas for several years as an undocumented immigrant. In 2012, when the Obama administration announced Deferred Action for Childhood Arrivals (DACA), Marina shared many aspects of Alma's story. The twenty-five-year-old was working below minimum wage at a local fast-food franchise. But, unlike Alma, Marina was eligible for DACA. Marina didn't expect that much about her life would change when she applied for it. Once she received the temporary reprieve from deportation and work authorization that DACA affords, though, she experienced almost immediate improvements in her labor market opportunities:

> Well, I think DACA made it easier for me to get a job. I think they [employers] consider you more for a job than an undocumented immigrant without DACA. I used to work in a Jack in the Box, and when I started working there, I made $6.80. Then, all of sudden, I got a raise to minimum wage of $7.25 once I got DACA. I felt good about that.

With a social security number in hand, Marina also took the chance to apply for a new job that she had sought years prior. At the time, the owner of another local fast-food franchise would not consider her because she lacked work authorization. Things were different now; the owner hired her with a starting hourly wage of $10. "I won't feel as much financial pressure as I did before," Marina explained with a sigh of relief. "And I will have the opportunity to move up; they're offering me a chance to learn how to become an assistant manager." As a result of the work authorization that she received from DACA, Marina now had the opportunity to translate her past labor market experiences into short- and long-term material gains.

Although work authorization is a first step in helping undocumented immigrants overcome some of the correlated hardships they face, it is not a cure-all. For her part, Marina arrived in Dallas when she was fifteen years old. She attended a local high school for a few years and, though she prefers to speak Spanish, can hold her own in an English-language conversation. She holds a high school diploma, which places her among a select group of undocumented immigrants with a relatively high level of education. She also has a few years of work experience. These qualities all reflect what economists call "human capital," or a person's education, knowledge, experience, and skills. People with high levels of human capital have, on average, access to a wider range of jobs and higher incomes than those with lower levels.[21]

Contrast Marina's experience with that of Yajaira and Javier. Both were permanent residents when we met but had previously lived in the country as undocumented immigrants. Javier arrived in 1985, at the age of seventeen, and became a permanent resident a few years later thanks to the 1986 Immigration Reform and Control Act (IRCA).[22] Yajaira followed Javier to Dallas in 1991, at the age of twenty-one, and lived as an undocumented immigrant until about ten years later. Although both have work authorization, they emphasized to me that their green cards did not offset all the overlapping hardships they face. Neither partner completed more than the equivalent of a middle-school education in Mexico; they both started working at a young age to support their families. Neither had more than a basic understanding of English. And neither could afford to pay for childcare for the children that they had gone on to have in the ten years it took for immigration officials to approve Yajaira's green card. Javier spends much of his time working as a subcontractor for a construction company, and Yajaira cleans neighbors' homes during those rare times when she's not tending to their five children. They told me they struggle to make ends meet on about $27,000 a year. "We work and work and work to provide for ourselves. That's why we came here—to try and get ahead," Yajaira reflected. Alongside Marina's example, these experiences highlight the possibilities and limitations of legalization programs for helping undocumented immigrants to overcome the hardships they face.[23]

Conflicting Roles

The overlapping hardships that undocumented immigrants endure are, to put it mildly, a source of consternation in their daily lives. They reflect the constraints of the laws, regulations, and policies that stifle their opportunities for making ends meet and for getting ahead. Although these hardships can manifest for undocumented immigrants with and without children, undocumented parents face a unique tension.[24] As individuals, federal and state laws, regulations, and policies prohibit the undocumented from accessing many service institutions that would help them offset some of the hardships they face. But, as parents, undocumented immigrants have access to—and often must engage with—service institutions to take care of their citizen children. Kids go to the doctor's office, where they regularly meet with a physician or nurse. They attend school, where teachers and staff monitor them almost daily. And, if these or other authorities determine that a child suffers from material scarcity or other maladies, case workers can intervene on their behalf. Therein lies a tension: the undocumented must be circumspect about the institutions they engage with on their own behalf but, given the intergenerational risks of the hardships they experience, more comprehensive with their institutional engagement on behalf of their children.

Numerous federal and state laws, regulations, and policies establish the conflicting responsibilities between one's social role as an undocumented immigrant and as a parent. And service institutions are a key setting in which this conflict manifests. Since at least 1882, the country's immigration laws have sought to exclude "any person unable to take care of himself or herself without becoming a public charge."[25] Who constitutes a public charge has shifted across time, but this label is rooted in racialized and classed stereotypes that depict immigrants as moving to this country in search of taxpayer-funded goods and services—usually, public assistance.[26] Yet, as sociologist Cybelle Fox has shown, federal laws blocking the undocumented from public assistance are a relatively recent invention; no such laws existed when the modern welfare state was established in 1935.[27] They instead emerged beginning in 1972, following the creation of the Supplemental Security Income (SSI) program, as part of a larger effort to rein in public spending on racial minorities. In quick succession, the federal government prohibited undocumented immigrants from receiving Aid to Families with Dependent Children (AFDC, which provided cash payments to children in certain low-income families) and Medicaid; from accessing food assistance in 1974; and from accepting unemployment insurance in 1976.[28] Applicants for these and other forms of public assistance would be required to verify their legal status and risk having their personal information turned over to immigration officials.[29]

Since the 1970s, the federal government has stepped up its efforts to exclude the undocumented from service institutions, with a continued emphasis on public assistance. In 1996, a bipartisan Congress passed, and the Clinton administration signed, two laws—the Personal Responsibility and Work Opportunity Reconciliation Act (PRWORA) and the Illegal Immigration Reform and Immigrant Responsibility Act (IIRIRA)—to further circumscribe undocumented immigrants' already limited access to these public goods. PRWORA reaffirmed these individuals' exclusion from federally funded public assistance, except in the case of limited emergency health care, and extended these exclusions to permanent residents who have lived in the country for fewer than five years. IIRIRA, meanwhile, outlined the criteria by which immigration officials could determine immigrants to be a public charge or likely to become one. In reviewing immigrants' visa applications, they consider immigrants' age, health, family status (e.g., whether they have dependent children), income, wealth, and education. In reviewing immigrants' eligibility for permanent residence or citizenship, they consider immigrants' use of cash-based public assistance, such as SSI or AFDC (now Temporary Assistance for Needy Families, or TANF). The Trump administration proposed a rule change in August 2019 that would require immigration officials to designate any noncitizen who "uses or receives one or more public benefits [namely, TANF, SSI, SNAP, nonemergency Medicaid, and federal housing assistance]" a public charge.[30] Officials began enforcing this rule in February 2020, with different lawsuits starting and stopping that enforcement until the Biden administration reverted to past practice in March 2021.[31] The consequences of a public charge designation are severe: prospective migrants may be denied visas to enter the country, current nonpermanent residents (i.e., undocumented immigrants or people hoping to apply for a green card) may be prevented from becoming permanent residents, and current permanent residents may be deported.

Undocumented immigrants must also contend with laws, regulations, and policies at the state level that govern their access to service institutions. Texas has a long history of (attempts at) excluding the undocumented from different service institutions. When the Social Security Act created the modern welfare state in 1935, it did not include any alienage-based restrictions; individual states, though, could implement their own.[32] Texas did so in 1936, prohibiting anyone who was not a U.S. citizen from accessing means-tested programs between 1936 and 1971, when the Supreme Court intervened.[33] The state narrowed its focus to excluding the undocumented in the 1970s and 1980s. Perhaps most infamously, Texas sought to deprive undocumented immigrants who arrived as children a right to a public education through high school. But the Supreme Court ruled in *Plyler v. Doe* that the state's efforts were unconstitutional.[34] Texas implemented its own welfare reform in 1995 via a state law known as HB 1863; alongside the 1996 PRWORA, this law laid the foundation for Texas' present-day approach to public assistance.[35] As of this writing, Texas excludes the undocumented from Medicaid, except in the case of emergency care or pregnancy; from cash welfare via SSI or TANF; from food assistance via SNAP; and from other forms of public assistance. In contrast, and building off the nationwide right to public education through high school, Texas was among the first states in the country to offer undocumented immigrants access to financial aid for higher education.[36]

Even as federal and state laws, regulations, and policies exclude the undocumented from many service institutions, their social role as parents all but demands their engagement with the same. Undocumented immigrants' exclusions do not formally extend to their children who were born in the United States. Nationwide, more than six million children who are U.S. citizens live with an undocumented parent; in Texas, that figure is one million; and, in Dallas, it is 180,000.[37] Most of these children are Latino.[38] Undocumented parents are no different from other parents in the most fundamental of ways. Like other parents confronting overlapping hardships, the hardships that undocumented parents face matter for their children's well-being—whether that is measured as food insecurity, psychological distress, or access to health care or education.[39] Like other parents, undocumented parents do not wish to pass on these hardships to their children.[40] And, like other parents, undocumented parents recognize the possible dangers of failing.

Central to this danger is a diverse cast of authorities in service institutions—whether doctors, nurses, teachers, social workers, or other authorities—whom they encounter through their children's routines. These authorities monitor children's well-being, often in ways that reflect and reproduce the overlapping hardships their parents they face.[41] They recognize when parents have few material resources and whether this scarcity affects a child they see regularly. For example, a teacher might notice that a child shows up to school hungry and doesn't have much to eat at lunch. Or a doctor might observe a child lose weight over time. These authorities can recommend that a parent solicit other public goods to offset this scarcity, such as a school's free-or-reduced meal program or CHIP or SNAP. These recommendations, as helpful or well-intentioned as they may be, are also fraught. Personally evading many of these services remains important for undocumented immigrants who do not wish immigration officials to view them as public charges down the road (in either removal proceedings or when submitting a legalization application); wholesale evasion nonetheless poses a more immediate risk of punishment for parents with young children. As in most states nationwide, Texas law does not allow authorities in service institutions to share information on individuals' legal status with immigration officials—but it does require them to report suspected cases of child abuse or neglect to the police and/ or Child Protective Services.[42] These reports can instigate a cascading series of events that threatens a family's stability, including an intrusive investigation and the removal of children from their parents' custody.[43] And, as established by the 1996 IIRIRA, accusations of child abuse and neglect can bring about parents' deportation, something that can afflict undocumented immigrants in even the most progressive of sanctuary jurisdictions nationwide.[44]

For the people I talked with, these myriad dynamics all boil down to an unavoidable tension between their social roles as undocumented immigrants and as parents. As we have seen, a requirement of this study's design is that each household interviewed contain at least one young child. A median of three citizen children are present in households with at least one undocumented parent, and the median age of the youngest child is five. All parents I spoke with described themselves as feeling "conflicted" over their engagement with service institutions. On the one hand, as undocumented immigrants, they told me they try to limit their own engagement with service institutions to the most exceptional of circumstances. Few have health insurance or a primary care provider for themselves; most have visited the emergency room or an urgent care clinic in response to acute ailments, and three acknowledged having received treatment through emergency Medicaid. A handful who arrived in the country at a young age attended a local public school, but none had gone on to college. On the other hand, as parents, they outlined substantial engagement with service institutions on behalf of their children. Every household in the study with at least one undocumented parent reported ever receiving WIC and CHIP, with all saying that they regularly attend their children's medical and dental appointments. They were more split on cash-based and cash-like public assistance, with sixteen reporting SNAP receipt and four reporting SSI receipt. Parents noted that their school-age children are enrolled in public schools, which they regularly visit for parent-teacher conferences or volunteer activities. In brief, institutional engagement and evasion go hand in hand for undocumented parents.

It's not hard to understand why undocumented immigrants with young children engage with service institutions. Given the correlated hardships they face, these parents simply need the public goods that these institutions make available. Samuel and Selena both described the hospital social workers who facilitated their applications for CHIP, SNAP, SSI, and public housing as "helpful," affording them the opportunity to treat their child's cancer and to provide for the rest of their children. Every six months or so, usually while the couple is at the hospital for another round of treatment for their child, a hospital social worker visits to help them submit renewal applications for these various services. Samuel explained how the paystubs he receives from his work are instrumental to this process: "The social worker asks us for a minimum of two months' worth of paystubs, or a letter from my employer that says how much I've made. That's why we always save the paystubs because, sooner or later, we know that we'll have to renew." Recall that Samuel works using *papeles chuecos*; his paystubs reflect the hardships he faces as an undocumented immigrant and establish his children's eligibility for life-saving public goods.

Across most interviews, undocumented immigrants recounted how the material hardships they face mean that their engagement with service institutions on behalf of their children is inevitable. Norma, who we met briefly in the previous chapter, fiddled with an empty roll of paper towels as she summed up what her and her husband Pablo's yearly income of about $19,000 enables them to do: "Here, you only work to survive." She wished that the pair could live off Pablo's earnings as a construction worker, but there was never money left at the end of the month for themselves and their two children once they had paid the household bills. Norma's older sister, who lives in the same apartment complex and who has struggled with similar hardships while raising her three children, taught Norma that she could apply for public assistance. Norma followed her sister's lead, and she ultimately secured CHIP, WIC, and SNAP—all services to which her citizen children are entitled. These public goods allow Norma to buy her children enough food each month and to take them for their regular checkups at the doctor—with no out-of-pocket copay. "That's all help for our kids," Norma declared. She took a moment to consider the statement before adding, "Well, it also helps us since we don't have money to pay for this ourselves. With just Pablo's income, it wouldn't be enough."

But engagement with service institutions goes beyond material need. Undocumented immigrants also consider the expectations that they believe the authorities within these institutions hold them to as undocumented parents. No one I talked with wanted to "burden the government," which is how study participants described their concerns about immigration officials viewing them as public charges one day. Yet engagement with service institutions has been a necessary feature of all study participants' routines for years. Samuel and Selena are both sensitive to "burdening the government" and noted how their engagement with service institutions began more than a decade ago when a nurse in the emergency room confirmed that Selena was pregnant. "They asked us if we had a social security number, and we told them we didn't, and that was it," Selena replied when I asked how the hospital social workers set them up with different public goods. And, as we saw at the start of this chapter, one reason they maintain this engagement is because they hope to show these authorities that they are protecting their children from the hardships their parents confront. Norma, who took her sister's advice and went to the doctor once she discovered she was pregnant, noted a similar dynamic about the social worker who visited her and Pablo: "They told me that they would help the kids, because they are children who were born here. But not me and Pablo because we do not qualify for that."

It was common for undocumented parents to identify pregnancy as their gateway to engagement with service institutions, undoubtedly a reflection of the study's design. Natalia, the seamstress from above, said she started engaging with service institutions when she learned that she was pregnant. She went to a local clinic after a positive at-home pregnancy test; a doctor at the clinic confirmed the result. Natalia was worried about how she would seek care during the pregnancy. Her doctor sent a social worker to help Natalia fill out the paperwork required for CHIP and WIC: "Before they were born, I was at the clinic, and they had me fill out some paperwork. They told me that they would cover my bills while pregnant and, once the kids were born, they would be covered." Natalia hesitated to sign up for the programs but felt like she had no other choice; she and her husband couldn't afford out-of-pocket care on $30,000 a year, and she was unsure what the social worker would do if she failed to enroll. She relented.

This engagement with service institutions continues beyond a child's birth. Parenthood regularly exposes people facing multiple hardships to empowered authorities in service institutions. From these parents' perspective, their interactions with institutional authorities can reproduce the same hardships that they are intended to counteract. Adriana, from chapter 1, is an undocumented mother of three children from Mexico. She receives a yearly income of $12,000 from the father of her children and stretches this limited income through several forms of public assistance—including CHIP, WIC, and SNAP. Adriana recognizes that the scope of her engagement with service institutions creates a unique tension for her as an undocumented parent. Yet she sees this engagement as important for caring for her children despite the material hardships she endures—and repelling authorities' accusations that she is an unfit mother:

> Many people say that you shouldn't ask for help. . . . But if the children were born here, they have a right to health insurance. And thank God they get it. I even signed them up for food assistance. Because I'm not rich. The children need health insurance. Imagine what would happen if they got sick. Or didn't have enough to eat. How would I pay their medical expenses? How would I pay for their doctors' visits when I take them for their checkups? How am I supposed to pay for their food?

The questions Adriana poses—how to cover her children's basic expenses with limited income and without public assistance—underscore her desire to be a good parent to her three children. And Adriana emphasized that she will maintain this engagement even if it renders her vulnerable to immigration officials' public charge accusations down the road: "I hear people say it will affect me if the government lets us fix our documents one day. I don't know if they want to scare us or are trying to warn people, if it's true or a lie. . . . But there is no time to stop and worry. . . . The children were born here, and it's my job to take care of them how I can."

Although engagement with service institutions on behalf of one's citizen children does not currently factor into public charge determinations, fears that it can or will are common. Pedro, whose wife Elizabet's story opened chapter 1, told me it is important to engage with service institutions— be they medical, educational, or public assistance—even if it means that immigration officials might one day classify them as public charges. When I asked him why, he noted that authorities in service institutions pose an everyday threat to his family's stability: "If I don't take my kids to the doctor or send them to school, the police come for them." Pedro, who has lived in the United States since 1992, did not think that immigration officials posed as immediate a threat: "I still hope to get my papers, and many people say I shouldn't apply for my kids because then the government won't give me papers. But they would have given me papers by now if they were going to do that. Besides, none of this help is for us; it's for our girls."

A key aspect of the tension between undocumented parents' two social roles is the perceived division between service institutions that offer cash-based (e.g., SSI or TANF) or cash-like assistance (e.g., SNAP) and those that do not (e.g., public schools or CHIP). Study participants universally (and correctly) saw public health insurance and schools as two institutions that were open to their citizen children. As Pedro put it, "There are no laws against us getting these things for our kids." They were more mixed on their views of institutions that provide cash-based and cash-like assistance. Everyone understood that they were personally ineligible, and that their citizen kids were potentially eligible, for this assistance. But they were less certain about the immigration consequences of receiving these public goods.

What separated those who received cash-based or cash-like assistance from those who did not was the context of their interactions with authorities in service institutions. In Natalia's case, for example, a hospital nurse offered to help enroll her in SNAP once her daughter was born. But Natalia, already nervous about the services she received, declined. She told me she didn't feel nervous declining the assistance because "we are [finan-cially] comfortable with the other assistance we receive, and we didn't need to take the money for food." But she also noted that she declined because it could limit her children's rights as citizens to sponsor their par-ents for a green card. "I don't know if it's true or not," she told me. "But I heard that if you are able to apply for your papers then we would have to pay back all the money that was given to us."

Contrast Natalia's case with that of Caridad. In her early forties with a self-deprecating sense of humor, Caridad has lived in Dallas without authorization since 2002. She arrived from Mexico with her two children, a daughter (then aged five) and a son (then aged three), and she has since given birth to three children in the United States. The family depends on an annual household income of $28,000, which Caridad's husband and her sister Felicidad bring in through irregular construction work and work at a nearby food-and-games establishment, respectively. This income is quickly depleted once the family's housing and utilities bills are accounted for, leaving Caridad desperate to provide for her children. The two oldest children, by virtue of lacking authorization to live in the country, largely do not qualify for public assistance; the youngest three, by virtue of being U.S. citizens, do. When Caridad was pregnant with each of her three youn-gest children, she recounted engaging with service institutions in ways like Natalia; she accepted a social worker's recommendation to sign up for CHIP and WIC but declined food assistance. Like Natalia, Caridad was reluctant to receive the cash-like assistance from SNAP. But as the kids have aged, and nutritional support from WIC has phased out, the family has struggled with food insecurity. A teacher noticed that the children sometimes arrived at school complaining to their friends that they were hungry. Caridad described what happened next:

> I went in for a meeting with the teacher, and she asked me to fill out some documents. . . . She told me that they didn't have anything to do with food stamps, but it was. My husband told me that it was best that I don't do that. . . . They said it had nothing to do with food stamps, but they had me fill out those documents. I filled them out and then we got food stamps and kept them. . . . I didn't know what it was for until my friend told me it was food stamps. But I kept them.

Caridad was uncertain about whether she did the right thing. On the one hand, she wanted to both care for her children and comply with the teacher's recommendation. On the other hand, she was so worried that she had just signed the dotted line on her and her husband's deportation that she hid the receipt of these services: "I haven't told my husband. He said it could hurt us [to receive SNAP]; immigration could catch us. I keep thinking he is going to find out." For Caridad, the easy-to-quantify monetary value of services like SNAP informs this uncertainty. Although not cash assistance, the food assistance her children receive, from Caridad's perspective, forms part of a ledger documenting her family's societal "cost." Every $120 in monthly food assistance is another $120 she fears immigration officials can use to label her and her husband as public charges. Yet declining this assistance didn't feel like an option for Caridad, who worried that the teacher might escalate the situation: "What would have happened? We were scared of them calling the police because we couldn't afford to take care of our kids."

Natalia and Caridad's stories reveal several important insights about undocumented immigrants' engagement with service institutions. First, it emerges in part from the overlapping hardships they face in this country. Second, these hardships raise the stakes of institutional engagement, particularly when children's well-being factors into the equation. Finally, conflicts between one's social role as an undocumented immigrant worried about relying on taxpayer-funded assistance and as a parent worried about caring for their children mediate this tension.

Worries that authorities in service institutions can bring about undocumented immigrants' policing do not extend to their children who are undocumented. In the two households in this study that have both undocumented and citizen children, parents noted how authorities in service institutions regularly enforce their undocumented children's exclusion from some service institutions. Caridad, whose two oldest children are undocumented, remembered how she had a hard time fulfilling her responsibilities as a parent when her kids were younger. Both her undocumented children have health conditions; one has a vision impairment and the other has a severe case of asthma. Caridad has struggled to get them medical care over the years. Part of the problem is that Caridad cannot afford private health insurance, and neither child qualifies for public health insurance. "When they find out we don't have insurance, they snatch the [intake] paper from me and kick us out," Caridad recalled of her experience moving from one medical office to another in search of a physician who would see her undocumented children. It was not until Caridad found a hospital with a program for low-income patients who are ineligible for public assistance that her children could get the help they need. She told me she has never experienced a similar situation with her three children who were born in the United States.

The tensions that undocumented parents face remain even if they find a way to legalize and become permanent residents. And, though these tensions are in some ways similar to those they experienced as undocumented immigrants, they feel like more is on the line. Yajaira and her husband, Javier, the permanent residents from the previous section, continue to face many overlapping hardships despite their legalization. Javier's employer does not offer health insurance, and the couple cannot afford to stretch their annual income to buy private health insurance. Both have been permanent residents for over five years, meaning that they could apply for public health insurance in Texas. But they hesitate to do so precisely because they are permanent residents, as Yajaira explained: "I have my social security number, and the government . . . knows everything about our lives." Concerned that they might become ineligible to naturalize as U.S. citizens if they accept public goods, they opt to pay cash for any infrequent medical care they receive. They nonetheless engage with service institutions on behalf of their four citizen children, who attend a nearby public school and receive public health insurance—but not food assistance. This selective engagement, as Yajaira sees it, allows the family to make ends meet while also anticipating concerns from immigration officials that she and Javier are public charges because "it costs our family money to live here." Taken together, Yajaira and Javier believe that the balance of their engagement with service institutions allows them to fulfill their dual social roles as immigrants compliant with the law and as good parents to citizen children.

Exceptional Hardship

Undocumented parents describe their selective engagement with service institutions as necessary to provide for their children, whom they recognize institutional authorities monitor on an almost daily basis. They pursue such engagement even when they believe it disqualifies them from any future legalization opportunities that may emerge. Against this backdrop, undocumented parents think about what might happen if, despite their best efforts every day, they wind up in removal proceedings. In these proceedings, they hope the records of their selective engagement with service institutions will both prevent their deportation and put them on the path toward becoming permanent residents. These outcomes are possible, so long as their records demonstrate to the immigration officials deciding their case that their deportation will cause their families what the Immigration and Nationality Act calls "exceptional and extremely unusual hardship."

Even as most undocumented immigrants will never experience a deportation, some will inevitably end up in removal proceedings. This possibility reflects the structure of interior immigration enforcement, reviewed in the previous chapter, which casts a wide dragnet as it polices undocumented immigrants for low-level offenses in communities nationwide.[45] Federal initiatives to prioritize the removal of undocumented immigrants with "serious" criminal records have, at the same time, deprioritized the removal of undocumented immigrants with immediate relatives (i.e., a parent, a spouse, or a child) who are U.S. citizens or permanent residents.[46] President Obama once characterized this prioritization as follows: ". . . [W]e're going to keep focusing enforcement resources on actual threats to our security. Felons, not families. Criminals, not children. Gang members, not a mom who's working hard to provide for her kids."[47] The trouble with this characterization, as scholars and advocates alike have observed, is that many people have criminal records in our era of mass criminalization—and many people with criminal records have families.[48] One study estimates that Immigration and Customs Enforcement (ICE) deported more than 231,000 people between 2013 and 2018 who reported having at least one citizen child; in 2019 alone, that figure was 27,980.[49] Another links these parents' removal to the growing number of U.S.-born children living in Mexico, about 500,000 as of 2015.[50] The reality, then, is that some undocumented parents will be shuttled into removal proceedings. We will learn more about what happens during removal proceedings in chapter 4.

Once in removal proceedings, undocumented immigrants have few legal avenues—known as "relief"—for escaping deportation. This stinginess is a relatively recent emergence.[51] Legal scholar Daniel Kanstroom describes how, in the early twentieth century, discretionary relief from removal was common.[52] Judges could advise against an undocumented immigrant's removal during criminal proceedings, and immigration officers had to comply. Such relief became formalized in 1940, when Congress passed the Alien Registration Act and allowed for "suspension of deportation" if removal would result in "serious economic detriment" to an immigrant's parent, spouse, or minor child who is a citizen or permanent resident.[53] Congress raised the bar for suspension of deportation in 1952, requiring not "serious economic detriment" but "exceptional and extremely unusual hardship."[54] Hardship to both the individual facing removal and their immediate relatives who are citizens or permanent residents could be considered.[55] Additional changes in 1962 would further constrain eligibility for suspension of deportation while preserving the tall "exceptional and extremely unusual hardship" standard.[56] Many of these restrictions are still found in the 1996 IIRIRA, which restructured contemporary relief from removal and gave rise to what is now known as cancellation of removal.[57]

Cancellation of removal for exceptional and extremely unusual hardship remains one form of relief available to undocumented parents of citizen children facing deportation.[58] To be sure, it may be the only form of relief available to them.[59] For an undocumented parent to have their removal canceled, they must meet several conditions. First, they must demonstrate that they have lived in the country for at least ten years and that they have done so with good moral character, itself an ambiguous standard.[60] Second, they must demonstrate that their deportation would result in exceptional and extremely unusual hardship for a citizen or permanent resident parent, spouse, or child. In practice, these requirements are difficult to meet. And it's not because undocumented parents lack good moral character or because their removal wouldn't cause exceptional and extremely unusual hardship for a qualifying relative. Rather, it's in part because these statutory requirements come with numerous caveats and bureaucratic obstacles.[61] What's more, these requirements are somewhat subjective; the federal government's own application instructions discourage people from applying unless "you are deserving of a favorable exercise of discretion on your application."[62] Central to this determination is what constitutes exceptional and extremely unusual hardship. The federal government does not consider the material, emotional, or social strains of a citizen child being separated from their parent as "exceptional" or "extremely unusual"; it considers these the "common consequences" of deportation.[63] Undocumented parents applying for cancellation of removal must instead marshal evidence that shows that their deportation would render these common consequences unusually difficult. The stakes are high: if successful, they not only avoid removal but are also granted permanent residence. (There is also cancellation of removal for permanent residents, but it operates differently.[64])

For the undocumented parents I spoke with, the statutory nuances of cancellation of removal were secondary to the hope that its existence offered them. These parents are not lawyers; they did not refer to the Immigration and Nationality Act or know all the eligibility criteria for cancellation of removal for exceptional and extremely unusual hardship. Yet they referred to cancellation of removal in its most general terms when answering a question about whether they saw a pathway for themselves to become permanent residents. Absent an amnesty like that from 1986's IRCA, undocumented parents without a citizen or permanent resident spouse universally saw themselves as having one of two options. First, they would have to wait to apply for permanent residence until their eldest citizen child reached twenty-one years of age. That wait could span years. The median age of the oldest citizen child in the study households is twelve, and it may take U.S. Citizenship and Immigration Services several years to approve such legalization applications. Second, and assuming they were swept into removal proceedings before that faraway future came to be, about half of the undocumented parents I talked with said they could "ask the judge for a permit to stay to take care of my kids" or "ask the judge for forgiveness since I need to be here for my kids." Each family recounted learning about cancellation of removal from a hospital or school social worker, always while addressing a child's new or existing health or educational concerns. Key to that perceived ability to stay are the records documenting families' selective engagement with service institutions.

I first learned about cancellation of removal from Samuel and Selena, whose story opened this chapter. As we saw on the opening pages, they referred to cancellation of removal when they noted how "we can use the help we received for our children to help us stay here since the kids can't live here without us." The hospital social worker had explained this idea to them when their child was admitted for cancer treatment: "We do everything with the social worker," Samuel told me. "She helps us with everything and explains how these things work." I was curious about this dynamic and looked into it; and, sure enough, there it was, written into the Immigration and Nationality Act. On their face, Samuel and Selena seemed to satisfy the requirements for cancellation of removal. When I met them, their oldest child was ten years old, and their youngest five, facts verified by their children's Texas-issued birth certificates. And, given the details surrounding their child's ongoing battle with a terminal illness, it seemed plausible that their deportation would make life extremely and unusually difficult for the child.

Over the course of subsequent interviews, I noticed more and more how hospital or school social workers instilled the possibility of cancellation for removal as a pathway to permanent residence for undocumented parents in the study. Alejandra and Mauricio, the couple from above who work for a party-planning business, have lived in the country since 2004. Their daughter was eight years old when I met the family. Over the years, Alejandra noticed that her daughter was having a hard time in school. "She doesn't learn like we do," Alejandra told me. "Her teachers say something to her and she understands it, but the next day she doesn't remember it." During a parent-teacher conference, the daughter's teacher encouraged Alejandra and Mauricio to consider enrolling the daughter in special education classes; the couple agreed, and the daughter has been making progress in the years since. School social workers also encouraged Alejandra to investigate the source of the disability. Since her daughter is a U.S. citizen and enrolled in CHIP, Alejandra has shuttled her from specialist to specialist to discern the nature of her condition. "To this day," she told me in 2015, "they haven't found anything."

> I took her to a neurologist, and they say she doesn't have anything. They say she has vision problems, but the ophthalmologist says there's nothing wrong with her. They sent me over to an ENT [ear, nose, and throat doctor] to check her throat and nose and all that and, no, they didn't find anything. They told me to take her to a physical therapist, so I did. But the insurance suspended that [because there didn't appear to be a medically necessary reason for physical therapy].

Even as the medical diagnosis remained indeterminate, Alejandra and Mauricio worried about their daughter. One day, as Alejandra explained to me when I visited her in 2018, the daughter fainted and regained consciousness only intermittently. Worried, Alejandra loaded her daughter into the car to rush her to the emergency room. On the way there, the daughter fainted again. Distracted, Alejandra crashed the car. An ambulance arrived and shuttled them both to the hospital, where they were treated for minor scratches and bruises. Doctors also evaluated the daughter more closely and diagnosed her with an autoimmune disease. A social worker visited Alejandra and her daughter in the hospital shortly thereafter, as Alejandra narrated to me:

> While we were in the hospital, the social worker came and told me that, because my daughter has a disability, perhaps my husband and I can qualify to fix our papers. The social worker said that, since my daughter has a disability, she won't be able to take care of herself if we were deported. We can't start the process now, but . . . there are lots of reports of the things that have happened to her. None of this is an easy process because you need to collect documents and prove and prove and prove your case.

Alejandra is mostly correct about the impressions that she derived from the social worker, with one important qualification. It is true that, if she and Mauricio can "prove and prove and prove" why their daughter will depend on them for care for the foreseeable future, they could qualify for permanent residence. But this process works through cancellation of removal for exceptional and extremely unusual hardship. As immigration lawyers and advocates advise, it can be dangerous to "start" this process if ICE has not initiated removal proceedings against someone because of how difficult it is to meet the hardship standard.[65] A practice advisory from the Immigrant Legal Resource Center, a national organization that supports the work of immigration attorneys, puts it plainly: "WARNING! It is risky to place your client in removal proceedings in order to apply for cancellation of removal."[66] Still, Alejandra holds out hope that the records of her family's engagement with service institutions on behalf of her citizen daughter will one day allow her and Mauricio formal societal membership.

Importantly, undocumented parents do not seek out engagement with service institutions because they are looking for a way to circumvent removal. Recall that study parents learned about cancellation of removal only after having engaged with service institutions for other reasons— namely, to provide for their kids despite the hardships imposed on the parents. The records emerging from these interactions just happen to have applicability to the cancellation of removal process, as institutional authorities explained to study parents.

Take the case of Maritza, an undocumented mother from Mexico with three citizen children who we met briefly in the last chapter. The children receive public health insurance and $300 per month in food assistance. Maritza's oldest daughter also qualifies for $600 per month in SSI. Her daughter has a severe case of epilepsy, which Maritza told me can produce up to three seizures a month. "The seizures erase everything," Maritza emphasized. "She depends on me for everything." Given the severity of her daughter's condition, Maritza spends much of her time outside of work engaging with myriad service institutions on behalf of her daughter. Treatment includes intensive physical, speech, and occupational therapy, which her daughter's pediatrician helps Maritza to arrange: "Thank God for the pediatrician. She is Latina and she has helped me a lot. When her [my daughter's] arm hurts, I go to see her [the pediatrician], and she gives me a referral to a specialist." Even with this assistance, Maritza has struggled over the years to maintain her daughter's therapies, largely due to insurance disputes about whether her daughter is making enough progress to justify the therapies' cost. But Maritza persists, striving each day to care for her daughter's numerous needs while also taking care of her two other kids.

These efforts are daunting in and of themselves, and they are more daunting under the threat of deportation. Maritza has lived in Dallas since 2001. Given that she has lived in the country for well over ten years, I asked Maritza whether she saw a pathway for herself to become a permanent resident. Like others in the study, she mentioned that one of her children could sponsor her legalization application when they reached twenty-one years of age; her eldest was twelve at the time of our conversation. She was cleareyed about how long that process might take, noting the risk that ICE might find her and initiate removal proceedings in the meantime. Maritza nonetheless hoped that her extensive efforts to care for her children would be enough to "ask for a permit from the judge to stay," as her daughter's social worker explained to her:

> If that happens to me, I can ask for a permit from the [immigration] judge to stay. . . . I can ask for a permit, and they say that they have to give it to me for her to be able to get the medicine, all of her things, and everything. . . . I cannot go to Mexico because, here, I can have the medication for my daughter. She needs three medicines, and each one costs $700; in Mexico, nobody is going to help me afford the medicine or the diapers she needs or anything. . . . She could maybe play by herself, but she is still my responsibility; if she finds something small, she will put it in her mouth and choke.

For undocumented parents like Maritza, cancellation of removal for exceptional and extremely unusual hardship represents a lifeline from the federal government. That lifeline recognizes several simple truths: that undocumented immigrants live in the United States, that they have citizen children, that they engage with service institutions on behalf of their children each day, and that their families are better off together than they are apart. Yet, for all this recognition, cancellation of removal is itself a limited avenue for relief for undocumented parents. Even if immigration officials determine that an undocumented parent meets all other criteria, the tall burden of proof for meeting exceptional and extremely unusual hardship renders this relief unavailable to many undocumented parents.

Conclusion

Service institutions, and the authorities staffing them, are responsible for distributing public goods such as health care, education, and public assistance. Most anyone will engage with at least one of these institutions at some point in life, whether for themselves or the children in their charge. But different laws, regulations, and policies at the federal and state level govern who can access these institutions and under what conditions. Deciphering them is essential for undocumented immigrants facing correlated hardships and raising citizen children. Informing these stakes are the multiple forms of surveillance that undocumented parents recognize as mattering not just for their daily lives but also for their societal membership. And service institutions, so common to all parents' lives, are one setting in which this surveillance occurs.

In the United States, to be undocumented typically means to navigate overlapping legal, material, and social hardships. Whether parents or not, undocumented immigrants experience these hardships in many spheres of life—including the workplace. Denied work authorization, and blocked from securing it in most cases, undocumented immigrants seek out work in labor-intensive, low-wage, and precarious jobs. Their employers offer them few opportunities for moving up. Instead, the undocumented immigrants I met report withheld wages and job instability. Many hold out hope that a legalization opportunity will allow them to overcome at least some of these hardships, though that depends on whether their existing human capital (e.g., education and work experience) is valued in their local labor market.

These hardships constitute just some of what undocumented immigrants endure every day. But undocumented immigrants do not exist in a vacuum. They have families, including children of their own who are U.S. citizens by birth, who suffer consequences arising from these same hardships. Undocumented immigrants recognize that they are prohibited from accessing the public goods that many service institutions provide, especially those related to public assistance, which might otherwise help them to offset these hardships. Some of this prohibition owes to the federal government (in that it excludes the undocumented from federally funded public assistance, lest they become public charges), and some of it owes to the state government (in that Texas has its own such exclusions from state-funded public assistance).

Yet, whatever exclusions they face as individuals, undocumented immigrants recognize that they are all but required to engage with these same institutions as parents. They feel they must, out of a fundamental concern for their children's welfare. Such engagement begins as early as pregnancy and continues well into children's adolescence, life stages during which all parents regularly shuttle their kids to medical appointments, school, and other service institutions. Authorities in these spaces monitor children's well-being, sometimes recommending that parents make use of additional services. These recommendations can be fraught for all parents; more fraught for parents navigating correlated hardships; and more fraught still for undocumented parents. Given concerns that immigration officials will one day deny them legalization opportunities for having used public goods, few undocumented immigrants express wanting to engage with service institutions. But the hardships they endure every day are felt to pose a more immediate danger: that different authorities will refer them to the police or Child Protective Services if they do not make use of service institutions on behalf of their kids. Such referrals are thought to escalate quickly and, ultimately, shuttle parents into removal proceedings.

Undocumented parents' selective engagement with service institutions emerges primarily out of love for their children and a desire to keep their families together. They nonetheless fear that immigration officials will use the records of their engagement to label them public charges and deny them the chance to legalize. Undocumented parents, therefore, worry about what might happen if they wind up in removal proceedings despite their efforts to manage everyday forms of surveillance. Cancellation of removal for exceptional and extremely unusual hardship emerges as a perceived lifeline for undocumented parents, which they understand is written into the law for exactly this situation. If undocumented parents can meet various eligibility criteria—in particular, that their citizen children will suffer their parents' deportation in "exceptional" and "extremely unusual" ways—immigration officials can grant them permanent residence. Informing this understanding are authorities in service institutions that undocumented parents interact with while caring for their children. Though this form of relief from deportation is rare in practice, undocumented parents hope that their selective engagement with service institutions will evidence to immigration officials that they are deserving of formal societal membership.

These dynamics point to the independent, interdependent, and successive import of legal status for undocumented immigrants and their families' life chances, showing how the effects of legal status depend on situational context. An interdisciplinary scholarship suggests that legal status is a "master status," one that overpowers all others to determine a person's social position. In his twelve-year study of how undocumented immigrants transition into adulthood following high school, sociologist Roberto G. Gonzales writes that undocumented status "frames their lives in such a way that years lived in the United States, acculturation to American norms and behavior, and educational attainment are all inconsequential to their everyday routines as undocumented immigrants."[67] Other scholars, such as Laura E. Enriquez, Zulema Valdez, and Tanya Golash-Boza, reach slightly different conclusions in their cross-sectional studies of undocumented young adults who either stopped out of college or who were enrolled in or completed college.[68] For these authors, legal status is the proverbial straw that broke the camel's back, another characteristic that adds to the many hardships that undocumented students navigate. My findings, based on undocumented immigrants who largely did not complete any formal schooling in the United States and who are raising citizen children, support both claims by calling attention to situational context. Legal status is a primary dimension of inequality for the undocumented immigrants I interviewed. More plainly, numerous laws, regulations, and policies constrain undocumented immigrants' life chances simply because they lack authorization to live in the country. These constraints range from whether, how much, and in what capacity they can work to whether, how much, and in what form they can access public goods like health care or public assistance. But their legal status is subordinate, or at least secondary, to the love they have for their children. They strive to insulate their kids from hardship, and these efforts unfold through their selective engagement with service institutions. Finally, their legal status and status as parents matter sequentially. It is their legal status that underlies the hardships that undocumented immigrants endure. It is their status as parents that informs the start of their engagement with service institutions. It is their legal status that signals the risk of institutional evasion. And it is their status as parents that might offer them relief from deportation. In brief, legal status matters—sometimes independently, sometimes interdependently, and sometimes successively—depending on situational context.

This reasoning helps clarify the increasingly mixed evidence of immigration enforcement's effects on undocumented immigrants and their families' societal participation. Whether in economics, education, political science, public health, or sociology, an established literature has observed the "chilling effects" of punitive laws, regulations, and policies that target undocumented immigrants.[69] The hypothesis goes that undocumented immigrants and their families will withdraw from mainstream societal institutions in anticipation of, or in response to, legal, regulatory, and policy changes that make deportation more likely. Evidence as far back as the 1970s supports this theory, with a similar dynamic observed in studies based on survey and interview data collected through the peak of immigration policing in about 2013.[70] More recent analyses based on the timing of infamous national or localized shocks—such as the partial implementation of Arizona's controversial SB 1070, Donald Trump's election to the presidency, the introduction of the Muslim Ban, or the Trump administration's proposed public charge rule—find something similar.[71] This literature establishes some of the negative effects of acute changes to immigration enforcement. Less discussed is what evidence of small or null chilling effects means, or what evidence of increased societal participation means. To be sure, as empirical work on the possible chilling effects of immigration enforcement accumulates, it tends to be much more mixed than our priors might have us expect.[72] This chapter suggests a couple reasons why: a focus on one unit of analysis (e.g., individuals or children), context of enforcement (e.g., the Secure Communities rollout or Trump's election), or outcome (e.g., work or school attendance or SNAP participation) provides a partial snapshot of how undocumented immigrants manage the tangled web of laws, regulations, and policies to which they are subject as they go about daily life. Attention to the meanings that undocumented parents hold about their engagement with service institutions, and how their engagement varies situationally given their multiple social roles and responsibilities, reveals a more complex dynamic: engagement with and evasion of myriad service institutions go hand in hand. In other words, it is one thing to examine what prompts people to evade a given institution; it is another to examine what brings or keeps them there despite the risk of their institutional engagement.

These insights, coupled with those presented in the previous chapter, round out our theoretical understandings of how subordinated populations manage surveillance in daily life. A dominant model of surveillance, particularly in studies of the criminal-legal system, poverty governance, and immigration, emphasizes what Michel Foucault called the "repressive" effects of punishment.[73] Research drawing inspiration from this model reveals how the government's capacity to surveil weighs heaviest on populations already worried about state punishment, such as people with criminal records, low-income people, and undocumented immigrants. And, because these labels are themselves reflective of broader racial and class inequalities in the United States, this research identifies punishment as one mechanism that exacerbates multiple forms of inequality. We have seen how scholars studying the criminal-legal system have linked the threat of punishment and people with criminal records' evasion of surveilling institutions.[74] Studies of poverty governance, such as those by Kelley Fong, likewise point to the threat of punishment to explain why low-income mothers experiencing material and social hardship (e.g., a lost job or housing insecurity) may withhold that information from authorities in service institutions and forgo public assistance; they worry about referrals to Child Protective Services that threaten their families. And, in immigration, much research suggests that the threat of punishment underlies undocumented immigrants and their citizen family members' avoidance of surveilling institutions, as in Sarah Desai, Jessica Houston Su, and Robert M. Adelman's study of the adult U.S. citizen children of undocumented immigrants in Los Angeles. My findings support the continued examination of the repressive effects of punishment while also resurrecting Foucault's call to "regard punishment as a complex social function" whose repressive effects must be "situate[d] . . . in a whole series of their possible positive effects, even if these seem marginal at first sight."[75] It is true that subordinated populations, such as the undocumented parents I interviewed for this book, are subject to everyday forms of surveillance that threaten both their well-being and societal presence.

But it is also true, as Foucault theorized, that "punishment is only one element of a double system: gratification-punishment."[76] Although studies of the criminal-legal system and poverty governance increasingly have paid attention to surveillance's dual functions, fewer studies of immigration have done the same.[77] Yet punishment and gratification (or assistance or reward) are mutually constitutive, particularly in the context of state efforts to manage people navigating correlated hardships. Authorities in service institutions surveil subordinated populations as they confer important material and symbolic resources—for example, public goods that offset financial hardship or formal records that catalog someone's involved parenting. They can also enforce subordinated populations' exclusion from material resources or document their noncompliance with various laws, regulations, or policies that might lead to greater surveillance from more punitive authorities in regulatory institutions (e.g., the police or Child Protective Services). Surveillance's rewards need not owe to the state's benevolence; they can instead be coercive, a way for the state to separate subordinated populations into categories of "good" and "bad."[78] Whereas those whom institutional authorities judge to be in the former category are granted rewards for their compliance with state rules, those whom institutional authorities sort into the latter category are punished for noncompliance. This chapter shows how undocumented parents manage the gratification-punishment duality of surveillance as they go about daily life. For the undocumented parents I met, risk is present in both their evasion of and engagement with service institutions. They evidence a relatively sophisticated understanding of the pervasive laws, regulations, and policies that set the parameters of their lives as not just undocumented immigrants but also undocumented parents. Their understandings are akin to what scholars studying criminal courts might variously refer to as "cultivated expertise"[79] or "jailhouse lawyering."[80] In other words, they develop lay understandings of how to manage surveillance through their own experiences engaging with regulatory and service institutions, as well as those of family or community members. Even though they don't always get all the details right (such as in the cases of cash-like public assistance or cancellation of removal for exceptional and extremely unusual hardship), their lay expertise offers them a blueprint for recognizing where surveillance occurs, the risks and rewards of this surveillance given their multiple social roles and responsibilities, and the best way to align their institutional engagement with the perceived expectations of the authorities monitoring them. Studying surveillance as both punishment and gratification takes nothing away from the power imbalance this dynamic entails. Subordinated populations, including the undocumented, learn to spot surveillance in part because they worry about state punishment. Still, undocumented immigrants' efforts to manage surveillance are based on a "reasonable bet that the incorporative workings of governmentality can retroact onto the more exclusionary logics of sovereignty," as Sébastien Chauvin and Blanca Garcés-Mascareñas posit.[81] In other words, they believe their selective engagement with everyday forms of surveillance offers them a way to "speak back" to the authorities they encounter regularly that they meet whatever tall expectations they have of them as undocumented immigrants and as undocumented parents.[82] Yet we will see in the next chapter how surveillance—and the records resulting from it—takes on new meanings if undocumented immigrants come to stand before immigration officials. Surveillance comes to represent as much about the threat of societal exclusion as well as the hope for inclusion.

CHAPTER FOUR

Surveillance and Societal Membership

ALTHOUGH MOST UNDOCUMENTED IMMIGRANTS will never encounter immigration officials once settled in the United States, such an encounter remains a menacing prospect. Their efforts to manage everyday surveillance, as we saw in the last two chapters, in part reflect their desire to avoid police referrals to immigration officials as they go about their routines. But, if they do come to stand before immigration officials as immigrants petitioning for formal societal membership, they also hope that their quotidian interactions with institutional authorities will offer them an important resource: formal records. Whether petitioning for legalization or to be spared from deportation, most can only speculate about whether their records will matter. This chapter rounds out this speculation through the vantage points of different study participants, including formerly undocumented immigrants (who have since secured a semi-legal status or green card), currently or formerly undocumented immigrants in removal proceedings, and immigration officials in Dallas Immigration Court. Doing so reveals how the contexts in which formal records are presented, including the laws, regulations, and policies governing their evaluation, circumscribe the meanings of those records for undocumented immigrants and immigration officials alike. Absent an affirmative opportunity to apply for permanent residence, they risk having to submit a defensive petition during removal proceedings in immigration court, where structural and organizational features are likely to coalesce to produce their deportation.

Like all the families I met, David and Maite selectively engaged with institutions that surveilled them as part of their daily lives. Recall from chapter 1 that David left his Guatemalan hometown, leaving behind Maite and their newborn daughter, at his dad's urging. David entered the United States with a tourist visa that he then overstayed, and Maite eventually used a fraudulent visa to enter with their daughter. The undocumented family initially struggled to rebuild the middle-class lifestyle they enjoyed back home. But, as we saw in chapter 2, Maite researched—online and by calling relevant authorities—about what rights her family had available to them in what they saw as "this country of opportunities." By the time I met them in 2013, they had learned to seize these few opportunities. Both had Individual Tax Identification Numbers (ITINs), which they used to work as independent contractors, selling housewares door-to-door. Their household's pretax income amounted to $52,000 a year, affording them a spacious two-bedroom apartment near a local private university. They paid for private health insurance for themselves and their now fourteen-year-old undocumented daughter, and they accepted public health insurance for their four-year-old daughter who was born in the United States. "We pay everything else ourselves," Maite declared proudly, "because we don't want to be a burden for the government."

Given their careful efforts, it surprised me to discover that David had almost been deported a few years before our first interview. But it should not have, as he reminded me: "You never know who the police will pick up and who immigration will kick out." In David's telling, a police officer arrested him following a traffic stop. His friend, also undocumented and from Guatemala, was driving when he rolled through a stop sign. A police officer pulled them over and asked for their driver's licenses, which they did not have because Texas does not allow undocumented immigrants a driver's license. Both men instead furnished a consular identification card, which immigrants of different national origins can secure from their sending country's consulate inside the United States. Known simply as a consular ID, it does not grant driving privileges. Many state and local authorities nonetheless recognize it as a valid form of identification.[1] Undocumented and documented immigrants alike can secure consular IDs, but many institutional authorities see them as more typical among the undocumented; in other words, they view a consular ID as an indication of unlawful presence in the country.[2] David suspected that something similar befell him and his friend here. The police officer inquired about their legal status, and both admitted to being undocumented. Things quickly escalated, as David recalled:

They first took us to a detention center and asked us for all our information. From there, they separated me from my friend and took me to a big detention center in El Paso. I hired a lawyer and saw an immigration judge. The lawyer got me out on bond, but I had to pay $8,000 to immigration to get out. Most people don't have that kind of money and will just ask to be deported instead. I told them that I would stay in detention until my wife could get the money to bail me out.

Over the next several years, David would fight his removal. His lawyer felt that David's best (and only) option for relief was cancellation of removal for exceptional and extremely unusual hardship, explaining that the odds looked good: David first entered the country a decade prior in 1999, with a tourist visa, and his only infraction was this recent incident of driving without a license—and he hadn't even been driving. It was still an open question as to whether he could meet the tall hardship standard. As we saw in the last chapter, immigration officials would not consider hardship to Maite or their eldest daughter since both were undocumented; their case would have to be built around their citizen daughter, who was an infant. Alongside David's lawyer, David and Maite worked to narrate the overlapping hardships that their family faces each day—and how these would pose an undue burden on their citizen daughter if David were deported.[3] From there, the family needed to provide as much evidence as possible to corroborate this narrative. Maite, a self-described hoarder of documents, was ready:

> I tell you, there are cases and then there are *cases*. For example, with my husband, it wasn't so bad because they looked into his background. He does not have any tickets. He pays his taxes on time. He doesn't owe the government anything. And we could prove it all because I always keep everything that I think I might need one day and, look, I did end up needing these documents. We put together a document of more than a hundred pages for his application.

One unexpected question that the couple had to contend with during David's removal case was whether to list Maite and their undocumented daughter on his application. Among other details, the application asks for the name, legal status, and contact information of the applicant's spouse and children. But, as undocumented immigrants themselves, Maite worried that providing this information would set her and her daughter up for deportation if the immigration judge rejected David's application. David's lawyer countered, reminding Maite that withholding their names might jeopardize David's case. What's more, if David's cancellation of removal application, based on exceptional and extremely unusual hardship to their citizen daughter, were successful, the lawyer pointed out to Maite that David would eventually be able to sponsor her and their undocumented daughter for a green card. "I had to think about it," Maite admitted. "If we said that he was single, then we would have been lying. If they had caught him in a lie, then it would have been a problem for his case, so we decided that it was better to tell the truth."

It had been years since David's arrest but, in 2014, David told me that his case was almost over: an immigration judge had all but granted his application. He had not yet received a green card, though, as only so many can be issued each year to undocumented immigrants approved for cancellation of removal.[4] When that cap is reached, any subsequent cases that an immigration judge wants to approve join a growing backlog awaiting formal approval. That backlog will take years to clear.[5] "They keep telling us to wait," Maite said with a shrug. "So, we wait. They give you the hope of waiting." As we'll see later this chapter, David never received a green card—and he, Maite, and their undocumented daughter would ultimately be deported.

———

So much about daily life as an undocumented immigrant is characterized by a palpable tension between a fear of societal exclusion and a hope for inclusion. This duality, though not explicitly stated in the laws, regulations, and policies governing immigration to the United States, has been one of this system's core features since at least 1986.[6] That year was the last time the federal government made a large-scale legalization opportunity, sometimes referred to as amnesty, available to undocumented immigrants. Alongside additional changes since 1996, the year 1986 also marks a turning point in the federal government's approach to border security and interior immigration enforcement, as we saw in chapter 2. For undocumented immigrants living in the United States, especially those from Mexico and Central America, it has become increasingly difficult to access a green card. Depending on where they settle and make a life for themselves and their families, it can be harder to make ends meet and, above all, to feel they have a long-term future here.[7] Still, every few years, a presidential administration or congressperson floats the possibility of another legalization program, rekindling many undocumented immigrants' flickering flames of hope. Those possibilities stall out, and the fear of exclusion again tempers the hope for inclusion.[8]

This chapter examines how this tension between exclusion and inclusion manifests as undocumented immigrants navigate consequential moments of immigration surveillance that will decide their formal societal membership, a phrase I use here to mean access to a green card that confers permanent residence and that offers a pathway to citizenship. None of the above implies that undocumented immigrants have zero chance of securing a green card. But the odds are long under current practice. Still, the undocumented immigrants I met were hopeful that their chance would come one day, perhaps via some new large-scale legalization program, or once their eldest citizen child reached twenty-one years of age, or if they had to demonstrate to an immigration judge the exceptional hardship that their removal would entail for their children. All they required, they believed, was a chance. Armed with the formal records that they had accumulated as part of their daily lives in this country, they felt that they would have enough evidence to prove to immigration officials that they deserve to be here permanently.

Although the meanings that undocumented immigrants assign to their records are essential for understanding how they manage everyday forms of institutional surveillance, these meanings beg another important question: Will their records of having engaged with regulatory and service institutions matter when it comes time to petition immigration officials for formal societal membership? It is difficult to answer this question from interviews with the most typical of undocumented immigrants; that is, those who have neither legalized nor faced removal. Most will hope the answer is yes. But the question becomes more directly answerable from interviews with both formerly undocumented immigrants (who have since legalized) and undocumented and formerly undocumented immigrants who have confronted removal proceedings, like David and Maite. It becomes more directly answerable, still, when we can peek inside immigration court to see how immigration officials—especially immigration judges and prosecutors from the Department of Homeland Security (DHS)—interpret some of these records in real time. Through these different vantage points, we can probe whether, when, and how the formal records that undocumented immigrants accrue every day matter for their formal societal membership.

An initial answer is found in the complex laws, regulations, and policies governing immigration surveillance. If they meet established eligibility criteria, undocumented immigrants will file either an *affirmative* or *defensive* application, also known as a petition.[9] The differences are substantial. Despite having spent a decade or more in the country, most undocumented immigrants remain ineligible for any affirmative petition as of this writing. When an undocumented immigrant submits an affirmative petition, they do so to U.S. Citizenship and Immigration Services (USCIS). An officer there processes the application and, for some petitions, invites the applicant to a "non-adversarial" interview that a USCIS training manual describes as intended to elicit information without "interrogat[ing] or argu[ing] with any interviewee."[10] In contrast, undocumented immigrants file defensive petitions in immigration court only after the DHS has initiated removal proceedings against them. Defensive petitions are almost always "adversarial," whereby "two parties oppose each other by advocating their mutually exclusive positions before a neutral arbiter until one side prevails and the other side loses," as the same training manual notes.[11] Of course, the stakes of winning and losing are higher than that sentence suggests. Whereas an undocumented immigrant who "wins" will escape removal (and perhaps secure permanent residence), any undocumented immigrant who "loses" will have to leave the country. The type of application, therefore, entails two very different contexts of submission that themselves imply situations with very different stakes.

Undocumented immigrants submit an affirmative petition when they believe they are eligible for some concrete, existing legalization opportunity. The process is ostensibly non-adversarial but, as the formerly undocumented immigrants I interviewed explained, it still felt adversarial when they had to submit their personal information to immigration officials whose scrutiny they had long tried to evade. As a relatively agentic process, study participants reported feeling conflicted about whether to begin an application, lest something go wrong and upset the life they had built. But their undocumented relatives or friends, themselves lacking a similar opportunity, spurred them on. Still feeling unsettled, the formerly undocumented immigrants I met reported relying on their networks to cobble together enough money to hire an immigration attorney. They saw these attorneys as offering not just professional expertise but also protection from an immigration system they viewed with suspicion. In all cases, they noted the comfort they felt as their attorneys pieced together their different records to ensure their eligibility for a legalization opportunity before submitting their application to immigration officials.

A defensive petition, by contrast, implies that the DHS has already initiated removal proceedings against an undocumented immigrant. And, as we saw in David and Maite's case, even the most cautious of undocumented immigrants have little control over this initiation. Those I interviewed who had experienced removal proceedings described how those proceedings compounded the overlapping hardships their families faced in daily life. For these study participants, local police had turned them over to Immigration and Customs Enforcement (ICE), who detained them until and often beyond their initial appearance in immigration court. Detention sapped their households of not just a partner or parent but also a key source of income and childcare. How long this detention, and these compounding hardships, lasted would depend on study participants' existing material and social resources, the formal records that led the DHS to initiate removal proceedings, and structural and organizational features of immigration court. Those with existing material resources, like David, could weather the compounding hardships that their detention imposed on their families long enough to hire an immigration attorney and secure bond. That attorney, in turn, could review the records that landed their client in removal proceedings and consider any available forms of relief. Those without these resources noted how they simply could not afford to do the same. Even if they could rely on family and friends to piece together the funds, many learned in early discussions with attorneys that things looked bleak: sometimes they discovered that their case would drag on for years with no guaranteed outcome, sometimes they realized that the records that brought them to immigration court would likely tank any defensive petition they could submit, and sometimes both were true. In these situations, they said they declined to submit a defensive petition, opting for a more immediate removal so they could attempt to reenter the country clandestinely via its southern border.

The in-depth interviews suggest that, at least in the context of removal proceedings, the records that undocumented immigrants accrue over their years in the country may not always be sufficient to access formal societal membership. My ethnographic observations in Dallas Immigration Court help explain why. I identify three structural and organizational features of immigration court that interrelate to promote immigration judges' interpretation of the balance of evidence in favor of the prosecution. The first is a high burden of proof on the defendant, which casts suspicion on any records defendants submit but uncritically accepts those of the prosecution. The second is a high proportion of removal proceedings conducted while defendants are detained, which complicates defendants' ability to gather evidence to counterbalance the prosecution's claims. And the third is a high proportion of defendants who lack attorney representation. To be sure, even attorneys representing defendants in immigration court sometimes struggle. But, without a constitutional right to a court-appointed lawyer, many defendants in immigration court have no choice but to go it alone as they attempt to decipher opaque court rules and challenge the prosecution's interpretation of evidence. In the cases I observed, these three constraints all contributed to immigration judges' denials of defendants' petitions.

These findings suggest that the contexts in which formal records are presented to immigration officials reflect distinct opportunities and constraints—outlined in myriad laws, regulations, and policies—that delimit the meanings of these records for undocumented immigrants' societal exclusion and inclusion. In other words, institutional surveillance can entail both punishments and rewards, which vary situationally. Selectively engaging with surveilling institutions, such as the IRS and schools, certainly helps undocumented immigrants secure important resources and avoid punishment in daily life. But living to fight another day is not the same as achieving formal societal membership. Opportunities for affirmative petitions are few and far between. Until such an opportunity emerges, the reality is that some undocumented immigrants will be swept into removal proceedings in immigration court. A defensive petition, then, will be their first and likely last chance at formal societal membership. But, as demonstrated below, the deck is stacked against them. Surveillance remains as much about the threat of exclusion as the promise of inclusion.

Affirmative Petitions

A common hope among undocumented immigrants settled in the United States is that they will, one day, be able to legalize—or, at least, to live with more rights and protections than their current legal status confers.[12] Every undocumented immigrant I interviewed taught me as much, expressing that they longed for the chance to submit an affirmative petition for immigration officials' consideration. They did not use this technical phrase to describe their hopes; they instead mentioned "applying for papers" or "fixing my papers" or "waiting for an amnesty." Nor did they know whether these opportunities would appear, if ever. But, for the formerly undocumented immigrants I met, these opportunities did appear. And, suddenly, something that they had hoped for transformed into something that they fretted over: Would they turn over their personal information to immigration officials whose gaze they had long averted? The answer turned out to be yes—but not before hiring an immigration attorney to review their formal records and confirm their eligibility.

As of this writing, most undocumented immigrants have no immediate pathway to formal societal membership. This truism belies the range of affirmative petitions that USCIS lists on their website.[13] In chapter 1, we reviewed the two broad categories of visas—nonimmigrant and immigrant. Whereas nonimmigrant visas do not always offer a pathway to permanent residence, immigrant visas do.[14] The few nonimmigrant visas that offer permanent residence are reserved either for victims of human trafficking (T visas) or criminal activity (U visas).[15] USCIS approves a maximum of 5,000 T visas, and 10,000 U visas, each year. No one I interviewed mentioned these visas as options for them.[16]

Immigrant visas—whether employment-, family-, or humanitarian-based—are, in theory, more available. In practice, though, these options are often as inaccessible to undocumented immigrants already living in the country as the nonimmigrant visas.[17] An employer could sponsor an undocumented immigrant's petition for an immigrant visa, but few will want to navigate the bureaucratic, and expensive, process for all but the most privileged of applicants.[18] A citizen or permanent resident spouse or twenty-one-year-old child could sponsor their relative's application, but most undocumented immigrants do not yet have a qualifying relative to begin this similarly bureaucratic and expensive process.[19] And an undocumented immigrant could apply to USCIS for asylum, assuming they fled persecution or torture in their home country, but the typical undocumented immigrant has lived in the country for far longer than the one year the federal government grants them to apply.[20] Still, some undocumented immigrants do eventually become eligible for an immigrant visa. Most relevant for the formerly undocumented immigrants I met were those visas concerning family sponsorship, especially from a citizen partner or child. About 12 percent of undocumented immigrants nationwide are married to a U.S. citizen, and about 33 percent of undocumented immigrants have at least one citizen child.[21] Each year, the Department of State and USCIS approve hundreds of thousands affirmative petitions from immigrants whose spouse or twenty-one-year-old child is a U.S. citizen; in fiscal year 2016, that number was 568,000.[22] Among the nine formerly undocumented immigrants I met who later became permanent residents via an affirmative petition, seven did so through family sponsorship (the other two legalized following IRCA's amnesty provisions).

Beyond nonimmigrant and immigrant visas, undocumented immigrants living in the United States may sometimes become eligible for what sociologist Cecilia Menjívar calls a "liminally legal" status—one that is not quite undocumented and not quite permanent residence.[23] Examples abound of these kinds of semi-legal statuses.[24] But the most relevant among the people I met is Deferred Action for Childhood Arrivals (DACA), for which an estimated 1.2 million undocumented immigrants nationwide are eligible.[25] Unlike the above nonimmigrant and immigrant visas that grant permanent residence and, ultimately, citizenship, DACA does not. It instead confers protection from deportation ("deferred action") and work authorization. Recipients must submit a renewal application for DACA every two years. Three of the formerly undocumented immigrants I interviewed for this book are DACA recipients.

If it seems obvious that an undocumented immigrant eligible for any affirmative petition will apply, it was less obvious to the formerly undocumented immigrants I spoke with. Though they had all spent a decade or more living in the country without authorization, they felt they had developed a routine. Life had its challenges—the hardships they confronted primary among them—but they had found ways to meet life's many demands. They feared that submitting an affirmative petition to immigration officials could render those efforts worthless. Accordingly, most reported a reluctance to apply, coaxed to do so instead by their partners or other relatives and friends. No one dared apply without the assistance of an immigration lawyer, whom they found through their family members and friends. Their lawyers constituted more than just a professional completing paperwork; they were also someone they trusted to review their cache of formal records to confirm that it was wise to apply in the first place.

Applying for an immigrant visa through family sponsorship was a nerve-wracking prospect for formerly undocumented immigrants in the study. An overview of the process, focusing on applicants whose sponsor is a U.S. citizen, reveals some reasons why.[26] It begins with the citizen submitting Form I-130, called "Petition for Alien Relative." The form asks for details about the citizen petitioner, including their relationship to the beneficiary, their biographical details (e.g., place of birth, address history, marital information, and employment history), and similar biographical details about the beneficiary. The citizen petitioner must also file Form I-864EZ, titled "Affidavit of Support Under Section 213A of the INA [Immigration and Nationality Act]." As USCIS notes on its website, this form shows that the beneficiary will "have adequate means of financial support [from their relatives] and are not likely to rely on the U.S. government for financial support." In other words, it establishes that they will not become a public charge. If the beneficiary entered the United States with a visa that they then overstayed, they can submit Form I-485, known as "Application to Register Permanent Residence or Adjust Status." This form asks for much of the same information about the beneficiary as Form I-130, in addition to a battery of questions regarding their criminal and immigration histories and general eligibility for permanent residence.[27]

Form I-689, titled "Report of Medical Examination and Vaccination Record," will also be required and demonstrates that the beneficiary complies with U.S. public health standards.[28] Other forms may also be necessary, as we will see below, especially for beneficiaries who entered the country without authorization or who have previously been deported.[29] Most forms have separate filing fees, which can total upward of $3,000.[30] Immigration officials with USCIS will first review the application and, if approved, turn over the materials to the Department of State's National Visa Center (NVC). An interview, which usually takes place in the U.S. Consulate in one's country of origin, is sometimes required before immigration officials will finalize application decisions.[31]

The stakes of these bureaucratic minutiae, surely tough to follow for even the immigration lawyers among us, are not always immediately apparent to undocumented immigrants eligible to legalize. Teresa, the Mexican-born naturalized citizen in her thirties we met briefly in chapter 2, laughed when I asked her to tell me the story of how she became a citizen. "It could have been a lot easier than it was," she said with a long exhale. As Teresa recalled, she entered the country without authorization at age seven alongside her mother in the early 1990s. The mother-daughter duo spent a few years in that status, sharing a bed in a cramped two-bedroom apartment that her mother rented with a friend who was also undocumented. Within two years, her mother fell hard for a man who is a U.S. citizen; they wed shortly thereafter. Her mom's new husband agreed to sponsor his new wife, and Teresa, for a green card. After consulting with an immigration attorney, he also offered to adopt Teresa; following her adoption and receipt of a green card, Teresa would automatically become a citizen.[32] Teresa refused. "I was young," she reasoned, "and I was jealous because he took my mom away from me." Though she didn't remember all the details given her youth at the time, Teresa did eventually receive a green card through her mother's sponsorship.

When Teresa met, and later married, Gerardo, the bureaucratic minutiae were much more evident to her this time around. Gerardo, in his thirties and from Mexico, was undocumented; he and Teresa shared two citizen kids under age seven. Though they had lived with these different legal statuses for years, Teresa realized during the height of interior immigration enforcement efforts in the 2000s that it was probably a good idea to sponsor Gerardo for a green card: "I was legal here," Teresa explained, "and he could be legal here, too. We didn't want to have to worry in case something happens, and he gets deported." One detail she learned from her own green card application was that "things would be easier if I became a citizen first." Whereas visa caps for permanent residents sponsoring their spouses for a green card can prolong the process, no such caps exist for citizens.[33] For Teresa, it was a no brainer: "I decided to become a citizen."

After that, Teresa relied on the same attorney who shepherded her naturalization application to start Gerardo's application for permanent residence. The attorney would fill out the several forms required to complete Gerardo's application, but Gerardo would need to be present to offer the details, to turn over the records that corroborated his answers, and, finally, to check that the attorney had filled out the application properly. "It took a long time," as Gerardo put it mildly. About a year later, Gerardo received a letter from the NVC that he would have to appear for an interview at the U.S. Consulate in Juarez, Mexico, because he entered the country without authorization (or "without inspection," in the parlance of the Immigration and Nationality Act). The trouble is that, by leaving the country, Gerardo could become subject to a yearslong ban on reentry as punishment for his initial entry.[34] But his attorney had filed Form I-601A, known as "Application for Waiver of Grounds of Inadmissibility." This form allows applicants in Gerardo's situation to avoid this ban if they can demonstrate "extreme hardship" (a lower standard than exceptional and extremely unusual hardship) to a citizen or permanent resident parent, spouse, or child. Forms of extreme hardship include the possible negative effects of the reentry bar on a qualifying relative's health, financial outlook, education, and personal life (e.g., because of family separation), among other factors. Fortunately, Gerardo's waiver had been provisionally approved prior to his interview.[35] "Everything went fine," Teresa remembered. "The only thing that was missing was a copy of a form, which our attorney had forgotten to include. I sent it via express mail overnight and, after a week, they approved him."

Managing the logistics of it all is critical to affirmative petitions and records are an important aspect underlying this process. Yajaira, who said in chapter 2 that she would not loan her social security number to the Virgin Mary, taught me as much. Though her husband Javier had become a permanent resident following the 1986 amnesty, Yajaira spent more than a decade living as an undocumented immigrant. Part of the reason for the delay was financial; she and Javier simply didn't have enough money to submit another application once they had finished his. Another reason was that Yajaira wasn't even sure she needed to invest the money. As the family's primary breadwinner, Javier felt that he had needed a green card; for her part, Yajaira felt that she had figured out daily life as an undocumented immigrant: "It was normal," she told me. But, once they had saved enough, Yajaira gave in to Javier's insistence that she apply.

Javier knew that they would need a lawyer to help with Yajaira's application, given his prior legalization experience and the peculiarities of Yajaira's case. The couple hired the same lawyer that Javier used for his own petition. What was most daunting about the application, according to Yajaira, were all the little details she had to remember: "You have to fill out the forms that immigration has. They ask you a lot of questions, even about the dates you entered, and they want proof. Immigration is outrageous." None of these details were straightforward for Yajaira, as she had crisscrossed the border several times throughout the 1990s so she could visit her parents in Mexico. Worse, still, she had been caught on several occasions: "My husband kept telling me, 'Remember how many times they catch you,' since he knew he was going to apply for my papers. He told me that all that information would be on my record with immigration." Her memory proved spotty, but the lawyer counseled her that rough guesses about each capture were better than omissions because "immigration has everything on the computer. They know when you got caught because they take your fingerprints." The lawyer finalized and submitted Yajaira's materials, including Form I-601A to account for her multiple unlawful entries.

It took a handful of years before Yajaira received a letter inviting her to a consular interview in Juarez, Mexico. Yajaira worried that immigration officials would deny her application and, therefore, be separated from her five children in the United States. Her lawyer reassured her that she had no reason to worry because they had been judicious about double checking the information on her application: "He told me, 'Just tell it like it is. When they interview you, they are going to ask you about what we put on the application, and you have to give them the same version of events we put on the form.'" Yajaira resolved to tell the truth: "If somebody lies, they get rejected, they don't get their residency, and they have to stay in Mexico." Shortly after her interview, Yajaira received notice that she would have to return to the consulate for a biometrics appointment. Her lawyer celebrated the news: "He said, 'You practically have your green card. When they ask for your fingerprints, it means that they want to check if you are lying and see if you have a criminal record or something like that before they give you the visa.'" Immigration officials approved her application thereafter, and Yajaira was soon on her way back to Dallas.

Formal records matter for formerly undocumented immigrants submitting affirmative applications, but they take on added weight in the time following their approval. Now squarely on the radar of immigration officials, they felt that they had to be even more cautious in how they engaged with the regulatory and service institutions that had long characterized their daily lives.[36] Gerardo saw it as follows: "I think the main thing is not to get in trouble with the law. . . . You don't want to have any of those things on your record because that will not help you if you want to stay here." Yajaira had a similar perspective: "I didn't feel I was so worried before getting my residency. . . . I see that [the undocumented] live more peaceful lives than me. . . . If I try to cheat, it'll appear in the system and immigration will take my residency away." Although undocumented immigrants are more likely than permanent residents to be deported, national survey data show that they fear deportation at comparable rates.[37] My interviews suggest that the records cataloging their lives as permanent residents are one reason for this pattern. Having secured formal societal membership, they wanted to try their best to maintain it.

This dynamic is also present among the formerly undocumented immigrants I spoke with who now have a semi-legal status—namely, those with DACA. In some ways, it is more palpable because of the contentious political battles that have surrounded DACA since its announcement in June 2012.[38] Take the case of Marina, the DACA recipient who we saw in the last chapter was training to become the assistant manager of a local fast-food franchise. DACA certainly produced material improvements to Marina's life, but she told me that she only applied because "my parents and my husband insisted." She had grown content with the routine she developed as an undocumented immigrant since her arrival in 2005, and it took her family's encouragement for her "to get it together" and "to take the opportunity to fix my papers."

A friend referred Marina to an attorney, who would take charge of the application. DACA has several eligibility requirements, which Marina easily recited during our interview.[39] Applicants must have been younger than age thirty-one on June 15, 2012; present in the United States before age sixteen; present in the country since June 15, 2007; be attending or graduated from high school (or be an honorably discharged member of the military); and not have a "significant" criminal record.[40] Marina recounted how she was able to cull together different records of her engagement with surveilling institutions to show that she met these criteria:

> I got here around July 2005. I went to a clinic to get some vaccinations that I needed for school. I still had that little vaccination card from the clinic. That proved the year I arrived. I also had the different leases for the apartments I had lived in. Apart from that, I had attended high school here, so everything from the school district helped. Two years after high school, I gave birth to my first daughter. And, to date, I'm filing taxes.

The extensive cache of records helped Marina prepare her application with her attorney, which they submitted to USCIS alongside a hefty application fee ($495, at the time of this writing). USCIS then requires applicants to schedule an appointment to have their biometrics taken. From there, applicants await notification of their application's approval or denial, with appeals of denied applications possible depending on the reason for denial.

Marina was ultimately approved for DACA. I asked her what she saw as its key benefits relative to having been undocumented: "The key benefit is my tax refund. I receive a lot more money back. . . . Secondly, it's also easier to find work. You have a valid social security number."[41] Notably, Marina did not mention the temporary reprieve from deportation as a "key benefit" of DACA. At around the time of our 2015 interview, campaigns for the 2016 presidential election were underway—with undocumented immigration among the most central and politicized of issues.[42] Donald Trump, in particular, launched his campaign with a promise to "terminate President Obama's illegal executive order on immigration immediately."[43] Marina picked up on this sentiment when she reported having felt more secure without DACA protections than with them: "This is something temporary. You never know, they may take it back. Then you'll go back to being just like the other millions of [undocumented] people."[44]

Formerly undocumented immigrants in the study worried about the personal information they surrendered to immigration officials in exchange for DACA's temporary deportation protections and work authorization. It was hard for some to know whether that trade would be worthwhile. Specifically, they agonized over what admitting their unlawful presence would mean to the immigration officials reviewing their applications. Araceli, whom we met in each of the previous chapters, told me that she was initially uncertain about applying for DACA—much to the chagrin of her undocumented husband, Rafael, who did not meet the age eligibility cutoffs. But Araceli distrusted what USCIS would do with her application. She ultimately gave in to her husband's wishes only when they saved up $1,500 to hire an attorney to manage the process.

> As a Mexican, you feel more suspicious about everything. Maybe because that has been our fate in this life. I don't know. At least that's my opinion. I feel suspicious about everything. I was not going to make such a strong move and go to immigration and say, "Hey, I'm here!" Just me all by myself. Because I think that you can. . . . But I didn't want to send all my information to them and have them find a mistake or something like that and, because of that mistake, I would receive my deportation notice, and this is over.

The attorney proved instrumental to calming Araceli's nerves. "I talked to her and explained my situation to her in the same way I have talked to you about many things," Araceli narrated. "She told me, 'Tell me the whole truth and nothing but the truth about everything you've done since you set foot in the United States.'" Araceli gave her attorney the highlights, at which point the attorney instructed her on the records she would need to fill out Araceli's application and, ultimately, secure DACA for her. Though Araceli understood DACA's benefits for her life, the political uncertainty surrounding its future continued to give Araceli pause about her family's long-term future in the country: "They have our future in their hands. My future. My husband's future. Our daughters' futures. Our family depends on this."

Fears over their prospects for long-term formal societal membership weighed on the DACA recipients I met. Maribel, who entered the country without authorization in 2002 at the age of ten, told me that she "had to think about whether she would ask for DACA or not." Like Marina and Araceli, the twenty-five-year-old was aware that DACA might be rescinded. But she decided to go for it: "It was a big opportunity. I knew that I would have more freedom to live and work. And I had hope that everything would turn out OK. I worked really hard to pay for the lawyer and the application." USCIS approved Maribel's DACA application in 2015.

By the time that I reconnected with Maribel in 2018, the political context had changed markedly. The Trump administration had rescinded DACA in September 2017, with various federal court decisions intervening to resuscitate or strangulate it over the next several years. The Supreme Court ultimately preserved DACA on an administrative technicality in June 2020, though a subsequent federal court decision in July 2021 allows only DACA renewal applications to be processed.[45] Against this backdrop, Maribel questioned whether it was wise to renew her DACA. She consulted with her lawyer, who cautiously reassured her that, "even though immigration has all our information, there is no reason for them to deport us unless we have committed a crime." For Maribel, the reassurances from her lawyer pointed to the importance of keeping in good with the various regulatory and service institutions she engages with in her daily life: "The lawyer helped me so much. She told me that immigration will only come for you if your record is dirty. But we pay our taxes. We haven't committed any crimes. I have a son who is a citizen. I don't think they will tell me: You know what? We don't want you here."

Formal records are necessary for undocumented immigrants to establish their eligibility for rare opportunities for legalization. But those records alone do not guarantee that undocumented immigrants will submit an affirmative petition. Study participants noted how they pursued these opportunities only when they could hire an attorney who, in turn, assured them that their records would constitute sufficient proof of their eligibility to the immigration officials reviewing their applications. That they could opt into the process offered study participants a sense of control over what they perceived to be an uncertain situation, one that they believed could be hostile to their and their families' long-term presence in the country. Although the formerly undocumented immigrants I met all had successful applications, an approved petition did little to erase these uncertainties. Their legal status, whether permanent residence or DACA, conferred a newfound visibility to immigration officials that they saw as raising the stakes of their future engagement with regulatory and service institutions in daily life.

Defensive Petitions

Most undocumented immigrants are not currently eligible for an affirmative petition. But, in a perverse twist of fate, some may become eligible for a defensive petition that offers the chance of facilitating their formal societal membership if they are swept into removal proceedings. Such was the experience of a handful of currently or formerly undocumented immigrants I interviewed. Although they had previously understood themselves to be ineligible for any kind of legalization opportunity, in immigration court, they learned that they might be eligible to legalize via a defensive petition. An immigration judge would confirm their eligibility but, for those allowed to submit a defensive petition, they had to decide whether they would pursue it. That decision was not always straightforward, even when they had formal records that would support their application. Rather, it depended on whether and how the overlapping hardships that characterized their daily lives outside court butt against the structural and organizational constraints of immigration court.

Undocumented immigrants can end up in removal proceedings in several ways. One of the most common for those settled in the country is following an arrest by a local police officer, who detains them until ICE assumes custody and the DHS initiates removal proceedings.[46] USCIS can initiate removal proceedings if they deny certain affirmative petitions or if they believe an applicant to have defrauded or misrepresented them; USCIS can also refer cases to ICE if they suspect an applicant is an "egregious public safety" risk.[47] Although not technically undocumented, immigrants who enter the country without prior authorization and request asylum are also placed in removal proceedings. Five study participants across four families reported having ever been placed in removal proceedings. Some reported multiple experiences, for a total of eight cases: five were initiated by the DHS following a negative police interaction (with four resulting in removal), two were initiated by USCIS (with both resulting in removal), and one was initiated by the DHS following an asylum claim (with the result pending as of this writing).[48]

Once in removal proceedings, the deck is stacked against defendants. Over a hundred years ago, the Supreme Court asserted that deportation is not a criminal punishment but rather a civil penalty.[49] This interpretation means that defendants in immigration court lack many of the rights available to defendants in criminal court, including the presumption of innocence, access to a court-appointed lawyer, and a speedy and public trial by an impartial jury. The absence of these legal rights matters in removal proceedings, where someone can be deported for a crime, even when they were not convicted of it in criminal court;[50] where they can be deported, even when they might be eligible to submit a defensive petition, because they cannot afford a lawyer or find one willing to work at low or no cost;[51] and where, given a backlog of 1.8 million removal cases that will take years to clear, they may spend months (and sometimes years) in detention until a single immigration judge decides their case.[52] In brief, this lack of basic rights can undermine defendants' opportunities for formal societal membership.

Many kinds of defensive petitions are available in removal proceedings, each with their own eligibility criteria. (Though these criteria are outlined in statute, we will see in the next section how they often require a subjective evaluation from the immigration judge or DHS prosecutor.) Two such petitions were relevant to the currently or formerly undocumented immigrants I interviewed. In the previous chapter and in David's story at the beginning of this chapter, we learned about cancellation of removal for exceptional and extremely unusual hardship. Asylum is the second. There are a few types of asylum, each with slightly different requirements.[53] But, in general, asylum applicants must prove that they have suffered, or will suffer, persecution in their home country due to their race, religion, nationality, membership in a particular social group, or political opinion. Three currently or formerly undocumented immigrants in the study reported submitting a defensive petition; two of them submitted cancellation of removal petitions and one submitted an asylum application.[54]

Submitting a defensive petition was not always possible for undocumented immigrants in the study. And, when relief via a defensive petition was available, not everyone pursued it. The reasons why have as much to do with the circumstances that triggered removal proceedings as they do with these individuals' perceived ability to withstand the hardships they faced and that the structural and organizational constraints of immigration court exacerbated. In most cases, the undocumented immigrants I interviewed told me that they declined to submit a defensive petition whose outcome was not guaranteed: simply put, it would take too much time and cost too much money—whether in terms of attorney costs, application fees, bond, or income lost in detention while awaiting their court date.[55] Those who submitted a defensive petition either had access to sufficient resources to weather these costs or felt that they had no viable alternative.

The overlapping hardships that characterize undocumented immigrants' daily lives matter in removal proceedings, too. Four currently or formerly undocumented immigrants I interviewed had been placed in removal proceedings following a negative police interaction. One had two such experiences, implying that people sometimes return to the country following their deportation. (One immigration judge I observed called this "the elephant in the room that we never talk about.") Maritza, who mentioned in the last chapter that she would ask an immigration judge for a permit to stay in the country to care for her daughter with special needs if she were ever placed in removal proceedings, pointed this out to me when she explained how her husband had been deported. Maritza told me that, a few months before our first interview in 2013, a police officer had arrested her undocumented husband for driving under the influence of alcohol. Her husband's arrest and subsequent detention exacerbated the hardships their family already faced. He is the primary breadwinner and finances were tight when he was arrested—their household income was about $20,000 a year—and Maritza could not afford to bail him out. Following Secure Communities protocol, ICE officers soon detained him.

Within a few weeks, the DHS initiated removal proceedings against her husband. I expected that Maritza would tell me that her husband applied for cancellation of removal for exceptional and extremely unusual hardship, because she had mentioned this possibility for herself. Though she said an immigration judge mentioned it as available to him, her husband declined to submit the petition. This outcome surprised me, but Maritza explained it bluntly: "We decided that he would just come back here [following his deportation]." For Maritza's family, paying a *coyote* several thousand dollars to help her husband reenter the country was less costly than the several thousand more dollars required to endure a prolonged detention and application process. Maritza, though, remained hopeful that she and her husband would one day be able to submit an affirmative petition: "Once my kids are of age, they can arrange for us to get papers." Although this remains a possibility for Maritza, given her husband's deportation and subsequent reentry, he may first be required to live outside the United States for ten or more years before applying.

For some undocumented immigrants I talked with, the perceived benefits of an immediate removal lay in the ease of navigating across the border again when compared with the perceived costs of navigating removal proceedings. Eduardo, with the sharp tongue, has been deported twice from inside the United States. The first time was ten years after his initial entry, around 2005. In Eduardo's telling, a police officer pulled him over for rolling through a stop sign but ended up arresting him after running Eduardo's license plate and discovering several unpaid tickets. Eduardo said he could not afford to pay the tickets. Local police held him until immigration officers picked him up and, before he knew it, he was in removal proceedings: "The police arrest you and these same police turn you over to immigration. You think you're being arrested because you owe money for two tickets, but no, they end up deporting you."

Eduardo made it back to Dallas before the start of the study. When I met him in 2014, he was not the single and childless man that he had been during his first deportation. He lived with his undocumented partner, Dorinda, though they were not married. And he had been helping to raise her three citizen children for about eight years. It was important to Eduardo to take care of his family, and he felt that he had developed a routine that allowed him to do so for the foreseeable future. "Just go from your home to your job, from your job to your home," he recited as a mantra of sorts. The routine worked for a while but, when I visited the family in 2018, Eduardo was nowhere to be found. When I got a hold of Dorinda, she told me why: Eduardo had been deported to Mexico. Dorinda explained during our interview that Eduardo's mother was diagnosed with cancer in early 2016, about six months after our prior interview. She said that Eduardo did not take the news well because he and his mother were so close, and he began drinking as a coping mechanism. One day in early spring, Eduardo left work and stopped at a bar for a drink; he poured a dose of oxycodone into his beer. A police officer pulled him over on his way home, as Dorinda recalled: "He ran a stop sign, and they didn't let him go after that."

Shortly thereafter, Eduardo was in immigration detention and back in removal proceedings. Dorinda said she tried to free Eduardo, but there was little she could do. She could not find a low- or no-cost immigration attorney willing to take Eduardo's case, and she could not afford one on her own; one attorney quoted her a fee of $15,000, which almost equaled her yearly annual income now that Eduardo was detained. In speaking with each of these attorneys, though, they suggested to Dorinda that Eduardo faced an uphill battle: Eduardo had been deported previously, was caught for driving under the influence of alcohol and drugs (the latter likely constituting an aggravated felony), and was not the biological or adoptive father of Dorinda's citizen children; legally speaking, there was nothing on which to base an application for cancellation of removal. She relayed the message to Eduardo: "I told him, 'Why don't you take the deportation, and then we can see if we can bring you back with a *coyote*?'" Dorinda was still saving up for that purpose when we last spoke, uncertain about when Eduardo would be reunited with his family.

The case of a formerly undocumented immigrant in the study who successfully petitioned for cancellation of removal suggests that a combination of formal records and preexisting resources is required to pursue defensive petitions in removal proceedings. Sebastián, in his mid-forties when I interviewed his family in 2015, has lived in the United States for almost three decades. His mother had left him with his grandparents in Mexico in the late 1970s so she could pursue work opportunities in Dallas. Although his mom had initially lived without authorization in the country, she eventually became a permanent resident following the amnesty provisions of the 1986 Immigration Reform and Control Act. By 1987, she sent for Sebastián, who crossed the border without authorization; she did not know how long it would take to sponsor him for a green card and, as Sebastián told me, she did not initially have enough money to do so.

Sebastián remained undocumented throughout his teenage years and well into adulthood. And he never felt the need to pursue a green card application, given the ease with each he engaged with different regulatory and service institutions in his daily life. Having attended a local public high school, he learned English shortly after his arrival in the country. This proficiency proved useful: "No one really asked me a lot of questions about my legal status back then. And, because I speak English, no one ever thought that I was undocumented." He was aware that he had to be careful in different spheres of his life, most especially in whether and how he engaged with regulatory institutions like the police: "When you don't have papers to prove that you're from here, they will send you right back [to Mexico] if you have some kind of criminal record." But he found work in construction using an ITIN, and he reported earning around $50,000 a year—more than enough in his view to take care of himself and his mom.

As with the two previous study participants, things changed for Sebastián after local police arrested him. Sebastián explained that he had been charged with felony aggravated assault following a fight at a bar. Though this does not always constitute a deportable offense in Texas, ICE picked him up shortly thereafter, and the DHS initiated removal proceedings against him.[56] Sebastián called his mom, who was still a permanent resident, to let her know what was happening. As he recalled, his mom took charge from there. She found a lawyer who was skilled in both criminal and immigration cases, and that lawyer had a simple strategy: to take advantage of the backlogged criminal-legal and immigration systems. "The lawyer delayed each of the courts every time he went," Sebastián explained, "because the longer it took, the less the prosecutors [in the criminal case] had to go on." After a year of this back-and-forth, the criminal case dropped to a misdemeanor charge and, as a result, Sebastián explained that his immigration case became more straightforward: "The immigration judge let me out with an ankle monitor for a year while we fixed my papers through my mom."[57] He fixed his papers through cancellation of removal for exceptional and extremely unusual hardship, naming his mom as the qualifying relative. Sebastián ultimately received his green card and, with it, formal societal membership.

That formal membership nonetheless remains precarious, suggesting the continued importance of everyday efforts to manage one's engagement with regulatory and service institutions. The case of a permanent resident in the study who landed in removal proceedings following a negative police interaction taught me as much. Javier, who is married to Yajaira, had lived as a green card holder without incident for over two decades. But, beginning around 2008, Javier said that his work in construction had started to wear on him. He used alcohol to cope. One day, he stopped at a local bar and had several drinks; on his way home, he was pulled over for driving while intoxicated. This was Javier's third offense, a third-degree felony in Texas.[58] The police officer arrested him and charged him accordingly. He ultimately pleaded guilty and was fined, placed on two years' probation, and ordered to complete alcohol counseling. Javier complied with his sentence but, once completed, the DHS initiated removal proceedings against him.

Although Javier and his family struggle to make ends meet, they hired an immigration attorney right away for $8,000. It was a steep price to pay on their $27,000 a year pretax income, but they relied on loans from Yajaira's several siblings in Dallas to scrape it together. They could not afford to

have Javier—a husband, a father, and the family's primary breadwinner—
deported. Javier's criminal record could amount to an aggravated felony,
given that his minimum prison sentence would have been one year; they
would need to submit a defensive petition for cancellation of removal to, as
Javier put it, "pardon" him. As the attorney pieced together the paperwork
to show that Javier had lived in the country for at least five years as a green
card holder before his conviction occurred, and for at least seven years in
any legal status before his conviction occurred, he put Javier's family to
work. The possible aggravated felony on his criminal record would likely
influence whether the immigration judge saw Javier as a moral person
who should retain his green card.[59] Javier's family needed to submit as
much evidence as possible to anticipate, and counteract, this possible
negative evaluation.[60] Yajaira mobilized the troops. She instructed their
oldest child to write a letter on behalf of his siblings in support of their
father, which noted how good of a dad he has been to them and how
hard he works to support the family. She asked Javier's friends who are
U.S. citizens to write letters of their own, outlining how they know him
to be a law-abiding person and a good member of the community. And,
finally, she contacted Javier's employer and their children's schoolteachers
to round out these perspectives. Javier told me that these endorsements
reflected well on him in immigration court, and the immigration judge
approved his cancellation petition: "The judge told me, 'A lot of people
wrote to support you. Don't let them down.'"[61]

Whereas the previous cases emerged from an initial negative police
interaction, USCIS can itself order undocumented immigrants' removal—
including those whose application for cancellation of removal was on the
verge of approval. David, whose story with his wife Maite opened this
chapter, exemplifies this dynamic. He was awaiting formal approval of his
application when I left him in 2015; his green card was imminent and,
once in hand, would sponsor Maite and their undocumented daughter
for one of their own. But, about a month following that interview, David's
father passed away in Guatemala. A devastated David wanted to attend
the funeral. But there was an important problem: David needed USCIS's
permission to leave the country since his green card had not yet been
approved, or they would consider his application abandoned. Overcome
with grief, David left for Guatemala without permission. "I don't think he
thought about the consequences," Maite reflected when we reconnected in
2018. "And believe me when I say that it was a really bad decision." Maite
said that she and her undocumented daughter, whose contact information
was listed on David's application, received removal orders from USCIS

one month after David left. "Because of him, we got deported." Maite considered not leaving, starting a life on the lam instead. "That would have been harder for everyone," she told me. "Personally, I think it's better to be in good shape, to have a good record. You live and work for a reason—to exist. And, besides, if the police found me, I might have gotten into more trouble." She would bring their second daughter, a U.S. citizen by birth, with them to Guatemala.

The importance of her formal records became even more apparent to Maite when she returned to the United States to seek asylum. She spent six months with David in his hometown before she fled Guatemala. According to Maite, gangs had started to threaten her daughters' safety. That was all it took for her to leave. She paid $8,000 to a *coyote* to transport her and her oldest daughter into and through Mexico, all the way to the U.S. border. Once there, Maite informed a U.S. Customs and Border Protection (CBP) officer that they were seeking asylum. That officer detained Maite and her daughter until they could both have a "credible and reasonable fear screening," which would inquire as to why they left Guatemala and whether those motivations constituted "credible" and "reasonable" fears. The CBP officer determined their claims to be both credible and reasonable, and the pair was transferred into ICE custody and placed into removal proceedings so that an immigration judge could decide their case.

Maite said that she and her daughter endured five weeks in detention before ICE determined that they were eligible for release. There are several factors that determine whether ICE will release someone from custody, including an officer's evaluation of a person's flight risk (i.e., will they show up to their scheduled court hearings?) and public safety risk (i.e., are they a danger to society?).[62] But not all people who meet these eligibility criteria end up released.[63] Maite pointed to the records cataloging her prior life in the country as making all the difference:

> They started investigating us and they found that we didn't have a bad record from when we lived here before—even our taxes were paid. That allowed us to get out of there quickly. . . . In the end, they let me out with an electronic monitor attached to my foot. They made me sign a consent form that said that I was doing this voluntarily. But I never requested this. . . . They said, "You have to sign, otherwise you won't leave here." . . . I spent about two weeks with the device on. . . . Then, one day, they told me, "We reviewed your record, and we didn't find anything wrong, so we're going to take it off." I couldn't believe it. Thank God they had a record of us since we had already lived here.

Maite was not out of the woods following her release from ICE custody. She still had to begin the arduous process of filling out Form I-589, formally called "Application for Asylum and for Withholding of Removal." It collects extensive personal information about the applicant—where they have lived, where they went to school, where they have worked, among other details—before probing for substantive details about the nature of their asylum claim. An immigration judge will consider the merits of the application at Maite's scheduled hearing. If approved, the judge will grant Maite asylum, allowing her to remain in the country as a permanent resident. If denied, the judge will consider whether Maite is eligible for other forms of relief from deportation before ordering her removed from the country. At the time of this writing, Maite has waited more than five years for her day in court. But, as many different lawyers have told Maite when declining to take her case, her odds don't look good: "It's getting harder and harder to be successful in an asylum case. Even the lawyers I talked to say I don't have a chance, which is why I don't have a lawyer yet. It's going to be very difficult."

Formal records are useful for undocumented immigrants seeking formal societal membership. In the context of removal proceedings, these records help them substantiate their eligibility for the few defensive petitions that might be available to them. Yet study participants noted how their own records were not always enough; they also needed legal, material, and social resources to withstand the structural and organizational constraints of immigration court. These resources made all the difference in whether they were willing to navigate the yearslong process of submitting a defensive petition—or whether they would accept a deportation and chance reentering the country unauthorized.

Inside Immigration Court

We now turn to my ethnographic observations of Dallas Immigration Court to consider how specific structural and organizational features of immigration court condition immigration officials' interpretations of undocumented immigrants' formal records, especially for those pursuing defensive petitions (recall that, by definition, affirmative petitions are not considered in immigration court). Although I never observed any of the people or families profiled throughout the book in this setting, I saw in real time how others who share many of these families' qualities—namely, national origin, legal status, long-term residence in the country, and parents of citizen children—navigated immigration court. What's more, I saw how immigration officials, whether judges or prosecutors, variously received, accepted, or contested undocumented defendants' formal records when considering their defensive petitions. These observations, therefore, offer another vantage point to examine when and why formal records mean the difference between undocumented immigrants' societal exclusion and inclusion.

Before moving forward, it is important to note that most undocumented immigrants whose cases are processed through Dallas Immigration Court end in deportation. In fiscal year 2015, which overlaps with the period of my ethnographic observations, deportation was the outcome of nearly 66 percent of completed cases in Dallas Immigration Court.[64] This rate was higher than the average for all immigration courts in Texas (57 percent) and much higher than the average for all immigration courts in the country (41 percent). Several reasons account for these variable rates, as scholars have considered elsewhere. Some reasons are structural, meaning that what happens in each immigration court reflects particularities of that context. For example, immigration courts are bound to the statutes, legal precedent, and court rules that govern one of the eleven federal circuit court districts they are a part of; that circuit, combined with the nonrandom distribution of defendants' cases across immigration courts, may well implicate their odds of being removed.[65] Other reasons are organizational. Some immigration courts have higher caseloads than others, which may result in higher removal rates if judicial norms there prioritize a quick disposition of cases.[66] Finally, immigration judges' own attitudes, biases, and motivations, reflected in their personal characteristics, policy predispositions, or attitudes toward specific national origin groups, may also contribute to these variable deportation outcomes.[67]

Rather than explain variation in deportation outcomes across immigration courts, my interest is in the structural and organizational features of one immigration court that inform immigration judges' interpretations of the records that undocumented defendants submit with their defensive petitions. I examine these features inside Dallas Immigration Court, where immigration judges approved defensive petitions in just over 2 percent of all completed cases in fiscal year 2015. Although this approval rate is low, it was also low in immigration courts statewide (almost 5 percent) and nationwide (10 percent) in that same year. I argue that structural and organizational constraints that plague many immigration courts but that are particularly salient in Dallas Immigration Court—specifically, a burden of proof on the defendant (rather than the prosecution); a high proportion of removal proceedings conducted while defendants are detained; and a high proportion of defendants without attorney representation—contribute to this low approval rate. They do so in part by casting suspicion on any records defendants submit but uncritically accepting those of the prosecution, by complicating defendants' ability to gather evidence that counterbalances the prosecution's claims, and by all but requiring defendants to decipher opaque court rules without professional assistance as they attempt to challenge the prosecution's interpretation of evidence. More often than not, these constraints promote immigration judges' interpretation of the balance of evidence in favor of the prosecution.

Observing officials in immigration court, especially immigration judges, is essential for understanding how this process unfolds. Immigration judges are career lawyers whom the U.S. attorney general has appointed to serve as administrative judges within the Department of Justice (DOJ).[68] They preside over proceedings between a DHS prosecutor, who represents the federal government, and a defendant, usually an undocumented immigrant. Their job is complex. As outlined in a handbook that the Executive Office of Immigration Review (EOIR; within the DOJ) uses to train them, "Immigration Judges are responsible for conducting Immigration Court proceedings and act[ing] independently in deciding matters before them. Immigration Judges are tasked with resolving cases in a manner that is timely, impartial, and consistent with the Immigration and Nationality Act, federal regulations, and precedent decisions of the Board of Immigration Appeals and federal appellate courts."

Immigration judges must sort through thousands of cases a year to determine which defendants may be eligible to submit a defensive petition. In Dallas Immigration Court, five immigration judges decided over 9,000 cases in fiscal year 2015; this figure does not include thousands more cases heard but not completed.[69] Most defendants will not be eligible to submit a defensive petition and, as we saw in the previous section, some who are will not submit one. I have considered this sorting process in greater detail elsewhere.[70] My focus here is on the structural and organizational constraints impacting immigration judges' evaluations of formal records in completed cases with undocumented defendants submitting defensive petitions. These defendants meet three criteria: (1) immigration judges have already determined them to be deportable, (2) immigration judges have already determined their eligibility for a defensive petition, and (3) they have submitted those petitions to immigration judges for review. I observed six such cases, with all defendants applying for cancellation of removal. None of these cases resulted in a petition's approval, itself telling of these constraints' weight on defendants.[71] Still,

I did observe one instance of immigration judges using their discretion in an ostensible attempt to circumvent the removal process when structural and organizational features of immigration court overwhelmed defendants whose records suggested they might have otherwise been deserving of formal societal membership.

The first structural constraint that conditioned immigration judges' interpretation of undocumented defendants' formal records was the burden of proof imposed on defendants. Although the DHS prosecutor has the burden to establish a defendant's deportability, this burden shifts to defendants once deportability has been established and defendants submit a defensive petition. In some ways, this burden is not unique to undocumented immigrants submitting defensive petitions; those submitting affirmative petitions to USCIS must also demonstrate that they are eligible for a legalization opportunity. Yet, in immigration court, this burden means something different. From the beginning of the case, the prosecution has evidence on the record—known as the I-213—that establishes a set of facts about the defendant that can undermine their defensive petition. Formally titled "Record of Deportable/Inadmissible Alien," the I-213 is an authoritative factsheet on each defendant. It summarizes information that CBP or ICE collected about the defendant when they apprehended them, including biographic data (e.g., name, place of residence in the United States and abroad, etc.), demographic data (e.g., sex, national origin, marital status, etc.), and data about their criminal or immigration violations in the United States (e.g., time and place of last entry into the country, where they were apprehended, etc.). The I-213 also displays the defendant's fingerprints and sometimes includes more narrative details about the defendant (i.e., "particulars under which alien was located/apprehended," as the form notes). I say authoritative because court precedent establishes the I-213, and all the information contained therein, as "inherently trustworthy."[72] One immigration judge I observed put it this way: "No one has proven to me that the I-213 is unreliable. It's taken by law to be reliable."

By contrast, no such assumption exists for defendants' own records, making for an imbalanced playing field from the start. Although defendants must demonstrate only "by the preponderance of evidence" that they qualify for a defensive petition (a lower evidentiary threshold than "beyond a reasonable doubt"), DHS prosecutors scrupulously vet any evidence that defendants submit for completeness, accuracy, or relevance. In addition, DHS prosecutors can leverage defendants' own records against them, reinterpreting evidence for immigration judges so that they are more likely to deny the defendant formal societal membership.

I observed this dynamic firsthand in Dallas Immigration Court. In the case of one undocumented defendant who applied for cancellation of removal, another immigration judge made explicit this dynamic at the start of the hearing that would decide the twenty-four-year-old man's fate: "One of the things that happens a lot . . . is a lack of candor, a lack of truthfulness, a lack of honesty. I depend on you to be honest." Of particular concern to the immigration judge were the application materials that the defendant, who did not have an attorney, submitted. "If we start and you go back and forth and say, 'Oh, yeah, I committed that crime, too,' that won't look good for you." The immigration judge asked the defendant whether he wanted to make any changes to his application packet. The defendant initially declined, but the immigration judge encouraged him to take a second look: "Well, you say you don't have any assets, but you didn't say for what years you filed tax returns to the IRS. You say you were convicted [of various drug-related crimes] and wrote, 'See attachment,' but you didn't attach anything to the application."[73] It was clear that the immigration judge was annoyed, his eyes slowly blinking as he explained these details. The defendant spent a few minutes reviewing his application, marking a few more changes before telling the immigration judge that he had no more changes to make.

Once the hearing began, the DHS prosecutor rose from her bench to indict different aspects of the defendant's application materials. She noted that one document listed in the application, a letter from someone who wrote in support of the defendant's character, was missing; that one document was a handwritten note in Spanish and not translated into English, as required; and that a report from a psychologist about the possible effects of the defendant's deportation on his young nephew was irrelevant because the qualifying relative for the cancellation petition was the defendant's mother, a naturalized citizen through a second marriage. On top of that, the prosecutor argued, the defendant neglected to account for a prior conviction that the prosecution recently discovered and listed on a new I-213 submitted to the court. The defendant had been convicted of stealing a car and, though sentenced to community service, the statute would have allowed for his incarceration for between three and seven years. This conviction, which had previously eluded the prosecutor due to a case management issue at the DHS that resulted in her delayed receipt of the defendant's background check, rendered the defendant ineligible for cancellation of removal and voided all his prior efforts to demonstrate through his own collection of records that he deserved formal societal membership.[74]

Meeting the burden of proof is that much more difficult for defendants who are detained as they prepare their case.[75] In fiscal year 2015, almost half (47 percent) of all completed cases in Dallas Immigration Court occurred while the defendant was detained, a rate higher than the state (36 percent) and national (22 percent) averages.[76] Detention complicates defendants' ability to gather evidence that might counterbalance the prosecution's claims for several reasons. These reasons include, but are not limited to, defendants' inability to search for evidence that might be at home and the difficulty of communicating with lawyers seeking to complete their petitions while they are held in a detention facility.

Detention's incapacitating effects on defendants' abilities to prepare successful defensive petitions were apparent in the case of another undocumented defendant I observed. The man, a Mexican national with three citizen children under the age of fourteen, submitted a cancellation of removal petition for another immigration judge to consider. Although he had been sober for almost eight years following several convictions for driving while intoxicated, the man relapsed in 2014. He was arrested several times by local police and, eventually, was transferred into immigration detention, where he remained until his appearance in immigration court. The defendant's attorney had prepared a cancellation of removal application on behalf of his client in advance of the court date and submitted it to the immigration judge. In reviewing it, the immigration judge asked about the discrepancies between the defendant's convictions listed on his application and those listed on the prosecution's I-213. The defendant's attorney explained that, given his client's detention in a facility several hours away from his Dallas office, he had filled out the application materials with the assistance of the defendant's wife. The attorney continued that he had many other clients facing similar removal proceedings and that he only had one chance to visit with his client to confirm the application's completeness and accuracy prior to its submission. The application, written entirely in English, was all but illegible to the defendant, who relied on the court-provided interpreter to follow the proceedings.

When weighed against the DHS prosecutor's records, the discrepancies proved too much for the defendant to overcome. The defendant could not recall how many times he had been caught while attempting to cross the southern border but, as the prosecutor noted, "Our records reveal that he was turned around at the border several times and that he was deported twice." The prosecutor went on to catalog the defendant's criminal record, including his several convictions for DWI, as well as a statement from the defendant's probation officer that he had violated the terms of his probation.[77] The immigration judge concluded that the defendant was not a credible witness because of the inconsistences between his application materials and DHS records. What's more, considering the defendant's multiple encounters with immigration officers at the border, the immigration judge did not believe the defendant had been forthright about his last date of entry into the United States—a key eligibility criterion for cancellation of removal. The judge denied the defensive petition and ordered the man deported.

The lack of a constitutional right to a court-appointed attorney in removal proceedings is the third structural constraint. As we have seen, this lack of a right to an attorney results from a longstanding Supreme Court precedent that treats deportation as a civil penalty rather than criminal punishment. About one-third of removal proceedings nationwide occurred without a defendant having an attorney in fiscal year 2015; that rate among Texas immigration courts was 56 percent and, in Dallas Immigration Court, it was 64 percent.[78] Legal scholars Ingrid Eagly and Steven Shafer show that attorney representation matters for undocumented defendants pursuing formal societal membership: those with attorneys were fifteen times more likely to submit a defensive petition, and 5.5 times more likely to have that petition approved, than similarly situated defendants without attorneys.[79] I suggest that one reason for this is the opaque court rules that undocumented defendants must decipher as they challenge the prosecution's interpretation of evidence, which, as hinted above and explored more fully below, trouble even immigration attorneys.

Attorneys are important because they help defendants manage the administrative burden of submitting a defensive petition. Prior to the start of my ethnographic observations in court, an immigration judge had determined one defendant, undocumented and from El Salvador, as possibly eligible for cancellation of removal. A father to two citizen children, the defendant would base his application on the exceptional hardships his kids would suffer if he were deported. The defendant requested time to find an attorney using a list of low- or no-cost legal service providers that judges in Dallas Immigration Court give to all defendants. The judge had agreed but warned the defendant that his application would be due at his next scheduled court date. At that date, I watched the defendant explain to the immigration judge that none of the legal service providers he contacted had the capacity to take his case. The judge rolled his eyes, incredulous at the delay. "These are fine legal service providers," he said. "But they can't help everyone. We have 10,000 cases a year!" The immigration judge offered the defendant a final extension but, when I saw him in court a few weeks later, the defendant was still without an attorney and without a completed application. "I'm trying my best, Your Honor," he told the immigration judge through the court-provided interpreter. "But I'm representing myself and my wife [at home] can barely help with my application because she works during the day because she is working now that I am in detention and is taking care of the kids at night." The DHS prosecutor opposed another extension as a matter of discretion, given that the defendant had two prior chances to turn in his completed application. The immigration judge agreed, finding that "the respondent has abandoned his right to turn in his application to court." But, in seeming recognition of the constraints that the defendant had to navigate, the immigration judge granted the defendant a voluntary departure. Whereas a deportation forecloses a person's possibility of applying for immigration benefits (e.g., visas) for five years or more, a voluntary departure leaves open that possibility. (Though, as the DHS prosecutor told me after court that day, she believed the defendant was likely to return to the United States without authorization, given that he has a wife and children here.)

Still, attorney representation offers no guarantee of overcoming a judge's ungenerous interpretation of a defendant's records or the compounding hardships of immigration detention, all of which often interrelate to complicate a defendant's due process. One defendant I observed, another Salvadoran national who entered the United States without authorization in 2003, hired an attorney to manage his cancellation of removal application. From my own vantage point, his odds seemed good. He had no criminal history except for a single DWI charge and shared a citizen daughter with his wife, who is also undocumented. He landed in removal proceedings after being rear-ended on his way home from work; when he went to the hospital to be evaluated, police officers investigating the accident arrested him there after smelling alcohol on his breath. The burden of proof was on the defendant to demonstrate his eligibility for cancellation of removal, something that he had worked on with his attorney, and the immigration judge would decide his fate during that day's hearing.

Much of the first part of the hearing focused on establishing the defendant's identity and tracking his movements since his arrival in the country. And, almost immediately, there were problems. The DHS prosecutor objected to several documents submitted as part of the man's application. She argued that his birth certificate, a copy of the original, lacked authentication from his home country's records office. What's more, she argued that the translation of the birth certificate was flawed, with the translator writing "Death Certificate" instead of "Birth Certificate." The implication, the DHS prosecutor argued, was that it was unclear whether this was the man's certificate and, even if it were, it shouldn't be accepted because it was poorly translated and therefore illegible to government officials. The judge sustained these objections.

The defendant was then called to the witness stand. The DHS prosecutor went first, and her questions aimed to establish the man's morality—or his lack thereof. The man said his wife, from Honduras, works as a house cleaner for a single family, earning about $300 per week. But, on his cancellation application, the DHS prosecutor noted, his wife is listed as unemployed. The DHS prosecutor carried on, identifying apparent discrepancies in the man's tax filing status with the IRS. In one year, he filed as head of household, which she argued was to secure a higher tax break; in the next, he filed jointly with his wife, which she argued was to secure a lower tax break. The man explained this discrepancy by referring to his wife's ITIN; she hadn't previously had one but, once she started working more regularly, she applied for one so that she could report and pay taxes on her earnings. The DHS prosecutor then asked how the man could work since, technically, undocumented immigrants aren't allowed to do so. The defendant admitted that he used *papeles chuecos*. He said he never actually acquired any physical documents, just the numbers, which he submitted to his various employers throughout his years in the country. The man said that he has a checking and savings account, but no money in them.

Another set of facts pertained to the situation of the defendant's citizen daughter, who he and his attorney argued would face exceptional and extremely unusual hardship were her father deported to El Salvador. In this case, the defendant argued that his deportation would hurt his daughter because he would have to take her with him to El Salvador, where he had concerns about the quality of education and health care relative to the United States. In addition, he worried about his family's safety in El Salvador; a relative had recently returned to El Salvador from the United States and was killed soon thereafter. (The specific nature of the death was not disclosed to anyone in the room, though the implication was that it was gang-related.) When questioned by the DHS prosecutor, the defendant disclosed that his mother and father live in El Salvador, as do some of his six siblings. The prosecutor asked why the information about his family members' whereabouts was not filled in on the application form:

DEFENDANT: [*to prosecutor*] I gave that information to my attorney.
JUDGE: [*to defendant*] Why didn't you do it?
DEFENDANT: [*to judge*] I thought my attorney had.

After this back and forth, the immigration judge took a fifteen-minute recess to deliberate. A guard who had escorted the defendant to court from his detention facility let out a deep sigh and offered me her assessment of the hearing: "That was brutal." The guard proved prescient. When the judge returned from the recess, he asked the courtroom interpreter to sit next to the defendant while he dictated his oral decision. The defendant began crying as the immigration judge outlined why he was denying the man's cancellation of removal petition:

> With respect to good moral character, the defendant failed to establish good moral character. He filed his IRS forms improperly, which affects his good moral character because he received a higher tax break as head of household than he was otherwise entitled to. He also has a DWI conviction, with another one pending. This serious criminal record means that he failed to demonstrate his good moral character.
>
> Exceptional hardship to a qualifying relative is also considered. He has a daughter who is a U.S. citizen and approximately six years of age. I find that the defendant didn't establish that his daughter would suffer exceptional hardship in the event of her father's deportation. No financial hardship was established; employment opportunities are available in El Salvador. The defendant's wife could also provide support for the daughter in the United States. In addition, no evidence was provided suggesting that there aren't quality schools in El Salvador that his daughter could attend. The daughter has no reported health issues, which means the quality of health care isn't an important factor in this determination. The defendant has demonstrated a lower threshold of extreme hardship—but not exceptional hardship.

In the end, the judge ordered the defendant deported to El Salvador. Even with attorney representation, the defendant could not overcome the immigration judge and DHS prosecutor's parsing of the validity of his records. Formal societal membership proved too elusive to secure.

Conclusion

Undocumented immigrants accumulate formal records over their years in the United States and, if ever they come before immigration officials, these records can mean the difference between their being allowed to stay or being kicked out. Sometimes these records are useful for affirmative petitions, which allow the undocumented to opt into rare legalization opportunities. Other times, these records are useful for defensive petitions that would allow the undocumented to demonstrate to an immigration judge why they should be allowed to remain in the country. In both cases, these records inform the consequential decisions that immigration officials make about each of the undocumented defendants before them. Thus, though the records the undocumented accumulate are primarily a reflection of the hardships they face in daily life, they also represent a resource that matters for their formal societal membership.

This chapter has shown that the records undocumented immigrants accumulate matter, in different ways, for their societal exclusion or inclusion. Underlying this dynamic are the laws, regulations, and policies that determine who is eligible to submit which petitions, as well as immigration officials' understandings of how well an applicant before them aligns with a given petition's eligibility criteria. For affirmative petitions, a small fraction of undocumented immigrants will have the opportunity to apply under current practice. Those with this opportunity recognize its stakes. But they express fears of immigration surveillance, outing themselves to officials whose gaze they have long averted. Although the formerly undocumented immigrants I talked with all eventually submitted an affirmative petition, no one dared to do so without the support of a trustworthy immigration attorney. In this way, ostensibly non-adversarial affirmative petitions can feel adversarial to applicants who fret about being excluded from society.

With few affirmative petitions available to most undocumented immigrants settled in the country, avoiding institutional interactions that result in their being turned over to immigration authorities is paramount. Inevitably, though, some do land in removal proceedings, usually following a negative interaction with local police. If that happens, undocumented immigrants may become eligible to submit a defensive petition that facilitates their formal societal membership. But, as the currently or formerly undocumented immigrants I interviewed explained, not all who are eligible will submit. With their families already facing overlapping hardships in daily life, and their arrest and subsequent detention compounding these hardships, many feel no choice but to forgo the protracted process of preparing and submitting a defensive petition. Those who do tend to have sufficient resources to withstand the structural and organizational constraints of immigration court. Thus, like what we saw in chapter 1 with visa applications, the resources undocumented immigrants have if they have their day in immigration court in part shape their access to opportunities for formal societal membership.

Removal is a common outcome for undocumented defendants processed through immigration courts across the United States. There are many reasons why, including defendants' access to resources. But an up-close examination of immigration officials reviewing undocumented defendants' petitions reveals one additional reason why: structural and organizational features of immigration court condition how officials in that context interpret defendants' records. With the burden of proof placed on the defendant, prosecutors and judges alike view defendants' application materials with suspicion; by contrast, judges assume prosecutors' records to be unimpeachable unless given a reason not to. This burden of proof is that much higher for undocumented defendants to meet while they are detained, separated from their homes where they might search for evidence, family members who might search on their behalf, and attorneys who might help them fill out their applications in a way that tips immigration judges' interpretations in their favor. It is higher, still, given that they must pay out of pocket for an attorney to manage the administrative burden of immigration court. These constraints often interrelate in practice, explaining in part low rates of approval for defensive petitions in Dallas Immigration Court and, likely, across the country.

I have argued throughout the book that, for undocumented immigrants, institutional surveillance is as much about a threat of societal exclusion as a hope for inclusion. Underlying this dynamic are formal records. By avoiding negative interactions with institutional authorities whom they encounter regularly, and maximizing positive ones, undocumented immigrants not only receive necessary resources for themselves and their families to get through each day but also accumulate records that they hope will facilitate their formal societal membership. Given that most undocumented immigrants will never experience a deportation, scholars have increasingly posited that these records will one day enable undocumented immigrants to submit affirmative petitions.[80] "In cases where few legalization avenues are available," Sébastien Chauvin and Blanca Garcés Mascareñas write, "being less illegal mostly boils down to becoming less deportable" and may be "tightly connected to the prospect of acquiring full legal status."[81]

Yet the meanings of formal records for undocumented immigrants' formal societal membership are themselves situational, dependent on the type of application available to undocumented immigrants (i.e., affirmative or defensive) when they encounter immigration officials. The typical undocumented immigrant has spent well over a decade in the United States, with the last large-scale affirmative opportunity to secure permanent residence occurring in 1986. In the almost four decades since, thousands of undocumented immigrants have landed in removal proceedings despite their best efforts to avoid that fate, a consequence of the institutional surveillance they encounter in their local communities. My findings suggest that undocumented immigrants' efforts to behave in ways that are "less illegal," such as those behaviors cataloged throughout the book, do not always come to matter in immigration court. Some feel compelled not to submit a petition in the first place. For those who do submit one, their prior efforts to align their institutional interactions with the perceived expectations of the authorities they encountered regularly do not always resonate with immigration officials reviewing their petition. In both cases, more and more undocumented immigrants who might have benefited from a future affirmative legalization opportunity are deported with each passing year, upending their lives and those of their family members. If such an opportunity emerges, many of them will likely be ineligible for having been deported. Others will likely be ineligible for having reentered the country without authorization to reunite with their families. In other words, they will come to represent a segment of a larger category of undocumented immigrants who are excluded from any future opportunities for formal societal membership.

Conclusion

MÓNICA, WHO HAD BEEN living without authorization in the United States since she entered in 2001, called to ask for a ride a few weeks after our interview in 2015. Almost forty years old, she had spent nearly half her adult life as an undocumented immigrant. But all my interview questions about her daily life as an undocumented immigrant had recently prompted her, albeit unintentionally, to search online for a nonprofit organization that might facilitate her legalization. Her U.S-born husband, Ignacio, helped her pick an organization and schedule a consultation but couldn't drive her there; he had to work during the day. As I drove her to the nonprofit for her appointment, Mónica recounted: "Ignacio told me, 'It took someone from Kentucky to come to Dallas to push you to legalize.'" I chuckled, reminding Mónica that I was from Wisconsin. "The point remains," she emphasized as we pulled up to an unremarkable office building, concrete except for four rows of glossy windows. We found the nonprofit's office tucked in a small corner suite on the second floor. A sign hung from its door: "Obtén la ciudadanía. La ciudadanía cambia tu vida." Get citizenship. Citizenship changes your life.

Mónica led us inside. A young woman, who appeared to be Latina and identified herself as the secretary, greeted us. She offered us an intake form. The form asked for all the information required for an affirmative petition for family sponsorship. As we saw in chapter 4, this includes biographical details about the sponsor, the beneficiary, and their shared life. Mónica had come prepared. She rifled through a red folder overstuffed with records—birth certificates for herself, her husband, and her three children; her marriage license; several years' worth of tax returns; her children's social security cards; and several copies of each of these documents that Mónica had brought "just in case"—as she filled out the form. She breezed through most questions but paused on the last: "Have you ever been arrested for or convicted of a crime in the United States?" We exchanged knowing glances, and Mónica marked a deflating "Yes" on the form.

Moments later, the secretary escorted us into the office of the nonprofit's staff immigration attorney. The attorney, who also appeared to be Latina, leafed through the completed intake form and homed in on the question about Mónica's criminal record. Mónica looked glum as she explained that she had been arrested in Paris, Texas, for stealing baby formula. She hadn't done so by choice; she had unwittingly joined an exploitative theft ring when a new employer in her rural hometown in the Mexican state of Guanajuato offered to smuggle her into the United States. The attorney seemed less concerned with the extenuating circumstances of Mónica's arrest than with what records Mónica might have accrued in the process: "Did you see a criminal or immigration judge? Were your fingerprints taken? Were you ever convicted?" Mónica remembered it was a criminal judge, but she could not recall whether she had been fingerprinted or convicted. The attorney explained how important the details were: "We can't take your case if you have a criminal record that might derail your application. We just don't have the capacity to handle complicated petitions. But, if your record is clean, we would be able to move forward." She encouraged Mónica to drive to Paris, about two hours northeast of Dallas, to ask local police if they had an arrest record on her. We thanked the attorney for her time and left the office. Mónica worried that this was the end of the road for her. I would be leaving Dallas the next morning but, as I dropped her off at home, Mónica assured me she would try.

Mónica never made it to Paris. When we caught up in 2018, she told me that she had hired a private immigration attorney to spearhead her affirmative petition. She found the attorney through her sister Maribel, a DACA recipient we met in the previous chapter. Mónica said that the attorney ran a thorough background check on her before preparing her application; her arrest appeared on her criminal record but no conviction did. After that, Mónica was told to gather as much evidence of her societal contributions as possible: "The attorney told me that immigration officials would want evidence that I am a good person and that I have not burdened the government." Mónica secured letters from the priest at her local church, and from her kids' schoolteachers, to help establish that she is a good person and an involved, doting parent. She also provided her attorney with a list of the public assistance that her family has received, including public health insurance and food assistance for her three children, as well as Social Security Insurance for her youngest child who has autism.

Her attorney compiled the documents and submitted Mónica's application to U.S. Citizenship and Immigration Services.

About ten months passed before Mónica received a letter from the National Visa Center inviting her to interview in Juarez, Mexico.[1] It was hard for Mónica not to feel nervous when it came time to travel: "I didn't know if they would reject me because of what happened in Paris and, if they did, then I wouldn't be able to see my kids again." Tying her long black hair into a loose ponytail, Mónica explained that her worst fears never came to be:

> The immigration official I talked to said that I do have a criminal record but that the crime was not an important one. He said he would give me papers so I could go back to Dallas and be with my kids. And thank God he did. I've been able to travel to Mexico twice to see my mother [for the first time in almost two decades] and meet siblings I never thought I'd meet.

Mónica told me that she feels "blessed" to now have a green card and live as a permanent resident: "This whole thing turned out to be a blessing. I never thought they would give me papers. When you live here illegally for so many years, you worry they won't want to." Still, no stranger to life as an undocumented immigrant, Mónica noted that her green card doesn't eliminate that old feeling of uncertainty: "Just because you have papers doesn't mean they won't kick you out of the country. Even with papers, you are not safe; one mistake and you must leave the country. You have to make sure your record stays clean, and that you are a good person."

———

In this moment of painfully partisan politics, it may be surprising to learn that most Americans want to overhaul the country's immigration system. It took decades but, regardless of one's political party, multiple nationally representative public opinion polls show this consensus to be real. Where there is disagreement, though, is on what that overhaul should look like. Majorities support a pathway to legalization, or amnesty, for undocumented immigrants.[2] But should amnesty be reserved for the fraction of undocumented immigrants who arrived as young children, or should it be extended to all who demonstrate that they meet certain civic benchmarks?[3] A minority of people support modifications to immigration enforcement itself. But should the federal government deport all undocumented immigrants, deport only those without citizen or permanent resident family members, or do away with deportation altogether?[4] The proposals are numerous, as are the disagreements over them, which explains in part the congressional stalemate over immigration reform.[5] It's unclear at the time of this writing whether Congress, which has the constitutional authority to change the laws that impact undocumented immigrants and their families, will act on even those reforms that enjoy broad bipartisan support.

Congressional inaction has meant that, for better and for worse, the executive branch has steered recent reform conversations.[6] Most presidential administrations since at least 1980 have conceded that mass deportations of undocumented immigrants are, to quote President George W. Bush, "neither wise nor realistic."[7] And, despite the significant uptick in deportations since then, the statistics reflect this reality: most undocumented immigrants will never be deported. In this era of mass deportability, undocumented immigrants and their families—especially those who are Latino—live under the threat of deportation. Sometimes presidential administrations have attenuated this threat through new regulations, policies, or guidance that establish or clarify their enforcement priorities.[8] Sometimes, though, they have magnified this threat. The Trump administration, for example, proposed or implemented more than four hundred policy changes in an attempt to "dismantle and reconstruct the U.S. immigration system."[9] Perhaps most notoriously, it separated hundreds of families recently arrived from Mexico and Central America, sparking a national outcry that brought a longstanding but previously fringe idea—to "Abolish ICE"—into the mainstream.[10] If anything, the relative ease with which the Trump administration destabilized immigrant life clued a broader public into the stakes of mass deportability.[11]

Political and public conversations about immigration reform have continued under the Biden administration. Early in its first term, the Biden administration called on Congress to pass an ambitious, multipronged, and progressive plan for immigration reform, including a large-scale amnesty for undocumented immigrants.[12] A few months later, the administration appeared ready to compromise for a more modest set of reforms, reserving amnesty for those undocumented immigrants who arrived as young children, and farmworkers who were lauded as essential workers in the early phases of the COVID-19 pandemic.[13] This limited amnesty would grant a green card, and a pathway to citizenship, to millions of undocumented immigrants who previously had almost zero chance at formal societal membership. But, almost two years later as of this writing, Congress remains gridlocked on this middle-ground approach.[14] We can and should tackle through legalization the immediate manifestation of the overlapping legal, material, and social hardships that undocumented immigrants face. A single reform that benefits a sliver of the existing undocumented population nonetheless merely kicks the can down the road. Fewer undocumented immigrants are arriving from Mexico, and more are entering from Central America.[15] What's more, immigrants from other national origins and world regions—especially from African and Asian countries—make up a growing share of the undocumented population.[16] Legalization is important, but it alone will not cure the overlapping hardships that undocumented immigrants endure; it will do even less for those who are ineligible for it.

Mónica's story illustrates the possibilities and limitations of reform efforts that focus on legalization alone. Mónica had been living in the country without authorization for over a decade when we met. She had been married to a U.S. citizen most of that time, but she had never attempted to legalize because there always seemed to be a reason not to: it was cost prohibitive to hire an attorney and pay all the associated application fees when money was already tight; it didn't feel like a necessary expense since her husband was a U.S. citizen; and, in the event that immigration officials denied her application due to her criminal record, it felt too risky to try. When she eventually did legalize, nudged to do so over the course of our several interviews, Mónica described her newfound permanent residence as both a blessing and a scourge. Her green card became something to protect—and something to protect herself against. In Mónica's view, legalization both changed her life for the better and left unchanged the institutional surveillance that haunts undocumented immigrants and permanent residents alike every day. Such surveillance is in part what dissuades some undocumented immigrants from legalizing, and it makes for an uneasy experience of formal societal membership for permanent residents.

Throughout the book, I have argued that undocumented immigrants manage two broad types of institutional surveillance that vary according to their multiple social roles and responsibilities. The first is immigration surveillance: the laws, regulations, and policies that circumscribe immigrant life at multiple levels of government. Even before leaving their country of origin, all prospective migrants must contend with the regulatory institutions governing immigration surveillance—especially that which delimits their access to visas that authorize them to enter the United States and establishes the stakes of crossing unauthorized. Most of the immigrants I met said they never tried to apply for a visa. For many, there was no need.

They were motivated to migrate because they felt deprived of material (e.g., income) and social (e.g., their family) resources, and these same resources are those they believed immigration officials would have expected to see on a visa application. They instead risked dangerous border-crossing conditions, including capture by immigration officers, to eventually settle in the United States without authorization.

The second is everyday surveillance: the laws, regulations, and policies that parameterize daily life for everyone in the country, and in each state and locality. Everyday surveillance weighs heaviest on people who occupy subordinated social positions, including undocumented immigrants navigating overlapping hardships. Although immigration surveillance remains an important consideration, it often takes a backseat to the surveillance of the authorities in regulatory and service institutions undocumented immigrants encounter as part of their daily lives in the United States. For the undocumented immigrants I met, everyday surveillance began with their engagement with regulatory institutions concerned with policing, employment, and taxation. They engaged selectively with these institutions, minimizing their negative interactions (especially with policing) and amplifying their positive ones (especially with employment and taxation) to demonstrate both their lack of criminality and their abundance of morality to authorities they felt view them with suspicion because of their legal status. Everyday surveillance eventually expanded to encompass undocumented immigrants' engagement with service institutions that distribute public goods (e.g., health care, education, and public assistance). Over their years in the country, every undocumented immigrant in the study navigating overlapping hardships became an undocumented parent navigating the same. Although their legal status means they are personally excluded from accessing many public goods, these exclusions do not apply to their citizen children. Many worried that accessing these public goods might render them ineligible for any future legalization opportunities— but they worried more about passing on the hardships they faced to their children. Under the gaze of various authorities (e.g., doctors, nurses, teachers, and social workers) who monitor their children's well-being, undocumented parents selectively engaged with service institutions to offset these hardships and to avoid giving these authorities reason to call the police or refer them to Child Protective Services.

Reforms that focus on immigration surveillance, and that overlook everyday forms of surveillance, are unlikely to obviate undocumented immigrants' societal exclusion or guarantee their inclusion. Legalization, coupled with reforms that circumscribe enforcement, would certainly go a long way toward blunting some of the societal exclusion that threatens the undocumented.[17] But, until these reforms are implemented, the undocumented continue to face overlapping—and compounding—hardships. They continue to work in jobs that do not pay them commensurate to their labor and that offer few opportunities for moving up. They continue to pay into Social Security but will lack retirement benefits of their own. They delay or forgo their own health care, lest they be seen as a public charge. And on and on and on. These compounding hardships will not vanish upon legalization. Nor will many of the vulnerabilities that characterize undocumented life, as Mónica reminds us. Permanent residents remain vulnerable to deportation and, depending on their state of residence, they remain excluded from many service institutions for several years. As I elaborate below, we must complement reforms to immigration surveillance with others that focus on the everyday surveillance that underlies the different hardships that undocumented immigrants confront and that stifle their opportunities for societal inclusion.

Exclusion, Inclusion, and Inequality

I have argued that surveillance is as much about the threat of exclusion as it is the promise of inclusion. Underlying this dynamic is a process of categorization, which involves the creation of two or more groups of people that hold differential rights and privileges. As Charles Tilly outlined in his influential book *Durable Inequality*, categorization is a mechanism that underlies the reproduction of inequality because myriad societal institutions use these groupings to differentially allocate important resources (whether material or symbolic or both).[18] But individuals may belong to more than one grouping, a reality that can render the relationship between categorization and inequality more complex than might otherwise be assumed. Philosopher Jonathan Wolff summarizes it as follows: "A given individual can be a member of many different groups that form for different purposes, and in virtue of membership of different groups can sometimes be treated as included, and sometimes as excluded."[19] The challenge, then, is to examine the conditions under which categorization implies inequality—and what it means if expected relationships between categorization and inequality do or do not manifest.

This book has shown how the exclusionary or inclusionary effects of institutional surveillance for a group of individuals worried about punishment depend on their multiple social roles and responsibilities. Undocumented immigrants do not evade surveilling institutions wholesale; they avoid specific interactions. They selectively engage with surveilling institutions in ways they believe align with the expectations of the authorities staffing them, given their multiple social roles and responsibilities. As we saw in chapter 1, these efforts begin long before undocumented immigrants ever set foot in the United States. They continue once undocumented immigrants settle in the country and carve out a life for themselves and their families amid the various laws, regulations, and policies that delimit what that life can look like.

Institutional surveillance is such an ingrained part of life today that most people probably do not register that different authorities record their attitudes, behaviors, or transactions almost everywhere they go. Not so for groups of people worried about punishment, who fear this trail of breadcrumbs will lead to their apprehension. Yet what institutional surveillance means varies—by the type of sanctionable status, by the type of surveilling institution, and by the demands of a given social role. Regarding the type of sanctionable status, the situation of people on the run from the police is often thought to parallel that of undocumented immigrants. But surveillance works differently for these groups. When someone has an outstanding arrest warrant, or violates the terms of their parole or probation, surveillance represents something to evade; police are on the lookout for that specific person and, in some cases, may be actively pursuing them.[20] Such active pursuit is less typical for most undocumented immigrants who have settled in the United States (and might better reflect some of their experiences entering the country). Policing is undoubtedly a risk that the undocumented see as inherent to their routines, but that risk is thought to be manageable. Some of this owes to a simple fact: immigration and police officers cannot pursue all undocumented immigrants. They often set enforcement priorities, which schematize the types of institutional interactions that are likely to lead to undocumented immigrants' apprehension— and those that are unlikely to do so.[21] Most undocumented immigrants will not pore over the complex laws, regulations, and policies governing these priorities. They will nonetheless come to internalize their essence— either from personal experiences or those of family members or coworkers or friends—and construct their own rules for how they believe these officers expect them to behave to avoid punishment. In brief, the type of sanctionable status that different groups of people hold matter both for how institutional surveillance operates and how members of these groups understand the risk of institutional surveillance.

The meanings of surveillance for people who share a sanctionable status also vary across institutional type. Although many institutions have surveilling functions, for the people subject to it, not all institutional surveillance is created equal. People with criminal records are more likely than those without criminal records to avoid medical care, to lack bank accounts, and to not work or be enrolled in school. For members of this group, routine interactions with surveilling institutions writ large represent a way for the police to track and apprehend them. Yet different surveilling institutions have different meanings for undocumented immigrants, who feel that they have something to prove through their interactions with authorities in these spaces. When it comes to regulatory institutions, undocumented immigrants hope that their selective engagement will counteract whatever racialized and classed tropes that some politicians, immigration officials, and members of the general public may hold of them as people living and working in the country without authorization. They do not always view these interactions, such as avoiding criminalized behaviors or paying taxes, as onerous; despite the added risks of noncompliance in the United States, many report they would have behaved similarly in their birth countries. In contrast, with an important exception reviewed below, undocumented immigrants believe their lack of interactions with service institutions point to both their morality (federal and state laws exclude most undocumented immigrants from most service institutions) and self-reliance (in that they are not public charges, people who subsist on public assistance, despite the hardships they face). The functions of regulatory and service institutions can, and often do, overlap. Still, conditional on the type of sanctionable status, the type of institution informs the perceived risk of surveillance.

Alongside the type of sanctionable status and surveilling institution, the meanings of surveillance vary according to a person's various social roles and responsibilities. People sharing a sanctionable status can certainly experience this group membership as a master status, one that overwhelms all other social roles and responsibilities to dictate their engagement with surveilling institutions. There is compelling evidence of this dynamic when studying people with criminal records.[22] Although their legal status signals the parameters of daily life that different laws, regulations, and policies impose on them, undocumented immigrants hold other social roles whose responsibilities variously supersede, overlap with, or are sidelined to their legal status. Parenthood, especially to citizen children, is one such social role and is perhaps most relevant to undocumented immigrants' engagement with service institutions. As individuals, they recognize—and, in some cases, are resigned to—the hardships that complicate their own well-being. But, as parents, they cannot accept passing on these hardships to their children. Whereas they minimize their interactions with service institutions on their own behalf, they amplify these interactions on behalf of their children. They have qualms about these new interactions because they had previously viewed their avoidance of them as signals of their morality and self-reliance. But, given their regular encounters with authorities in service institutions over the course of their children's lives, undocumented parents feel they have little alternative. This selective engagement both results in children's receipt of important resources (e.g., health care, food assistance, and the like) and is thought to prevent these authorities from intervening more forcefully in family life. In this way, for people holding multiple social roles and responsibilities, a sanctionable status can entail diverse meanings of and experiences with surveillance.

It is reasonable for scholars to study, and for the general public to understand, categorization as a process that generates inequality through exclusion from institutional spaces. This reasonability is that much clearer in studies of how different subordinated populations engage with or evade surveilling institutions. We can assign people into two or more groups, such as those with a criminal record and those without, and quantify all the inequalities in institutional engagement between them: in health care access, in educational attainment, and in employment. Quantifying inequalities in observable outcomes such as these is essential; doing so unearths social problems, mobilizes political and/or public will to address them, and allows for the efficacy of any implemented solutions to be evaluated. There is nonetheless a danger here. If small differences are observed between two groups, or no differences at all, then the groups might be assumed to be "equal" in terms of the metrics of institutional engagement we have selected as our benchmark. This idea—that the absence of categorical differences implies the absence of inequality—runs through many conversations about inequality. In their influential account of immigrant assimilation, for example, sociologists Richard Alba and Victor Nee posit that assimilation occurs when the distinction between immigrants and U.S.-born citizens "attenuates in salience, that the occurrences for which it is relevant diminish in number and contract to fewer and fewer domains of social life." When that happens, immigrants become part of mainstream society, which Alba and Nee take to mean "a core set of interrelated institutional structures and organizations . . . that weaken, even undermine, the influence of ethnic origins per se."[23] They are careful to acknowledge the numerous structural hurdles that impede assimilation for undocumented immigrants, and books by sociologists Douglas S. Massey, Frank D. Bean,

Susan K. Brown, and James D. Bachmeier, among others, have examined these hurdles' effects on inequalities between undocumented immigrants and permanent residents or U.S. citizens.[24] When we observe the expected relationships between categorization and inequality, such as in the case of undocumented immigrants relative to U.S. citizens, it supports the conclusion that these groups have unequal life chances. In other words, inequality remains an outcome of categorization. What, then, when inequalities between two groups go undetected or unobserved?

Categorization is as an indicator of inequality, even in the absence of quantifiable differences between two or more groups. Put differently, categorization itself constitutes inequality. To be sure, a sanctionable status signals the rights and privileges that different laws, regulations, and policies grant the people holding it, or the lack thereof, relative to people who do not hold it. And these differential rights and privileges can imply unequal access to institutional resources. Additional categories that correspond to the multiple social roles and responsibilities of people sharing a sanctionable status may nonetheless become more salient under certain conditions and attenuate some of these quantifiable measures of inequality. As outlined in chapters 2 and 3, and more fully elaborated in appendix B, I did not always observe in national data the inequalities I expected between Latino U.S.-born citizens and Latino noncitizens' (whether undocumented or permanent residents) engagement with surveilling institutions. But, as I hope has been clear, this result points to the meanings of institutional surveillance for undocumented immigrants navigating overlapping hardships and multiple social roles and responsibilities—rather than categorical equality per se.[25] I would not have known this were it not for the interviews with undocumented immigrants I collected. Undocumented immigrants' institutional engagement reflects their understandings of who authorities in these spaces want in the country: people with morals greater than those of any U.S. citizen; workers with the grit to labor in strenuous jobs that offer limited pay and few opportunities for advancement; and superlative parents who raise their children amid tremendous legal, material, and social constraints and with minimal public assistance. These understandings, which have consequences for both undocumented immigrants and their citizen children, are rooted in the laws, regulations, and policies that govern both immigration surveillance and more everyday forms of surveillance. They are themselves reflections of inequality rooted in categorization (e.g., based on the designation of some people as undocumented and others as U.S.-born citizens), and they can have effects that may be hard to quantify or interpret with large-scale data alone. Asking for whom, when, and why categorization does—and does not—yield quantifiable differences in inequality teaches us that the meanings of institutional surveillance for the exclusion and inclusion of people with and without a sanctionable status are situational.[26]

What institutional surveillance means also depends on social context, changes to which can upend both how people with a sanctionable status understand the risk of their engagement with surveilling institutions each day and their opportunities for formal societal membership. Undocumented immigrants' exclusion from or inclusion in surveilling institutions depends on when (e.g., before or after a law is implemented, or during a specific presidential administration) and where (e.g., state or county) they live. Dallas police may today decline to turn over an undocumented immigrant to immigration officers for one DWI, but that was not their policy a decade ago.[27] A small number of undocumented or semi-legal immigrants in states like California, Oregon, and Pennsylvania may be eligible for state-funded cash assistance, but they are ineligible in most other states.[28] The list goes on. This geographic and temporal unevenness creates a hodgepodge of laws, regulations, and policies to which undocumented immigrants are subject, with real consequences for their formal societal membership. To extend the previous example, though state-funded cash assistance may not have disqualified those few undocumented and semi-legal immigrants from a green card when they first received it, that receipt became disqualifying on February 24, 2020, when the Trump administration implemented its new public charge rule (and, as of this writing, it is no longer disqualifying because the rule has been rescinded). These contradictory rules have real effects. We can celebrate those who figure it all out despite these contradictions—but the contradictions are themselves a form of hardship that stifle undocumented immigrants and their families' societal inclusion.

Confronting Surveillance

Mónica's story at the start of this chapter exemplifies the multiple forms of surveillance that undocumented immigrants manage as they journey to and settle in the United States. It also shows how decisions to pursue legalization are weighty for undocumented immigrants, including those who have likely been eligible for a green card for years. One lesson that we could take from Mónica's story is that undocumented immigrants need only be encouraged to consult with immigration attorneys to determine their eligibility for legalization. This takeaway isn't itself novel; many immigration attorneys, whether working in private practice or in the non-profit space, do this work every day. It is, however, consequential: for eligible undocumented immigrants, legalization can allow them to overcome some of the hardships they face.

Although this solution does move some people from one sanctionable status to another that is relatively less vulnerable, it does little to address the diffuse forms of institutional surveillance cataloged throughout the book. This surveillance can dissuade some immigration attorneys, especially those who work at low- or no-cost, from accepting cases like Mónica's that appear complicated; given high and ongoing demand for their services, they make the most of their scarce resources by prioritizing cases that they believe have a high likelihood of success under current practice. Nor does legalization cure the correlated hardships undocumented immigrants and their families face. We can address some of these dynamics via changes to immigration surveillance, and others via changes to everyday forms of surveillance. I want to close by proposing solutions in this spirit. The below discussion generally follows the organization of the book, with the first set of solutions corresponding to immigration surveillance (e.g., visa allocations; legalization and naturalization; and interior enforcement) and the second set corresponding to everyday forms of surveillance (e.g., policing, taxation, employment, and public assistance). Throughout, I consider what the purpose of these different institutions should be as we change some of their underlying laws, regulations, and policies that currently allow categorical inequalities to take hold and grow.

Much of the current political and public discourse about immigration reform is rooted in an implicit question: How can the United States move from having 10.5 million undocumented immigrants to zero?[29] Since at least the mid-1980s, the federal government has looked to additional investments in border personnel or technologies in an ostensible attempt to raise the costs, and decrease the benefits, of entry without authorization.[30] These investments backfired, discouraging undocumented immigrants from leaving once they had made it across the border.[31] More of these investments are unlikely to work. The undocumented population overall is shrinking, largely due to reduced undocumented immigration from Mexico during the Great Recession, and most recent undocumented immigrants first entered with a visa that they then overstayed.[32] More guards and more walls and more drones are, simply put, a waste of money.

Instead, one of the simplest reforms we can make is to create more clarity in how we distribute visas. There is a mismatch between the visas available to immigrants who bypass or overstay them and the visas that they require to live with authorization in the United States. One reason for this mismatch is the per-country limits on visa allocation, especially for immigrant visas related to family sponsorship.[33] No one country may receive more than 7 percent of these visas each year. These restrictions are outlined in the Immigration and Nationality Act and, as the State Department argues, help "avoid the potential monopolization of virtually all the annual [visa] limitation by applicants from only a few countries."[34] These limitations nonetheless create massive visas backlogs for applicants from countries with established histories of immigration, who might otherwise use these visas to enter and live in the country with authorization.[35] For example, more than 1.2 million family-sponsored visa applications from Mexico await adjudication; that number amounts to 31 percent of all such pending applications.[36] It will take at least twenty years to clear this backlog under the current system (and even that assumes that no additional applications are submitted, which is obviously not realistic).[37] Increasing or eliminating the cap would reduce the size of the undocumented population and blunt some of the hardships these individuals and their families might otherwise endure.[38]

More generally, though, the process for distributing immigrant visas is itself responsible for at least some fraction of undocumented immigration. The most common immigrant visas related to employment and family reunification require having a sponsor who is either an employer or an immediate family member, respectively. As we saw in chapter 1, these requirements privilege applicants with existing material and social resources and, therefore, lead to visa allocations that reflect inequalities in prospective migrants' birth countries.[39] Aware that some people simply lack these connections, the current system awards a limited number of "diversity visas" each year to qualified applicants from countries with historically low rates of U.S. immigration. Applicants from El Salvador, Guatemala, Honduras, and Mexico, among other countries, are not eligible to apply. These countries' exclusion from diversity visas belies a simple reality that demographers studying international migration have established: international migration flows become less selective over time.[40] This means that the earliest immigrants from a country will have higher levels of education or income or wealth, on average, relative to the most recent ones. And it means that more recent arrivals may themselves come from families or communities new to immigration. Thus, they are less likely to have the material and social resources required for securing the most common immigrant visas under the current system. Expanding the Diversity Visa Program to consider these applicants, who represent a growing fraction of the country's undocumented population, would attenuate some of these inequalities.[41]

Such reforms are unlikely to be effective absent changes to the application process. The current system imposes a heavy administrative burden on new and renewing visa applicants.[42] It is at once confusing, expensive, and time-consuming to get, and keep, a visa for applicants from some countries. The Obama administration streamlined aspects of this process—for example, by moving to online applications (though this, too, has its challenges) as part of an effort to "reduce redundant systems, improve the experience of applicants, and enable better oversight."[43] More can be done in this spirit. For example, application fee waivers can be expanded to encompass all visa applications rather than a select few, and fees can be waived automatically, rather than by request, for all low-income applicants based on the information contained in their application materials. Likewise, the Visa Waiver Program allows citizens of select countries (mostly those in the Global North) to enter the United States for tourism or business reasons without obtaining a visa; the list can be expanded to include countries in the Global South with historically high rates of U.S. immigration.[44] Finally, visa expiration dates can be stretched or eliminated altogether, which would ease the system's administrative bloat for immigration officials and immigrants alike; to be sure, no green cards issued between January 1977 and August 1989 had expiration dates.[45] These changes would build flexibility into an otherwise inflexible system, allowing immigrants who might otherwise enter the country without authorization to enter with it.

The preceding reforms, which will primarily benefit those who have yet to immigrate to the United States, must be complemented by a legalization program for the 10.5 million undocumented immigrants already here. Half of these individuals are aged thirty-five years or older, and most have lived in the country for over a decade.[46] Although some undocumented immigrants' eligibility for legalization is a matter of time, a legalization program would allow us to reach more undocumented immigrants and to more quickly interrupt the hardships imposed upon them.[47] Many are eligible to legalize now, such as the 21 percent of undocumented immigrants married to U.S. citizens or permanent residents. Many others will become eligible as soon as their oldest child reaches twenty-one years of age, such as the 35 percent of undocumented immigrants who have least one citizen child under the age of eighteen. Lowering the age eligibility threshold from twenty-one to eighteen or even sixteen would hasten these individuals' eligibility, too. Finally, the legalization program must consider the situation of undocumented immigrants who lack qualifying relatives and who have limited recourse for legalization in our current system; 39 percent of the undocumented are unmarried, and 59 percent do not have children. To aid in these efforts, the federal government should partner with, and invest in, immigrant-serving nonprofits. One example is the Refugee and Immigrant Center for Education and Legal Services (known as RAICES) which, among other legal services, provides low- or no-cost assistance with legalization applications in Texas. As sociologist Jacqueline Hagan has shown, buy-in from community-based nonprofits was essential for the success of the last large-scale legalization program in 1986.[48]

Legalization would disrupt some of the hardships that undocumented immigrants face but leave others intact. As we have seen, permanent residents enjoy more rights and privileges than the undocumented; they also share some of their vulnerabilities—including to deportation.[49] Most permanent residents become eligible to naturalize as U.S. citizens within three (if they are married to a U.S. citizen) or five (if they are not) years of their legalization. Yet just 61 percent of eligible immigrants pursue legalization (and the rate is even lower for immigrants from Mexico and Central America).[50] This stems in part from the high financial costs of naturalization, and in part from the perceived risks of naturalization for some permanent residents with undocumented family members or who themselves are marked by any number of low-level infractions.[51] One simple solution would be to take seriously the permanence of the permanent resident designation when someone has lived in the United States for a sufficient period of time; permanent residents who have lived in the country for three (or five or ten) years under that status should become immune to deportation. An alternative would be to move toward an automatic naturalization process once all eligibility requirements for citizenship are met, like the one enjoyed by permanent resident children adopted by U.S. citizens. Another would be to skip the three- or five-year probationary period altogether, with the federal government immediately naturalizing all undocumented immigrants in recognition of the hardships that have characterized their lives in the country.[52] These latter two reforms, though perhaps more idealistic given ongoing political efforts to limit access to citizenship, would nonetheless safeguard would-be citizens from deportation.[53]

Immigration courts are one setting in which the overlapping hardships that the undocumented endure manifest. Most will never set foot in them, but these courts process hundreds of thousands of undocumented immigrants for deportation each year. Given that the federal government considers deportation a civil penalty rather than a criminal punishment, it denies defendants in immigration court the presumption of innocence, access to a court-appointed public defender, and the right to a speedy and public trial by an impartial jury. Defendants' outcomes have less to do with any infraction they may have committed and more to do with whether their existing material and social resources allow them to hire an attorney.[54] A lack of basic due process rights, therefore, both exacerbates inequalities among undocumented immigrants (i.e., those who can and cannot secure lawyers) and worsens an already stark power imbalance between undocumented defendants and immigration officials. Granting defendants the right to a public defender in immigration court would help level these imbalances. The Vera Institute of Justice's Safety and Fairness for Everyone (SAFE) Network, which has piloted one such program for undocumented defendants since 2017, finds that having an attorney matters: among completed cases in immigration court, SAFE has helped more than one in three undocumented defendants win the right to remain in the United States.[55]

Efforts to make public defenders available in immigration court must occur alongside efforts that allow these courts, and the judges within them, to operate independently of the executive branch of the federal government. The U.S. attorney general, a presidential political appointee, oversees immigration courts; they can appoint judges, pressure them to make decisions that align with their own ideologies, and if they do not comply, remove them from the bench.[56] This means that immigration courts— including judges' authority within them and immigrants' opportunities for relief from deportation—can vary widely from one presidential administration to the next.[57] As representatives of both the National Association of Immigration Judges, the American Immigration Lawyers Association, the National Immigrant Justice Center, and twelve other organizations have argued, this lack of independence not only undermines the credibility of the immigration courts but also makes them less efficient.[58] It is difficult for undocumented immigrants to overcome the hardships they face in such a system. The Federal Bar Association, which counts a diverse profile of attorneys and federal judges among its members, offers one proposal: to abolish the Executive Office for Immigration Review in the Department of Justice and transfer its functions to a new U.S. Immigration Court managed by the Administrative Office of the U.S. Courts (like the Bankruptcy Court).[59]

Up to now, many of the above suggestions have been predicated on preventing additional undocumented immigration while also helping current undocumented immigrants legalize. But, for the foreseeable future, undocumented immigrants will count among most countries' populations. This owes to several reasons, which boil down to the laws, regulations, and policies that different countries use to govern immigration and delimit the boundaries of who can secure a visa or green card—and who cannot. These laws, regulations, and policies tend to be reactive rather than pro-active. In other words, they respond to historical conditions that gave rise to some fraction of the existing undocumented population; seldom do they address more nascent or emergent dynamics (e.g., climate change) that are generating, or will generate, new undocumented populations.[60] Given this inevitability, perhaps a more prudent question for political and public dis-course to ask is not how to shrink the existing undocumented population but rather how to limit the categorical inequalities imposed upon it.

One answer to this question begins with accepting that the reason some people are undocumented is because a country's laws, regulations, and policies have "illegalized" them. This illegalization occurs in the name of a country's sovereignty, or its authority to govern itself and the people who not only inhabit its territory but who also seek to cross its borders. Yet, as political scientist Joseph H. Carens argues, there is another way forward—but it requires a fundamental "transformation both of current immigration policies and of conventional moral thinking about the ques-tion of immigration."[61] In Carens' view, "Our social institutions and pub-lic policies must respect all human beings as moral persons" and grant as part of this respect "the freedom and equality of every human being." The freedoms that Carens writes about include the freedom of movement from one country to another, without regard to their national origin, their legal status, race or ethnicity, or other categorical markers. Some object to this idea, of freedom of movement, contending that such freedoms might imperil a country's economy or cultural heritage.[62] For Carens, these con-cerns are secondary, especially in the context of immigrants leaving their birth countries because of the material and social deprivation they face. Carens does not offer concrete steps for change, but he notes that rede-signing our societal institutions to support the freedom to move and to live would be essential to this vision.[63]

My own view is that, alongside or even absent the reforms cataloged above, we strive to promote undocumented immigrants' freedom to live. This perspective aligns with conversations among scholars and organiz-ers in the criminal-legal space who see "non-reformist" reforms—those that "reduce the power of an oppressive system while illuminating the system's inability to solve the crises it creates"—as necessary intermedi-ate steps for achieving more transformational changes to systems that are as inequitable as they are intransigent.[64] The federal government has the authority to implement many reforms to the immigration system that move us closer to this vision. I have suggested some of these reforms above, many of which are intended to facilitate immigration (and, therefore, afford greater freedom of movement). These reforms, no matter how sustained or successful, will nonetheless be insufficient to address the overlapping hardships described throughout the book without others. And that is in part because they do little to address the everyday forms of surveillance that characterize daily life for undocumented immigrants.[65] The federal government can enact some of these changes but, as sociologist Cecilia Menjívar writes, states and localities might need to take the lead if federal reform remains elusive.[66] And the criminal-legal system, which includes policing and civil and criminal courts, is a natural starting point for this change.

At present, getting arrested by a police officer is the primary pathway into immigration court for undocumented immigrants who live in the country.[67] But cooperation between federal immigration officers and local police is counterproductive; it reduces undocumented immigrants' willingness to collaborate with the police to solve crime and, therefore, threatens public safety.[68] To grapple with this reality, eleven states and 178 additional counties have adopted a sanctuary policy at the time of this writing.[69] These policies do not prohibit all cooperation between immigration and police officers; they instead circumscribe this cooperation by, for example, requiring immigration officers to have arrest warrants for undocumented immigrants.[70] Study after study shows that states and counties with sanctuary policies have reduced deportations without increasing crime rates.[71] Adopting a nationwide sanctuary policy—in which the federal government itself reins in its immigration officers' cooperation with state and local police—would help temper many undocumented immigrants' worries about policing, including in states or localities with existing sanctuary policies of their own but where informal cooperation between immigration and police officers continues unabated.[72] There is precedent for such a policy; sanctuary was federal policy between 1935 and the early 1970s.[73]

Though an important step, the inequality-ameliorating effects of limiting police and immigration officer collaborations will be that much stronger when implemented alongside reforms to criminal laws that have allowed for mass criminalization in daily life. This mass criminalization affects us all, but a simple criminal case can quickly become grounds for deportation for an undocumented immigrant depending on the nature of their arrest, charge, or conviction (including the state in which it occurred). The mechanisms behind this process are complex, requiring multiple solutions. Two are of particular relevance. First, we must recognize that the reason many undocumented immigrants land in removal proceedings is because of an insidious, and still-growing, shift to the penal code. Alongside changes to the criminal-legal system that made use of mandatory minimum sentences for many offenses, the federal government deports thousands of undocumented immigrants a year for crimes whose potential conviction amounts to one year or more in prison. The trouble, as we saw in chapter 2, is that these so-called aggravated felonies can range from jumping a subway turnstile to first-degree murder. Decriminalizing undocumented immigration, by repealing Sections 1325 and 1326 of the U.S. Code (which make it a criminal offense to enter the country once or more without authorization) and by outlawing the transfer into immigration detention of undocumented immigrants who have served criminal sentences, will interrupt some of these dynamics.[74] Short of this, restoring the definition of an aggravated felony to its original meaning—that is, murder and drug or firearms trafficking—should unclog some of the bloated pipeline between the criminal-legal and immigration systems.[75] Reinstating criminal judges' authority to advise against an undocumented defendant's deportation, which disappeared in 1990, should help, too.[76]

Second, defense attorneys in criminal cases must be apprised of the seemingly unrelated immigration consequences of a criminal conviction for their undocumented clients. The reality is that most criminal cases terminate in plea deals.[77] Try as they might, many defense attorneys— especially those working at low or no cost to their clients—simply do not have the capacity or resources to nail down the complexities of immigration law on top of those of criminal law. And those who try sometimes get it wrong despite their best efforts, with disastrous consequences for their clients.[78] For example, pleading "no contest" to a charge in criminal court constitutes a conviction in immigration court; this conviction may foreclose an undocumented immigrant's eligibility to submit a defensive petition and lead to their deportation. These complexities are why some public defenders and legal aid offices have moved toward a holistic defense model, which includes both traditional legal representation and wraparound services that seek to address the underlying causes or consequences of a criminal case (e.g., mental health, employment, or immigration, among others).[79] For example, in Alameda County, California, the Office of the Public Defender established its Immigration Representation Unit (IRU) in 2014. The IRU's attorneys consult with public defenders on their undocumented clients' criminal cases, minimizing the chance that these clients will face immigration consequences on top of whatever criminal penalties might be imposed. Federal and state investments in public defenders' offices nationwide could scale up these efforts. Additional support for nonprofits engaged in legal advocacy or defense—such as the Immigrant Defense Project, the National Immigration Project of the National Lawyers Guild, and the Immigrant Legal Resource Center—would likewise help improve defense attorneys' representation of their undocumented clients in criminal court.[80]

Beyond the criminal-legal system, reforms to other regulatory as well as service institutions could go a long way toward interrupting the correlated hardships that undocumented immigrants confront in daily life. In the spirit of Carens' idea that our societal institutions and public policies must respect all human beings, the goal here would be to remove legal status (namely, permanent residence or U.S. citizenship) as a criterion for accessing the institutional resources necessary to get through each day and to make ends meet. In the case of regulatory institutions, granting undocumented immigrants the right to a social security number that confers work authorization and a driver's license are two simple reforms that would advance this goal. These reforms have the added benefit of not being especially novel or unconventional. As discussed in chapter 2, the undocumented had the right to a social security number for almost four decades beginning in 1935.[81] A social security number that offers undocumented immigrants work authorization allows the federal and state governments to streamline their collection of income and payroll taxes. Similarly, eligibility for a driver's license would smooth out some of the unevenness in identification that afflicts undocumented immigrants' lives.[82] Seventeen states and Washington, D.C., already offer driver's licenses to undocumented immigrants, though the federal government prohibits these individuals from holding driver's licenses that comply with federal standards.[83] Given that the undocumented already work and drive every day in this country, the above changes have the added benefit of obviating some of the fear that working or driving without authorization will upend their and their families' stability in the country.

In the case of service institutions, such as hospitals, schools, and public assistance, reforms that expand access—regardless of citizenship or legal status—can promote all people's freedom to live.[84] A common argument against this idea is that it is cost prohibitive to expand this access; instead, federal and state governments should prioritize services for U.S. citizens and permanent residents. But this argument is a red herring. If we commit to public policies that treat all human beings as moral persons, then we can reallocate funding from policies that are antithetical to this idea—for example, border security and immigration detention—and toward service institutions.[85] As we learned throughout chapter 3, what varies by citizenship and legal status is not the desire to maximize health, or education, or well-being but rather the access to the institutions that allow everyone to thrive. What's more, excluding (or otherwise limiting) undocumented immigrants from service institutions has negative consequences not just for their own access but also for that of their citizen family members. Investing in service institutions is an investment in all people who access them—especially the most marginalized among us. And, for the fiscally minded, such investments entail fiscal payoffs, too. Undocumented immigrants who have lived in the country for a decade or more already pay into federal and state tax bases in ways that more than offset the services they receive.[86] Their continued exclusion from service institutions will cost federal and state governments more each year, whether in terms of lost wages or productivity or human capital, than would including them.

Many reforms can establish or facilitate undocumented immigrants' access to service institutions. One would be to rescind the sections of the Immigration and Nationality Act that codify the public charge ground of inadmissibility and deportability.[87] As we have seen, undocumented immigrants worry about this designation in ways that can undermine their and their children's well-being. Even without rescission, additional reforms can promote undocumented immigrants' access to service institutions. In health care, and as a first step, the federal government could allow undocumented immigrants to buy into the Affordable Care Act's Health Insurance Marketplace, which would allow this population more affordable health coverage (via tax credits or other savings). A longer-term goal would be to allow undocumented immigrants to sign up for federally or state-funded health programs for low-income people. Advocates in California have worked for years to expand this access to undocumented young people and seniors, with the new state budget poised to expand this access to the remainder of the state's undocumented population by 2024.[88] This expansion could serve as a blueprint for how to achieve similar expansions in other states. In education, undocumented immigrants already hold the right to a public education through high school. Expanding this right to include community colleges and public institutions of higher education would mean allowing undocumented immigrants access to federally funded financial aid, including Pell Grants. Finally, in public assistance, federal and state governments could begin by making undocumented immigrants younger than eighteen eligible for public health insurance and food assistance—two programs critical for child development. A longer-term goal would be to expand eligibility for these services to all undocumented immigrants who need them.

Moving away from laws, regulations, and policies that threaten the societal exclusion, and toward those that promote the inclusion, of undocumented immigrants and their families is easier said than done. Every victory that immigration advocates and organizers have achieved over the last several decades has been preceded by one or more failures. But victories big and small have been possible before and, whether at the local, state, or federal level of government, they remain so. The categorical inequalities inherent to the institutional surveillance that undocumented immigrants confront each day are corrosive and, given undocumented immigrants' multiple social roles and responsibilities, they have consequences both for their citizen family members and for the health of the United States as a whole. The hardships imposed on undocumented immigrants today will be the hardships that their citizen children and grandchildren inherit tomorrow. We can begin to counteract these hardships through changes to our societal institutions, which enforce the very inequalities that we hope to interrupt.

APPENDIX A

Methodological Narrative

DESPITE OUR BEST INTENTIONS or efforts as scientists, the research process is messy. And this is true whether we are natural or social scientists.[1] It may not always look it when you leaf through a well-manicured academic book or article, but that messiness is part of the research process that gives rise to that publication.[2] What messiness constitutes can vary. Maybe a scientist had intended to answer one question but ended up discovering an answer to another. Or perhaps the project they designed had not produced the expected result, owing to an oversight in the study's procedures that they had no way of anticipating until they started their research. Messiness could also look like a need to design one or more additional studies to confirm, refine, or challenge the results of the first study, with each of these studies entailing their own set of contributions and limitations to the broader scientific endeavor. And, of course, there is real life—and all its own messiness—that frames everything we do as scientists.

For social scientists, the messiness or complexity of real life happens to be our laboratory. Most of us do not work in controlled or sterile environments (though some do with wonderful consequence). That would be beside the point in some ways. We study, and learn from, real people navigating real structural opportunities and constraints to their daily life. Who has access to an opportunity, and who does not, is seldom random; in this way, the complexity becomes patterned. The questions we ask about these patterns lend themselves to different methods to answer them but, even then, we may have to adjust our question or methods (or both!) over the course of the research process as we begin to uncover an answer. Studies that rely on in-depth interviews or ethnographic observations almost inevitably grapple with this complexity.[3] We often know that we have a general interest in something—in my case, how Latino immigrants perceive and respond to deportation threat—but what specific angle or analytic lens we end up using seldom emerges in the first interview or observation.[4] Research that relies on any number of quantitative or statistical methods also grapples with the complexity of the real world, albeit in different ways concerning operationalization (what do our questions measure, and how do we know?) and analysis (what models best align with our theoretical and empirical expectations, and how do we know?).[5] And, once we have assembled our data and gathered our evidence, writing our findings in a way that upholds the strengths of each method while buffering against their limitations is painstaking.[6]

The purpose of this appendix is to narrate the yearslong efforts at data collection and analysis that inform this book. Throughout, I pay attention to the complexities of real life that informed the evolution of the in-depth interviews, the need to gather ethnographic observations of Dallas Immigration Court, and the importance of adding statistical analyses. I also outline how and why I iterated between each method—interviews, ethnography, and statistical analysis—as I wrote the book to help make sense of the myriad structural conditions that the people in my study not only faced but also managed. Finally, I reflect on the complexities of the real world that I managed while writing this book, and how that informs the product you hold today.

Data Collection and Analysis

PHASE I: TEAM-BASED IN-DEPTH INTERVIEWS (2013–2014)

I first happened upon the families whose perspectives inform this book while I was a graduate student in sociology.[7] In 2013, I accepted an invitation to join a research project known as How Parents House Kids (HPHK). The project directors, Professors Stefanie DeLuca and Kathryn Edin, assembled a large team of researchers to study how low-, middle-, and high-income Black, White, and Latino families make decisions about where to live.[8] I name these researchers in the book's acknowledgements. With funding provided by the John D. and Catherine T. MacArthur Foundation and the Annie E. Casey Foundation, our team would conduct semi-structured, in-depth interviews with race- and class-diverse families in two selected counties: Cuyahoga County, Ohio, and Dallas County, Texas. Given my broad interests in questions of race, immigration, and inequality, I opted to join the team in Dallas County.[9]

Sampling procedures for the study were time- and labor-intensive, relying on the efforts of the entire team of researchers. We pulled a random sample of addresses selected from a stratified random sample of block groups, which were stratified by the median annual income of households in the block group and by the block group's racial composition. In other words, we identified low- (less than $25,000), middle- ($25,000 to $50,000), and high-income (greater than $50,000) block groups with Black, White, and Latino majorities. We selected block groups within each race-class pairing at random and, within each selected block group, selected addresses at random for possible inclusion in the study. We oversampled from poor and non-White block groups to ensure an in-depth examination of these residents' perspectives.

Members of the research team visited, sometimes as many as six times, each address that we pulled at random to determine a household's eligibility for the study. A household was eligible if at least one child between the ages of three and eight lived there. If the household met this criterion, the team member would ask the child's primary caregiver for an interview. If the household did not meet this criterion—such as in the case of a household with older children or with no children at all—they would be deemed ineligible and excluded from the study.

Language emerged as one unforeseen—but ultimately happy—complication during this initial sampling and recruitment phase. At many of the addresses we visited in majority-Latino block groups, and at a handful of the addresses in the majority-White or Black block groups, the team's researchers sometimes found themselves unable to communicate with potential study participants who spoke only Spanish. As a fluent Spanish speaker, I could communicate with these households if I happened to be present when the team knocked on a door. In my absence, a team member would usually call me and pass the phone to the potential participant to verify their eligibility for the study. We thought this would be an infrequent occurrence but, as fieldwork progressed, it occurred more and more. Shortly thereafter, I devoted almost exclusive attention to the majority-Latino block groups to facilitate these households' screening.

By the end of the summer of 2013, the research team had recruited twenty-eight Latino-headed households in Dallas County for in-depth, semi-structured interviews. Most interviews had two researchers present, excepting some of the Spanish-language interviews I conducted. As a team-based project, the initial interview guide included questions that spanned researchers' myriad interests. Topics covered in the 2013 interviews included each family's household roster and dynamics; their perceptions of their past and present neighborhoods; their perceptions of their past and present housing situations; their educational and employment backgrounds; their health; their children's schooling; and their residential mobility and neighborhoods. Given that HPHK was not designed as a study about immigration, questions that inquired about this topic directly were almost entirely absent from the 2013 interview guide. Still, themes related to immigration or to the unique position of immigrant families often emerged in these families' responses to our standard battery of questions. The HPHK team also fielded a short demographic survey to all families we interviewed, which revealed that twenty of the twenty-eight Latino families interviewed contained at least one household head who was born outside the United States. In other words, they constituted Latino immigrant families.

The large number of Latino immigrant families in our sample surprised me, but it should not have: in Dallas County, three-quarters of all Latino households who have children between the ages of three and eight have at least one immigrant parent.[10] Our small sample of immigrant families would by no means offer a statistically representative account of life in the county. Yet I was intrigued. Unlike most research on how immigrants families experience the threat of deportation, our study did not rely on churches, community-based organizations, detention centers, or legal aid clinics to aid our recruitment. In fact, we had not gone looking for immigrant households at all, but they formed a sizable share of our data. Here we had a rare opportunity to study how Latino immigrant families recruited from their residential environments, rather than institutional or organizational settings that foretold their engagement with or evasion of different institutions, managed surveillance in everyday life. I received permission from the HPHK codirectors to pursue an independent line of inquiry with these families.

We returned to Dallas in 2014 to follow up with all the families interviewed the prior year and to interview thirteen additional families whom we were unable to speak with before our time in the field had elapsed.[11] I focused my efforts on the twenty Latino immigrant families we identified in 2013; sixteen (or 80 percent) completed a second interview. I also interviewed eight Latino immigrant families who turned out to be a part of the thirteen leftover households. The 2014 interviews allowed me to probe more specifically about these families' experiences as immigrants (without regard to anyone's specific legal status) in the same topic areas we asked about in the prior year's interviews. In addition, I gathered details about how each family ended up in Dallas; the perceived strengths and limitations of living among co-ethnics; whether the families thought that their everyday worries differ from those of their U.S.-born neighbors; and whether and how these families felt that their nativity complicates some aspects of their daily life. As before, we also fielded a brief demographic survey to study participants.

PHASE II: INDEPENDENT IN-DEPTH INTERVIEWS AND ETHNOGRAPHY (2015)

The first two years of interviews with Latino immigrant families proved rich. Interviews in 2013 allowed matters of immigration to emerge only when this topic was salient to a householder's perceptions of their daily life. In 2014, I gleaned more systematic insights about the role of nativity—that is, being an immigrant—in this equation. Most families did not view their lives as substantially different from those of nonimmigrant families, though they did acknowledge that perhaps their day-to-day worries as they went to work or raised their children were tinged with more fears of surveillance. Some even went so far as to say that this everyday surveillance could be at once helpful and detrimental to their long-term presence in the country, depending on the formal records that they accrued over the years. I was intrigued by these ideas, and I wanted to pursue them further.

I returned to Dallas in the summer months of 2015. My priority was to recontact all twenty-eight Latino immigrant families who participated in at least one interview in 2013 or 2014. I had the phone numbers and residential addresses for each family, as well as the names and contact information each family had provided for up to three people in their lives who would know how to find them, should the HPHK team return for subsequent follow-up interviews. I was able to reestablish contact with all twenty-eight Latino immigrant households that summer, and twenty-seven of these families (96 percent) completed an interview that summer. Most remembered the study, and many joked that my annual visit was something they had come to expect over the years. The one refusal that summer was Natalia, who had indicated over several phone calls that she had wanted to participate. Other aspects of her life, which I review below in the section on positionality, nonetheless prevented me from completing an interview.

The questions in 2015 probed about whether the families had experienced any big changes in their lives since our last interview; details about life in their country of origin and the factors that motivated their U.S. migration; how they perceive themselves in relation to society more broadly; whether and how their specific legal status factors into their routines; and their awareness of immigration enforcement at the local, state, and national levels. At the conclusion of each interview, I fielded a brief demographic survey to all families to track any changes to household dynamics since the prior interview.

Interviews in 2015 had gone as well as any researcher could have hoped. But, as instructive as these conversations were, I felt that the study was missing something—namely, the perspectives of the immigration officials who make the legalization or deportation decisions that the Latino immigrant families I had come to know worried about. It's not that I doubted these families' perceptions; on the contrary, I took the meanings they expressed throughout our conversations as orienting their social action.[12] Still, I wondered if it made any difference to immigration officials that these families tried to align their social roles and their engagement with surveilling institutions. This thinking was inspired by the perspective of relational ethnography, which challenges qualitative researchers to incorporate "at least two types of actors or agencies occupying different positions within the social space and bound together in a relationship of mutual dependence or struggle."[13]

The range of actors contained within the umbrella term of "immigration officials" is vast. I didn't want to study officers who work within U.S. Customs and Border Protection (including Border Patrol) because mine was a study of Latino immigrant families who live and work inside the United States and outside the hundred-mile border zone where these officers are most visible. Nor did I want to study officers who work within Immigration and Customs Enforcement, the agency primarily concerned with the apprehension, detention, and removal of noncitizens inside the United States. Though important to the larger dynamics of policing and immigration enforcement in chapter 2, they do not oversee any legalization applications. I could have tried to study officers who work within U.S. Citizenship and Immigration Services, the agency primarily concerned with processing immigrants' visa and legalization applications. But, given that most people in the study had no immediate legalization prospects, I felt that this seemed less relevant to their daily lives than I would have liked. Yet the possibility of deportation hangs over many study participants, even if they will likely never experience one. In the end, I decided to study Dallas Immigration Court. All noncitizens processed through this setting face removal, but some can escape that outcome via various applications for "relief."[14]

Table A.1 uses data from Syracuse University's Transactional Records Access Clearinghouse to summarize key details of all completed cases in

Table A.1. Comparison of Matters Completed by Immigration Judges in Dallas Immigration Court, Texas Immigration Courts, and Nationwide Immigration Courts, FY2015

	Dallas	Texas	Nationwide
Number of Judges (N)	5	31	247
Completed Cases (N)	9,492	35,833	199,382
Concluded with Removal Order (%)	65.8	56.5	41.2
Concluded with Voluntary Departure (%)	7.53	5.18	5.26
Concluded with Terminations (%)	10.9	9.32	14.3
Concluded with Relief Granted (%)	2.25	4.72	10.1
Concluded with Administrative/ Other Closure (%)	9.84	14.2	24.5
Conducted with Attorney Representation (%)	35.6	43.9	63.3
Conducted as Detained Proceedings (%)	47.4	35.8	21.5
Average Days to Completion	435	236	816

Source: Author's tabulations of TRAC. 2018. "Immigration Court Backlog Tool, Pending Cases and Length of Wait in Immigration Courts." https://bit.ly/2JLMD5E.

Note: Number of judges in Dallas accurate as of June 2015. Number of judges in Texas and nationwide accurate as of June 2015. Completed cases represent fiscal year 2015. Data on cases conducted with attorney representation and as detained proceedings in Dallas are author's tabulations of TRAC (2018), based on "current status" of case.

Dallas Immigration Court during fiscal year 2015 (which overlaps with the fieldwork period) and compares them to all completed cases in Texas overall and nationwide.[15] Among all cases completed nationwide, about 41 percent ended in removal, compared with 57 percent in Texas and 66 percent in Dallas. Noncitizens in Dallas Immigration Court are less likely than noncitizens statewide and nationwide to have attorney representation, and they are more likely to be detained. Simply stated, noncitizens processed through Dallas Immigration Court face an uphill climb relative to those processed in other immigration courts. But some do succeed in finding relief. In brief, Dallas Immigration Court offers a site for examining how the dual realities of exclusion and inclusion that immigrants confront daily play out through judges' evaluations of formal records.

I started observing Dallas Immigration Court in early June 2015. As a site open to the public, I did not require permission to sit in on most proceedings (apart from asylum determination hearings, which required permission from the immigrant in question and/or their attorney). Dallas had five immigration judges at the time, and I spent the first two days of fieldwork in one judge's courtroom. My goal was to become a familiar, reliable presence in that courtroom. I did not write field notes until immediately after court. At the end of my second day of observations, the judge asked me about my interest in the court. I started to explain that I was a graduate student at Harvard University, but the judge interrupted excitedly to introduce me to the courtroom's Spanish-language interpreter—a Harvard College alumna. The judge encouraged my observations and granted me permission to take notes during the proceedings. (Although such permission wasn't strictly necessary.) My university affiliation would facilitate access to the other judges' courtrooms as well, who heard about me from this first judge.

By the end of the summer, I had spent about two hundred hours in Dallas Immigration Court. I interacted not only with immigration judges but also courtroom interpreters, marshals, Department of Homeland Security prosecutors, as well as the family members and private attorneys of some immigrants with cases before the court. I divided my time among the five judges' courtrooms in a roughly equal fashion. I produced over 150 single-spaced pages of field notes while observing Dallas Immigration Court. Over the course of fieldwork, the judges made deportation decisions regarding noncitizens in a range of legal situations, including but not limited to: unaccompanied minor cases, with many of the youths coming from Central America; cases involving the undocumented parents of U.S.-citizen children (and vice versa); and cases of noncitizens detained in two separate facilities for crimes such as driving while intoxicated, drug possession or distribution, and domestic violence. In the book, I focus on completed cases in which an undocumented defendant aged eighteen or older submitted a defensive petition, since their experiences would approximate most closely what the undocumented immigrants I interviewed would experience were they to end up in immigration court. Although Department of Homeland Security regulations precluded formal interviews of the judges, the judges would usually remain in the courtroom to answer questions about the cases I had observed that day.

Table A.2 summarizes the completed cases observed and outcomes, as well as several observable characteristics of the undocumented defendants. All but one of the six completed cases involving a defensive petition that I observed ended in removal; the other ended in a voluntary departure, which also results in the defendant leaving the country. Among these defendants, all appeared to be men and all were detained. Most designated Mexico as their home country. Most had lawyers, and most used an interpreter to communicate with the court.

Archival materials from Dallas Immigration Court, downloaded from the court's website that same summer, supplement this ethnographic

Table A.2. Summary of Completed Cases with Defensive Petitions Submitted, Outcomes, and Undocumented Defendants Observed in Dallas Immigration Court (N = 6)

	N
Completed Cases Observed with Defensive Petitions Submitted, by Type[a]	
Cancellation of Removal	6
Observed Outcomes	
Ordered Removed	5
Voluntary Departure	1
Observable Characteristics of Undocumented Defendants	
Male	6
Detained	6
National Origin	
Mexico	4
El Salvador	2
Represented by Attorney	5
Used Courtroom Interpreter	5

Source: Author's tabulations of ethnographic field notes.

[a] Tabulations include only completed cases observed in which adult undocumented defendants submitted a defensive petition and an immigration judge made a final decision on that application.

fieldwork. They include documents from the Executive Office of Immigration Review instructing judges on how to advise noncitizens of their rights at the start of court proceedings and describing evidentiary standards in immigration court, as well as myriad templates for judges to complete during court proceedings. I use the archival materials to better understand judicial decision-making in immigration courts nationwide, to interpret the structural and bureaucratic contexts within which the court operates, and to examine what the law is on the books versus how it is applied on the ground.

PHASE III: INDEPENDENT IN-DEPTH INTERVIEWS (2018)

There was much reason for optimism among Latino immigrant families since the 2013 interviews, and that optimism appeared to be validated by the close of our 2015 interviews. Despite legitimate criticism of President Barack Obama as a "Deporter-in-Chief" (a reference to the unprecedented number of deportations his administration executed through his first term), his administration pivoted in its second term.[16] The administration recognized that it was unlikely to pass comprehensive immigration reform through a polarized Congress, and it marshaled some of the powers of the Executive to change key dimensions of immigration enforcement. First, it formalized its commitment to deport immigrants with "serious" criminal convictions (for better and for worse; see chapter 2). Second, it instituted Deferred Action for Childhood Arrivals (DACA), which it then expanded to cover more undocumented immigrants who arrived in the United States as young children. Finally, though its implementation was blocked when several states sued the federal government, the Obama administration announced Deferred Action for Parents of Americans and Lawful Permanent Residents (DAPA). These events gave the families I interviewed through 2015 reason to hope, even as they heard rumblings of xenophobic rhetoric from a longshot candidate jockeying for the Republican Party's presidential nomination for the upcoming election cycle. It seemed inevitable that Democrat Hillary Clinton would be elected president and that she would facilitate comprehensive immigration reform. When I shut off my audio recorder after the final interview that year, I felt that the story I would tell in this book would reflect the earnest optimism of the families I had come to know.

Nothing quite worked out as we had expected. As we all know by now, Donald Trump was elected president. It didn't take long before the world learned what that might mean for immigrants generally, and I for the Latino immigrant families I interviewed specifically. On his first day in office, President Trump began the yearslong project of simultaneously dismantling pathways to lawful immigration and expanding immigration enforcement. (The nonpartisan Migration Policy Institute ultimately tallied more than four hundred such changes between 2016 and 2020.[17]) Any optimism I had previously felt vanished against this backdrop, and I wondered whether the same was true of the families I last saw in 2015. Would another round of interviews be possible? I had kept in touch with only a handful of families since our last conversations, with some texting me every now and again to gush about their child, to ask a question about something a presidential candidate had promised, or to tell me about a new health condition that they had just discovered. But I had not been diligent in checking in with families each year, as had been my practice; I hadn't felt that I had a good reason to take up any more of their valuable time. Still, I decided to give it a go; I returned to Dallas in 2018 and relied on the same contact information I had used in 2015 to track down and interview as many families as possible.

Table A.3. Summary Characteristics of 28 Latino Immigrant Families in Dallas, TX, Interviewed between 2013 and 2018

	N or Median	Minimum	Maximum
Number of Households	28		
Number of Adult Respondents Per Household	2	1	4
Total Number of Adult Respondents	60		
Interview Characteristics			
Total Number of Interviews	89		
Number of Interviews Per Household	3	2	4
Single Interview Time (Hours)	1.94	0.45	4.96
Total Interview Time Per Household (Hours)	6.62	1.07	13.20
Total Interview Time for Study (Hours)	185.35		
Immigration Characteristics			
Legal Status at Last Interview			
U.S.-born Citizen	5		
Naturalized Citizen	4		
Permanent Resident	12		
Semi-legal (DACA, TPS)	4		
Undocumented	35		
Country of Origin			
Mexico	50		
El Salvador	2		
Guatemala	2		
Honduras	1		
USA	5		
Year of First U.S. Arrival (Immigrants Only)	1996	1969	2007
Demographic Characteristics			
Gender			
Man	25		
Woman	35		
Birth Year	1979	1940	1993
Educational Attainment			
< High School	35		
High School	20		

Continued on next page

Table A.3. (*continued*)

	N or Median	Minimum	Maximum
Some College	3		
College+	2		
Married or Partnered	54		
Number of Children in Household	100	2	7
Number of U.S. Citizen Children in Household	97	1	7
Age of Oldest U.S. Citizen Child in Household	12	6	23
Age of Youngest U.S. Citizen Child in Household	5	1	11

Source: Author's tabulations of interview data and demographic questionnaire.

Note: Legal status observed in household's year of last interview. Children's ages observed in 2015.

It did not necessarily prove more difficult to find the twenty-eight Latino immigrant families in 2018, but it did prove more difficult to reinterview some of them. I successfully reinterviewed eighteen of the twenty-eight families (64 percent). Of the ten I could not reinterview, three I could not schedule due to reported work or family obligations, two I could not locate, two refused, one had moved to Mexico, one was visiting Mexico for the summer, and one had decided three years prior that the 2015 interview would be their last. I have no reason to believe that the three families I could not schedule misrepresented their availability or interest. Although they historically had been the most difficult to pin down over the years, two had completed three interviews between 2013 and 2015, and the other had completed two interviews in 2014 and 2015. Of the two I could not locate, repeated attempts at visiting their prior addresses, and calling and emailing their three designated contacts, proved fruitless. The two refusals were connected to relationship dynamics within the household, described in the positionality section below, that I could not address. Neither family in Mexico had time or occasion to chat. And I did not recontact the lone household that ceased participation after 2015.

More important than the fact of not completing some interviews, though, is the rare opportunity to follow up with most of the families I had come to know. In completing these interviews, I could compare families' understandings of their pre-2016 lives with their understandings of their post-2016 lives. Rather than prompt the families to talk about any deleterious effects the Trump administration may have had on their lives, most of the questions I asked in 2018 did not mention President Trump or his administration at all. This was purposeful, as I wanted to see whether and how the families I interviewed made sense of the national politics that seemed to consume an embroiled country each day. In addition to some of the same questions from 2015, I asked families about the possibility of their legalization and the possibility of their deportation. Near the end of each interview, I asked families what they made of the Trump administration to gauge whether and how their answers to the prior questions might change once asked directly about it. In their estimation, and to my surprise, very little changed about their daily lives. They saw the Trump administration as a natural extension of immigrant life in this country; some politicians make promises to help immigrants, and others make promises to harm them. Over their many years in the country, the families noted that they had learned to temper their expectations and to keep on with their daily lives for as long as possible.

Table A.3 summarizes the characteristics of the Latino immigrant families I interviewed between 2013 and 2018. Across these families, I interviewed sixty adults, fifty-five of whom are immigrants. Most of the immigrant participants were undocumented (thirty-five/fifty-five) by the time of our last interview. The remainder held a semi-legal status (e.g., DACA or TPS; four/fifty-five), a green card (twelve/fifty-five), or had naturalized to become a U.S. citizen (four/fifty-five). Most were born in Mexico (fifty), with a handful each from El Salvador (two), Guatemala (two), and Honduras (one). The median year of their arrival in the United States is 1996. Of the sixty adults, twenty-five identified as men and thirty-five as women. Their median birth year is 1979, meaning that the median study participant was about thirty-six years old in 2015. More than half of the people I interviewed never completed high school (thirty-five/sixty), one-third graduated high school (twenty/sixty), and a small fraction completed some college or more (five/sixty). Most study participants were married or partnered at the time of our last interview (fifty-four/sixty). In total, the households they lived in contained a hundred children, ranging from two to seven children per household; this figure falls to ninety-seven children when considering only those kids born in the United States, ranging from one to seven children per household. In 2015, the median age of the oldest child who is a U.S. citizen child was twelve, and the median age of the youngest was five.

PHASE IV: STATISTICAL ANALYSES (2020)

When I started writing this book, I did not anticipate including any statistical analyses. I believed in—and still do—the ethnographic and interview data I had collected over the years. Central to that belief is the *depth* of the data I had amassed, allowing me to "illuminate meaning— particularly the micro-level nuances of attitudes and daily behaviors" that might have escaped scrutiny absent the multiyear design.[18] In particular, this depth excavated the complex ways that the Latino immigrant families I came to know managed everyday forms of surveillance. I felt that they could and should stand alone in characterizing the processes described in the book.

Yet, for all my belief in these data, I struggled to convince other social scientists to see their value during peer review. This was, in part, my own fault. Junior scholars often go through growing pains as we learn to do sociology: figuring out the right way to frame a paper, the right way to discuss the limitations of existing research, and the right way to explain the value of our methodologies. I was no exception. But, on this last point, I also encountered resistance from editors and peer reviewers. All agreed that the data offered an "in-depth look" at the dynamics I studied, but they disagreed with my argument that the processes I had uncovered with this specific sample of families in this specific site were generalizable. One reviewer wrote, "Given that the data come from a non-random sample, it is not clear how to judge the significance of the apparent finding[s]." Another argued that my "sample of less than 60 immigrants, most of them of a single nationality and in a single city, provides feeble grounds for generalization." In other words, and as one editor summarized in their rejection decision, mine was a "rich study of a relatively small set of respondents (representing a still smaller number of households), in one specific setting. Consequently, the empirical basis for the argument is limited."

Researchers writing qualitative studies of immigration often face these kinds of comments from peer reviewers who apply the logic of quantitative social science to qualitative social science. As sociologist Mario Luis Small observes, "Ethnographic studies in . . . immigration operate in an environment at once thirsty for in-depth case studies that describe conditions in . . . immigrant . . . groups, neighborhoods and communities, *and* either skeptical or uncertain about the relationship between these 'small-*n*' studies and the larger population of groups, neighborhoods, and communities that the case studies are expected to represent" (emphasis in original).[19] The comments I received frustrated me (and likely frustrate many of us who use in-depth interviews) because they dismiss the method outright without appreciating its core contributions. They are akin to criticizing analyses of nationally representative survey data because they tell us nothing about how people experience statistical trends on the ground.

Setting aside my frustrations, I decided to add quantitative analyses of national data in anticipation of this possible objection. I thought long and hard about the kinds of data I required to complement the design of the qualitative study. As a growing body of scholarship on multimethod research highlights, aligning how the qualitative and the quantitative data are sampled ensures that scholars can make generalizable claims across the two methods.[20] I, therefore, required quantitative data that met several criteria so that they complemented and extended the existing qualitative design. First, the data had to include a national sample of Latino households, as these families form the crux of the book's argument. Second, the data had to include households with and without children, as this would enable me to examine whether and how the presence of children mattered to the processes I identified. And, finally, the data had to include information about whether and how these households navigated a range of surveilling institutions (both regulatory and service), as the core idea emerging from the qualitative data is that immigrants worried about deportation synchronize their different social roles with their institutional engagement. My search ultimately led me to the American Time Use Survey (ATUS), which, as I explain more fully in appendix B, is a national study of how people—including oversamples of Latino households with and without children—spend a typical day. I would use the ATUS both to contextualize study participants' claims and to test whether national data supported the findings from the in-depth interviews.

Appraisal of Data Collection and Analysis

TEAM SCIENCE

Instrumental to the interview data on display in the book is the team-based science that went into the initial recruitment of each family. As explained above, HPHK's sampling strategy required knocking on strangers' doors in different neighborhoods across a sprawling county, sometimes as many as six times, just to verify a household's eligibility (never mind recruiting and completing interviews with each household). I could not have followed these same procedures working alone. I am grateful for the opportunity to have collaborated with the dozens of researchers who invested in this project. Their efforts, especially during the early years of the study, helped locate, recruit, and interview the twenty-eight Latino immigrant households whose stories fill the pages of this book.

I am particularly indebted to Jessica Tollette (2013) and Hilario Domin-guez (2014), who knocked on doors with me and conducted some of the Spanish-language interviews when I could not be present.

As valuable as teamwork is, some may worry that it trades off with more "purist" approaches to ethnography or in-depth interviewing, in which a lone researcher collects all their own data.[21] That may be true at the margins of data collection, such as if a participant expected a differ-ent fieldworker to show up for the interview or if a teammate neglects to ask an important follow-up question. I saw inconsistent evidence of the first dynamic. My conversation with Norma in 2013 ran for 2.5 hours and, over the next several months, she regularly answered my follow-up phone calls. And, when I informed her that I would be in Dallas again in 2014, she seemed eager to participate in a second interview. Given the relative ease with which I had recruited and followed up with her, I asked Hilario to conduct Norma's second interview. But Norma resisted Hilario's efforts, telling him, "Yes, I remember the study, but I don't know who you are." Norma agreed to be reinterviewed when I had the opportunity to return to her door. In contrast, we had no such difficulty with Mónica, who Hilario had recruited but who completed her interview with me. She was surprised when she opened the door to her home, telling me, "There was a handsome guy coming before, but they sent a different handsome guy instead!" Her overblown compliment notwithstanding, our experience with Mónica was more typical.

The second concern, about data quality, is important. In the context of this study, though, this concern is less relevant for a few reasons. First, all fieldworkers shared intensive training blocks before and during field-work. Once in the field, we regularly checked in with one another about the interview process and debriefed about emerging ideas or themes to follow up on. Second, having interviewed every household in the study at least twice, I did not notice any systematic differences in the quality of interviews, or the themes contained therein. Nor did I expect there to be. While it is important to be attentive to these issues, the core benefit of in-depth interviews is the opportunity for people to share their stories. Different researchers may pick up on different dimensions of truth, reality, or the social world, but they all coalesce into creating a richer description and resolving inconsistencies in what aspects of which stories are impor-tant.[22] Even if a handful of participants may be concerned about who is sitting in front of them or how a particular question is phrased, increas-ingly, different studies suggest that people are who they are and generally will share their unfiltered stories when asked about them.[23]

DEPTH AND EXPOSURE

To be sure, the primary strengths of this study lie in the depth of the interview data and in its exposure to the families contained therein. Depth, as sociologists Annette Lareau and Aliya Rao define it, refers to "obtaining textured insights into social phenomen[a] . . . without invok[ing] the reliability of quantitative methods . . . as a way to legitimize" the work. These textured insights come from the meanings that study participants attach to "large-scale social structural forces" and the impacts that these forces have "on the rituals of daily life as well as many other spheres of life."[24] As explained throughout the book, sometimes seismic and sometimes mundane shifts in politics and policy at federal, state, and local levels of government characterized the five-year period during which I interviewed the families. Repeated interviews over this time enabled me to inquire about these changes and to examine whether and how these families perceived any effects on their daily lives. A cross-sectional study can do the same, of course, by recruiting and interviewing a new group of participants any time social structure changes. But a longitudinal study offers the analyst an opportunity to explicate how theoretically relevant changes to social structure matter for the social processes they identify using the same set of participants. In so doing, we learn more about whether changes to social structure frame any opportunities and constraints that people perceive, and along what characteristics they may vary.

Whereas depth is first and foremost about the texture of the data, exposure is about the intensity of the data collection. Sociologists Mario Luis Small and Jessica Calarco define exposure as the amount of time a researcher spends interviewing people.[25] According to this perspective, one study that gives a hundred people a ten-minute survey has as much exposure as one that interviews ten people for a hundred minutes each. Each study's exposure totals a thousand minutes or almost seventeen hours. This exposure adds up, doubling for every hundred people surveyed and every ten people interviewed. Neither study is better or worse than the other based on this metric alone, but each study has different goals. The survey learns a little about a lot of people, and the interviews learn a lot about a few people. Researchers analyzing the survey data are likely to investigate questions of prevalence or correlation, and those analyzing the interview data are likely to investigate questions of meaning-making or process. Both have the potential to generalize and contribute to a broader scholarly conversation.

Relying on exposure to evaluate the qualitative social science on display in this book, we transform what some might have identified as this study's

Achilles' heel into its strength. It is true that mine is a study of twenty-eight Latino immigrant families in a single place. But looking beyond sample size, table A.3 shows that these data benefit from a high level of exposure. I completed eighty-nine interviews across the years, with a minimum of two interviews per household and a maximum of four. The median interview lasted almost two hours, with the shortest at twenty-seven minutes and the longest about five hours. (For reference, each ATUS survey lasts twenty minutes.[26]) The median household completed about seven hours of interviews, ranging from one to thirteen hours. In total, I have more than 185 hours of interview data.

Taken together, the study's depth and exposure afford several analytical payoffs. First, they allow for iterative interviews. Each interview yields new, unexpected insights that may not be apparent to the researcher at the time of the initial interview. Interviews over several years allowed me to ask questions based on careful analyses of prior interviews and, in so doing, helped me move toward a theoretical and empirical contribution faithful to families' daily lives. Second, the study's depth and exposure enabled me to evaluate how consistent participants' accounts are across time. It becomes more difficult to dismiss families' perceptions about the effects of structural forces on their lives when the accounts they provide are stable over a half decade. Third, and as mentioned at the outset of this appendix, real life is complicated. Successful interviewing sometimes requires that researchers confirm, refine, or expand upon details learned from prior interviews. And, above all, depth and exposure breed familiarity. This familiarity becomes the basis of a mutual—albeit imbalanced—relationship between the researcher and study participants, as discussed in the next section.

POSITIONALITY

Positionality refers to the idea that a researcher's social position can influence their relationship with their study participants, with possible consequences for data collection and quality. After all, researchers are people who interview other people. And, whether our gender, race/ethnicity, class, nativity, sexuality, or something else, it is likely that aspects of our multidimensional personhood matter for how we relate to our study participants—and how they relate to us.

Many scholarly discussions about positionality begin with a statement about where the researcher falls in relation to the social group they study. On a spectrum of positionality, they are either "insiders" to the group (meaning that they share the social positions most relevant to their study participants, be it race/ethnicity, gender, or nativity) or "outsiders" to the group (meaning that they do not share the social positions most relevant to the study participants). In between these poles are "partial insiders," or researchers who share at least one important social position with their study participants but who occupy others that make full insider status impossible.[27] Of course, partial insiders may also be rebranded as "mostly outsiders" (in the same way partly sunny may be thought of as mostly cloudy). I see myself as a mostly outsider. And, for reasons explained below, I think many academics who study subordinated populations fit this bill, too.

On the surface, there are reasons why I might be branded a partial insider. I do share some important social positions with the people I interviewed. Although I am not an immigrant, my parents are; my own social position is, therefore, closer to study participants' U.S.-born children. And, though I am not descended from Latino immigrants, many assumed I was either Latino or Hispanic (i.e., Spanish). There are several reasons for this. My complexion affords me an ethnic ambiguity, which, when coupled with my Spanish-language fluency, made this scenario plausible for at least one participant in each household I interviewed.

But partial insiders are still strangers, and that matters at the onset of a study such as this. A shared social position hardly guarantees that prospective study participants would open the doors to their homes after an unexpected knock, entertain my explanation of the study, agree to schedule an interview, and, ultimately, follow through on that interview. I also had to convince people that I was a graduate student interested in having a simple conversation about their daily lives and ordinary routines. The rub is that many state authorities—whether police officers looking to make an arrest or case workers looking to check on a child's welfare—can follow a similar protocol. To guard against this possibility, I made several choices that I hoped would lead study participants to read me as friendly, even nonthreatening. I kept a short beard to ensure that my one dimple would be visible any time I smiled. My uniform consisted of an athleisure top and chino shorts, which kept me cool in the summer heat and seemed less stuffy than what state authorities might wear on a similar visit. When I arrived to a potential participant's neighborhood, I parked at least one block away from their home. I left my clipboard in the car, neatly folding and tucking away in my back pocket only the bare necessities in terms of recruitment materials. Finally, I always backed away from the door after knocking so that the prospective participant could see me from any vantage point they preferred from within the safety of their home. I held a smile with a pleasant expression the entire time.

In general, the above efforts paid off. Among the people who enrolled in the study, many commented that, because I "looked like a student," they felt comfortable agreeing to an interview. Alma, whose story opened the book, was one exception. With a wry smile, she admitted in 2014 that she "almost didn't schedule an interview with you last year." Her reason was that I hadn't "come in a suit, so I didn't think you were actually doing interviews." I joked that I would have melted in the hundred-degree heat had I worn a suit. After a bit of laughter from us both, she noted that she "thought for a second that maybe you weren't telling me the truth because you weren't wearing a suit." This may also explain why I had difficulty recruiting Esmeralda and Paco, as well as Luciano and Cecilia, for their household's first interview. Despite my efforts to appear nonthreatening, I was still unknown to them. What's more, I had shown up unannounced to their door asking to interview them. It's easy to forget just how strange that situation is for most people—not only for people worried about state surveillance.

That strangeness explains why two Latino immigrant households that were eligible for the study declined to enroll. One would-be participant noted that, though I seemed like a nice person, she worried that the interview was simply a way to enter her home to burglarize it. It had happened to her recently, she told me, with a young man taking advantage of her willingness to help him with a school project. (A quick search of local news reports from around the same time suggests that her worries were not unfounded.) The study's sampling procedures, whereby her household was selected for inclusion in the study but not her neighbors', only added to these suspicions. My attempts to reassure her were futile. Another would-be participant was less concerned about a potential burglary and more put off by the research team's regular attempts to schedule an interview. The weekly phone calls and/or text messages annoyed the prospective participant, who found it odd that we were so interested in speaking with her.

Although my various social positions likely mattered for how friendly or nonthreatening others perceived me to be when I knocked on their door, they also mattered for building rapport during the interviews each year. Study participants often told me at the conclusion of each interview that they enjoyed the process and that few of them had ever sat for over an hour thinking about how they go about their daily lives. Everyone welcomed me back at least once and, more typically, two or three more times. The few who formally dropped out of the study reported doing so for several reasons. Some, such as Esmeralda, Paco, Luciano, and Cecilia, could not overcome the strangeness of the study. As Cecilia told me in 2015, "We're not scared of you or anything, but the idea that someone would knock on our door, offer us money to talk about our lives, and keep coming back is something that we've never experienced before." This also explains why I could gather only one hour total of interview data with their household over the years. Others, such as Natalia, as well as Arturo and Rosario, experienced relationship dynamics within their household that my presence complicated. In Natalia's case, she apparently never disclosed the study to her husband, Roberto, who wondered why a man was regularly calling and texting his wife to schedule an interview. When Roberto answered Natalia's phone one afternoon in 2018, he asked me with more than a hint of anger, "Why are you calling my wife?" I first reassured him that nothing out of sorts had transpired between Natalia and me. Then, I explained the study to him, which he compared to the Mexican Census ("el INEGI," as Roberto astutely named by its Spanish initials). I informed him that he had the right to decline to participate, which he did, noting that the interview "doesn't do anything for our lives." Finally, after two prior interviews in 2013 and 2015, Arturo declined to participate in 2018. I never found him at home that summer; his teenage son had instead answered the door one day, calling his dad to ask whether he wanted to participate again. I couldn't hear the specifics of Arturo's response, but I did hear an expletive or two. My hunch is that, given the content of the 2015 interview, I had shown too much interest in Rosario (who is an immigrant and preferred to interview in Spanish) and not enough in Arturo (who is U.S. born and does not speak Spanish). I do not believe that Arturo appreciated this differential interest, despite my efforts to include him.

I was attentive to my social positioning in Dallas Immigration Court, too. Whether any of the five sitting immigration judges caught my (very ethnic) name, I am not certain. They instead referred to me by nicknames associated with my academic credentialing at the time—such as "Harvard" or "Harvard Man." This was often an asset, with the judges using this moniker when introducing me to other court actors (e.g., prosecutors, immigration attorneys, and interpreters). My identity as a man probably facilitated this rapport among the five male judges, as well. Over time, they came to depend on my showing up to court each day. When an interview with one of the study families took me away from court for one day, a judge remarked upon my return, "Harvard! We missed you yesterday." The judges also recounted discussing my reliable presence with one another. One judge quipped at the end of proceedings one day, "We were all talking at lunch yesterday about how you're at court so much we should probably just start paying you!" Shortly before lunch on another day, I found three of the five judges lingering in the hallway. A fourth emerged from the restroom and teased, "I'm not going to tell them [the other judges] who you said was the *best* judge!" Another retorted, "I'm not going to tell them who you said the *best dressed* judge was!" We all shared a laugh before we parted ways for lunch.

Whatever social positions we share with our study participants, or how comfortable we are with them or they with us, I think most of us leave each study as we found one another: as strangers. To be sure, every researcher learns something important from the people or families they study. We take this knowledge and abstract from it to generate a broader explanation about the social world. Yet, no matter our social position, we rarely become full insiders. Just as we are complex and multidimensional individuals, so too are our study participants. We may share some aspects of ourselves with our study participants, but the goal is to probe for their truth about a given topic in a given context. The meanings associated with that truth are important data points for us. No one researcher will uncover the unequivocal truth about the social world, nor should they try to. We instead are engaged in a collective and ongoing conversation about societal structures. Our study participants inform our contributions to this conversation, given our different social positions. In this way, we move together toward better understanding society.

Putting It Together

ANALYSIS

It can be challenging for studies to make use of multiple forms of data, particularly if the researcher does not have a clear vision of what those data contribute to the final write-up. My own view is that this book benefits from an iterative and sequential design. By iterative, I mean that I conducted repeated interviews with each household over the years, asking new questions once I reflected upon the interviews I had collected previously. By sequential, I mean that I added new modes of data collection that flowed from the early findings suggested by interviews—rather than collecting all forms of data simultaneously.[28] Data analysis, though iterative in some ways, followed the sequential design of the data collection.

I started by analyzing the in-depth interviews, relying on a coding process suggested by sociologists Nicole Deterding and Mary C. Waters.[29]

First, I imported all interview transcripts into Atlas.ti, a software program that allows researchers to code or "tag" text. Second, I assigned the multiple transcripts per household I had collected over the years into a larger "Document Group" for each household; this allowed me to scrutinize each household's experiences with surveillance and punishment. Third, and before doing any formal coding of the transcripts, I wrote memos that summarized the key themes from each household's several interviews. The memos paid close attention to the everyday forms of surveillance that undocumented study participants experienced, in addition to the consequences they believed this surveillance entailed for their short- and long-term societal membership. Fourth, and with an eye toward these dynamics of surveillance, I read through all interview transcripts again and coded for any mention of surveilling institutions. These included references to immigration and law enforcement officers, as well as the medical, financial, educational, labor market, and social service institutions that are typical to research on surveillance and system avoidance.

Following this initial round of coding, I took a moment to reflect on the data before me. I used Atlas.ti to "export" each code into a separate document, internally sorted by each household, to read each set of quotations together. Doing so enabled me to observe how, despite the myriad surveilling institutions contained within the interview data, they coalesced around two broad types: regulatory and service.[30] As we saw in chapter 2, regulatory institutions focus on the administration or enforcement of law; in this study, these include employment, financial, immigration, and law enforcement institutions. In contrast, and as explained in chapter 3, service institutions focus on the provision of public goods; in this study, these include medical, educational, and social service institutions. I reanalyzed the interview data with this typology of surveilling institutions in mind, writing new memos that tracked emergent themes. It was at this stage that I observed how study participants' forms of engagement varied by their multiple social roles and responsibilities—as immigrants, as immigrant workers, as immigrant parents, and as possible permanent members of society. I reviewed study participants' mentions of their engagement with surveilling institutions to categorize which role or roles motivated their interaction. In most cases, study participants discussed their engagement with regulatory institutions as revolving around their social roles as immigrants or immigrant workers; they described their engagement with service institutions, in all but a handful of cases, as revolving around their social roles as immigrants or immigrant parents. In a third round of coding, I scrutinized the character of study participants' engagement with each broad type of surveilling institution. These characterizations gave rise to the subsections in each empirical chapter.

After identifying how study participants understood their engagement with surveilling institutions, I considered whether and how they believed this engagement to impact their long-term relationship to U.S. society. All study participants linked these institutional engagements with their own, or a family member's, possible societal membership. Specifically, I focused on how they related the formal records, or lack thereof, associated with institutional engagement to the possibility of deportation and/or the possibility of legalization (to become a permanent resident) or naturalization (to become a citizen). For most study participants, who were undocumented at the time of our interview, I focused on their perceptions of these dynamics; I contextualized these perceptions within those of study participants who were permanent residents or naturalized citizens at the time of our interview. What's more, among the few study participants who began the study as undocumented but later legalized or naturalized, I could evaluate these dynamics among the same person over time. My goal here was not to identify a causal relationship between institutional engagement and societal membership; rather, it was to identify social processes that might have otherwise eluded empirical scrutiny.[31]

Analyses of the ethnographic data from Dallas Immigration Court followed those of the interview data. Though many of these observations focused on whether and how immigration judges in that context decided to deport noncitizens, underlying much of this decision-making were formal records.[32] I used these data to bolster the latter argument that emerged from the in-depth interviews—namely, to interrogate when and how formal records mattered to deportation or legalization outcomes among noncitizens processed through immigration court. I analyzed field notes and archival materials with this idea in mind, reading and coding them multiple times. In a first read, I worked to understand the legal and organizational contexts within which immigration judges worked. Whether statutes, legal precedent, or court rules, immigration judges are bound by various standards set forth in federal law.[33] In a second read, I searched for any mention of noncitizens' formal records and coded them in Atlas.ti. In a third read of the "formal records" code, I added subcodes for the type of formal records mentioned—such as immigration records (e.g., I-213), criminal records, medical records, financial records, employment records, school records, or public assistance records. In a final read of these subcodes, I linked them to whether and how judges used them to frame the relief available to noncitizens before them.

After analyzing the interview and ethnographic data, I turned to the data from the American Time Use Survey as a final step. I describe this analysis more fully in appendix B. Overall, I relied on this analysis to test core processes emerging from interview findings.

TIMING

When introducing me in advance of a seminar discussion, a colleague once remarked to the audience that they have been "eagerly awaiting Dr. Asad's book for a long time." The sentiment was kind, a reflection that the colleague wanted the book so that they could engage with the ideas I have been developing for a few years. Even as I understood the complimentary nature of the comment, it also unsettled me. I had never written a book before this one, and I certainly underestimated how long it would take to finish a single publication. But the well-meaning comment also saddened me, for a few reasons that the colleague had no way of knowing.

I began this methodological narrative with the acknowledgment that real life is complicated. The longer data collection for a study goes, the higher the likelihood that aspects of everyday life will impact the study. Structural changes—such as legal, regulatory, or policy changes bearing on the surveillance of immigrant families—can steer a project down a new path and delay data analysis and writing. But so can changes to the researcher's own life. As I explain below, I sometimes wanted to resist these changes to meet the expectations that I felt others had for me, and those I had for myself. But making room for these changes, as I would ultimately learn, meant creating a product that reflected these changes and better aligned with the realities of my study participants' daily lives—and my own.

Much can happen to push and pull a research in different directions once data collection has started. I do not think this is unique to studies of immigration, but this is one topic where structural conditions are as prone to fluctuation as they are stability. Researchers must collect sufficient data to understand not only how study participants make sense of their structural conditions but also what specific structural features matter to this sense-making. We must also know when to cease all data collection efforts. The first idea is about saturation, the second about maturation, and the third about affiliation.

Saturation refers to the point in the collection of ethnographic or interview data when no new properties of a theoretically relevant pattern emerge.[34] In other words, it describes the point when the researcher believes they have learned all there is to learn about a particular phenomenon, given the questions they have asked or the interactions they have had. Such saturation inevitably takes longer in a study like this one, which began as part of a larger project on residential decision-making. Yet, when worries of surveillance bubbled up as relevant to study participants' daily lives, it became clear to me that the 2015 interviews would need to inquire about these dynamics. And I needed to observe and interact with immigration officials if I hoped to understand whether and how the interview data mapped on to these officials' own ideas of surveillance and social control. By the end of summer 2015, and coupled with the interviews from 2013 and 2014, I felt that I had reached saturation as to how surveillance is as much about the threat of exclusion as the hope for inclusion.

I nonetheless worried about the argument's maturation in the ensuing years. By maturation, I mean whether the data collection and analysis would be not only timely but also timeless. It was not enough for the study to reflect present-day dynamics of surveillance and control among immigrant families; it also had to withstand anticipated and unanticipated structural changes to the laws, regulations, and policies governing these dynamics. And Donald Trump's ascendancy to the U.S. presidency, as noted above, eventually compelled my return to the field. This fieldwork did not alter my conclusions in any fundamental way. If anything, it validated the insight that emerged from the prior years' interviews: the threat of exclusion was more palpable among study participants, but so too were their hopes of inclusion. I realized that achieving maturation was not about returning to the field every time something "big" happens. Instead, it was about identifying a generalizable conclusion that allows researcher and reader alike to make sense of any structural changes that may follow the book's publication.

This realization freed me from the anxieties that always accompany "closing" data collection, and it allowed me to consider how I would manage any continued affiliation with study participants. Here, I define affiliation broadly to mean any interpersonal interaction beyond the scope of the study. Stanford undergraduates who enroll in a course I teach about "Race and Immigration" often ask during my office hours how I maintain relationships with study participants once data collection concludes. Implicit in the question is that study participants *want* such a relationship; in reality, most do not. As much as they reported enjoying the interview process, I am, at the end of the day, someone outside their daily lives and ordinary routines. I could continue to inject myself into these routines once data collection finished, but that would feel unethical. Instead, I offer study participants my name and contact information, and I encourage them to check in about matters large and small at any time that they would like.

Only a handful of study participants have taken me up on that offer over the years. And, mostly, I think that's a good thing. As I outline in the above section on positionality, the researcher-participant dynamic is imbalanced, with a relatively empowered researcher learning from a relatively disempowered study participant. Yet that imbalance can become dangerous if data collection is ongoing and a researcher proposes possible interventions to their participants' lives. Here, I do not mean to indict situations like that described at the start of the concluding chapter; Mónica decided to investigate the legalization process and asked me to accompany her to an appointment that she booked herself. But I felt that the situation would have become murky had I pushed Mónica into legalization with the expectation of using that process—whether successful or unsuccessful—as another data point for this book. Likewise, Maite has kept in close contact with me over the years, usually to offer me an update on her health or her business. When she asked for help with her eldest daughter's college applications, I helped revise personal statements and pushed the high-achieving daughter to apply to more selective colleges. When she asked for help with her (still ongoing, as of this writing) immigration case, though, I decided to never include the resulting dynamics in any published research (much to the chagrin of some who read over this book prior to its publication). The power I would have held over an important aspect of Maite's life in that situation was simply too great to justify its inclusion. Researchers must be attentive to their empowered position and recognize when data collection should stop.

Beyond saturation, maturation, and affiliation, the timing of this book also reflects personal hardships I encountered. It goes without saying that the onset of the COVID-19 pandemic upended the world, exacerbating long-standing fissures by race/ethnicity, class, gender, and legal status, among others. Some of these consequences are invisible to the naked eye. I have privileges as a professor at a well-resourced institution. Early in the pandemic, the worst thing that had happened to me was that I fell off my bike on my way to buy a cupcake and fractured my right elbow (I got my cupcake a few weeks later). But, try as I might, my own privileges do not always extend to my family in Milwaukee. Suffice it to say, the material, social, and psychological strains of the early stages of the pandemic weighed on some of them more than on me. No one felt these strains more than my brother, Samer, who died by suicide five days after his 38th birthday in June 2020. I was (and remain) devastated. In the months that followed, I dealt with sometimes-paralyzing grief. My grief was but a small sliver of the mounting collective grief around the world, but it consumed me. It was hard to find purpose or joy, let alone motivation to write. I prioritized self and community care over productivity.

I wish I had good advice for others navigating their own grief journey as they wind their way through the publication pressures of academia. What I can offer instead is what worked for me. I found that I needed time. Time to cry. Time to mourn. Time to accept. (I don't know that there is enough time in the world to heal from such a loss.) With a lot of self and community work, I eventually found purpose enough to get back to writing. This newfound purpose did not cause my grief to dissipate, but it offered me one way to reclaim some of the energies that grief sapped from me. As sociologist Karina Santellano reminds us in her own reflections about the grief she experienced during the pandemic, "While we cannot control what the next few months and years have in store for us, we . . . can seek ways to take care of ourselves and our loved ones. . . ."[35] It is a nice reminder, and one that I hope we all carry with us in the years to come.

National Evidence
of Latinos' Engagement
with Surveilling Institutions

I HAVE ARGUED THROUGHOUT the book that Latino immigrants consider the perceived expectations of the authorities they encounter as part of their daily routines when making decisions to engage with surveilling institutions. Underlying this dynamic are Latino immigrants' multiple social roles and responsibilities. This argument has several testable implications. First, Latino noncitizens should exhibit a selective engagement with surveilling institutions on their own behalf. This means that their engagement with regulatory institutions should be similar to that of Latino U.S. citizens (whose perceived morality they hope to match), and their engagement with service institutions should be lower (given public charge concerns). Second, Latino noncitizens who are parents should broaden their engagement with service institutions on behalf of their citizen children. This means that we should expect them to approach U.S. citizens' level of engagement with service institutions. I evaluate these ideas using sixteen years of survey data from the American Time Use Survey (ATUS). [1]

The American Time Use Survey (ATUS) is a federal study conducted by the Bureau of Labor Statistics and the U.S. Census Bureau to assess how people in this country spend a typical day. Although it is a cross-sectional survey, interviewing each person only once, the ATUS regularly samples individuals from households wrapping up their participation in the Current Population Survey (CPS). And the criteria for inclusion in the ATUS are conducive to an examination of Latino immigrants' engagement with surveilling institutions.[2] The ATUS selects households from the CPS according to a stratification procedure that accounts for the race/ethnicity of the householder; the presence and age of children in the household; and the number of adults in adult-only households. Latino households are oversampled to improve estimates. Within each ATUS household, one person aged fifteen or older completes a one-day time diary, described more fully below. I use surveys and time diaries from 25,665 Latinos aged eighteen or older to examine how adults across citizenship groupings spend their time. Sampling weights that account for sample construction, nonresponse, and the days covered by the diaries enable a snapshot of what the average Latino—citizen or not—was doing on a typical day during the survey period; survey year fixed-effects allow for a similar interpretation in the average year.

Key Variables

Time diaries are used to construct the dependent variables. Each diary reflects the 24-hour period preceding the morning on which respondents completed the time diary via telephone, in either English or Spanish. Respondents list their activities for the period, in their own words, and the interviewer records that activity. The number of activities reported varies. In 2003, an average of twenty separate activities, and a maximum of seventy-one, were reported for any 24-hour period; the minimum number of activities across all survey years was five and the maximum was ninety-one. At the end of each survey, respondents are asked to identify all activities during which they had a child under the age of thirteen in their care. Additional questions are used to identify all volunteer activities. At the conclusion of the ATUS data collection, researchers recode the activities listed in the time diaries into various categories.[3] I rely on different categorizations of these activities for the main analyses, which are summarized in table B.1 and constructed using IPUMS-ATUS.[4] No respondent used the language of "surveilling" or "nonsurveilling" institutions in their time diaries; these are analytical decisions I made for the purposes of this analysis. Given the cross-sectional nature of the time diaries, an examination of changes over time in institutional engagement within respondents is not possible. ATUS's one-diary-per-household restriction likewise prevents an examination of time-use differences within households.

The main dependent variables are a series of binary indicators that measure engagement with surveilling institutions.[5] *Overall surveilling* is defined as individual-level engagement with one or more institutions that keep formal records for at least one minute. *Overall regulatory* refers to at least one minute of engagement with regulatory institutions (financial, work, government/civic). *Overall service* is constructed similarly but focuses on service institutions (medical, school). I also include measures for each of the constituent surveilling institutions to examine whether any one type of institution may underlie the results. *Financial* describes individual-level engagement with banking and other financial services for at least one minute. *Government/civic* reflects individual-level engagement with government services or civic activities for at least one minute. *Work* captures individual-level engagement with work for at least one minute. *Medical* refers to individual-level engagement with health and care services inside and outside the home for at least one minute. *School* refers to individual-level engagement with school inside and outside the home for at least one minute.

These measures of institutional engagement are multidimensional, including numerous activities that relate to each surveilling institution, and offer a more capacious definition of engagement than might otherwise be possible in research that relies on one dimension of engagement with each surveilling institution.[6] For example, research on surveillance and system avoidance tends to rely on whether an individual has a checking or savings account to code engagement with or evasion of financial institutions. The ATUS encompasses a broader set of actions related to a person's finances, including doing banking (depositing, transferring, or withdrawing money); talking with a bank manager, teller, or loan officer; and talking with an accountant, claims adjuster, or insurance agent. Someone can at once lack a bank account and engage with a financial institution. Moreover, these measures capture institutions where respondents recently spent their time and, therefore, offer insights into whether and how hypothesized relationships between surveillance and system avoidance manifest in daily life. Requiring at least one minute of engagement with each institution aligns with existing research that tends to compare engagement (coded as 1) and evasion (coded as 0) as separate options. The distribution of time reported involved in these institutions is right skewed; most respondents, regardless of citizenship status, reported no time spent in any surveilling institution.[7]

All the preceding indicators measure respondents' time spent engaging with surveilling institutions on their own behalf. But, for parents, these measures may underestimate their total engagement if it does not include engagement motivated by their children. To address this concern, the analysis also makes use of indicators that account for time spent engaging with surveilling institutions on behalf of respondents' children. These indicators are available only for medical and educational institutions. In the

Table B.1. Coding of Surveilling and Nonsurveilling Institutions in ATUS Data, 2003–2019

Measure	Definition	Examples
Surveilling Institutions		
Main Analysis		
Overall Surveilling	Individual-level engagement with one or more surveilling institutions (medical, financial, work, school, government/civic)	Individual-level engagement with any of the activities described within this category
Overall Regulatory	Individual-level engagement with one or more regulatory institutions (financial, work, government/civic)	Individual-level engagement with any of the activities described within this category
Financial	Individual-level engagement with banking and other financial services	Doing banking (depositing, transferring, or withdrawing money)
		Talking with a bank manager, teller, or loan officer
		Talking with an accountant, claims adjuster, or insurance agent
Government/Civic	Individual-level engagement with government services or civic activities	Using government services (police, fire, social services)
		Paying fines or fees
		Fulfilling government-mandated duties (jury duty, parole meetings, court appearances)
		Civic participation (voting, town hall meetings)
Work	Individual-level engagement with work	Going to work
		Attending conferences, conventions, or trainings
Overall Service	Individual-level engagement with one or more service institutions (medical, school)	Individual-level engagement with any of the activities described within this category
Medical	Individual-level engagement with health and care services inside and outside the home	Having a (dental, eye, or medical) doctor's appointment
		Having specialty care (chiropractic, therapeutic)
		Paying for health care services
		Talking with a medical professional (doctor, nurse, pharmacist)
School	Individual-level engagement with school	Attending class
		Attending conferences, conventions, or trainings
		Doing homework or research
		Reviewing notes

Parenthood Analysis

Overall Surveilling	Engagement with one or more surveilling institutions on behalf of oneself (medical, financial, work, school, government/civic services) and one's children (medical, school)
Overall Service	Engagement with one or more service institutions (medical, school) on behalf of oneself and one's children
Medical	Engagement with health and care services inside and outside the home, for oneself or one's children
School	Engagement with school on behalf of oneself or one's child
	Engagement with any of the activities described within this category on behalf of oneself or one's children
	As above, but with the inclusion of time spent on children
	As above, but with the inclusion of time spent on children
	Attending class
	Attending parent-teacher conferences or PTA meetings
	Doing homework or research
	Checking child's homework for completeness
	Meeting with child's principal, teacher, guidance counselor, or school psychologist
	Reviewing notes

Nonsurveilling Institutions

Overall	Individual-level engagement with one or more nonsurveilling institutions (volunteer or religious)
Volunteer	Individual-level engagement with unpaid activities for individuals or institutions through formal organizations
Religious	Individual-level engagement with religious services
	Individual-level engagement with any of the activities described within this category
	Computer use (e.g., e-mail, website design)
	Donating (e.g., collecting clothing, school supplies, or toys)
	Fundraising (e.g., bake sales, collecting donations)
	Organizing and preparing (e.g., filings, mailings, paperwork)
	Attending religious services (church, mosque, synagogue, temple)
	Participation in religious practices (e.g., praying, religious retreats)

subsample analyses by parenthood, *medical* is measured as engaging with health and care services inside and outside the home, for oneself or one's children, for at least one minute. Likewise, *school* is measured as engaging with school on behalf of oneself or one's child for at least one minute. The *overall surveilling* and *overall service* indicators are updated to reflect these additional time commitments. It is possible that the other indicators for surveilling institutions capture engagement on behalf of respondents' children. For example, *government/civic* includes situations in which respondents make use of social services, which, as we saw in chapter 3, is more than likely on behalf of their children. Unfortunately, the time-use data do not allow for such a fine-grained analysis. Nonetheless, considering time spent on behalf of one's children in medical and educational institutions offers a more complete snapshot of how parents go about their lives than might otherwise be possible.

One possible limitation of the ATUS data is that they do not specify the character—"positive" or "negative," "good" or "bad"—of the reported institutional engagement. For example, the indicator for government/civic engagement captures interactions that include the use of police, fire, or social services; the payment of fines and fees; court appearances; and participating in town hall meetings. Some of these activities can represent a source of risk for immigrants worried about deportation. The time diaries nonetheless reflect the 24-hour period preceding the survey; whatever the character of the interaction, then, all respondents in the dataset "survived" it. Accordingly, the results may both underestimate and overestimate institutional engagement. Results may be underestimates if they omit Latino noncitizens who experienced an arrest or a deportation following their engagement with a surveilling institution; institutional engagement among noncitizens would therefore be higher than what is reported below. In contrast, results may be overestimates if noncitizens who experienced an arrest or a deportation were less likely to be engaged with surveilling institutions in the first place than noncitizens who did not experience these events. Engagement may be further inflated if survey fears prevented the individuals most fearful of arrest or deportation—whether noncitizens fearful for themselves or U.S. citizens fearful for a family member or friend in the household—from participating in the survey. The effects of underestimation and overestimation for differences in institutional engagement between Latino U.S. citizens and noncitizens are unclear. Depending on dynamics of survey response and nonresponse among Latino U.S. citizens and noncitizens, differences in institutional engagement may be larger or smaller than observed. Although the sampling weights account for sample construction and nonresponse, future work attuned to these possible selection effects would help assuage these concerns.

Analyses of nonsurveilling institutions allow for an examination of whether any observed differences in engagement with surveilling institutions between Latino citizens and noncitizens is likely attributable to these institutions' collection of formal records. If fears of surveillance jeopardize noncitizens' engagement with surveilling institutions, then these fears should not manifest in institutions that do not keep formal records. Measures of engagement with these nonsurveilling institutions are constructed in a similar fashion as the indicators for surveilling institutions and summarized in table B.1. *Volunteer* describes individual-level engagement with unpaid activities for individuals or institutions through formal organizations for at least one minute. *Religious* reflects individual-level engagement with religious services for at least one minute. *Overall nonsurveilling* is defined as individual-level engagement in one or more of the nonsurveilling institutions for at least one minute.

The primary independent variable is Latino respondents' citizenship status. Those born in the United States or a U.S. territory, and those born abroad to a U.S.-citizen parent, are U.S.-born citizens; they are about 48 percent of the pooled ATUS sample. Naturalized citizens are born abroad to foreign-born parents and report holding U.S. citizenship; they are about 18 percent of the pooled sample. Noncitizens are any immigrant who lacks U.S. citizenship and are, therefore, vulnerable to deportation; they are about 34 percent of the pooled sample. This group includes a diverse mix of individuals—including undocumented immigrants, visa holders, and permanent residents—who have unequal vulnerabilities to deportation. Latinos who are noncitizens, regardless of their specific legal status, nonetheless have feared deportation at similar rates through at least 2018.[8] This reality emerges in part from policy changes since the 1980s that have made it easier to fall out of a legal status—through requirements for more frequent renewals, expensive legal fees, and confusing rules governing each legal status—than to fall into one. It also partly reflects growing rates of deportation among permanent residents; at least 20 percent of all deportations between 1997 and 2007 were of green card holders.[9] Accordingly, relying on a single noncitizen category should appropriately capture whether worries about surveillance and punishment inform these individuals' engagement with surveilling institutions.

In secondary analyses, I distinguish between noncitizens who are likely permanent residents and those who are likely undocumented. The ATUS does not include information about noncitizens' specific legal status.

Accordingly, I follow previous research and "logically impute" legal status on the basis of other indicators available in the dataset.[10] Noncitizens who meet one or more of the following criteria are classified as likely permanent residents: (1) arrived in the United States before 1980; (2) reported any time spent using social services (e.g., collecting social security); (3) is a veteran or currently in the U.S. Armed Forces; (4) works in the government sector; (5) was born in Cuba; (6) works in an occupation where over 60 percent of jobs require certification (as reported in the 2019 Current Population Survey); and (7) is married to a legal immigrant (determined using these same criteria) or citizen. Any remaining noncitizens are placed into a residual category of likely undocumented immigrants.[11] It is possible that this residual category includes some visa holders. Research nonetheless suggests that former visa holders constitute a growing fraction of the undocumented population; accordingly, their experiences should be more similar to undocumented immigrants than permanent residents.[12] The sample size for this analysis (n = 7,902) is about 30 percent of the full sample because information necessary for the logical imputation, such as public and social service use for ATUS respondents and their spouses, is only collected in the Annual Social and Economic Supplement (ASEC) of the CPS. Adjusted sampling weights account for possible differences in the characteristics of respondents with and without these supplemental data.[13]

The analysis includes a suite of demographic controls known to be associated with citizenship status and engagement with surveilling institutions. These controls include sex (1 = male, relative to female), national origin (1 = Mexican, relative to not Mexican), age (in years), age squared, years living in the United States (>10 years or 5–10 years, relative to less than five years), education (college graduate or more, some college, or high school graduate, relative to < high school), marital status (1 = married, relative to not married), household income (1 = > $50,000, relative to $50,000 or less), the number of adults in the households, parenthood (1 = parent, relative to nonparent), employment status (1 = employed, relative to not employed), and school enrollment (1 = enrolled, relative to not enrolled).

Table B.2 presents survey year-adjusted descriptive statistics of Latino ATUS respondents by citizenship for each of the demographic indicators. U.S.-born citizens and noncitizens differ along most characteristics. Noncitizens are more likely to be male, of Mexican descent, and short-term residents of the United States. They have lower levels of educational attainment (and are less likely to be enrolled in school) and have lower household incomes. Noncitizens are also more likely to live in larger households, to be married, and to be parents of children under eighteen years of age. However, employment rates are similar among citizens and noncitizens.

Table B.2. Survey Year-Adjusted Descriptive Statistics for Latino Respondents in ATUS Data, 2003–2019

Variables	All Respondents (N = 25,665)		U.S.-Born Citizens (N = 12,352)		Naturalized Citizens (N = 4,716)		Noncitizens (N = 8,597)	
	Mean	Std. Err.	Mean	Std. Err.	Mean	Std. Err.	Mean	Std. Err.
Male	0.504	0.002	0.491	0.005	0.494	0.010	0.526*	0.005
Mexican	0.637	0.004	0.649	0.007	0.513*	0.010	0.678*	0.007
Age	39.729	0.122	38.062	0.198	48.091*	0.309	38.041	0.179
Age Squared	1,819.710	11.080	1,724.981	17.156	2,545.217*	30.323	1,608.065*	15.204
Years Living in U.S.								
Less than 5 Years	0.059	0.002	0.009	0.001	0.026*	0.003	0.142*	0.006
5–10 Years	0.077	0.002	0.008	0.001	0.061*	0.006	0.177*	0.006
Greater than 10 Years	0.864	0.003	0.983	0.001	0.912*	0.006	0.682*	0.008
Education								
Less than High School	0.332	0.004	0.189	0.005	0.324*	0.009	0.523*	0.008
High School Graduate	0.310	0.004	0.331	0.007	0.290*	0.010	0.293*	0.007
Some College	0.156	0.003	0.222	0.005	0.136*	0.007	0.078*	0.004
College Graduate	0.202	0.003	0.258	0.005	0.249	0.008	0.107*	0.004
Married	0.535	0.004	0.416	0.006	0.665*	0.009	0.631*	0.007
Household Income >$50K	0.356	0.005	0.446	0.007	0.395*	0.011	0.220*	0.006
Number of Adults in Household	2.574	0.014	2.512	0.018	2.563	0.030	2.659*	0.021
Parent	0.431	0.004	0.336	0.006	0.422*	0.010	0.560*	0.007
Employed	0.667	0.004	0.662	0.006	0.669	0.010	0.673	0.007
Enrolled in School	0.102	0.003	0.146	0.005	0.050*	0.005	0.068*	0.004

Note: N = 25,665. * $p < 0.05$ (indicating a significant difference with U.S.-born citizens). Estimates are predictive margins from regression models with controls for survey year. Sample was limited to Latino respondents aged eighteen and older.

These demographic characteristics are associated with nativity and, conditional on being an immigrant, citizenship status. Table B.3 shows these results from two separate logistic regression models among Latinos in the ATUS data. Net of other controls in the models, immigrants are significantly less likely (p < 0.001; exceptions indicated) to be Mexican, to have lived in the United States for over ten years, to be a high school graduate or higher, and to have higher household incomes; they are more likely to be older, to be married, to live with more adults, to be parents, and to work. Conditional on being an immigrant, U.S. citizens are more likely to be women (p < 0.05), to not be descended from Mexico, to be longer-term residents of the United States, to be a high school graduate or higher, to have higher household incomes, and to be employed (p < 0.05). Employment differences by nativity and citizenship, not present in table B.2, emerge in table B.3 after statistical adjustment for other demographic characteristics.

Analytic Strategy

The analysis uses Stata 16 to estimate a series of logistic regression models predicting the odds of engagement with surveilling institutions relative to nonengagement (what existing research might call avoidance). It compares Latino U.S.-born citizens with noncitizens and naturalized citizens. I calculate and interpret differences in average marginal effects to facilitate interpretation of results.[14] Given the theoretical expectations reviewed at the start of this appendix, the below discussion foregrounds comparisons between the U.S. born and noncitizens. Results comparing U.S.-born and naturalized citizens are presented in the tables for reference.

Results

Table B.4 presents survey year-adjusted descriptive statistics of Latino ATUS respondents by citizenship. The hypothesized association between citizenship and engagement with surveilling institutions is apparent. Relative to U.S.-born citizens on a typical day in a typical year, noncitizens not only spend time in fewer surveilling institutions (0.62 v. 0.57) but also have lower average rates of engagement (56.6% v. 53.2%) with them. Their average rate of engagement with regulatory institutions overall is similar to that of U.S.-born citizens, though the typical noncitizen engages less with financial institutions (2% v. 1.4%). Noncitizens have lower average rates of engagement with service institutions overall when compared with the U.S. born (11.6% v. 6.4%), which extends to both medical and

Table B.3. Logistic Regressions Predicting Nativity and Citizenship Status for Latino ATUS Respondents, 2003–2019

Variables	Nativity (1 = Foreign Born) Model 1	Citizenship Status (1 = U.S. Citizen) Model 2
Male	1.087+	0.875*
	(0.048)	(0.052)
Mexican	0.769***	0.692***
	(0.033)	(0.040)
Age	1.162***	1.016
	(0.009)	(0.014)
Age Squared	0.999***	1.000**
	(0.000)	(0.000)
Years Living in U.S. (Ref: <5 Years)		
5–10 Years	1.241	2.187***
	(0.233)	(0.391)
>10 Years	0.045***	6.568***
	(0.007)	(0.966)
Education (Ref: Less than High School)		
High School Graduate	0.357***	1.947***
	(0.019)	(0.144)
Some College	0.226***	3.885***
	(0.015)	(0.400)
College Graduate	0.226***	3.884***
	(0.013)	(0.323)
Married	1.728***	1.032
	(0.077)	(0.073)
Household Income >$50K	0.545***	1.685***
	(0.026)	(0.124)
Number of Adults in Household	1.266***	0.955
	(0.029)	(0.032)
Parent	1.594***	0.941
	(0.086)	(0.068)
Employed	1.289***	1.213*
	(0.062)	(0.092)
Enrolled in School	0.957	1.152
	(0.080)	(0.158)
Year Dummy	YES	YES
Constant	0.491**	0.013***
	(0.108)	(0.005)
Sub-Population Observations	25,665	13,313

Note: Standard errors in parentheses. *** p<0.001, ** p<0.01, * p<0.05, +p<0.1. Model 2 predicts citizenship conditional on being an immigrant. The sample in all models is limited to Latino respondents aged eighteen or older.

Table B.4. Latino ATUS Respondents' Survey Year-Adjusted Engagement with Surveilling and Nonsurveilling Institutions by Citizenship, 2003–2019

Variables	All Respondents (N = 25,665)		U.S.-Born Citizens (N = 12,352)		Naturalized Citizens (N = 4,716)		Noncitizens (N = 8,597)	
	Mean	Std. Err.	Mean	Std. Err.	Mean	Std. Err.	Mean	Std. Err.
Surveilling Institutions								
Count of Engagement	0.599	0.005	0.623	0.008	0.602	0.011	0.567*	0.008
Overall Engagement	0.553	0.004	0.566	0.007	0.562	0.010	0.532*	0.007
Regulatory	0.493	0.004	0.489	0.007	0.506	0.010	0.493	0.007
Financial	0.020	0.001	0.024	0.002	0.022	0.003	0.014*	0.002
Government/Civic	0.006	0.001	0.006	0.001	0.005	0.001	0.006	0.001
Work	0.479	0.004	0.473	0.007	0.492	0.011	0.482	0.007
Service	0.091	0.002	0.116	0.004	0.081*	0.006	0.064*	0.004
Medical	0.027	0.001	0.030	0.002	0.039*	0.004	0.017*	0.002
Education	0.065	0.002	0.087	0.004	0.042*	0.005	0.047*	0.003
Nonsurveilling Institutions								
Count of Engagement	0.122	0.003	0.110	0.004	0.153*	0.007	0.124*	0.005
Overall Engagement	0.112	0.002	0.101	0.003	0.140*	0.006	0.115*	0.004
Volunteer	0.030	0.001	0.035	0.002	0.028*	0.003	0.025*	0.002
Religious	0.090	0.002	0.074	0.003	0.123*	0.006	0.097*	0.004

Note: N = 25,665. * p<0.05 (indicating a significant difference with U.S.-born citizens). Estimates are predictive margins from regression models with controls for survey year. Sample was limited to Latino respondents aged eighteen and older.

educational institutions. In contrast, for nonsurveilling institutions over-all, noncitizens are more likely to engage them than are U.S.-born citizens (11.5% v. 10.1%). For both volunteer and religious institutions, noncitizens' average rates of engagement are higher than those of U.S.-born citizens. These associations suggest that, on a typical day in a typical year, Latinos' institutional engagement varies by citizenship in a way consonant with existing research on surveillance and system avoidance.

Table B.5 presents predictive margins from discrete logistic regressions examining the relationship between citizenship and institutional engage-ment, adjusting for individual-level demographic characteristics and sur-vey year-fixed effects. On a typical day in a typical year, Latino noncitizens are as likely as Latino U.S.-born citizens to spend time in surveilling insti-tutions overall. This pattern extends to regulatory institutions overall, as well as service institutions overall. Looking more closely at each individual institution, Latino noncitizens are less likely than the U.S. born to engage with medical institutions but as likely to engage with the others in the fully adjusted models. As in table B.4, noncitizens in table B.5 are more likely than the U.S. born to engage with nonsurveilling institutions.

The preceding analyses focus on how Latino respondents who are U.S.-born citizens and noncitizens spend their time on a typical day in a typical year. It is nonetheless possible that patterns of institutional engagement vary in relation to these individuals' social role as parents. If so, then mea-sures that do not also account for the time respondents spend engaged with surveilling institutions on behalf of their children may misdiagnose the conditions under which citizenship and institutional engagement are associated. Table B.6 offers support for this idea. It distinguishes between parents and nonparents and, within each group, examines year-adjusted differences in institutional engagement across citizenship categories. The first part of table B.6 uses the indicators that have guided the analyses thus far—those that capture time spent in surveilling institutions on behalf of oneself. Among Latino parents, noncitizens are less likely than U.S.-born citizens (p < 0.05) to report spending time in surveilling institutions overall, and financial and service institutions in particular; this pattern is similar among nonparents. Notably, average rates of engagement with sur-veilling institutions overall, and medical institutions specifically, among noncitizens are higher among nonparents than parents when accounting only for time spent on behalf of oneself.

Indicators that measure respondents' engagement with surveilling institutions on behalf of themselves and their children are presented in the bottom part of table B.6. These indicators are available for medical

Table B.5. Predictive Margins from Logistic Regressions Predicting Engagement with Surveilling and Nonsurveilling Institutions among Latino ATUS Respondents by Citizenship, 2003–2019

	Surveilling Institutions								Nonsurveilling Institutions		
		Regulatory Institutions				Service Institutions					
	All	Overall Reg.	Finance	Govt./Civic	Work	Overall Service	Medical	Educ.	All	Vol.	Relig.
Variable	Mod. 1	Mod. 2	Mod. 3	Mod. 4	Mod. 5	Mod. 6	Mod. 7	Mod. 8	Mod. 9	Mod. 10	Mod. 11
Engagement by Citizenship											
U.S.-Born Citizen	0.553	0.494	0.019	0.006	0.466	0.091	0.024	0.063	0.096	0.030	0.071
	(0.005)	(0.005)	(0.002)	(0.001)	(0.007)	(0.003)	(0.002)	(0.003)	(0.004)	(0.002)	(0.003)
Naturalized Citizen	0.582*	0.508	0.019	0.004	0.517*	0.104	0.026	0.076*	0.110*	0.024*	0.091*
	(0.008)	(0.007)	(0.003)	(0.001)	(0.010)	(0.006)	(0.003)	(0.005)	(0.005)	(0.003)	(0.005)
Noncitizen	0.539	0.486	0.016	0.005	0.479	0.085	0.016*	0.063	0.112*	0.026	0.091*
	(0.006)	(0.006)	(0.002)	(0.001)	(0.007)	(0.004)	(0.002)	(0.004)	(0.005)	(0.002)	(0.004)
Sociodemographic Controls	YES	YES	YES	YES	YES	YES	YES	YES	YES	YES	YES
Year Dummy Control	YES	YES	YES	YES	YES	YES	YES	YES	YES	YES	YES

Note: N = 25,665. * p<0.05 (indicating a significant difference with U.S.-born citizens). Estimates are predictive margins from regression models with controls for survey year. Sociodemographic controls include sex, national origin, age, age squared, number of years living in the United States, education level, marital status, household income, number of adults in household, parenthood status, employment status (except Model 5), and school enrollment (except Model 8). Sample was limited to Latino respondents aged eighteen and older.

Table B.6. Latino ATUS Respondents' Survey Year-Adjusted Engagement with Surveilling Institutions by Parenthood and Citizenship, 2003–2019

	Parent			Nonparent		
	U.S.-Born Citizen	Naturalized Citizen	Noncitizen	U.S.-Born Citizen	Naturalized Citizen	Noncitizen
Engagement for Oneself						
Surveilling Institutions	0.557	0.554	0.526*	0.570	0.568	0.539*
	(0.008)	(0.011)	(0.007)	(0.007)	(0.010)	(0.008)
Regulatory	0.511	0.525	0.508	0.478	0.492	0.475
	(0.009)	(0.011)	(0.007)	(0.007)	(0.011)	(0.009)
Financial	0.024	0.022	0.013*	0.025	0.024	0.015*
	(0.002)	(0.003)	(0.002)	(0.002)	(0.003)	(0.002)
Government/Civic	0.008	0.006	0.007	0.007	0.005	0.006
	(0.001)	(0.001)	(0.001)	(0.001)	(0.001)	(0.001)
Work	0.495	0.512	0.497	0.462	0.478	0.463
	(0.009)	(0.012)	(0.007)	(0.007)	(0.011)	(0.009)
Service	0.074	0.044*	0.036*	0.137	0.108*	0.100*
	(0.004)	(0.006)	(0.004)	(0.005)	(0.007)	(0.005)
Medical	0.024	0.035*	0.013*	0.034	0.044*	0.022*
	(0.002)	(0.004)	(0.002)	(0.002)	(0.005)	(0.002)
Education	0.051	0.010*	0.023*	0.106	0.065*	0.078*
	(0.004)	(0.005)	(0.003)	(0.004)	(0.005)	(0.005)

Continued on next page

Table B.6. (*continued*)

	Parent			Nonparent		
	U.S.-Born Citizen	Naturalized Citizen	Noncitizen	U.S.-Born Citizen	Naturalized Citizen	Noncitizen
Engagement for Oneself+Kids						
Surveilling Institutions	0.619	0.611	0.597*	0.573	0.565	0.551*
	(0.008)	(0.011)	(0.007)	(0.007)	(0.010)	(0.008)
Service	0.194	0.165*	0.161*	0.143	0.113*	0.110*
	(0.006)	(0.009)	(0.007)	(0.005)	(0.008)	(0.006)
Medical	0.036	0.044	0.025*	0.034	0.043	0.024*
	(0.003)	(0.005)	(0.003)	(0.002)	(0.005)	(0.002)
Education	0.166	0.126*	0.140*	0.112	0.072*	0.086*
	(0.006)	(0.008)	(0.006)	(0.005)	(0.007)	(0.005)

Note: N=25,665. Standard errors in parentheses. * p<0.05 (indicating a significant difference with U.S.-born citizens within each parent category). Estimates are predictive margins from regression models with controls for citizenship, parenthood status, and survey year. Sample was limited to Latino respondents aged eighteen and older.

and educational institutions and are also reflected in the indicator for overall engagement with surveilling institutions. Among Latino parents, noncitizens are less likely than U.S.-born citizens ($p < 0.05$) to spend time in surveilling institutions overall on a typical day in a typical year. This difference reflects noncitizens' lower likelihood of spending time in medical and educational institutions on their own behalf. Although the measure that adds time spent on behalf of one's children roughly doubles noncitizen parents' reported engagement with medical institutions, and multiplies their engagement with educational institutions six-fold, they are still less likely to engage with these institutions than the U.S. born. Among nonparents, noncitizens are less likely than the U.S. born to engage with surveilling institutions; this pattern is the result of their lower average rates of engagement with medical and educational institutions.

Table B.7 presents predictive margins from fully adjusted logistic regression models examining institutional engagement separately for Latino (a) parents and (b) nonparents. One set of results uses the indicators that do not account for time spent on behalf of one's children, whereas the other set includes time spent on behalf of one's children. In the left-hand side of table B.7A, which measures parents' time spent engaging surveilling institutions on behalf of themselves, noncitizens are less likely than U.S.-born citizens ($p < 0.05$) to spend time in surveilling institutions. But, when including time spent on behalf of respondents' children, overall rates of engagement with surveilling institutions are similar for noncitizens and citizens.

Table B.7B offers a similar analysis for Latino nonparents. Among nonparents, noncitizens and U.S.-born citizens have similar rates of engagement with surveilling institutions overall. Noncitizens are nonetheless less likely than U.S.-born citizens ($p < 0.05$) to engage with medical institutions. Adding time spent on behalf of one's children leaves these results unchanged since nonparents, by definition, do not have children.

These results are similar when distinguishing among noncitizens who are likely permanent residents and those who are likely undocumented. Table B.8 presents predictive margins from fully adjusted logistic regression models that examine the relationship between legal status and institutional engagement. Relative to the U.S. born, likely undocumented immigrants are as likely to report engaging surveilling institutions overall on a typical day in a typical year, though they are

Table B.7. Predictive Margins from Logistic Regressions Predicting Institutional Engagement by Citizenship Status among Latino ATUS Respondents, 2003–2019

	Time Spent on Self				Time Spent on Self + Kids			
	Surveilling Model 1	Service Model 2	Medical Model 3	Education Model 4	Surveilling Model 5	Service Model 6	Medical Model 7	Education Model 8
A. Parents[a]								
U.S.-Born Citizen	0.554	0.057	0.021	0.035	0.617	0.170	0.031	0.144
	(0.009)	(0.004)	(0.003)	(0.004)	(0.009)	(0.009)	(0.004)	(0.009)
Naturalized Citizen	0.571	0.053	0.018	0.034	0.627	0.180	0.025	0.158
	(0.012)	(0.006)	(0.004)	(0.005)	(0.012)	(0.012)	(0.005)	(0.011)
Noncitizen	0.523*	0.046	0.015	0.027	0.595	0.174	0.026	0.146
	(0.007)	(0.004)	(0.003)	(0.003)	(0.008)	(0.008)	(0.004)	(0.007)
Controls								
Sociodemographic	YES	YES	YES	YES	YES	YES	YES	YES
Year Dummy	YES	YES	YES	YES	YES	YES	YES	YES

B. Nonparents[b]

	(1)	(2)	(3)	(4)	(5)	(6)	(7)	(8)
U.S.-Born Citizen	0.552	0.119	0.024	0.087	0.555	0.125	0.024	0.093
	(0.007)	(0.005)	(0.003)	(0.005)	(0.007)	(0.005)	(0.003)	(0.005)
Naturalized Citizen	0.588*	0.142*	0.029	0.102	0.592*	0.148*	0.030	0.108
	(0.011)	(0.010)	(0.005)	(0.007)	(0.011)	(0.010)	(0.005)	(0.007)
Noncitizen	0.562	0.115	0.015*	0.094	0.568	0.124	0.016*	0.102
	(0.010)	(0.007)	(0.002)	(0.008)	(0.010)	(0.007)	(0.003)	(0.008)
Controls								
Sociodemographic	YES	YES	YES	YES	YES	YES	YES	YES
Year Dummy	YES	YES	YES	YES	YES	YES	YES	YES

Note: * p<0.05 (indicating a significant difference with U.S.-born citizens). Sociodemographic controls include sex, national origin, age, age squared, number of years living in the United States, education level, marital status, household income, number of adults in household, survey year, employment status, and school enrollment (except Model 4 and 8).

[a] N=11,075. Sample was limited to Latino parent respondents aged eighteen and older.

[b] N=14,590. Sample was limited to Latino nonparent respondents aged eighteen and older.

Table B.8. Predictive Margins from Logistic Regressions Predicting Engagement with Surveilling and Nonsurveilling Institutions among Latino ATUS Respondents by Legal Status, 2003–2019

Variable	Surveilling Institutions								Nonsurveilling Institutions		
	Regulatory Institutions					Service Institutions					
	All	Overall Reg.	Finance	Govt./ Civic	Work	Overall Service	Medical	Educ.	All	Vol.	Relig.
	Mod. 1	Mod. 2	Mod. 3	Mod. 4	Mod. 5	Mod. 6	Mod. 7	Mod. 8	Mod. 9	Mod. 10	Mod. 11
Engagement by Citizenship											
U.S.-Born Citizen	0.535	0.484	0.012	0.006	0.459	0.081	0.023	0.049	0.088	0.026	0.063
	(0.010)	(0.010)	(0.003)	(0.001)	(0.013)	(0.006)	(0.004)	(0.005)	(0.007)	(0.004)	(0.005)
Naturalized Citizen	0.549	0.488	0.016	0.004	0.499	0.091	0.023	0.069	0.107*	0.026	0.088*
	(0.014)	(0.014)	(0.004)	(0.001)	(0.018)	(0.012)	(0.005)	(0.010)	(0.009)	(0.005)	(0.008)
Likely Permanent Resident	0.540	0.507	0.011	0.008	0.482	0.058	0.017	0.048	0.083	0.017	0.068
	(0.015)	(0.015)	(0.004)	(0.002)	(0.020)	(0.009)	(0.005)	(0.008)	(0.010)	(0.005)	(0.008)
Likely Undocumented	0.562	0.514	0.009	0.004	0.527*	0.075	0.018	0.045	0.099	0.022	0.083
	(0.014)	(0.015)	(0.003)	(0.001)	(0.019)	(0.009)	(0.006)	(0.009)	(0.012)	(0.004)	(0.011)
Sociodemographic Controls	YES	YES	YES	YES	YES	YES	YES	YES	YES	YES	YES
Year Dummy Control	YES	YES	YES	YES	YES	YES	YES	YES	YES	YES	YES

Note: N=7,902. Standard errors in parentheses. * p<0.05 (indicating a significant difference with U.S.-born citizens). Sociodemographic controls include sex, national origin, age, age squared, number of years living in the United States, education level, marital status, household income, number of adults in household, survey year, employment status (except Model 5), and school enrollment (except Model 8). Sample was limited to Latino respondents aged eighteen and older. The likely permanent resident category includes noncitizen respondents who fit one or more of the following criteria: (1) arrived before 1980; (2) reported any time spent using social services (e.g., applying for unemployment benefits, collecting social security); (3) is a veteran or currently in the U.S. Armed Forces; (4) works in the government sector; (5) was born in Cuba; (6) works in an occupation where over 60 percent of jobs require certification (as reported in the 2019 Current Population Survey); and (7) is married to a legal immigrant (using these same indicators) or citizen. Employment-level data on spouses are captured between two and five months before the ATUS interviews in the CPS. Data on receipt of public and social services are from the Annual Social and Economic Supplement (ASEC) of the CPS. These data are linked through the CPSIDP unique identifier that IPUMS-CPS constructs to link individuals across CPS samples. Analysis weights are adjusted based on the documentation provided by IPUMS because not all ATUS respondents have CPS supplemental data.

more likely to report working ($p < 0.05$). Likely permanent residents are as likely as the U.S. born to report engaging with surveilling institutions overall, with no discernible differences in time use across surveilling institutions.

Examining differences in institutional engagement by legal status and parenthood reinforces the idea that Latinos worried about state punishment maintain complex processes of institutional engagement. Table B.9 predicts institutional engagement separately for Latino (a) parents and (b) nonparents in each of the four legal status categories. On the left-hand side of table B.9A, which measures parents' personal institutional engagement, likely undocumented immigrants and permanent residents are as likely as U.S.-born citizens to spend time in surveilling institutions overall. Measures that include time spent on behalf of children increase the overall likelihood of engagement for all groups, but the likelihood of engagement remains similar between the U.S. born and likely undocumented or permanent resident immigrants.

Table B.9B offers a similar analysis for nonparents. Likely undocumented and permanent resident respondents have similar rates of engagement as the U.S. born. Likely permanent residents are nonetheless less likely than the U.S. born to engage with service institutions.

Conclusion

The above analyses validate and extend some of the core arguments developed throughout the book. First, they confirm that Latino immigrants align their institutional engagement with their multiple social roles and responsibilities. Second, they urge theoretical and empirical work that accounts for the complex dynamics of societal exclusion and inclusion that surveillance imposes on daily life. Research that relies on any one surveilling institution, such as hospitals or banks, to make a claim about the relationship between citizenship and system avoidance captures just one dimension of engagement with surveilling institutions; these measures, therefore, underestimate Latino noncitizens' full scope of institutional engagement. Third, the analysis highlights the importance of quotidian institutional engagement for Latino immigrants worried about deportation. Measuring engagement in a way that considers how people spend their time on a typical day, not just for themselves but also for their children, offers a more holistic snapshot of the complex ways through which surveillance informs Latino noncitizens' multiple forms of institutional engagement.

Table B.9. Predictive Margins from Logistic Regressions Predicting Institutional Engagement by Legal Status among Latino ATUS Respondents, 2003–2019

	Time Spent on Self				Time Spent on Self + Kids			
	Surveilling	Service	Medical	Education	Surveilling	Service	Medical	Education
	Model 1	Model 2	Model 3	Model 4	Model 5	Model 6	Model 7	Model 8
A. Parents[a]								
U.S.-Born Citizen	0.524	0.056	0.016	0.033	0.566	0.133	0.024	0.108
	(0.015)	(0.009)	(0.006)	(0.007)	(0.015)	(0.014)	(0.007)	(0.014)
Naturalized Citizen	0.529	0.063	0.014	0.040	0.560	0.142	0.030	0.108
	(0.025)	(0.013)	(0.007)	(0.011)	(0.023)	(0.021)	(0.011)	(0.018)
Likely Permanent Resident	0.507	0.047	0.015	0.022	0.567	0.153	0.032	0.109
	(0.019)	(0.011)	(0.008)	(0.008)	(0.020)	(0.019)	(0.011)	(0.016)
Likely Undocumented	0.542	0.036	0.011	0.015*	0.592	0.120	0.020	0.088
	(0.018)	(0.008)	(0.005)	(0.005)	(0.019)	(0.015)	(0.007)	(0.014)
Controls								
Sociodemographic	YES	YES	YES	YES	YES	YES	YES	YES
Year Dummy	YES	YES	YES	YES	YES	YES	YES	YES

B. Nonparents[b]

U.S.-Born Citizen	0.541	0.100	0.022	0.063	0.544	0.109	0.023	0.072
	(0.012)	(0.009)	(0.005)	(0.008)	(0.012)	(0.009)	(0.005)	(0.008)
Naturalized Citizen	0.561	0.107	0.021	0.086	0.565	0.113	0.022	0.092
	(0.019)	(0.018)	(0.006)	(0.016)	(0.019)	(0.018)	(0.006)	(0.016)
Likely Permanent Resident	0.582	0.061*	0.014	0.071	0.586	0.070*	0.016	0.077
	(0.022)	(0.015)	(0.005)	(0.015)	(0.022)	(0.016)	(0.006)	(0.015)
Likely Undocumented	0.584	0.114	0.018	0.074	0.589	0.116	0.018	0.077
	(0.023)	(0.019)	(0.009)	(0.020)	(0.024)	(0.019)	(0.009)	(0.020)
Controls								
Sociodemographic	YES	YES	YES	YES	YES	YES	YES	YES
Year Dummy	YES	YES	YES	YES	YES	YES	YES	YES

Note: Standard errors in parentheses. * p<0.05 (indicating a significant difference with U.S.-born citizens). Sociodemographic controls include sex, national origin, age, age squared, number of years living in the United States, education level, marital status, household income, number of adults in household, survey year, and, with the exceptions of Model 3 and 6, employment status and school enrollment.

[a] N = 3,397. Sample was limited to Latino parent respondents aged eighteen and older.

[b] N = 4,505. Sample was limited to Latino nonparent respondents aged eighteen and older.

ACKNOWLEDGMENTS

GROWING UP, I NEVER ENVISIONED that I would write a book. It's not that I actively doubted myself; the thought simply never crossed my mind. I enjoyed reading, a habit my parents supported, but that was the extent of my relationship with books: reader. And, now, author. It's a relationship that I have not yet embraced. I experienced many moments of excitement and pride throughout the research and writing process—and many more moments of confusion and doubt that I think any first-time book author would encounter. This book is as much a product of my efforts as it is those of an extensive community that has propelled me across the finish line.

Nothing in this life would have been possible without my parents and siblings. My parents, Lugman and Naziha, left the West Bank decades ago, hoping for a new life in the United States on behalf of those they left behind. I am thankful that Baba and Mama dared to hope, and that they encouraged me to pursue my own dreams. My siblings championed all my educational pursuits. I have always had a great role model in Sara, the first in the family to graduate from a four-year college and to show me that I could do it, too. For as long as I can remember, Wisam has sacrificed so that the rest of us didn't have to. Samer, my late brother, never lost sight of me even as he lost sight of himself. I miss him every day. I don't know anyone with a more generous soul than Amani, who showed me how to be a compassionate student and teacher. And life just wouldn't make sense without Amjad, my twin brother, harshest critic, and biggest cheerleader. I am lucky to have been born with someone who has always been there. This book exists because of all of them, with a special dedication to my parents and Samer.

My extended family, too, offered support. Huda, who felt like a sister the moment she joined the family, is unsurpassed in her dedication to her community. To my nieces and nephews, near and far, I hope you remember to challenge the world as it's presented to you. I will give a special mention to Adam and Jenna, who have already grown into wonderful young adults. Thanks also to my many aunts, uncles, and cousins for their support over the years.

Although the earliest version of the book was born in graduate school, I don't think I would have gone to graduate school without supportive college mentors at the University of Wisconsin. I am especially grateful to Scott Gehlbach, Kenneth R. Mayer, and Kathryn Sanchez. At Harvard,

Mary C. Waters served as a devoted doctoral advisor and taught me how to have serious ideas without taking myself too seriously. Filiz Garip reminded me to trust my instincts and be courageous as a researcher and writer. Mario Luis Small challenged me to demand more from myself as a thinker. And William Julius Wilson emphasized the importance of linking sociological theory and research to actionable policy solutions. Thanks also to Steve Bloomfield, Nancy Branco, Deb De Laurell, Dorothy Friendly, Jessica Gauchel, Ted Gilman, Gretchen Gingo, Eudeen Green, Kristen Halbert, Rebecca Haley, Mervi Karttunen, Laura Kistler, Dotty Lucas, Kimberly Lyle, Jessica Matteson, Pam Metz, Lisa McAllister, Suzanne Ogungbadero, Clare Putnam, Laura Thomas, and the late Judy Vichniac for their support.

A postdoctoral fellowship at Cornell University's Center for the Study of Inequality (CSI) afforded me time to develop as a researcher and writer. My deepest appreciation goes to Filiz Garip, Matthew Hall, and Kim Weeden for the opportunity. I met and learned from so many wonderful scholars while at Cornell, including Steven Alvarado, Kendra Bischoff, Shannon Gleeson, Anna Haskins, Dan Lichter, Kelly Musick, Peter Rich, and Sharon Sassler. Filiz Garip, Shannon Gleeson, and Beth Lyon read an early version of this book with a constructive eye, and Meaghan Mingo and Yoselinda Mendoza kept track of the many suggestions for improvement offered. Staff at CSI, the Cornell Department of Sociology, and the Cornell Population Center—including Meg Cole, Clara Epi, Sue Meyer, Alice Murdock, Dave Nelson, John Niederbuhl, Mary Newhart, and Marty White—made me feel welcome and supported. I would also like to thank Michael Jones-Correa, who offered me an affiliation with and office space at the University of Pennsylvania for whenever life brought me to Philadelphia during my postdoctoral fellowship.

I wrote the book in earnest as a faculty member at Stanford, a position that has overlapped with the COVID-19 pandemic. Dean Debra Satz and Senior Associate Dean Ran Abramitzky have made the School of Humanities and Sciences a supportive environment, especially for junior faculty, throughout. Michael Rosenfeld and Jeremy Freese both have been attentive department chairs. The rest of my colleagues in the sociology department, including but not limited to David Grusky, Jackelyn Hwang, Michelle Jackson, Tomás Jiménez, Aliya Saperstein, Forrest Stuart, Florencia Torche, and Xueguang Zhou, have served as founts of kindness and knowledge. With Karen Cook's help, the Institute for Research in the Social Sciences offered me office space during my research leave, from which I finalized several portions of this book. Jennifer DeVere Brody and Paula

Moya have stewarded a vibrant intellectual community at the Stanford Center for Comparative Studies in Race and Ethnicity (CCSRE). Thanks also to Mariette Conway, Afrooz Emami, Sihla Koop, Edwin Mendoza, Randy Michaud, Natasha Newson, Morgan Speer, and Chrissy Stimmel for their attentive administrative support. A book manuscript workshop, organized by the thoughtful Jenny Martinez and funded by the Stanford Humanities Center and CCSRE, allowed me to receive essential substantive feedback on a later version of the book from Cybelle Fox, David Hausman, Tomás Jiménez, Cecilia Menjívar, Emily Ryo, and Jayashri Srikantiah. I appreciate their efforts to help me transform the manuscript into the book I intended. Tomás Jiménez, a steadfast mentor and friend, has provided additional rounds of valuable feedback on portions of the book since the conference. And, for their research assistance that contributed to different sections of the book, I thank Livia Baer-Bositis, Daniella Efrat, Joshua Pe, Apollo Rydzik, and Tristyn Thomas.

Scholars depend on feedback, both positive and constructive, to develop their research. In addition to benefitting from the people already named, this book reflects conversations or feedback accumulated over the years from others kind enough to share their insights: Amada Armenta, Jason Beckfield, Stefan Beljean, Frank Bean, Monica Bell, Bart Bonikowski, Hana Brown, Silvia Domínguez, Frank Edwards, Kelley Fong, Roberto Gonzales, Hope Harvey, Jackelyn Hwang, Tiffany Joseph, Michéle Lamont, Jennifer Lee, Abena Mackall, Helen Marrow, Margot Moinester, Katherine Ann Morris, Michela Musto, Devah Pager, Ben Rissing, Apollo Rydzik, Aliya Saperstein, Ariela Schachter, Florencia Torche, Alba Villamil, Jocelyn Viterna, Nathan Wilmers, Andreas Wimmer, and Chris Winship. David Lobenstine deserves a special mention for his sharp edits and comments on previous versions of the manuscript. Audiences at the Colegio de México, Columbia, Cornell, Harvard, Princeton, Rice, Stanford, the University of Michigan, the University of Pennsylvania, the University of Toronto, the University of Washington, the University of Wisconsin, Yale Law School, and the Vera Institute of Justice also offered helpful suggestions. So did editors and anonymous reviewers at several journals, especially *American Behavioral Scientist, Journal of Ethnic and Migration Studies, International Migration Review, Law & Society Review*, and the *Proceedings of the National Academy of Sciences*. Finally, my thanks to audiences at several conferences, including the American Sociological Association, the Eastern Sociological Society, the Population Association of America, the Society for Epidemiological Research, and the Society for the Study of Social Problems.

Without the efforts of the whole How Parents House Kids (HPHK) team, there would have been no book manuscript on which to solicit feedback. HPHK was funded by the Annie E. Casey Foundation and the John D. and Catherine T. MacArthur Foundation. My most immense gratitude to Kathy Edin and Stefanie DeLuca, the co-principal investigators, for having me on the team and allowing me to pursue the line of research that led to this book. In addition to myself, the HPHK fieldworkers include Monica Bell, Melody Boyd, Brielle Bryan, Sophie Damas, Jennifer Darrah, Hilario Dominguez, Kaitlin Edin-Nelson, Jennifer Ferentz, Kelley Fong, Philip Garboden, Meredith Greif, Hope Harvey, Barbara Kiviat, Holly Howell Koogler, Margot Moinester, Ann Owens, Kristin Perkins, Kathryn Reed, Anna Rhodes, Eva Rosen, Beth Schueler, Angela Simms, Elizabeth Talbert, Jessica Tollette, and Siri Warkentien. Jessie Albee, Megan Prior, and Terri Thomas at Johns Hopkins University provided crucial logistical support. As detailed in appendix A, my ability to write this book is in large part a testament to this team.

I received generous funding and support from multiple sources for the later stages of fieldwork, data analysis, and writing. At Harvard, thanks to the Harvard Center for American Political Studies, the Harvard Program on Criminal Justice, the Radcliffe Institute for Advanced Study, and the Weatherhead Center for International Affairs. At Cornell, thanks to the Center for the Study of Inequality and the Cornell Population Center. At Stanford, thanks to the Department of Sociology, the School of Humanities and Sciences, and the Vice Provost of Undergraduate Education. Finally, on the ground in Dallas, thanks to the Barakat Family. They embraced me as an honorary member in both 2015 and 2018, with Maher, Mazena, and Omar going out of their way to support me and my work while I was in the field.

This research would have been impossible without willing participants. My deepest gratitude to all study participants, families and immigration officials alike, for inviting me in.

Despite blowing past the deadline I had set for myself to finish this manuscript, the team at Princeton University Press led with kindness and efficiency as they saw the book through peer review and into production. It has been a privilege to work with Meagan Levinson and Erik Beranek, whose enthusiasm for the manuscript I appreciated. Thanks also to Natalie Baan, Leah Caldwell, Kate Hensley, Katie Osborne, Kathryn Stevens, and Erin Suydam for their work.

Family and friends, near and far, have kept me going through the ups and downs of research and writing. Monica Bell invests in her people with everything she has. Monica, thank you for being the first friend I made in graduate school, and for encouraging me to evolve over the years. I have long thought of Anthony Jack as a mentor, friend, and brother wrapped into one. Tony, thank you for always looking out. Alix Winter is the most empathetic listener, one who is always ready to offer a critical but non-judgmental ear. Alix, thank you for your thoughtfulness and care. Many other friends, some spanning multiple states and phases of this project, also have offered support. Back home in Wisconsin, I thank Natasha Anderson, Alecia Corbett, Kelly Hennigan, Samir Jaber, Eva Lam, Myra Lam, Clara Rose Tracey, and Sema Taheri. For sharing their time in Massachusetts, I thank Ralph Bouquet, Rachel Bradshaw, Brian Clair, Kyrah Daniels, Charity Glass, Yennice Linares, Katherine Morris, Kelsey Palder, Luke Palder, Michael Paydos, Tyler Payne, Lumumba Seegars, Taylor Seegars, Jessica Tollette, Nathan Wilmers, Alba Villamil, and Xiaolin Zhuo. For sharing their time in New York, I thank Catherine Clepper, Jessica Cooper, Lucas Drouhot, Frank Edwards, Leslie Fair-Page, Brandon Gray, Briahna Gray, Hope Harvey, Patrick Ishizuka, Neil Lewis, Devon Magliozzi, Devin McCauley, Erin McCauley, Meaghan Mingo, Yoselinda Mendoza, Mario Molina, Kelly Nielsen, Archie Page, Camille Portier, Cassandra Robertson, and Youngmin Yi. Special thanks to Neil, Erin, Meaghan, and Yoselinda, whose everyday warmth and generosity helped make Ithaca gorgeous. For sharing their time in Pennsylvania, I thank Lola Agabalogun, Asli Bashir, Naveen Mohan, Shivani Mohan, Amanda Woog, and Tom Wooten. For sharing their time in Tennessee, I thank Drs. Walter Clair and Deborah Webster-Clair, as well as Dawn and Steve Sabin. To the Clairs: I am so humbled by your acceptance, your generosity, and your kinship. And, for sharing their time in California, I thank Jon Atwell, Rebecca Atwell, Daniel Colvard, Jesse Izzo, Natalie Jabbar, Hakeem Jefferson, Nova Jiménez, Hayden Kantor, Roanne Kantor, Barbara Kiviat, Mao-Mei Liu, Meagan Mauter, Brittany Northcross, Alvin Pearman, Kristin Pearman, David Pedulla, Matt Salisbury, Jonathan Sands, Chris Schenk, Dave Szymaszek, and Saron Tesfalul.

I cannot close without acknowledging Rita, the best dog in the world. She will never read this book but cared enough to offer her support throughout the writing process.

And, last but not least, Matthew Clair. Anyone who knows him understands how special he is. From my vantage point, he is all that and more. Matt, I am in awe of your brilliance, your charm, your patience, and above all, you. Thank you, for everything.

Preface

1. (Chávez 2013)

2. (Martinez-Aranda 2020). For a review, see Kalhan 2014; Menjívar, Gómez Cervantes, and Alvord 2018.

3. (Massey, Durand, and Malone 2002)

4. (Massey, Durand, and Pren 2016)

5. (Warren and Kerwin 2017)

6. (Kalhan 2014)

7. (Armenta 2017; Moinester 2018)

8. (Meissner et al. 2013)

9. (De Genova 2002)

10. (Batalova et al. 2017)

11. (Zong et al. 2017)

12. (Shear and Davis 2017)

13. (Asad 2020b; Burciaga and Malone 2021; Patler et al. 2019)

14. (Liptak and Shear 2020)

15. (Jordan 2021; Lederman and Ainsley 2022)

16. Source of all tabulations in the preface, unless otherwise noted: USC Equity Research Institute analysis of 2017 five-year American Community Survey (ACS) microdata from IPUMS-USA, or author's tabulations of the same. I thank Justin Scoggins and Carolina Otero for analyzing the ACS data.

17. (Asad 2020a)

18. For a helpful synthesis of the dominant academic theories on this topic, see Garland 2012a.

19. (Foucault 1991 [1978]; Garland 2012a)

Introduction

1. All study participants' names are pseudonyms. Note that I have previously published details about Alma's story under the pseudonym Josefina. That name is changed throughout the book for editorial reasons.

2. See, generally, Chávez 2012 [1992]. For alternate accounts, see Enriquez and Saguy 2016; García 2019; Prieto 2018.

3. On the of morality of decisions to migrate without authorization, see Ryo 2013.

4. Undocumented immigrants could receive social security numbers until 1972, when the Social Security Administration prohibited them from doing so. See Fox 2016.

5. (Hagan 1994; Hondagneu-Sotelo 2007)

6. (Horton 2016; Horton and Heyman 2020)

7. For tax returns that report wages, the IRS requires ITIN filers to include the social security number under which they earned wages on the Form W-2. The IRS

accepts tax returns with mismatched ITINs and social security numbers, with almost one million of these returns accepted in 2018. See, generally, U.S. Office of General Accountability 2020. See also Horton 2016.

8. (Dreby 2015; Menjívar, Abrego, and Schmalzbauer 2016)

9. A federal lawsuit, led by Texas, blocked DAPA before it could be implemented.

10. For a helpful synthesis of different theoretical perspectives on surveillance and punishment, see Garland 2012a.

11. (E.g., Brayne 2014; Goffman 2009; Haskins and Jacobsen 2017; Lanuza and Turney 2020)

12. (Brayne 2014, 2020)

13. (Haskins and Jacobsen 2017; Lanuza and Turney 2020)

14. Many studies on surveillance and system avoidance parallelize the situation of people with criminal records and people who are undocumented immigrants. See Brayne 2014: 387; Fong 2019: 1788; Goffman 2009: 356; and Haskins and Jacobsen 2017: 679.

15. (Brayne 2020; Foucault 2007 [1977]; Garland 2001; Giddens 2013 [1990]; Haggerty and Ericson 2000; Lyon 2003, 2007)

16. (Abarca and Coutin 2018; Chauvin and Garcés-Mascareñas 2012; Chauvin and Garcés-Mascareñas 2014; Coutin 1998, 2003; Hallett 2014; Horton and Heyman 2020)

17. (Massey 2007; Menjívar 2006; Menjívar and Abrego 2012)

18. (Passel and Cohn 2019)

19. For example, see Bachmeier, Van Hook, and Bean 2014; Desai, Su, and Adelman 2020; Gonzalez and Patler 2021; Patler and Gonzalez 2020; Waters and Kasinitz 2015.

20. For a generative discussion about this idea in the context of undocumented immigrants' secondary and postsecondary schooling, see Enriquez 2017; Gonzales 2015; Gonzales and Burciaga 2018; Valdez and Golash-Boza 2018.

21. (Foucault 1991 [1977]: 180)

22. For a helpful overview of role theory, see Biddle 1986. There are different theoretical perspectives and traditions on role theory—functional role theory, symbolic interactionist role theory, structural role theory, organizational role theory, and cognitive role theory—each with its own unique contributions. In this book, I primarily draw on the symbolic interactionist and cognitive traditions. The former shows how social roles "reflect norms, attitudes, contextual demands, negotiation, and the evolving definition of the situation as understood by the actors"; the latter pays attention to "social conditions that give rise to expectations . . . and to the impact of expectations on social conduct" (Biddle 1986: 71–74). To the extent that I pay attention to the structural contexts enabling or constraining expectations, the analysis I offer is also compatible with structural role theory.

23. How these different terms are used likely varies across scholarly and popular writings on immigration.

24. (Asad 2020b; Joseph 2018; Massey and Bartley 2005)

25. Contemporary efforts to strip citizenship from immigrants who have acquired U.S. citizenship, known as denaturalization, are an important exception with historical precedent. See Lind 2018; Ryo and Peacock 2019; Weil 2012.

26. (Menjívar 2006: 1008)

27. Visa overstays have exceeded undocumented entries in their contribution to the total number of undocumented immigrants in the United States since 2007. In 2014, visa overstays accounted for two-thirds of the new undocumented immigrants in the country. See Warren and Kerwin 2017.

28. (Abrego 2019; Enriquez 2015; López 2015; Rodriguez 2016)

29. This typology is adapted from Marrow 2009, 2011.

30. Definition of social roles is from Hughes 1956: 3. Definition of social responsibilities is from Biddle 1996: 10. For foundational theoretical statements on symbolic interactionism, see Blumer 1986; Mead 1934; Znaniecki 1965.

31. (Dreby 2015; Gonzales 2015; Massey 2007; Menjívar 2006)

32. (Enriquez 2017; Enriquez and Millán 2019; Valdez and Golash-Boza 2018)

33. (Foucault 1991 [1978]). On this more general point of intersectionality, see Crenshaw 1990.

34. (Golash-Boza and Hondagneu-Sotelo 2013)

35. (Dreby 2015)

36. (Golash-Boza 2015a; Martínez, Slack, and Martínez-Schuldt 2018). As we will see in chapter 4, the Supreme Court does not consider deportations to be a punishment in the criminal-legal sense, with important implications for their due process rights in removal proceedings.

37. The number of deportations from the United States does not necessarily reflect the number of people deported from the country; the same person may be deported multiple times (U.S. Department of Homeland Security 2020).

38. For a richer historical treatment of these developments, see Goodman 2015; Minian 2018; Ngai 2004.

39. The overall number of removals is from U.S. Department of Homeland Security 2020. The number of interior removals is from U.S. Immigration and Customs Enforcement 2020. The denominator is the size of the undocumented population in the United States in the respective year. In 2010, Passel and Cohn (2011) estimate that 11.4 million undocumented immigrants lived in the United States; the figure in 2017 was 10.5 million (Passel and Cohn 2019). I linearly interpolate the denominators for the years between 2010 and 2017. Absent information on the trend since 2017 at the time of this writing, I assume the 2018 denominator to equal the 2017 denominator.

40. According to Moinester 2019, between one-third and three-fifths of all interior removals between fiscal years 2003 and 2015 were of individuals who had previously been deported. Throughout this period, interior removals increasingly targeted noncitizens who had been deported previously; this rate was 30.3 percent in 2003 and 57.7 percent in 2015.

41. (Passel and Cohn 2019)

42. (De Genova 2002)

43. (Passel and Cohn 2019)

44. Human Rights Watch (2009) estimates that 20 percent of all immigrants deported between 1997 and 2007 were permanent residents.

45. All remaining figures in this paragraph come from USC Equity Research Institute's analysis of 2017 five-year American Community Survey microdata from IPUMS-USA on behalf of the author.

46. (Abrego 2019)

47. This figure doubles to forty million people and 12 percent of the population if we consider all noncitizens and their citizen family members.

48. Historian Torrie Hester (2015) uses the phrase "mass deportability" to describe the precarity faced by undocumented laborers.

49. (Golash-Boza and Hondagneu-Sotelo 2013; Passel and Cohn 2019)

50. All remaining figures in this paragraph come from USC Equity Research Institute's analysis of 2017 five-year American Community Survey microdata from IPUMS-USA on behalf of the author.

51. (Asad 2020a)

52. Coutin (2003) characterizes these contradictions as undocumented immigrants being physically present but legally absent.

53. The Immigration and Nationality Act makes no mention of "undocumented immigrants." Some people we understand as undocumented are either "inadmissible" or have "unlawful presence." The phrase "illegal alien" is used to describe a noncitizen who has been convicted of a felony.

54. (E.g., Bachmeier, Van Hook, and Bean 2014; Desai, Su, and Adelman 2020; Gonzalez and Patler 2021; Patler and Gonzalez 2020; Waters and Kasinitz 2015)

55. (Dominguez and Watkins 2003)

56. (Schmalzbauer 2014)

57. (Del Real 2019; Cervantes and Menjívar 2020)

58. (García 2019)

59. (E.g., Fong 2019; Hughes 2019, 2021)

60. (Menjívar, Gómez Cervantes, and Alvord 2018; Pickett 2016; Stumpf 2006)

61. For a detailed summary, see Abrego et al. 2017.

62. (Chávez 2013; Hirota 2016; Molina 2006)

63. (Armenta 2017; Provine et al. 2016)

64. (Marrow 2012; Marrow and Joseph 2015)

65. Quotation is from Cornelius, Chavez, and Castro 1982: 72. Writing in Southern California, Cornelius and his collaborators wrote that undocumented immigrants "dislike living in isolation here, wanting to go places and do many things, but [are] unable to because of the risk of apprehension and deportation" (Cornelius 1982: 399; Cornelius, Chavez, and Castro 1982, for a review). One additional report concluded that "99% of the undocumented parents of U.S. citizen children will not complete . . . applications [for public assistance] for their children because they fear detection and deportation" (Health Research Services and Analysis 1978: 399–400, cited in Cornelius, Chavez, and Castro 1982). Compare the quotation in the main text with findings from Menjívar and Abrego 2012, who offer a similar characterization as they outline the concept of legal violence.

66. (Perreira and Pedroza 2019)

67. (Armenta and Rosales 2019; Correia 2010; Menjívar et al. 2018; Nguyen and Gill 2016; Theodore and Habans 2016)

68. (Golash-Boza 2015b; Holmes 2013; Lopez 2019; Menjívar and Abrego 2012)

69. (Armenta and Sarabia 2020; Castañeda et al. 2015; Derose, Escarce, and Lurie 2007; Grace, Bais, and Roth 2018; Holmes 2006; Lopez et al. 2017; Marrow 2012; Marrow and Joseph 2015; Perreira and Pedroza 2019; Van Natta 2019)

70. (Menjívar and Abrego 2012: 1410)

71. For the original treatment of "master status" as a concept, see Hughes 1945. For an application of the concept to the situation of undocumented immigrants, see Gonzales 2015.

72. (Abarca and Coutin 2018: 12; Chauvin-Garcés-Mascareñas 2012)

73. (Abarca and Coutin 2018: 9; see also Coutin 2003; Coutin 1998)

74. (Horton and Heyman 2020)

75. (Coutin 1998, 2003; Galli 2020; Hagan 1994; Hallett 2014)

76. (Menjívar and Lakhani 2016)

77. (Chauvin and Garcés-Mascareñas 2014; Coutin 2003; Galli 2020; Hagan 1994; Lakhani 2013). Menjívar and Lakhani (2016: 1833) write: "While we focus on those immigrants who have lived in legal limbo in the United States but who have the opportunity to enter the legalization process, we would like to underscore that many immigrants in our studies could not realistically contemplate legalization. . . . Their situation poses a counterfactual to our argument, as these immigrants did not seem to alter their behaviors and practices in the ways we observed among those who began the legalization process. . . . Thus, the current immigration regime and its system of exclusionary practices that closes doors to [undocumented] immigrants . . . is sustained by those immigrants who do transform their lives in legally attractive ways."

78. In their respective books, both set in Southern California, sociologists Angela S. García and Greg Prieto show the different ways undocumented immigrants manage their relationship with local police as they go about daily life worried about the threat of deportation. For Prieto, deportation threat underlies his study of participants' engagement with social movements. He uses the concept of "instrumental activism" to show how activists in his study focused on "the prospect of achieving concrete and material improvements in [undocumented immigrants'] daily lives" to motivate their participation (pp. 108–9). For García, worries about policing as immigration enforcement produced her study participants' "legal passing," which she defines as "a strategic presentation of self to the outside world that takes on characteristics associated with mainstream, U.S.-born groups to mask unauthorized immigration status" (p. 134). García's focus is on the behavioral, material, and mental adaptations her study participants make—styling their hair in "American" ways, dressing in "American" ways, walking the "American" way (i.e., with confidence), and driving "American-looking" vehicles (i.e., well-kept cars)—to avert the gaze of local police as well as the consequences of these adaptations for undocumented immigrants' assimilation. Regarding recruitment from immigrant-serving nonprofits, Chauvin and Garcés-Mascareñas (2014: 425) write: "As studies on undocumented migrants tend to recruit informants through NGOs and support organizations, they run the risk of overemphasizing the peculiar situation of these not-yet-integrated newcomers who are more visible, more vulnerable and more in need of assistance."

79. (Horton and Heyman 2020; Menjívar and Lakhani 2016)

80. This is a typology, implying that immigration surveillance and everyday surveillance often interrelate in practice.

81. This definition groups García's (2019) "immigration" and "immigrant" policy typology because both sets of policies inform a broader web of immigration surveillance in how the undocumented immigrants I interviewed experience them.

82. To read the original policy, see Morton 2011. Although this policy has been in place since 2011, ICE has made numerous exceptions over the years. For one journalistic account, see Blitzer 2017.

83. (Tilly 1999)

84. (E.g., Wolff 2017). Massey (2007) shows how progress on one front of categorical inequality often comes at the expense of progress in another. Brubaker (2015) offers a rejoinder to Tilly, arguing that categorization need not imply inequality. He posits this is less likely among noncitizens, who face formal categorical exclusion (especially relative to increasingly informal categorical exclusions based on gender or race). Brubaker nonetheless urges analyses that identify the situational contexts in which categorical differences do and do not produce inequality. This book broadly aligns with that idea. Specifically, as I outline more fully in the conclusion, I offer legal status and parenthood as two overlapping and crosscutting categories that have complex associations with the production of inequality.

85. (Carré 2015; Lee 2018: 1627)

86. (Lee 2016; Reich 2012; Roberts 2009)

87. See Title 5, Subtitle B, Chapter 151 of Texas State Family Code: "Rights and Duties in Parent-Child Relationship."

88. (Altman, Heflin, Jun, and Bachmeier 2021; Iceland 2021)

89. (E.g., Berger Cardoso, Scott, Faulkner, and Lane 2018; Wildeman, Edwards, and Wakefield 2020). The cumulative risk of investigation, confirmed maltreatment, foster care placement, and termination of parental rights by Child Protective Services by age 18 in the 20 most populous U.S. counties is 34.5 percent, 9.1 percent, 3.5 percent, and 0.7 percent, respectively; in Dallas County, these risks for Latinos are about 30 percent, nine percent, three percent, and 0.5 percent (see Wildeman, Edwards, and Wakefield 2020: pp. 2–3).

90. (Lipsky 2010 [1980]; see also Brehm and Gates 1999)

91. (Chiarello 2013; Lara-Millán 2014; Watkins-Hayes 2009)

92. (Brayne 2020; Hull 2012; Lageson 2020)

93. (E.g., Abarca and Coutin 2018; Chauvin and Garcés-Mascareñas 2014; Kim 2019, 2022; Menjívar and Lakhani 2016)

94. (Armenta and Rosales 2019; Correia 2010; Menjívar et al. 2018; Nguyen and Gill 2016; Theodore and Habans 2016)

95. (Armenta and Sarabia 2020; Castañeda et al. 2015; Derose, Escarce, and Lurie 2007; Grace, Bais, and Roth 2018; Holmes 2006; Lopez et al. 2017; Marrow 2012; Marrow and Joseph 2015; Perreira and Pedroza 2019; Van Natta 2019)

96. (Alsan and Yang 2018; Bernstein et al. 2019; Dondero and Altman 2022; Espenshade, Baraka, and Huber 1997; Fix and Passel 1999; Hagan et al. 2003; Kaushal and Kaestner 2005; Lichter and Jayakody 2002; Singer 2004; Van Hook 2003; Watson 2010)

97. (Allen 2018; Allen and McNeely 2017; Ro, Bruckner, and Duquette-Rury 2020)

98. (Andrews 2017; Armenta and Rosales 2019; García 2019; Prieto 2018)

99. For a fuller discussion of this point, see Eagly 2020.

100. For a general overview of role conflict, see Stryker and Macke 1978.

101. For helpful explications and reviews of symbolic interactionist theory, see Fine 1993 and Stryer 2008.

102. (Mead 1934)

103. (Blumer 1986)

104. (Goffman 1959, 1963)

105. See, generally, Crenshaw 1990.

106. (Lamont 1992; Tilly 1999)

107. See also Enriquez 2017; Enriquez and Millán 2019; Valdez and Golash-Boza 2018.

108. (E.g., Brayne 2014; Goffman 2009; Haskins and Jacobsen 2017; Lanuza and Turney 2020)

109. See, generally, Becker 2008 [1963]; Lemert 1967.

110. For an early treatment of this idea, see Goffman 1963.

111. (E.g., Brayne 2014; Goffman 2009)

112. (Foucault 1901 [1977])

113. (E.g., Bruch, Ferree, and Soss 2010; Reich 2012; Roberts 2009; Soss 2005; Soss et al. 2011; Watkins-Hayes 2009)

114. (Edin and Lein 1997; Gilliom 2001; Gustafson 2011)

115. (Fong 2019)

116. (Hughes 2019, 2021).

117. (E.g., Gilliom 2001; Rosales 2020; Stuart 2016)

118. For an illustrative example, see Bryan 2022.

119. (Small 2009, 2013)

120. (Lamont and Swidler 2014)

121. This is common in ethnographic studies of respondents in privileged professional positions, including immigration officials. See Gilboy 1991.

122. As Lara-García (2022: 3) argues, "Migration scholars should endeavor to move past population criteria when selecting research sites and to study the full range of contexts where immigrants are settling." One way to do that, as Lara-García notes, is to study cities as contexts in their own right.

123. All figures in this paragraph come from USC Equity Research Institute's analysis of 2017 five-year American Community Survey microdata from IPUMS-USA on behalf of the author.

124. (Garip 2016; Massey, Durand, and Pren 2016)

125. (Chávez 2013)

126. (Massey, Durand, and Pren 2016)

127. (De Trinidad Young and Wallace 2019)

128. (Grissom 2015; Jacome 2018)

129. The City of Dallas established an Office of Welcoming Communities and Immigrant Affairs in March 2017. Part of a larger network of "Welcoming Cities" sponsored by the nonprofit Welcoming America (2021), the goal of this office is to "promote and advance the economic, civic and social engagement of immigrants and refugees residing in Dallas" (City of Dallas 2020). These efforts are ongoing but, as Wasem (2020) notes, even this progressive initiative can include dichotomies: local government is very supportive of these efforts, but Dallas scores at the bottom of indices that bear on the dynamics on display in this book as they relate to undocumented immigrants: livability measures (e.g., homeownership rate, overcrowded dwellings, rent burden, share of people with health insurance, and education levels), job opportunities (e.g., labor force participation rate, employment rate, and shares of people in high prestige occupations, part-time work, and self-employed). For a scholarly discussion of these and related initiatives, see De Graauw and Bloemraad 2017.

130. Political scientist Abigail Williamson writes that local contexts are immigrants' "most accessible experiences of the state." See Williamson 2018. See also Coleman 2007, 2012; Coleman and Kocher 2011, 2019.

Chapter 1: Deprivation and Deportability

1. (De Haas 2021; Schewel 2020)

2. (Borjas 1987; Chiquiar and Hanson 2005; Feliciano 2005; Massey et al. 1990; Massey and Espinosa 1997; Massey and Zenteno 1999; McKenzie and Rapoport 2010; Orrenius and Zavodny 2005)

3. Appendix B, table B.2.

4. For reviews, see Garip 2016; Massey et al. 1993.

5. (Harris and Todaro 1970; Sjaastad 1962)

6. (Stark and Bloom 1985; Taylor 1987)

7. (Massey 1990)

8. (FitzGerald and Arar 2018; Hernández León 1999)

9. To be sure, most immigrants (77 percent) live in the United States with authorization. But Mexicans and Central Americans are overrepresented among the undocumented population. See Passel and Cohn 2019.

10. In other work, I show this to be the case using large-scale survey data from the Mexican Migration Project. See Asad and Hwang 2019a, 2019b.

11. Appendix B, table B.3.

12. See also Le and Pastor 2022.

13. Recall bias is less likely in accounts of major life events such as international migration that occur infrequently and that stand out as an important aspect of a person's life story. On the general point, see Berney and Blane 1997.

14. For a helpful discussion, see Desmond and Western 2018. Matthew Desmond distinguishes deprivation from severe deprivation, with the latter defined as "economic hardship that is (1) acute, (2) compounded, and (3) persistent." (Desmond 2015)

15. There is a long body of work on "relative deprivation" or "the judgment that one or one's ingroup is disadvantaged compared to a relevant referent and that this judgment invokes feelings of anger, resentment, and entitlement." For a review, see Pettigrew 2015. For the original concept, see Stouffer et al. 1949. For extensions of the concept, see Merton 1957; Runciman 1966. In poverty studies, "absolute" deprivation describes individuals who cannot afford life's basics such as food, shelter, and clothing, whereas "relative" deprivation describes individuals who cannot afford what most others in their social context can. See Sen 1983; Townsend 1979, 1985. The concept has also been applied to the case of international migration, as in Stark and Taylor 1991. In all cases, relative deprivation implies a subjective evaluation of one's own position relative to someone else's. It need not be the case, then, that someone suffer from extreme poverty to be "deprived" of income or wealth. Rather, an individual might feel deprived by simply acknowledging that they lack something, seeing that others have it, and believing that they too can acquire it. De Haas (2021: 2) builds on this literature, specifically Sen's (1999) capabilities framework, to define human mobility "as people's capability (freedom) to choose where to live—including the option to stay—instead of a more or less automated, passive and 'cause-and-effect' response to a set of

static push and pull factors." This definition is compatible with that presented in this chapter, with study participants all turning to international migration as a response to their perceived material, social, or psychological deprivation.

16. (Stark and Taylor 1991; Stark, Taylor, and Yitzhaki 1988)

17. Wage differentials: (Harris and Todaro 1970; Sjaastad 1962). Wealth: (Stark and Bloom 1985; Taylor 1987). Interdependence: (Castells and Laserna 1989; Sassen 1988, 2013). Colonialism: (Dunbar-Ortiz 2021). History of U.S. immigration: (Massey 1990). These theories are not mutually exclusive and should be interpreted as complementary, see Garip 2012, 2016.

18. (Asad and Garip 2019; Garip and Asad 2016)

19. Mexico experienced three *peso* devaluations in quick succession, in 1976, 1982, and 1985.

20. A robust, interdisciplinary literature traces the roots of this lost sense of safety in El Salvador, Guatemala, and Honduras to the imperial or colonial interventions of Western powers—including the United States. For reviews, see Dunbar-Ortiz 2021; Massey and Pren 2012; Massey and Riosmena 2010. Among Mexican study participants, similar motivations appeared not as reasons for migration but as reasons for settlement in the United States.

21. For reviews, see Kalleberg and Sorensen 1979; Rogerson, Shimer, and Wright 2005.

22. (Spring et al. 2017)

23. (Bruch and Mare 2006; Charles 2003; Harvey et al. 2020; Rosen 2017)

24. Formally, the 1965 Immigration and Nationality Act created a seven-category preference system, which includes (1) the unmarried adult children of U.S. citizens, (2) the spouses and (unmarried) children of permanent residents, (3) professionals and scientists and artists of exceptional ability, (4) the married children of U.S. citizens, (5) the siblings of U.S. citizens age twenty-one and older, (6) workers in occupations for which there is insufficient labor supply, and (7) refugees.

25. There is also a fourth category of immigrant visas, known as the diversity visa, though people from Mexico and Central American countries are ineligible for it. See the book's conclusion for a fuller discussion of the diversity visa.

26. (U.S. Department of State 2021a)

27. On employment visas, see Rissing and Castilla 2014. On family reunification visas, see Jasso and Rosenzweig 1986; Massey and Malone 2002.

28. 101(a)(42) of the Immigration and Nationality Act (INA).

29. A key difference between refugees and a similar group—asylees—is the nature and location of their application process. Refugees' applications are *affirmative*, meaning that they apply before arriving to the United States; asylees' applications are *defensive*, meaning that they apply after arriving to the United States and face removal if their application is unsuccessful. Whereas there are limits to the number of refugees resettled in the United States each year, there is no similar limit for asylees. See FitzGerald 2019; FitzGerald and Arar 2018.

30. In the United States, a person seeking refuge or asylum because of gang violence must still prove a "well-founded fear" of persecution based on political opinion, race, religion, nationality, or another protected social group.

31. As of this writing, thirty-nine countries participate in the Visa Waiver Program, which allows them to travel to the United States for business or tourism for stays of up to ninety days without a visa. Only one of these countries, Chile, is in Latin America.

32. Author's tabulation of 2019 Encuesta Nacional sobre Disponibilidad y Uso de Tecnologías de la Información en los Hogares. In Mexico, access to information technology is unequal by age, educational attainment, income, occupation, and geography, among other factors. See Martínez Domínguez 2018.

33. Author's tabulation of 2019 American Community Survey (five-year estimates). As in Mexico, access to information technology in the United States is also unequal by age, educational attainment, income, occupation, and geography, among other factors. See Talukdar and Gauri 2011.

34. (U.S. Department of State 2021b)

35. (U.S. Department of State 2021c)

36. (E.g., Kim 2018)

37. This is a common idea among undocumented immigrants. See Ryo 2013, 2015, 2021.

38. Access to these resources is itself a reflection of the history of immigration between Mexico and Central America and the United States. See Asad and Hwang 2019a, 2019b; Garip 2016; Massey, Durand, and Malone 2002.

39. On this general point, see Small 2013.

40. (Weil 2012)

41. See the Immigration and Nationality Act of 1952 (Public Law 82–414). Today, the requirements governing citizenship acquisition for someone born outside the United States to one citizen parent require five years of physical presence preceding the child's birth, with at least two of those five years occurring after the parent's fourteenth birthday (8 USC § 1401). For a careful analysis of birthright citizenship, see Chavez 2020.

42. Legalization petitions at the time would not be approved if the sponsor died before the petition had been accepted. See Chavez 2020.

43. (Donato, Durand, and Massey 1992; Garip 2016; Hagan 1998; Massey and Espinosa 1997)

44. (Cornelius 2001; Martínez et al. 2014; Soto and Martínez 2018)

45. Recent scholarship shows that undocumented immigrants from Mexico experience surveillance at the United States' southern border as "normal," evincing a sophisticated understanding about U.S. Border Patrol surveillance and technology use. See Newell, Gomez, and Guajardo 2017.

46. Average costs for *coyotes* (in 2013 dollars) have increased steadily from about $500 in 1990 to almost $3,000 in 2010. See Massey, Durand, and Pren 2016.

47. (Ryo 2021)

48. (Massey, Durand, and Malone 2002; Massey, Durand, and Pren 2014, 2016; Massey and Pren 2012)

49. (Massey, Durand, and Malone 2002; Massey, Durand, and Pren 2016). After 1986, most Mexican migrants who attempted to enter the United States without authorization made it in eventually. See Donato, Wagner, and Patterson 2008.

50. Congress had authorized a 50 percent increase in the budget for enforcement operations at the border in 1986, and, in 1990, Congress passed additional laws that authorized the hiring of a thousand more federal immigration officers to patrol the border. See Massey, Durand, and Pren 2016; Massey and Pren 2012.

51. According to analyses from the Mexican Migration Project (MMP), the probability that an undocumented immigrant from Mexico would be apprehended on their journey to the United States fluctuated across time, ranging from a high of about 0.40 in 1965 to a low of about 0.02 in 2013. Most people in the study entered the

United States during a time when the probability of capture hovered around 0.30, meaning that, on average, three out of every ten undocumented immigrants from Mexico would be captured on their way in—and seven out of ten would not be.

52. (Massey, Durand, and Pren 2016; Massey and Pren 2012)

53. Massey and colleagues estimate that the probability that an immigrant from Mexico crosses into the United States with a *coyote* on an unauthorized trip since the late 1990s is over 0.90 and, in 2010, was 1.00. See Massey, Durand, and Pren 2016.

54. Following the September 11 attacks, the Department of Homeland Security (DHS) was created. Immigration and Naturalization Services (INS), previously managed by the U.S. Department of Justice, was dissolved. The DHS began managing the immigration system, and U.S. Citizenship and Immigration Services, U.S. Customs and Border Protection, and U.S. Immigration and Customs Enforcement were created to take over INS' functions. For a full review, see Donato and Armenta 2011.

55. This strategy is likely less feasible for more recent entrants to the United States. In 2005, the Border Protection, Antiterrorism, and Illegal Immigration Control Act instituted a timeline for making the United States Visitor and Immigrant Status Indicator Technology (US-VISIT) available at ports of entry. This system, managed by U.S. Customs and Border Protection, collected and analyzed immigrants' biometric data. In 2009, most noncitizens became subject to US-VISIT requirements. In 2013, and excepting specific aspects of the system, US-VISIT became the Office of Biometric Identity Management. For a detailed overview of these myriad changes, see Kalhan 2014.

56. (Donato, Wagner, and Patterson 2008)

57. (Massey and Pren 2012)

58. On the prevalence of visa overstays, see Warren and Kerwin 2017. The 1996 Illegal Immigration Reform and Immigrant Responsibility Act authorized the federal government to create an automated system to record visa recipients' entries to, and departures from, U.S. ports of entry. Several laws since then—including the 2002 Enhanced Border Security and Visa Entry Reform Act and the Intelligence Reform and Terrorism Prevention Act of 2004—authorized U.S. Customs and Border Protection (CBP) to collect biometric data, which it has done on visa entrants since 2004. In 2013, CBP has sought to integrate biometrics to verify travelers' departure from the country. In 2018, this program formally launched as the Traveler Verification Service. See Kalhan 2014.

59. (Border Angels n.d.; U.S. Customs and Border Protection 2019). See also De León 2015; Hernández 2010.

60. For a comprehensive review and analysis, see Garip 2016; Massey et al. 1993; Massey and Espinosa 1997.

61. (Harris and Todaro 1970; Massey 1990; Sjaastad 1962; Stark and Bloom 1985; Stark and Levhari 1982; Stark and Taylor 1991)

62. (Chiquiar and Hanson 2005; Feliciano 2005; Hanson 2006; McKenzie and Rapoport 2010; Orrenius and Zavodny 2005; Palloni et al. 2001)

63. (Fussell and Massey 2004; Massey 1990)

64. (Asad and Hwang 2019a, 2019b; Faist 2016)

65. (Garip 2016; Massey et al. 1993; Massey and Espinosa 1997)

66. (Asad and Hwang 2019a, 2019b; Faist 2016)

Chapter 2: Deportable but Moral Immigrants

1. Flores and Schachter (2018) develop the concept of "social illegality" to refer to how people rely on shared stereotypes to assign "illegality" to certain bodies—usually, but not exclusively, Latinos. National origin is an important component of social illegality, with Mexicans viewed as highly suspect among the White American study participants completing Flores and Schachter's survey, as are other nationalities in Latin America.

2. Flores and Azar (Forthcoming) identify "perceived immigrant composition" as one factor that shapes attitudes toward immigration generally, and toward immigrants specifically. Perceived immigrant composition describes individual assessments of who makes up the immigrant population, assessments that are deeply subjective. Using Latent Class Analysis, Flores and Azar find five main immigrant archetypes in how White Americans imagine who makes up the immigrant population: 1) the high-status Asian or European worker; 2) the poor, non-White immigrant with an undefined national origin; 3) the rainbow undocumented immigrant who is poor, non-White, and undocumented but from all over the world; 4) the upwardly mobile Latina, who is poor, doesn't speak English, and holds a low-status job but who is highly educated and immigrates with her family; 5) the undocumented Latino man, who is poor, uneducated, employed in a low-status job, and from Mexico, Central America, or South America.

3. (Garip 2016)

4. Goffman (2009) posited in her study of Black men "on the run" from the police in one Philadelphia neighborhood was comparable to the situation of undocumented immigrants, imagining them to share a similar desire to "dodge" the police gaze. Waters and Kasinitz (2015) find this framework compelling in the context of undocumented immigrants as well, outlining how undocumented immigrants and Black men wanted by the police face similar forms of legal exclusion in the contemporary United States. Additional immigration scholars have either relied on this same theoretical framework or invoked similar ideas of being on the lam (e.g., Bernstein et al. 2019; Cheong 2021; Desai, Su, and Adelman 2020; Maggio 2021; Núñez and Heyman 2007; Patler and Gonzalez 2020). These studies, like this one, are set in a given time and place and describe some of the effects of a particular set of laws and policies that govern daily life in that moment or in that setting (Coleman 2007, 2012; Coleman and Kocher 2011, 2019).

5. (Flores and Schachter 2018; Massey 2007)

6. Andrews 2017; Armenta and Rosales 2019; García 2019; and Prieto 2018 find similar evidence of this internalization process in their respective studies of undocumented immigrants in several locales in California and Pennsylvania. The moral boundaries the undocumented immigrants in their studies draw tend to center on individual behavior in relation to one regulatory institution—policing. Here, I consider the importance of these moral boundaries across several regulatory institutions.

7. See Garland 2012a, 2018 for an extensive historical discussion of how Western market societies came to relate punishment and welfare in their regulation of subordinated populations. For subordinated populations facing correlated legal, material, and social hardships, regulatory institutions related to policing (Bell 2017; Fine, Padilla, and Tom 2020; Stewart et al. 2009) and taxation and employment (Brown 2007; Gustafson 2011) undergird many of the market-based logics giving rise to the forms of social control they experience.

8. Both occasions were as I drove northwest of downtown, along I-35E, which is in the direction of the ICE Field Office in Dallas. This office sits just about a mile away from the Consulate of Mexico.

9. (Golash-Boza 2015b; Lopez 2019; Romero 2008)

10. An interdisciplinary scholarship has considered undocumented immigrants' bureaucratic incorporation (e.g., Jones-Correa 2005; Lewis and Ramakrishnan 2007; Marrow 2009, 2011; Menjívar et al. 2018). I follow this scholarship but focus on not just the fact of these immigrants' incorporation but also what this incorporation means to them in light of ongoing dynamics of immigration and everyday surveillance.

11. Even though undocumented immigrants are statistically more likely than permanent residents to be deported, these groups express fears of deportation at similar rates (Asad 2020a).

12. (Armenta 2017; Provine et al. 2016; Theodore and Habans 2016)

13. (ACLU 2019)

14. For a rich discussion of the relationship between immigration officers and subnational police, see Armenta 2017; Jain 2019.

15. (Michaud 2010)

16. (Menjívar and Kanstroom 2013)

17. According to the Immigrant Legal Resource Center (2019), "100% of Texas' current 287(g) contracts have begun since Donald Trump was elected." For greater legal and policy context about 287(g) agreements, see Menjívar and Kanstroom 2013. For additional information about which counties or police departments sought a 287(g) agreement but where one was never formalized, see Pedroza 2019.

18. See ICE's listing of 287(g) communities between 2009 and 2017, as detailed in their reply to FOIA 2017-ICFO-33429 (n.d.).

19. (Cantor, Noferi, and Martinez 2015; Macías-Rojas 2016; Moinester 2019)

20. (Cantor, Noferi, and Martinez 2015; Gardner and Kohli 2009)

21. (Cantor, Noferi, and Martinez 2015)

22. Enforcement priorities under the Priority Enforcement Program ostensibly focus on immigrants with criminal—not civil—convictions. Priority 1 includes noncitizens deemed threats to national security, apprehended as they cross the border, identified as gang affiliated, or convicted of a criminal or aggravated felony. Priority 2 includes noncitizens convicted of three or more misdemeanors, convicted of a "serious" misdemeanor such as domestic violence, those who entered without authorization after July 1, 2014, or those who "abused" visa privileges. Priority 3 includes noncitizens with an outstanding deportation order issued on or after January 1, 2014.

23. The Immigration and Nationality Act designates certain crimes as "aggravated felonies." See INA § 101(a)(43), 8 USC § 1101(a)(43).

24. Fine (1997) called this change a "miscarriage of justice" in advocating for the reinstatement of judicial recommendations against deportation.

25. As legal scholar Nancy Morawetz (2000: 1944) summarizes, "It is now more likely than ever that a person convicted of a crime will serve a prison sentence, and that sentence will probably be longer than sentences have been in the past. To the extent that the immigration law bases its assessment of the seriousness of the crime on the length of the [criminal] sentence, it is simply more likely that the same crime committed today will carry a sentence that meets . . . requirements for deportability and exclusion from relief."

26. (Kalhan 2014)

27. (Michaud 2010; Santos et al. 2017; Torche and Sirois 2018)

28. (Ewick and Silbey 1998; Scott 2008)

29. (Ewick and Silbey 1998)

30. This "Morton Memo" did not reduce the deportation rate, but, over time, the rate of deportations of people with little or no criminal history fell more quickly than the rate of people with serious convictions (Hausman 2022).

31. (Hausman 2022)

32. As this book went to press, two lawsuits in the federal circuit courts reached opposing conclusions about the legality of the Biden administration's enforcement priorities. The Department of Justice is continuing litigation in defense of the enforcement priorities, but the Supreme Court ruled in July 2022 that the priorities cannot be implemented while litigation is pending. The Supreme Court will hear arguments about the legality of the enforcement priorities in December 2022. Some legal scholars see the outcome of this litigation as beside the point. As Shalini Bhargava Ray (2022) writes: "Selective or partial immigration enforcement is inevitable in the U.S., given its vast deportable population and limited resources for enforcement (however staggering in absolute terms)."

33. (Hausman 2020). For more information on the history, content, and effects of sanctuary policies, see Ascherio 2022; Fox n.d.; Gulasekaram and Villazor 2009; Lasch et al. 2018; Martínez-Schuldt and Martínez 2019, 2021; Ortiz et al. 2021.

34. Study participants sometimes mentioned other forms of caution as well, including having a licensed driver shuttle them to and from work or, if they had to drive, taking side roads early in the day or after evening rush hour when they believed the police might be less active or visible. Though important, these forms of caution are more exceptional than those cataloged in the main text of the book.

35. (Clair 2020; Small 2014)

36. But see Sanchez et al. (2022) for a discussion of how other financial penalties exploit undocumented immigrants who are jailed and seeking to avoid immigration detention.

37. (City of Dallas n.d.)

38. Individuals eligible for employment include U.S. citizens and permanent residents or, absent these statuses, holders of visas or other permits that authorize the individual to work. Establishing eligibility occurs via Form I-9 ("Employment Eligibility Verification"), which all employers must use during the hiring process.

39. (Fox 2022)

40. (Fussell 2011; Golash-Boza 2015a)

41. For example, Jacqueline Hagan (1994, 1998) finds in her study of a Maya community in Houston that women who worked under the table (e.g., as house cleaners or nannies) had a harder time than men who worked in more public spheres (e.g., construction sites) documenting how long they had lived in the United States.

42. An employer who "knowingly" hires an undocumented immigrant may face legal or financial sanctions; repeated infractions may result in prison time of up to six months. On the symbolism of employer sanctions, see Wishnie 2007.

43. (National Conference of State Legislatures 2015)

44. George W. Bush's presidential administration aggressively prosecuted undocumented immigrants for using *papeles chuecos*, until the Supreme Court ruled in

Flores-Figueroa v. United States that such prosecutions needed to demonstrate that the individual in question intended to defraud a specific individual (rather than just use any old number to work).

45. (Goss et al. 2013)

46. (Goss et al. 2013)

47. See T.D. 8671, 1996–1 C.B.314, which notes: "The Social Security Administration generally limits its assignment of social security numbers to individuals who are U.S. citizens and alien individuals legally admitted to the United States for permanent residence or under other immigration categories which authorize U.S. employment. Therefore, this change is designed to help taxpayers (who need a TIN but cannot qualify for a social security number) maintain compliance with TIN requirements under the Code and regulations."

48. Evidence might include a non-U.S. passport or at least two other identification documents, with at least one that contains a photograph, along with the ITIN application. These other documents include a national identification card, a U.S. driver's license, a foreign driver's license, a foreign voter's registration card, a foreign military identification card, or a visa.

49. (U.S. Office of General Accountability 2020). The GAO generally believes this to be a lower-bound estimate.

50. (Somashekhar 2022)

51. (Internal Revenu Service 2014)

52. (American Immigration Council 2021a)

53. The quotation about immigration law's complexity comes from Hull 1985. The TurboTax quotation is reported in American Bar Association 2017.

54. (Passel and Cohn 2016)

55. (Valverde 2019)

56. The firing of undocumented workers following I-9 audits is known as a "silent raid" (Preston 2010 and Jordan 2011, as cited in Valverde 2019).

57. (National Immigration Law Center 2020; U.S. Immigration and Customs Enforcement 2018)

58. (Kerwin and Warren 2020)

59. (Mayorkas 2021a)

60. (Internal Revenue Service 2021)

61. (Lockhart III 2006)

62. (Horton 2016)

63. On penalties regarding social security fraud, see 42 U.S.C. 408 §208(a).

64. (Tyler 2017; Tyler 2021; Tyler and Huo 2002; but see Nagin and Telep 2017)

65. (Bell 2016; Carr, Napolitano, and Keating 2007; Kirk and Matsuda 2011; Sampson and Bartusch 1998)

66. (Andrews 2017; Armenta 2017; Armenta and Rosales 2019; García 2019; Prieto 2018)

67. (Bell 2016)

68. See also Clair (2020), who finds that disadvantaged criminal defendants who mistrust their lawyers nevertheless retain a faith in legal tools and procedures.

69. For exceptions, see Ryo 2013, 2015, 2021.

70. (Williamson 2017: xi)

71. This dynamic may also help explain why many undocumented immigrants seeking immigration legal services report scams to the Federal Trade Commission (Pedroza 2022).

72. (Becker 2008 [1963]; Bernburg 2019; Lemert 1967; Pager 2008)

73. (Brayne 2014; Goffman 2009)

74. (Chua and Engel 2019)

75. (Ewick and Silbey 1998)

76. (Ewick and Silbey 1998: 136)

Chapter 3: Good Immigrants, or Good Parents?

1. For a general overview of the research on the effects of these correlated hardships on immigrant families, see Dreby 2012, 2015; Enriquez 2015; Lopez 2019; Mathema 2017; Menjívar, Abrego, and Schmalzbauer 2016; Rodriguez and Hagan 2004; Schmalzbauer 2014.

2. For two earlier treatments of the unique tensions undocumented parents face raising citizen children, see Bean, Brown, and Bachmeier 2015; Yoshikawa 2011. Bean et al. focus on schooling, and Yoshikawa focuses on public assistance such as food assistance and childcare. Both books are based on data collected during the proliferation of interior immigration enforcement through the first decade of the 2000s, which precedes formal efforts by the federal government to prioritize interior enforcement.

3. (Asad and Clair 2018; Perreira and Pedroza 2019)

4. Sociologist Kelley Fong (2017, 2019, 2020) observes a similar dynamic in her research on low-income mothers worried about Child Protective Services. Sociologist Cayce Hughes (2019, 2021) likewise shows how low-income Black mothers encounter undue scrutiny from authorities in service institutions.

5. Sociologist Spencer Headworth's (2020, 2021) research draws on the perspectives of welfare fraud investigators to offer a powerful illustration of the effects of this racialized and classed scrutiny.

6. (Edwards 2016, 2019; Edwards, Wakefield, Healy, and Wildeman 2021; Fong 2017, 2019, 2020)

7. To classify whether study families lived in poverty, I used the 2015 Poverty Guidelines from the U.S. Department of Health and Human Services (HHS). In contrast to poverty thresholds, which are often used for statistical purposes by the U.S. Census Bureau, HHS uses poverty guidelines for administrative purposes such as determining eligibility for federally funded public assistance. In 2015, a single-person household is classified as living in poverty if they earned $11,770 or less each year. Adding $4,160 for each additional person in the household gives the poverty guideline for additional household sizes. See U.S. Department of Health and Human Services 2015.

8. (Fussell 2011; Hall, Greenman, and Farkas 2010; Kossoudji and Cobb-Clark 2002)

9. (Chávez and Altman 2017; Hall and Greenman 2015; Orrenius and Zavodny 2009)

10. (Gleeson 2010, 2012, 2016; Griffith 2009)

11. This perspective is most aligned with the "spatial assimilation" model, which views material resources as the primary constraint to individuals' mobility (Logan and Alba 1993; Massey 1988; Massey and Denton 1993; Massey and Denton 1985; Massey and Mullan 1984).

12. (Gleeson 2010, 2012; Gleeson and Gonzales 2012; Gleeson 2016; Griffith 2009; Kreisberg 2022)

13. (Bean, Leach, and Lowell 2004; Hall, Greenman, and Yi 2019; Hudson 2007; c.f. Hagan, Lowe, and Quingla 2011)

14. (Fussell 2011; Hall, Greenman, and Farkas 2010; Kossoudji and Cobb-Clark 2002)

15. (Golash-Boza 2015a; Gomberg-Muñoz and Nussbaum-Barberena 2011; Menjívar 2011)

16. (U.S. Immigration and Customs Enforcement 2018; Griffith and Gleeson 2019; Mayorkas 2021b; Marienbach and Wroe 2017)

17. All statistics in this paragraph come from Migration Policy Institute (2018).

18. In segmented labor markets theory (Piore 1980), undocumented immigrants occupy low-status and low-wage jobs that native-born workers find undesirable.

19. This dynamic of a promotion without an accompanying raise is common in industries with high shares of low-wage workers. See Wilmers and Kimball 2021.

20. (Gonzales, Terriquez, and Ruszczyk 2014)

21. For a comprehensive review, see Becker 2009. Gowayed (2022) argues that human capital, and the extent to which an immigrant can leverage theirs for material gain, depends on the laws and policies of the destination country.

22. It is possible that Javier was not eligible for IRCA, whose amnesty provision covered immigrants in the country without authorization prior to January 1, 1982. But, as Hagan (1994) has shown, men sometimes could access this opportunity with the help of their employers in a way that women could not.

23. See also García, Diaz-Strong, and Rodriguez-Rodriguez 2022.

24. (Altman et al. 2021; Iceland 2021)

25. The Immigration Act of 1882 was the first to use the phrase "public charge." On the history of the public charge rule, and the idea of immigrants as dependent on government funds, see Hirota 2016; Molina 2006.

26. (Hirota 2016; Molina 2006)

27. (Fox 2016)

28. (Fox 2016: 1059)

29. (Cornelius, Chavez, and Castro 1982; Cornelius 1982, 1986)

30. Capps, Gelatt, and Greenberg (2020) suggest that, given their already limited eligibility for these services under federal law, the rule change would have affected about 167,000 noncitizens—about 1 percent of the noncitizen population.

31. Research suggests that the fear and uncertainty surrounding the proposed changes to the public charge rule had a substantial impact despite its limited reach and short-lived implementation. One of every seven immigrants who heard about the proposed rule change said they would minimize their engagement with institutions that offer public assistance; this rate was one in three among undocumented adults, and one in nine among permanent residents (Bernstein et al. 2019).

32. (Fox 2016)

33. (Fox 2016)

34. (Gonzales 2015)

35. (Pindus et al. 1998; Capps et al. 2001)

36. For a comprehensive database on the different laws and policies to which immigrants are subject across states nationwide, see Koball, Stinson, and Martinez 2021.

37. USC Equity Research Institute analysis of 2017 five-year American Community Survey (ACS) microdata from IPUMS-USA, or author's tabulations of the same.

38. Ibid. Among Latinos, five million U.S.-citizen children nationwide, 969,000 in Texas, and 161,000 in Dallas County live with an undocumented parent.

39. (Asad and Clair 2018; Bean, Brown, and Bachmeier 2015; Perreira and Pedroza 2019; Van Hook and Balistreri 2006; Yoshikawa 2011)

40. (Dreby 2012, 2015)

41. (Edwards 2016; Fong 2017, 2019; Garland 2018; Hughes 2019, 2021)

42. (Capps et al. 2001; Gelatt and Koball 2014)

43. Such fears may be especially palpable in states like Texas, where state authorities contract with community-based organizations to facilitate applications to public assistance (Gelatt and Koball 2014). No study participant mentioned this dynamic throughout our interviews, and studies of the effects of this collaboration suggest that it is beneficial for improving undocumented immigrants' access to service institutions (Yoshikawa et al. 2014).

44. (Amuedo-Dorantes and Arenas-Arroyo 2018; Dettlaff, Earner, and Phillips 2009; Hall, Musick, and Yi 2019; Hong and Torrey 2019)

45. (Jain 2019)

46. (Hausman 2022)

47. (White House 2014)

48. (Cházaro 2016; Clair 2020; Enns et al. 2019; Hausman 2022)

49. (American Immigration Council 2021b)

50. (Masferrer, Hamilton, and Denier 2019)

51. (Family 2016)

52. (Kanstroom 2007)

53. (Kanstroom 2007)

54. (Family 2016)

55. (Family 2016)

56. (Family 2016)

57. (Kanstroom 2007)

58. Formally, this form of cancellation of removal is for "non-permanent residents," a category that includes undocumented immigrants and visa holders.

59. (Immigrant Legal Resource Center 2018)

60. (Lapp 2012)

61. (Family 2016)

62. (Executive Office for Immigration Review 2015)

63. (Family 2016)

64. (Immigrant Legal Resource Center 2020b)

65. (Immigrant Legal Resource Center 2018)

66. (Immigrant Legal Resource Center 2018)

67. (Gonzales 2015: 15). Gonzales's study tracks undocumented young adults through various educational and developmental transitions, including as they discover their legal status, "learn to be illegal," make decisions about their educational trajectories (i.e., stopping out before or after completing high school, or going on to college or more), and, regardless of educational attainment, as they enter the low-wage labor market. See also Dreby 2015; Massey 2007; Menjívar and Abrego 2012.

68. (Enriquez 2017; Enriquez and Millán 2019; Valdez and Golash-Boza 2018; c.f., Gonzales and Burciaga 2018). To be sure, Gonzales and Burciaga (2018: 182) note that these perspectives need not be in tension. As they write, undocumented immigrants "have many other traits that shape who they are and that either constrain or open up possibilities in their everyday lives. These may be other traits or statuses that are otherwise dominant but, in most situations, become subordinate to their undocumented status." In this way, Gonzales and Burciaga also point to the importance of situational context.

69. For examples or full reviews, see Asad and Clair 2018; Castañeda et al. 2015; Perreira and Pedroza 2019; Street, Jones-Correa, and Zepeda-Millán 2017; Vernice et al. 2020; Viladrich 2012.

70. (Alsan and Yang 2018; Cervantes and Menjívar 2020; Cornelius, Chavez, and Castro 1982; Cornelius 1986; Dee and Murphy 2018; Fix and Passel 1999; Friedman and Venkataramani 2021; Hagan et al. 2003; Huang, Kaushal, and Wang 2020; Kaushal and Kaestner 2005; Kirksey and Sattin-Bajaj 2021; Menjívar and Abrego 2012; Menjívar, Abrego, and Schmalzbauer 2016; Singer 2004; Van Hook 2003; Van Hook and Balistreri 2006; Van Hook, Glick, and Bean 1999; Vargas 2015; Vargas and Pirog 2016; Watson 2010)

71. (Bernstein et al. 2019; Gemmill et al. 2019; Samari et al. 2020; Torche and Sirois 2018)

72. (Allen and McNeely 2017; Allen 2018; Armenta and Rosales 2019; Armenta and Sarabia 2020; Bruhn 2022; Crookes, Stanhope, Kim, Lummus, and Suglia 2022; Crookes, Stanhope, and Suglia 2022; Cuevas 2021; De Trinidad Young and Wallace 2019; Dondero and Altman 2022; Hamilton, Hale, and Savinar 2019; Hamilton, Patler, and Hale 2019; Jiménez et al. 2021; McCann and Jones-Correa 2020; Ruszczyk 2021; White 2014)

73. (Foucault 2007 [1977]: p. 23, 215). See also Foucault 1991 [1978]. For a review, see Lyon 2007; Rose, O'Malley, and Valverde 2006. See also: Garland 2012a, 2012b; Giddens 2013 [1990].

74. (e.g., Brayne 2014; Goffman 2009)

75. (Foucault 1991 [1977]: p. 23)

76. (Foucault 1991 [1977]: p. 180)

77. (Lyon 2003; Garland 2012a, 2018)

78. But see Parreñas 2021 for an example of "pastoral empowerment."

79. (Clair 2020: 77; 2021)

80. (Milovanovic 1988)

81. (Chauvin and Garcés-Mascareñas 2012: 254)

82. (Abarca and Coutin 2018)

Chapter 4: Surveillance and Societal Membership

1. (Varsanyi 2007)

2. (Lewis and Ramakrishnan 2007; Menjívar 2020; see De Graauw 2014 for a related discussion on municipal identification cards)

3. As explained later in the chapter, Maite remains in removal proceedings at the time of this writing. I, therefore, omit some details to maintain her confidentiality.

4. Formally, an immigration judge "reserved" the final decision on David's case. Section 240A(e)(1) of the Immigration and Nationality Act specifies that not more than 4,000 cancellation petitions can be approved in any fiscal year.

5. See O'Leary 2012 for the procedures that immigration judges follow for handling cancellation of removal petitions when the cap has been reached in a fiscal year.

6. As legal scholar Daniel Kanstroom (2007) shows, this duality likely extends farther back in time, too.

7. (See, e.g., De Trinidad Young and Wallace 2019; Varsanyi et al. 2012)

8. (Jones-Correa and de Graauw 2013; McCann and Jones-Correa 2020)

9. Some petitions can be either affirmative or defensive. Asylum, for example, can be either affirmative (when someone applies to USCIS within a year of their arrival) or defensive (when someone is placed in removal proceedings upon their arrival and applies).

10. (U.S. Citizenship and Immigration Services 2019: 15)

11. (U.S. Citizenship and Immigration Services 2019: 15)

12. (González-Barrera, Krogstad, and Noe-Bustamante 2020)

13. (U.S. Citizenship and Immigration Services n.d.)

14. (Obinna 2020)

15. (Berger 2009; Lakhani 2013; Menjívar and Lakhani 2016)

16. A nonimmigrant visa is also available for survivors of domestic abuse perpetrated by a U.S. citizen or permanent resident parent, partner, or child. This is an important form of relief available to some undocumented immigrants via the Violence Against Women Act and may eventually result in permanent residence (see Berger 2009). No one I interviewed mentioned this possibility as available to them.

17. As Menjívar and Lakhani (2016: 1821) note, "The great majority of undocumented immigrants in the United States simply have no recourse for legalization."

18. (Rissing and Castilla 2014)

19. Eighty-two percent of undocumented immigrants aged fifteen and older in the United States have never been married, are married to a noncitizen who is not a permanent resident, or are divorced, separated, or widowed. And 67 percent of undocumented immigrants either do not have children or have only a noncitizen child. All tabulations come from the Migration Policy Institute (2018).

20. Seventy-eight percent of undocumented immigrants have lived in the United States for at least five years, and 62 percent have done so for at least ten years (Migration Policy Institute 2018).

21. (Migration Policy Institute 2018)

22. (Kandel 2018: 10)

23. (Menjívar 2006)

24. (Abrego and Lakhani 2015; Chacón 2014)

25. (Zong et al. 2017)

26. See U.S. Department of State (n.d.) for a stylized summary of this process.

27. https://www.uscis.gov/sites/default/files/document/forms/i-485.pdf.

28. https://www.uscis.gov/i-693.

29. Form I-601 is formally titled "Application for Waiver of Grounds of Inadmissibility." Form I-212 is formally titled "I-212, Application for Permission to Reapply for Admission into the United States After Deportation or Removal."

30. Other fees are possible too. For I-485, applicants between the ages of fourteen and seventy-eight must pay an additional $85 fee for biometric services. For I-864, applicants for consular processing must pay an additional fee.

31. About 45 percent of immediate relatives of U.S. citizens approved for a green card in fiscal year 2016 adjusted to permanent resident status from inside the United States; the remainder did so after first leaving the country (Kandel 2018).

32. Section 320 of the Immigration and Nationality Act provides that a child born outside the United States will automatically become a U.S. citizen after birth if the person is a child of a U.S. citizen (by birth or naturalization); the child is under age eighteen, the child is a permanent resident; and the child resides in the legal and physical custody of the citizen parent.

33. See Kandel 2018 for a helpful explanation.

34. (Gomberg-Muñoz 2015, 2016)

35. (Gomberg-Muñoz 2015)

36. (Asad 2020b)

37. (Asad 2020a)

38. (Burciaga and Malone 2021; Patler et al. 2019)

39. All details in this paragraph from U.S. Citizenship and Immigration Services 2021.

40. See Immigrant Legal Resource Center 2012 for a simple discussion of what constitutes a "significant" criminal record.

41. (Gonzales, Terriquez, and Ruszczyk 2014)

42. (Lamont, Park, and Ayala-Hurtado 2017; Ogan et al. 2018; Winders 2016)

43. (Trump 2015)

44. (Burciaga and Malone 2021; Patler et al. 2019; Patler and Pirtle 2018)

45. (Jordan 2021; Liptak and Shear 2020; Shear and Davis 2017)

46. (Hausman 2022)

47. In general, see U.S. Citizenship and Immigration Services 2011. The Trump administration expanded these conditions, and the Biden administrated reverted to 2011 guidance set by the Obama administration.

48. This count refers to experiences with interior enforcement, plus the one asylum claim. I do not consider experiences with border security or enforcement in this chapter (but see chapter 1).

49. (García Hernández 2014; Markowitz 2010)

50. (Das 2011; Jain 2015)

51. (Eagly and Shafer 2015)

52. (TRAC Immigration 2021)

53. The types are asylum, withholding of removal, and relief under the Convention Against Torture. Formally, these are distinct forms of relief (American Immigration Council 2020).

54. In other words, out of eight total cases in immigration court among interview participants, three cases involved a respondent submitting a defensive petition.

55. See also Patler and Gonzalez 2021.

56. (Immigrant Legal Resource Center 2020a)

57. See Martinez-Aranda 2020 for an extended discussion of how different forms of electronic monitoring—such as ankle devices—are forms of surveillance that extend undocumented immigrants' punishment beyond a detention center and into their most intimate spheres of life.

58. In Asad (2020b), I noted how this was Javier's second offense based on his and Yajaira's reports of his case. Revisiting the consequences that he and Yajaira described, it is more likely that this was Javier's third offense.

59. More formally, they needed to show that Javier did not commit a crime involving moral turpitude—one "that shocks the public conscience as being inherently base, vile, or depraved, contrary to the rules of morality and the duties owed between man and man, either one's fellow man or society in general" (Board of Immigration Appeals 1988).

60. Even when a crime does not involve moral turpitude, immigrants in removal proceedings for DWI are still required to show that they are not a "habitual drunkard" and that they have "good moral character." See Rathod 2013 for a fuller discussion.

61. Farrell-Bryan (2022) shows in her observations of immigration judges hearing cancellation of removal petitions in a northeastern immigration court how common Javier's reports of what the immigration judge told him are.

62. (American Immigration Council 2019)

63. (Ryo 2016, 2018a, 2018b)

64. For all figures cited in the next two paragraphs, see appendix, table A.1.

65. (Asad 2019; Eagly and Shafer 2018; Moinester 2018)

66. (Baum 2010; Legomsky 2005; Markowitz 2010; Marks 2012)

67. (Keith et al. 2013; Rottman et al. 2009; Ryo 2016, 2018a, 2018b; Schrag et al. 2009)

68. (Asad 2019)

69. See appendix, table A.1.

70. (Asad 2019)

71. In an ideal world, I would have observed one or more successful defensive petitions to further delineate the conditions under which structural and organizational features of immigration court shape immigration officials' interpretations of defendants' formal records. This is a rare outcome to begin with in Dallas Immigration Court. Other factors may also have come into play. Although I observed hundreds of cases over one summer, many cases were right censored, in that I never observed a defendant's final outcome. This is, in part, a reflection of the protracted nature of removal proceedings that, in fiscal year 2015, took over 400 days to complete on average. Even so, many cases in which an immigration judge determined that a defendant was possibly eligible to submit a defensive petition were completed when those defendants declined to submit a petition. I use those cases to round out my interpretations of the six cases considered here.

72. Matter of Barcenas, 19 I&N Dec. 609 (BIA 1988); Matter of Mejia, 16 I&N Dec. 6 (BIA 1976).

73. According to the Immigration and Nationality Act, drug crimes include everything from simple possession to the sale of controlled substances that have the potential for abuse. A single incident involving thirty grams or fewer of marijuana does not constitute an aggravated felony.

74. (Brady 2017)

75. See Levesque et al. 2022 for another example of how detention disadvantaged detained noncitizens during removal proceedings.

76. See appendix, table A.1.

77. Alcohol-related crimes such as driving while intoxicated (DWI) are not always considered aggravated felonies but, in Texas, three or more DWI convictions become an aggravated felony for immigration purposes, because they are a third-degree criminal felony with a minimum sentence of no fewer than two years and a maximum sentence of no more than ten years.

78. See appendix, table A.1.

79. (Eagly and Shafer 2015)

80. (Abarca and Coutin 2018; Chauvin and Garcés-Mascareñas 2012; Chauvin and Garcés-Mascareñas 2014; Coutin 1998, 2003; Horton and Heyman 2020)

81. (Chauvin and Garcés-Mascareñas 2014: 426)

Conclusion

1. Mónica first entered the United States without inspection. Undocumented immigrants who enter without inspection are "inadmissible" and, therefore, generally ineligible to adjust their legal status without first leaving the United States. This contrasts with undocumented immigrants who first entered the country on a visa, even when they have overstayed it; these individuals have "unlawful presence" but can legalize while they are physically present in the United States. On entry without inspection, see INA 212(a)(6)(A); on unlawful presence, see INA 212(a)(9)(B).

2. Gallup News asked a national sample of adults in 2016 and 2019 whether they support "allowing immigrants living in the U.S. illegally the chance to become U.S. citizens if they meet certain requirements over a period of time." In 2016, 84 percent of adults favored this idea; in 2019, 81 percent did (Gallup Group n.d.)

3. In a national poll completed in April 2021, 69 percent of Americans said that there should be a way for undocumented immigrants to stay in the country legally, if certain requirements are met. That figure was down slightly from previous polls, which tallied support in the mid- to high-seventies. Accounting for this change are Americans who identify as Republicans; whereas 61 percent of these voters supported this proposal in March 2017, 48 percent did in April 2021 (Pew Research Center 2021).

4. In 2019, 37 percent of adults in the United States favored deporting "all immigrants who are living in the United States illegally back to their home country"; these adults vote overwhelmingly Republican (Gallup Group n.d.). For an account on prioritization of immigration enforcement by family ties, see Hausman 2022. In a 2018 poll, 21 percent of adults in the United States said they supported abolishing ICE; these adults vote overwhelmingly Democrat (Robillard and Marans 2018).

5. (Kamarck 2021)

6. (Cox and Rodríguez 2009, 2015)

7. (Bush 2006). For a historical overview of presidential administrations' approaches to contemporary immigration law and policy, see Coleman (2021).

8. (Cox and Rodríguez 2009, 2015)

9. See Pierce and Bolter (2020) for extensive details about each legal, policy, or regulatory change bearing on immigration during the Trump administration.

10. (Pew Research Center 2021; Robillard and Marans 2018)

11. (Asad 2020a)

12. (White House 2021)

13. (Jordan 2020; Ordoñez 2021)

14. (Ordoñez 2021)

15. (Passel and Cohn 2019)

16. (Kim and Yellow Horse 2018; Hanna and Batalova 2021)

17. (Wong et al. 2021; Wong, Shklyan, and Silva 2021)

18. Tilly (2003) distinguishes between exploitation and opportunity hoarding, which underlie the relationship between categorization and inequality. The former implies the unequal allocation of resources, and the latter implies that the dominant group withholds access to these resources. But see Brubaker (2015) for a rejoinder to Tilly.

19. (Wolff 2017: 179)

20. (Brayne 2014; Goffman 2009; Haskins and Jacobsen 2017; Lanuza and Turney 2020)

21. As noted in chapter 2, two lawsuits in the federal circuit courts reached opposing conclusions about the legality of the Biden administration's enforcement priorities as this book went to press. The effects of these lawsuits, if any, remain unclear given a large undocumented population and limited resources for enforcement (Ray 2022).

22. Haskins and Jacobsen (2017) find mixed evidence of a relationship between surveillance and system avoidance among parents: they do not find an effect for the primary caregiver (usually the mother), though they do find an effect for the father.

23. (Alba and Nee 2009: 6). Though Alba and Nee do not engage with Charles Tilly, their theory of immigrant assimilation is consonant with Tilly's ideas. For one, their theory is rooted in institutions ("interrelated norms . . . [that] govern social relationships," 36) and that make resources available to people in organizations (which we have called here surveilling institutions). People are agentic in Alba and Nee's model, as they are in Tilly's, but their context circumscribes the actions available to them and, therefore, their ability to resist institutional structures.

24. (Bean, Brown, and Bachmeier 2015; Massey 2007)

25. Tilly notes that people can engage in "adaptation," whereby they learn to cope with, and therefore reproduce, the exclusions they face in their daily interactions. As a result, people can unintentionally reify the categories that produce their inequalities.

26. Alba and Nee note that "parity in life chances" does not mean free from discrimination.

27. (Jacome 2018)

28. (Capps, Gelatt, and Greenberg 2020)

29. (Passel and Cohn 2019)

30. (Massey, Durand, and Pren 2016)

31. (Massey, Durand, and Pren 2016)

32. (Massey, Durand, and Pren 2014, 2016; Passel and Cohn 2019; Villarreal 2014)

33. As of this writing, the federal government limits family-sponsored visas to 226,000 per year and employment-based visas to 262,000. For a full discussion of per-country limits on visa distribution, and their impact on wait times for lawful immigration to the United States, see Obinna 2020.

34. (U.S. Department of State 2020)
35. (Kerwin and Warren 2019)
36. (U.S. Department of State 2020)
37. (Bureau of Consular Affairs 2021)
38. (Bergeron 2013)
39. (Asad and Hwang 2019a; Faist 2016; Massey 1990; Massey et al. 1993)
40. (Fussell and Massey 2004; Massey 1990)
41. (Asad and Hwang 2019a)
42. (Heinrich 2018; Herd and Moynihan 2019; Ray, Herd, and Moynihan 2020)
43. (The White House 2015: p. 4)
44. The United States makes available a border crossing card for Mexican nationals who want to enter for business or tourism reasons, which are good for ten years after issuance. Adding this country to the Visa Waiver Program would eliminate the need for renewals.
45. (U.S. Citizenship and Immigration Services n.d.)
46. All percentages in this paragraph come from Migration Policy Institute 2018.
47. (García, Diaz-Strong, and Rodriguez-Rodriguez 2022)
48. (Hagan 1994)
49. (Asad 2020b)
50. (Budiman 2020; Gonzalez-Barrera 2017; Warren and Kerwin 2015)
51. (Aptekar 2015; Gomberg-Muñoz 2016; Hainmueller et al. 2018; Le and Pastor 2022)
52. (Bosniak 2000, 2013, 2017)
53. (Ryo 2021; Ryo and Peacock 2019; Stevens 2011)
54. (Eagly and Shafer 2015)
55. (Kenney et al. 2021)
56. (Asad 2019)
57. (Kim 2018; Kocher 2019; Lynch and Voigt 2020)
58. (Pew Research Center 2017)
59. (Federal Bar Association 2021)
60. (Garip 2016)
61. All quotations from (Carens 1987: pp. 264–5).
62. For a thorough discussion and review, see Song (2018b). Song (2018a) outlines what she describes as an "intermediate ethical position" on immigration reform that balances the claims of immigrants alongside the democratic countries that receive them. See also Song and Bloemraad (2022).
63. See Gowayed 2020 for an application of Carens' idea in the context of refugee migrations.
64. The quotation comes from Berger, Kaba, and Stein (2017). For a fuller explication of abolitionist theorizing and organizing, including the importance of including the immigration system in this work, see Davis 2016 and Kaba 2021. Clair and Woog (2022) apply an abolitionist perspective when discussing transformations to the criminal courts. Koh (2021) offers several practical steps for "downsizing the deportation state" in ways that align with abolitionist theorizing and organizing.

65. (Jain 2019)

66. (Menjívar 2022)

67. (Hausman 2022)

68. (Wong, Kang, Valdivia, Espino, Gonzalez, and Peralta 2021)

69. Author's own extension and tabulation of data by Hausman 2020. I thank Livia Baer-Bositis for research assistance.

70. (Gulasekaram and Villazor 2009; Ortiz et al. 2021)

71. (Hausman 2020; Martínez-Schuldt and Martínez 2019)

72. (Schmalzbauer 2014; Wong, Shklyan, Isorena, Peng 2019; Wong, Kang, Valdivia, Espino, Gonzalez, and Peralta 2021)

73. (Fox 2022)

74. (Eagly 2020)

75. INA § 101(a)(43)(Q), (T), 8 U.S.C. § 1101(a)(43)(Q), (T).

76. (Fine 1997)

77. (American Bar Association 2021)

78. To be sure, this idea in part motivated the Supreme Court's decision in *Padilla v. Kentucky*, holding that criminal defense attorneys must advise their noncitizen clients about the deportation risks of a guilty plea. For a general discussion of this idea, see Lasch (2013, 2014).

79. (Anderson, Buenaventura, and Heaton 2018; Kwon 2016; Steinberg 2013)

80. (Project 2021)

81. (Fox n.d.)

82. (Horton and Heyman 2020)

83. For a fuller description of federal-state dynamics pertaining to driver's licenses that comply with federal standards, see Newton 2018.

84. (Williamson 2018)

85. (Koh 2021)

86. (National Academies of Sciences and Medicine 2017). See also (Orrenius 2017).

87. These are Sections 212(a)(4) and 237(a)(5) of the INA.

88. (Karlamangla 2022)

Appendix A: Methodological Narrative

1. (Lieberson and Lynn 2002)

2. (Lareau 2021: 226)

3. (Glaser and Strauss 2009 [1967]; Miles and Huberman 1994; Weiss 1995)

4. (Small 2009)

5. (Luker 2009: 43)

6. (Small 2011)

7. Lareau (2021: 2) laments the serendipity element, rightly noting that this is hard to recreate. It's nonetheless important to follow through on one's research projects because one never knows where they will lead.

8. Some publications emanating from different facets of this research include Asad 2020b; Asad and Rosen 2018; Bell 2020; Darrah–Okike, Harvey, and Fong 2020; Harvey et al. 2020. For another example of a "spinoff" study, see Harvey 2022.

9. More than 90 percent of Cuyahoga County's residents identify as White (61 percent) or Black (29 percent). In contrast, 54 percent of Dallas County's residents identify as White (32 percent) or Black (22 percent), and 39 percent identify as Latino. And, perhaps even more striking, 93 percent of Cuyahoga County residents were born in the United States, whereas that figure for Dallas County residents is 77 percent. 2013 ACS (five-year estimates).

10. All figures in this paragraph come from USC Equity Research Institute's analysis of 2017 five-year American Community Survey microdata from IPUMS-USA on behalf of the author.

11. At the conclusion of fieldwork in 2014, the HPHK team had interviewed eighty-three of 109 eligible families across twenty block groups in Dallas County. Of the seventy interviews completed in 2013, sixty-seven families were eligible for a follow-up interview in 2014 (excluding those who had moved out of state or whose household head was incarcerated); fifty-six families (84 percent) were reinterviewed.

12. (Lamont and Swidler 2014; Pugh 2013; Reed 2010)

13. On relational ethnography, see Desmond (2014: 554). On getting the main connections right, see (1992: 36) as cited in Desmond 2014. See also Emirbayer 1997.

14. Although most removals occur outside formal removal proceedings in immigration court, the Latino immigrant families I interviewed would likely be processed through this setting if they received a deportation order. They have lived in the United States for several years and have young children who are U.S. citizens, two characteristics that may require an immigration judge to adjudicate the complexities of their cases.

15. (TRAC Immigration 2021)

16. (Chishti, Pierce, and Bolter 2017)

17. (Pierce and Bolter 2020)

18. (Lareau and Rao 2016)

19. (Small 2009: p. 9; emphasis in original)

20. (Hancock, Sykes, and Verma 2018; Small 2011)

21. (May and Pattillo-McCoy 2000)

22. (May and Pattillo-McCoy 2000)

23. For different illustrations of this point across a variety of contexts, see Buford May 2014; Clair 2020; Reyes 2020; Vasquez-Tokos 2017.

24. (Lareau and Rao 2016)

25. (Small and Calarco 2022: p. 19)

26. (Hofferth et al. 2020)

27. (Chávez 2013)

28. (Small 2011: 67)

29. (Deterding and Waters 2018)

30. This typology is adapted from Marrow 2009.

31. (Small 2013)

32. (Asad 2019)

33. (Asad 2019)

34. (Charmaz 2014: 96; Glaser and Strauss 2009 [1967]: 191). For a fuller discussion of the theoretical ideas underlying saturation, see Low 2019.

35. (Santellano 2022: 6)

Appendix B: National Evidence of Latinos' Engagement with Surveilling Institutions

1. For research assistance, I thank Livia Baer-Bositis. For funding, I thank the Stanford School of Humanities and Sciences and the Stanford Department of Sociology.

2. See, generally, Bureau of Labor Statistics (2020) for the ATUS User's Guide. See Hamermesh, Frazis, and Stewart 2005) for a rich description of the ATUS's utility for social-scientific research.

3. Shelley (2005) explains how this coding scheme was developed. These categories include seventeen major groupings: personal care; household activities; caring for and helping household members; caring for and helping nonhousehold members; working and work-related activities; education; consumer purchases; professional and personal care services; household services; government services and civic obligations; eating and drinking; socializing, relaxing, and leisure; sports, exercise, and recreation; religious and spiritual activities; volunteer activities; telephone calls; and traveling.

4. (Hofferth et al. 2020)

5. The construction of the dependent variables used in this appendix aligns with recent advances in the study of surveillance and system avoidance in the criminal-legal context (e.g., Haskins and Jacobsen 2017; Lanuza and Turney 2020).

6. Compare with Brayne (2014), who considers separately medical (whether respondents reported not obtaining necessary medical care in the past twelve months), financial (whether respondents reported not having a checking account), school/work (whether respondents reported not being enrolled in school or work), and public supports (whether respondents reported not being involved in SNAP and/or TANF) institutions.

7. This is common in ATUS-based studies. As others have observed (e.g., Hamermesh and Trejo 2013), ATUS respondents report spending about 60 percent of their time sleeping, working for payment, and watching television.

8. (Asad 2020a)

9. (Human Rights Watch 2009)

10. See Borjas (2017), whose method reverse engineers the classification scheme that the Pew Research Center uses (Passel and Cohn 2014). Although cautions are warranted about any method for imputing legal status (Spence et al. 2020; Van Hook et al. 2015), I rely on the logical imputation method because the ATUS data align most closely with the method's data requirements.

11. According to the classification scheme used, about 14.6 percent of respondents are likely permanent residents and about 18.3 percent are likely undocumented. These estimates are comparable with other national estimates of the Latino noncitizen population.

12. (Warren and Kerwin 2017)

13. (ATUS-X 2010)

14. (Long and Mustillo 2018)

Abarca, Gray Albert, and Susan Bibler Coutin. 2018. "Sovereign Intimacies: The Lives of Documents within U.S. State-Noncitizen Relationships." *American Ethnologist* 45: 7–19.

Abrego, Leisy. 2019. "Relational Legal Consciousness of U.S. Citizenship: Privilege, Responsibility, Guilt, and Love in Latino Mixed-Status Families." *Law & Society Review* 53: 641–70.

Abrego, Leisy, Mat Coleman, Daniel E. Martínez, Cecilia Menjívar, and Jeremy Slack. 2017. "Making Immigrants into Criminals: Legal Processes of Criminalization in the Post-IIRIRA Era." *Journal on Migration and Human Security* 5: 694–715.

Abrego, Leisy, and Sarah M. Lakhani. 2015. "Incomplete Inclusion: Legal Violence and Immigrants in Liminal Legal Statuses." *Law & Policy* 37: 265–93.

ACLU. 2019. "The Constitution in the 100-Mile Border Zone." https://www.aclu.org /other/constitution-100-mile-border-zone.

Alba, Richard, and Victor Nee. 2009. *Remaking the American Mainstream: Assimilation and Contemporary Immigration.* Cambridge, MA: Harvard University Press.

Allen, Chenoa D. 2018. "Who Loses Public Health Insurance When States Pass Restrictive Omnibus Immigration-Related Laws? The Moderating Role of County Latino Density." *Health & Place* 54: 20–28.

Allen, Chenoa D., and Clea A. McNeely. 2017. "Do Restrictive Omnibus Immigration Laws Reduce Enrollment in Public Health Insurance by Latino Citizen Children? A Comparative Interrupted Time Series Study." *Social Science & Medicine* 191: 19–29.

Alsan, Marcella, and Crystal Yang. 2018. "Fear and the Safety Net: Evidence from Secure Communities." The National Bureau of Economic Research.

Altman, Claire E., Colleen M. Heflin, Chaegyung Jun, and James D. Bachmeier. 2021. "Material Hardship among Immigrants in the United States: Variation by Citizenship, Legal Status, and Origin in the 1996–2008 SIPP." *Population Research and Policy Review* 40: 363–99.

American Bar Association. 2017. "Panelists Urge Help for Those Facing Removal at Immigration Program on Trump." Accessed October 1. https://www.americanbar .org/news/abanews/aba-news-archives/2017/02/panelists_urge_help/.

———. 2021. "Steps in a Trial: Plea Bargaining." Accessed October 1. https://www.americanbar.org/groups/public_education/resources/law_related _education_network/how_courts_work/pleabargaining/

American Immigration Council. 2019. "Seeking Release from Immigration Detention." American Immigration Council. Accessed December 4. https://www .americanimmigrationcouncil.org/research/release-immigration-detention.

———. 2020. "Asylum in the United States."

———. 2021a. "Immigrants in the United States."

———. 2021b. "U.S. Citizen Children Impacted by Immigration Enforcement."

Amuedo-Dorantes, Catalina, and Esther Arenas-Arroyo. 2018. "Split Families and the Future of Children: Immigration Enforcement and Foster Care Placements." In *American Economic Association Papers and Proceedings* 108: 368–72.

Anderson, James M., Maya Buenaventura, and Paul Heaton. 2018. "The Effects of Holistic Defense on Criminal Justice Outcomes." *Harvard Law Review* 132: 819.

Andrews, Abigail L. 2017. "Moralizing Regulation: The Implications of Policing 'Good' Versus 'Bad' Immigrants." *Ethnic and Racial Studies* 41: 2485–2503.

Aptekar, Sofya. 2015. *The Road to Citizenship: What Naturalization Means for Immigrants and the United States*. New Brunswick, NJ: Rutgers University Press.

Armenta, Amada. 2017. *Protect, Serve, and Deport: The Rise of Policing as Immigration Enforcement*. Oakland: University of California Press.

Armenta, Amada, and Heidy Sarabia. 2020. "Receptionists, Doctors, and Social Workers: Examining Undocumented Immigrant Women's Perceptions of Health Services." *Social Science & Medicine*: 112788.

Armenta, Amada, and Rocío Rosales. 2019. "Beyond the Fear of Deportation: Understanding Unauthorized Immigrants' Ambivalence Toward the Police." *American Behavioral Scientist* 63: 1350–69.

Asad, Asad L. 2019. "Deportation Decisions: Judicial Decision-Making in an American Immigration Court." *American Behavioral Scientist* 63: 1221–49.

——. 2020a. "Latinos' Deportation Fears by Citizenship and Legal Status, 2007 to 2018." *Proceedings of the National Academy of Sciences*.

——. 2020b. "On the Radar: System Embeddedness and Latin American Immigrants' Perceived Risk of Deportation." *Law & Society Review* 54: 133–67.

Asad, Asad L., and Matthew Clair. 2018. "Racialized Legal Status as a Social Determinant of Health." *Social Science & Medicine* 199: 19–28.

Asad, Asad L., and Filiz Garip. 2019. "Mexico-U.S. Migration in Time: From Economic to Social Mechanisms." *The Annals of the American Academy of Political and Social Science* 684: 60–84.

Asad, Asad L., and Jackelyn Hwang. 2019a. "Indigenous Places and the Making of Undocumented Status in Mexico-U.S. Migration." *International Migration Review* 53: 1032–77.

——. 2019b. "Migration to the United States from Indigenous Communities in Mexico." *The Annals of the American Academy of Political and Social Science* 684: 120–45.

Asad, Asad L., and Eva Rosen. 2018. "Hiding within Racial Hierarchies: How Undocumented Immigrants Make Residential Decisions in an American City." *Journal of Ethnic and Migration Studies* 45: 1857–82.

Ascherio, Marta. 2022. "Do Sanctuary Policies Increase Crime? Contrary Evidence from a County-Level Investigation in the United States." *Social Science Research* 106: 102743.

ATUS-X. 2010. "General Documentation for Linked ATUS-CPS Supplement Files."

Bachmeier, James D., Jennifer Van Hook, and Frank D. Bean. 2014. "Can We Measure Immigrants' Legal Status? Lessons from Two U.S. Surveys." *International Migration Review* 48: 538–66.

Batalova, Jeanne, Ariel G. Ruiz Soto, Sarah Pierce, and Randy Capps. 2017. "Differing DREAMs: Estimating the Unauthorized Populations that Could Benefit under Different Legalization Bills." Fact Sheet. Migration Policy Institute, Washington, D.C.

Baum, Lawrence. 2009. "Judicial Specialization and the Adjudication of Immigration Cases." *Duke Law Journal* 59: 1501.

Bean, Frank D., Susan K. Brown, and James D. Bachmeier. 2015. *Parents without Papers: The Progress and Pitfalls of Mexican American Integration.* New York: Russell Sage Foundation.

Bean, Frank D., Mark Leach, and B. Lindsay Lowell. 2004. "Immigrant Job Quality and Mobility in the United States." *Work and Occupations* 31: 499–518.

Becker, Gary S. 2009. *Human Capital: A Theoretical and Empirical Analysis, with Special Reference to Education.* Chicago: University of Chicago Press.

Becker, Howard S. 2008 [1963]. *Outsiders: Studies in the Sociology of Deviance.* New York: Simon and Schuster.

Bell, Monica C. 2016. "Situational Trust: How Disadvantaged Mothers Reconceive Legal Cynicism." *Law & Society Review* 50: 314–47.

———. 2017. "Police Reform and the Dismantling of Legal Estrangement." *Yale Law Journal* 126: 2054.

———. 2020. "Located Institutions: Neighborhood Frames, Residential Preferences, and the Case of Policing." *American Journal of Sociology* 125: 917–73.

Berger, Dan, Mariame Kaba, and David Stein. 2017. "What Abolitionists Do." *Jacobin.* https://jacobin.com/2017/08/prison-abolition-reform-mass-incarceration.

Berger, Susan. 2009. "(Un)Worthy: Latina Battered Immigrants under VAWA and the Construction of Neoliberal Subjects." *Citizenship Studies* 13: 201–17.

Berger Cardoso, Jodi, Jennifer L. Scott, Monica Faulkner, and Liza Barros Lane. 2018. "Parenting in the Context of Deportation Risk." *Journal of Marriage and Family* 80 (2): 301–16.

Bergeron, Claire. 2013. "Going to the Back of the Line: A Primer on Lines, Visa Categories, and Wait Times." Issue Brief. Migration Policy Institute, Washington D.C. https://www.migrationpolicy.org/research/going-back-line-primer-lines-visa-categories-and-wait-times.

Bernburg, Jon Gunnar. 2019. "Labeling Theory." In *Handbook on Crime and Deviance,* edited by Marvin D. Krohn, Alan J. Lizotte, and Gina Penly Hall. New York: Springer.

Berney, Lee R., and David B. Blane. 1997. "Collecting Retrospective Data: Accuracy of Recall after 50 Years Judged against Historical Records." *Social Science & Medicine* 45: 1519–25.

Bernstein, Hamutal, Dulce Gonzalez, Michael Karpman, and Stephen Zuckerman. 2019. "One in Seven Adults in Immigrant Families Reported Avoiding Public Benefit Programs in 2018." Urban Institute Brief, May 22. https://www.urban.org/research/publication/oneseven-adults-immigrant-families-reported-avoiding-public-benefitprograms-2018.

Biddle, Bruce J. 1986. "Recent Development in Role Theory." *Annual Review of Sociology* 12: 67–92.

Blitzer, Jonathan. 2017. "After an Immigration Raid, a City's Students Vanish." *New Yorker.* March 23.

Blumer, Herbert. 1986. *Symbolic Interactionism: Perspective and Method.* Oakland: University of California Press.

Board of Immigration Appeals. 1988. "Matter of Danesh." Decision #3068.

Border Angels. n.d. "OUR SERVICES: WATER DROPS." Accessed May 26. https://www.borderangels.org/water-drops.html.

Borjas, George J. 1987. "Self-Selection and the Earnings of Immigrants." *American Economic Review* 77: 531–53.

———. 2017. "The Labor Supply of Undocumented Immigrants." *Labour Economics* 46: 1–13.

Bosniak, Linda. 2000. "Universal Citizenship and the Problem of Alienage." *Immigration & Nationality Law Review* 21: 373.

———. 2013. "Amnesty in Immigration: Forgetting, Forgiving, and Freedom." *Critical Review of International Social and Political Philosophy* 16 (3): 344–65.

———. 2017. "Being Here: Ethical Territoriality and the Rights of Immigrants." In *Migrants and Rights*. Routledge: 53–74.

Brady, Kathy. 2017. "Aggravated Felonies." In *Practice Advisory*. Washington, D.C.: Immigrant Legal Resource Center.

Brayne, Sarah. 2014. "Surveillance and System Avoidance: Criminal Justice Contact and Institutional Attachment." *American Sociological Review* 79: 367–91.

———. 2020. *Predict and Surveil: Data, Discretion, and the Future of Policing*. NY: Oxford University Press, USA.

Brehm, John O., and Scott Gates. 1999. *Working, Shirking, and Sabotage: Bureaucratic Response to a Democratic Public*. Ann Arbor: University of Michigan Press.

Brown, Dorothy A. 2007. "Race and Class Matters in Tax Policy." *Columbia Law Review* 107: 790.

Brubaker, Rogers. 2015. *Grounds for Difference*. Cambridge, MA: Harvard University Press.

Bruch, Elizabeth E., and Robert D. Mare. 2006. "Neighborhood Choice and Neighborhood Change." *American Journal of Sociology* 112: 667–709.

Bruch, Sarah K., Myra Marx Ferree, and Joe Soss. 2010. "From Policy to Polity: Democracy, Paternalism, and the Incorporation of Disadvantaged Citizens." *American Sociological Review* 75: 205–26.

Bruhn, Sarah. 2022. "Intersectional Recognition: Immigrant Motherhood in a Gentrifying Sanctuary City's Schools." *Journal of Ethnic and Migration Studies*: 1–20.

Bryan, Brielle. 2022. "Housing Instability Following Felony Conviction and Incarceration: Disentangling Being Marked from Being Locked Up." *Journal of Quantitative Criminology*: 1–42.

Budiman, Abby. 2020. "Key Findings about U.S. Immigrants." Pew Research Center. https://www.pewresearch.org/fact-tank/2020/08/20/key-findings-about-u-s-immigrants/.

Buford May, Reuben A. 2014. "When the Methodological Shoe Is on the Other Foot: African American Interviewer and White Interviewees." *Qualitative Sociology* 37: 117–36.

Burciaga, Edelina M., and Aaron Malone. 2021. "Intensified Liminal Legality: The Impact of the DACA Rescission for Undocumented Young Adults in Colorado." *Law & Social Inquiry* 46: 1–23.

Bureau of Consular Affairs. 2021. "Visa Bulletin for August 2021." U.S. Department of State.

Bureau of Labor Statistics. 2020. "American Time Use Survey User's Guide: Understanding ATUS 2003 to 2019." U.S. Census Bureau.

Bush, George W. 2006. "President Bush Addresses the Nation." Speech. The Oval Office.

Cantor, Guillermo, Mark L. Noferi, and Daniel Martinez. 2015. "Enforcement Overdrive: A Comprehensive Assessment of ICE's Criminal Alien Program." American Immigration Council. https://www.americanimmigrationcouncil.org/research /enforcement-overdrive-comprehensive-assessment-ice%E2%80%99s-criminal -alien-program.

Capps, Randy, Julia Gelatt, and Mark Greenberg. 2020. "The Public-Charge Rule: Broad Impacts, but Few Will Be Denied Green Cards Based on Actual Benefits Use." Migration Policy Institute, Washington D.C. https://www.migrationpolicy .org/news/public-charge-denial-green-cards-benefits-use.

Capps, Randy, Nancy M. Pindus, Kathleen Snyder, and Jacob Leos-Urbel. 2001. "Recent Changes in Texas Welfare and Work, Child Care and Child Welfare Systems." Assessing the New Federalism: An Urban Institute Program to Assess Changing Social Policies. The Urban Institute, Washington D.C.

Carens, Joseph H. 1987. "Aliens and Citizens: The Case for Open Borders." *The Review of Politics* 49: 251–73.

Carr, Patrick J., Laura Napolitano, and Jessica Keating. 2007. "We Never Call the Cops and Here Is Why: A Qualitative Examination of Legal Cynicism in Three Philadelphia Neighborhoods." *Criminology* 45: 445–80.

Carré, Françoise. 2015. "(In)dependent Contractor Misclassification." Economic Policy Institute, Washington, D.C. https://www.epi.org/publication/independent -contractor-misclassification/.

Castañeda, Heide, Seth M. Holmes, Daniel S. Madrigal, Maria-Elena De Trinidad Young, Naomi Beyeler, and James Quesada. 2015. "Immigration as a Social Determinant of Health." *Annual Review of Public Health* 36: 375–92.

Castells, Manuel, and Roberto Laserna. 1989. "The New Dependency: Technological Change and Socioeconomic Restructuring in Latin America." *Sociological Forum* 4: 535–60.

Cervantes, Andrea Gómez, and Cecilia Menjívar. 2020. "Legal Violence, Health, and Access to Care: Latina Immigrants in Rural and Urban Kansas." *Journal of Health and Social Behavior* 61: 307–23.

Chacón, Jennifer M. 2014. "Producing Liminal Legality." *Denver Law Review* 92: 709.

Charles, Camille Zubrinsky. 2003. "The Dynamics of Racial Residential Segregation." *Annual Review of Sociology* 29: 167–207.

Charmaz, Kathy. 2014. *Constructing Grounded Theory*. Washington D.C.: Sage Publishing.

Chauvin, Sébastien, and Blanca Garcés-Mascareñas. 2012. "Beyond Informal Citizenship: The New Moral Economy of Migrant Illegality." *International Political Sociology* 6: 241–59.

———. 2014. "Becoming Less Illegal: Deservingness Frames and Undocumented Migrant Incorporation." *Sociology Compass* 8: 422–32.

Chávez, Leo R. 2020. *Anchor Babies and the Challenge of Birthright Citizenship*. Redwood City, CA: Stanford University Press.

———. 2013. *The Latino Threat: Constructing Immigrants, Citizens, and the Nation*. Redwood City, CA: Stanford University Press.

———. 2012 [1992]. *Shadowed Lives: Undocumented Immigrants in American Society*. Boston: Cengage Learning.

Chávez, Sergio, and Claire E. Altman. 2017. "Gambling with Life: Masculinity, Risk, and Danger in the Lives of Unauthorized Migrant Roofers." *American Journal of Industrial Medicine* 60: 537–47.

Cházaro, Angélica. 2016. "Challenging the 'Criminal Alien' Paradigm." *UCLA Law Review* 63: 594.

Cheong, Amanda R. 2021. "Legal Histories as Determinants of Incorporation: Previous Undocumented Experience and Naturalization Propensities among Immigrants in the United States." *International Migration Review* 55: 482–513.

Chiarello, Elizabeth. 2013. "How Organizational Context Affects Bioethical Decision-Making: Pharmacists' Management of Gatekeeping Processes in Retail and Hospital Settings." *Social Science & Medicine* 98: 319–29.

Chiquiar, Daniel, and Gordon H. Hanson. 2005. "International Migration, Self-Selection, and the Distribution of Wages: Evidence from Mexico and the United States." *Journal of Political Economy* 113: 239–81.

Chishti, Muzaffar, Sarah Pierce, and Jessica Bolter. 2017. "The Obama Record on Deportations: Deporter in Chief or Not?" Migration Policy Institute, Washington D.C.

Chua, Lynette J, and David M. Engel. 2019. "Legal Consciousness Reconsidered." *Annual Review of Law and Social Science* 15: 335–53.

City of Dallas. 2020. "Welcoming Dallas Strategic Plan." Welcoming Communities and Immigrant Affairs. Dallas, TX, Dallas City Hall.

———. n.d. "Court & Detention Services: Frequently Asked Questions & Forms." Accessed October 1. https://dallascityhall.com/departments/courtdetentionservices /Pages/Frequently-Asked-Questions.aspx#Arrested.

Clair, Matthew. 2020. *Privilege and Punishment: How Race and Class Matter in Criminal Court*. Princeton, NJ: Princeton University Press.

———. 2021. "Being a Disadvantaged Criminal Defendant: Mistrust and Resistance in Attorney-Client Interactions." *Social Forces* 100: 194–217.

Clair, Matthew, and Amanda Woog. 2022. "Courts and the Abolition Movement." *California Law Review* 110: 1.

Coleman, Mathew. 2007. "Immigration Geopolitics beyond the Mexico–U.S. Border." *Antipode* 39: 54–76.

———. 2012. "The 'Local' Migration State: The Site-Specific Devolution of Immigration Enforcement in the U.S. South." *Law & Policy* 34: 159–90.

Coleman, Mathew, and Austin Kocher. 2011. "Detention, Deportation, Devolution and Immigrant Incapacitation in the U.S., Post 9/11." *The Geographical Journal* 177: 228–37.

———. 2019. "Rethinking the 'Gold Standard' of Racial Profiling. 287(g), Secure Communities, and Racially Discrepant Police Power." *American Behavioral Scientist* 63 (9): 1185–1220.

Coleman, Sarah. 2021. *The Walls Within: The Politics of Immigration in Modern America*. Princeton, NJ: Princeton University Press.

Cornelius, Wayne A. 1982. "Interviewing Undocumented Immigrants: Methodological Reflections Based on Fieldwork in Mexico and the U.S." *International Migration Review* 16: 378–411.

———. 1986. *From Sojourners to Settlers: The Changing Profile of Mexican Migration to the United States*. Americas Program, Stanford University.

———. 2001. "Death at the Border: Efficacy and Unintended Consequences of U.S. Immigration Control Policy." *Population and Development Review* 27: 661–85.

Cornelius, Wayne, Leo Chavez, and Jorge Castro. 1982. *Mexican Immigrants and Southern California: A Summary of Current Knowledge*. La Jolla, CA: Center for U.S.-Mexican Studies, University of California, San Diego.

Correia, Mark E. 2010. "Determinants of Attitudes Toward Police of Latino Immigrants and Non-immigrants." *Journal of Criminal Justice* 38: 99–107.

Coutin, Susan Bibler. 1998. "From Refugees to Immigrants: The Legalization Strategies of Salvadoran Immigrants and Activists." *International Migration Review* 32: 901–25.

———. 2003. *Legalizing Moves: Salvadoran Immigrants' Struggle for U.S. Residency*. Ann Arbor: University of Michigan Press.

Cox, Adam B., and Cristina M. Rodríguez. 2009. "The President and Immigration Law." *Yale Law Journal* 119: 458.

———. 2015. "The President and Immigration Law Redux." *Yale Law Journal* 125: 104.

Crenshaw, Kimberlé. 1990. "Mapping the Margins: Intersectionality, Identity Politics, and Violence against Women of Color." *Stanford Law Review* 43: 1241.

Crookes, Danielle M., Kaitlyn K. Stanhope, Ye Ji Kim, Elizabeth Lummus, and Shakira F. Suglia. 2021. "Federal, State, and Local Immigrant-Related Policies and Child Health Outcomes: A Systematic Review." *Journal of Racial and Ethnic Health Disparities*: 1–11.

Crookes, Danielle M., Kaitlyn K. Stanhope, and Shakira F. Suglia. 2022. "Immigrant-Related Policies and the Health Outcomes of Latinx Adults in the United States: A Systematic Review." *Epidemiology* 33 (4): 593–605.

Cuevas, Stephany. 2021. *Apoyo Sacrificial, Sacrificial Support: How Undocumented Latinx Parents Get Their Children to College*. New York: Teachers College Press.

Darrah–Okike, Jennifer, Hope Harvey, and Kelley Fong. 2020. "'Because the World Consists of Everybody': Understanding Parents' Preferences for Neighborhood Diversity." *City & Community* 19: 374–97.

Das, Alina. 2011. "The Immigration Penalties of Criminal Convictions: Resurrecting Categorical Analysis in Immigration Law. *NYU Law Review* 86: 1669.

Davis, Angela Y. 2016. *Freedom Is a Constant Struggle: Ferguson, Palestine, and the Foundations of a Movement*. Chicago: Haymarket Books.

De Genova, Nicholas P. 2002. "Migrant 'Illegality' and Deportability in Everyday Life." *Annual Review of Anthropology* 31: 419–47.

De Graauw, Els. 2014. "Municipal ID Cards for Undocumented Immigrants: Local Bureaucratic Membership in a Federal System." *Politics & Society* 42: 309–30.

De Graauw, Els, and Irene Bloemraad. 2017. "Working Together: Building Successful Policy and Program Partnerships for Immigrant Integration." *Journal on Migration and Human Security* 5: 105–23.

De Haas, Hein. 2021. "A Theory of Migration: The Aspirations-Capabilities Framework." *Comparative Migration Studies* 9: 1–35.

De León, Jason. 2015. *The Land of Open Graves: Living and Dying on the Migrant Trail*. Oakland: University of California Press.

De Trinidad Young, Maria-Elena, and Steven P. Wallace. 2019. "Included, but Deportable: A New Public Health Approach to Policies That Criminalize and Integrate Immigrants." *American Journal of Public Health* 109: 1171–76.

Dee, Thomas, and Mark Murphy. 2018. "Vanished Classmates: The Effects of Local Immigration Enforcement on Student Enrollment." National Bureau of Economic Research.

Del Real, Deisy. 2019. "Toxic Ties: The Reproduction of Legal Violence Within Mixed-Status Intimate Partners, Relatives, and Friends." *International Migration Review* 53 (2): 548–570.

Derose, Kathryn Pitkin, José J. Escarce, and Nicole Lurie. 2007. "Immigrants and Health Care: Sources of Vulnerability. *Health Affairs* 26: 1258–68.

Desai, Sarah, Jessica Houston Su, and Robert M. Adelman. 2020. "Legacies of Marginalization: System Avoidance among the Adult Children of Unauthorized Immigrants in the United States." *International Migration Review* 54: 707–39.

Desmond, Matthew. 2014. "Relational Ethnography." *Theory and Society* 43: 547–79.

———. 2015. "Severe Deprivation in America: An Introduction." *RSF: The Russell Sage Foundation Journal of the Social Sciences* 1: 1–11.

Desmond, Matthew, and Bruce Western. 2018. "Poverty in America: New Directions and Debates." *Annual Review of Sociology* 44: 305–18.

Deterding, Nicole M., and Mary C. Waters. 2018. "Flexible Coding of In-Depth Interviews: A Twenty-First-Century Approach." *Sociological Methods & Research* 50: 708–39.

Dettlaff, Alan J., Ilze Earner, and Susan D. Phillips. 2009. "Latino Children of Immigrants in the Child Welfare System: Prevalence, Characteristics, and Risk." *Children and Youth Services Review* 31: 775–83.

Dominguez, Silvia, and Celeste Watkins. 2003. "Creating Networks for Survival and Mobility: Social Capital among African-American and Latin-American Low-Income Mothers." *Social Problems* 50 (1): 111–35.

Donato, Katharine M., and Amada Armenta. 2011. "What We Know about Unauthorized Migration." *Annual Review of Sociology* 37: 529–43.

Donato, Katharine M., Jorge Durand, and Douglas S. Massey. 1992. "Stemming the Tide? Assessing the Deterrent Effects of the Immigration Reform and Control Act." *Demography* 29: 139–57.

Donato, Katharine M., Brandon Wagner, and Evelyn Patterson. 2008. "The Cat and Mouse Game at the Mexico-U.S. Border: Gendered Patterns and Recent Shifts." *International Migration Review* 42: 330–59.

Dondero, Molly, and Claire E. Altman. 2022. "State-Level Immigrant Policy Climates and Health Care among U.S. Children of Immigrants." *Population Research and Policy Review* 41.

Dreby, Joanna. 2012. "The Burden of Deportation on Children in Mexican Immigrant Families." *Journal of Marriage and Family* 74: 829–45.

———. 2015. *Everyday Illegal: When Policies Undermine Immigrant Families*. Oakland: University of California Press.

Dunbar-Ortiz, Roxanne. 2021. *Not 'A Nation of Immigrants': Settler Colonialism, White Supremacy, and a History of Erasure and Exclusion*. Boston: Beacon Press.

Eagly, Ingrid V. 2020. "The Movement to Decriminalize Border Crossing." *Boston College Law Review* 61: 1967.

Eagly, Ingrid V., and Steven Shafer. 2015. "A National Study of Access to Counsel in Immigration Court." *University of Pennsylvania Law Review* 164: 1.

Edin, Kathryn, and Laura Lein. 1997. *Making Ends Meet: How Single Mothers Survive Welfare and Low-Wage Work*. New York: Russell Sage Foundation.

Edwards, Frank. 2016. "Saving Children, Controlling Families: Punishment, Redistribution, and Child Protection." *American Sociological Review* 81: 575–95.

———. 2019. "Family Surveillance: Police and the Reporting of Child Abuse and Neglect." *RSF: The Russell Sage Foundation Journal of the Social Sciences* 5 (1): 50–70.

Edwards, Frank, Sara Wakefield, Kieran Healy, and Christopher Wildeman. 2021. "Contact with Child Protective Services Is Pervasive but Unequally Distributed by Race and Ethnicity in Large U.S. Counties." *Proceedings of the National Academy of Sciences* 118 (30): e2106272118.

Emirbayer, Mustafa. 1997. "Manifesto for a Relational Sociology." *American Journal of Sociology* 103: 281–317.

Enns, Peter K., Youngmin Yi, Megan Comfort, Alyssa W. Goldman, Hedwig Lee, Christopher Muller, Sara Wakefield, Emily A. Wang, and Christopher Wildeman. 2019. "What Percentage of Americans Have Ever Had a Family Member Incarcerated?: Evidence from the Family History of Incarceration Survey (FamHIS)." *Socius* 5.

Enriquez, Laura E. 2015. "Multigenerational Punishment: Shared Experiences of Undocumented Immigration Status within Mixed-Status Families." *Journal of Marriage and Family* 77: 939–53.

———. 2017. "A 'Master Status' or the 'Final Straw'? Assessing the Role of Immigration Status in Latino Undocumented Youths' Pathways out of School." *Journal of Ethnic and Migration Studies* 43: 1526–43.

Enriquez, Laura E., and Daniel Millán. 2019. "Situational Triggers and Protective Locations: Conceptualising the Salience of Deportability in Everyday Life." *Journal of Ethnic and Migration Studies* 47: 1–20.

Enriquez, Laura E., and Abigail C. Saguy. 2016. "Coming Out of the Shadows: Harnessing a Cultural Schema to Advance the Undocumented Immigrant Youth Movement." *American Journal of Cultural Sociology* 4: 107–30.

Espenshade, Thomas J., Jessica L. Baraka, and Gregory A. Huber. 1997. "Implications of the 1996 Welfare and Immigration Reform Acts for U.S. Immigration." *Population and Development Review* 23: 769–801.

Ewick, Patricia, and Susan S. Silbey. 1998. *The Common Place of Law: Stories from Everyday Life*. Chicago: University of Chicago Press.

Executive Office for Immigration Review. 2015. "Application for Cancellation of Removal and Adjustment of Status for Certain Nonpermanent Residents." U.S. Department of Justice.

Faist, Thomas. 2016. "Cross-Border Migration and Social Inequalities." *Annual Review of Sociology* 42: 323–46.

Family, Jill E. 2016. "The Future Relief of Immigration Law." *Drexel Law Review* 9: 393.

Farrell-Bryan, Dylan. 2022. "Relief or Removal: State Logics of Deservingness and Masculinity for Immigrant Men in Removal Proceedings." *Law & Society Review* 56: 167–87.

Federal Bar Association. 2021. "Article I Immigration Court." Accessed August 10, 2022. https://www.fedbar.org/government-relations/policy-priorities/article-i-immigration-court/.

Feliciano, Cynthia. 2005. "Educational Selectivity in U.S. Immigration: How Do Immigrants Compare to Those Left Behind?" *Demography* 42: 131–52.

Fine, Adam D., Kathleen E. Padilla, and Kelsey E. Tom. 2020. "Police Legitimacy: Identifying Developmental Trends and Whether Youths' Perceptions Can Be Changed." *Journal of Experimental Criminology* 18: 1–21.

Fine, Gary Alan. 1993. "The Sad Demise, Mysterious Disappearance, and Glorious Triumph of Symbolic Interactionism." *Annual Review of Sociology*: 61–87.

Fine, Lisa R. 1997. "Preventing Miscarriages of Justice: Reinstating the Use of Judicial Recommendations against Deportation." *Georgetown Immigration Law Journal* 12: 491.

FitzGerald, David Scott. 2019. *Refuge beyond Reach: How Rich Democracies Repel Asylum Seekers*. Oxford: Oxford University Press.

FitzGerald, David Scott, and Rawan Arar. 2018. "The Sociology of Refugee Migration." *Annual Review of Sociology* 44: 387–406.

Fix, Michael E., and Jeffrey S. Passel. 1999. "Trends in Noncitizens' and Citizens' Use of Public Benefits following Welfare Reform: 1994–97." Office of the Assistant Secretary for Planning and Evaluation.

Flores, René D., and Ariel Azar. Forthcoming. "Who Are the 'Immigrants'?: How Whites' Diverse Perceptions of Immigrants Shape Their Attitudes." *Social Forces*.

Flores, René D., and Ariela Schachter. 2018. "Who Are the 'Illegals'?: The Social Construction of Illegality in the United States." *American Sociological Review* 83: 839–68.

Fong, Kelley. 2017. "Child Welfare Involvement and Contexts of Poverty: The Role of Parental Adversities, Social Networks, and Social Services." *Children and Youth Services Review* 72: 5–13.

———. 2019. "Concealment and Constraint: Child Protective Services Fears and Poor Mothers' Institutional Engagement." *Social Forces* 97: 1785–1809.

———. 2020. "Getting Eyes in the Home: Child Protective Services Investigations and State Surveillance of Family Life." *American Sociological Review* 85: 610–38.

Foucault, Michel. 1991 [1978]. *The Foucault Effect: Studies in Governmentality*. Chicago: University of Chicago Press.

———. 2007 [1977]. *Discipline and Punish: The Birth of the Prison*. Durham, NC: Duke University Press.

Fox, Cybelle. 2016. "Unauthorized Welfare: The Origins of Immigrant Status Restrictions in American Social Policy." *The Journal of American History* 102: 1051–74.

———. 2022. "Rethinking Sanctuary: The Origins Non-Cooperation Policies in Social Welfare Agencies." *Law & Social Inquiry*.

Friedman, Abigail S., and Atheendar S. Venkataramani. 2021. "Chilling Effects: U.S. Immigration Enforcement and Health Care Seeking among Hispanic Adults: Study Examines the Effects of U.S. Immigration Enforcement and Health Care Seeking among Hispanic Adults." *Health Affairs* 40: 1056–65.

Fussell, Elizabeth. 2011. "The Deportation Threat Dynamic and Victimization of Latino Migrants: Wage Theft and Robbery." *Sociological Quarterly* 52: 593–615.

Fussell, Elizabeth, and Douglas S. Massey. 2004. "The Limits to Cumulative Causation: International Migration from Mexican Urban Areas." *Demography* 41: 151–71.

Galli, Chiara. 2020. "Humanitarian Capital: How Lawyers Help Immigrants Use Suffering to Claim Membership in the Nation-State." *Journal of Ethnic and Migration Studies* 46: 2181–98.

Gallup Group. n.d. "Immigration." Accessed August 11, 2022.

García, Angela S. 2019. *Legal Passing: Navigating Undocumented Life and Local Immigration Law*. Oakland: University of California Press.

García, Angela S., Daysi X. Diaz-Strong, and Yunuen Rodriguez Rodriguez. 2022. "A Matter of Time: The Life Course Implications of Deferred Action for Undocumented Latin American Immigrants in the United States." *Social Problems*.

García Hernández, César Cuauhtémoc. 2014. "Immigration Detention as Punishment." *Immigration & Nationality Law Review* 35: 385.

Gardner, Trevor George, and Aarti Kohli. 2009. "The CAP Effect: Racial Profiling in the ICE Criminal Alien Program." Policy Brief. University of California, Berkeley Law School, The Chief Justice Earl Warren Institute on Race, Ethnicity & Diversity.

Garip, Filiz. 2012. "Discovering Diverse Mechanisms of Migration: The Mexico–U.S. Stream 1970–2000." *Population and Development Review* 38: 393–433.

———. 2016. *On the Move: The Changing Dynamics of Mexico-U.S. Migration*. Princeton, NJ: Princeton University Press.

Garip, Filiz, and Asad L. Asad. 2016. "Network Effects in Mexico-U.S. Migration: Disentangling the Underlying Social Mechanisms." *American Behavioral Scientist* 60: 1168–93.

Garland, David. 2001. *Mass Imprisonment: Social Causes and Consequences*. London: SAGE Books.

———. 2012a. *Punishment and Modern Society: A Study in Social Theory*. Chicago: University of Chicago Press.

———. 2012b. *The Culture of Control: Crime and Social Order in Contemporary Society*. Chicago: University of Chicago Press.

———. 2018. *Punishment and Welfare: A History of Penal Strategies*. New Orleans: Quid Pro Books.

Gelatt, Julia, and Heather Koball. 2014. "Immigrant Access to Health and Human Services." Urban Institute. https://www.urban.org/sites/default/files/publication/33551/2000012-Immigrant-Access-to-Health-and-Human-Services.pdf.

Gemmill, Alison, Ralph Catalano, Joan A. Casey, Deborah Karasek, Héctor E. Alcalá, Holly Elser, and Jacqueline M. Torres. 2019. "Association of Preterm Births among U.S. Latina Women with the 2016 Presidential Election." *JAMA Network Open* 2.

Giddens, Anthony. 2013 [1990]. *The Consequences of Modernity*. Hoboken, NJ: John Wiley & Sons.

Gilboy, Janet A. 1991. "Deciding Who Gets In: Decisionmaking by Immigration Inspectors." *Law and Society Review* 25: 571–99.

Gilliom, John. 2001. *Overseers of the Poor: Surveillance, Resistance, and the Limits of Privacy*. Chicago: University of Chicago Press.

Glaser, Barney G., and Anselm L. Strauss. 2009 [1967]. *The Discovery of Grounded Theory: Strategies for Qualitative Research*. New Brunswick, NJ: Transaction Books.

Gleeson, Shannon. 2010. "Labor Rights for All? The Role of Undocumented Immigrant Status for Worker Claims Making." *Law & Social Inquiry* 35: 561–602.

———. 2012. *Conflicting Commitments: The Politics of Enforcing Immigrant Worker Rights in San Jose and Houston*. Ithaca, NY: Cornell University Press.

———. 2016. *Precarious Claims: The Promise and Failure of Workplace Protections in the United States*. Oakland: University of California Press.

Gleeson, Shannon, and Roberto G. Gonzales. 2012. "When Do Papers Matter? An Institutional Analysis of Undocumented Life in the United States." *International Migration* 50: 1–19.

Goffman, Alice. 2009. "On the Run: Wanted Men in a Philadelphia Ghetto." *American Sociological Review* 74: 339–57.

Goffman, Erving. 1959. *The Presentation of Self in Everyday Life*. London: Harmondsworth London.

———. 1963. *Stigma: Notes on the Management of Spoiled Identity* New York: Simon and Schuster.

Golash-Boza, Tanya. 2015a. *Deported: Immigrant Policing, Disposable Labor and Global Capitalism*. New York: NYU Press.

———. 2015b. *Immigration Nation: Raids, Detentions, and Deportations in Post-9/11 America*. Abingdon, UK: Routledge.

Golash-Boza, Tanya, and Pierrette Hondagneu-Sotelo. 2013. "Latino Immigrant Men and the Deportation Crisis: A Gendered Racial Removal Program." *Latino Studies* 11: 271–92.

Gomberg-Muñoz, Ruth, and Laura Nussbaum-Barberena. 2011. "Is Immigration Policy Labor Policy?: Immigration Enforcement, Undocumented Workers, and the State." *Human Organization* 70: 366–75.

Gomberg-Muñoz, Ruth. 2015. "The Punishment/El Castigo: Undocumented Latinos and U.S. Immigration Processing." *Journal of Ethnic and Migration Studies* 41: 2235–52.

———. 2016. *Becoming Legal: Immigration Law and Mixed Status Families*. Oxford: Oxford University Press.

Gonzales, Roberto G. 2015. *Lives in Limbo: Undocumented and Coming of Age in America*. Oakland: University of California Press.

Gonzales, Roberto G., and Edelina M. Burciaga. 2018. "Segmented Pathways of Illegality: Reconciling the Coexistence of Master and Auxiliary Statuses in the Experiences of 1.5-Generation Undocumented Young Adults." *Ethnicities* 18: 178–91.

Gonzales, Roberto G., Veronica Terriquez, and Stephen P. Ruszczyk. 2014. "Becoming DACAmented: Assessing the Short-Term Benefits of Deferred Action for Childhood Arrivals (DACA)." *American Behavioral Scientist* 58: 1852–72.

Gonzalez, Gabriela, and Caitlin Patler. 2021. "The Educational Consequences of Parental Immigration Detention." *Sociological Perspectives* 64: 301–20.

Gonzalez-Barrera, Ana. 2017. "Mexican Lawful Immigrants among the Least Likely to Become U.S. Citizens." Pew Research Center. https://www.pewresearch.org/hispanic/2017/06/29/mexican-lawful-immigrants-among-least-likely-to-become-u-s-citizens/.

González-Barrera, Ana, Jens Manuel Krogstad, and Luis Noe-Bustamante. 2020. "Path to Legal Status for the Unauthorized Is Top Immigration Policy Goal for Hispanics in U.S." Pew Research Center. https://www.pewresearch.org/fact-tank/2020/02/11/path-to-legal-status-for-the-unauthorized-is-top-immigration-policy-goal-for-hispanics-in-u-s/.

Goodman, Adam. 2015. "Nation of Migrants, Historians of Migration." *Journal of American Ethnic History* 34: 7–16.

Goss, Stephen, Alice Wade, J. Patrick Skirvin, Michael Morris, K. Mark Bye, and Daniella Huston. 2013. "Effects of Unauthorized Immigration on the Actuarial Status of the Social Security Trust Funds." Social Security Administration. *Actuarial Note*.

Gowayed, Heba. 2022. *Refuge: How the State Shapes Human Potential*. Princeton, NJ: Princeton University Press.

Grace, Breanne L., Rajeev Bais, and Benjamin J. Roth. 2018. "The Violence of Uncertainty: Undermining Immigrant and Refugee health." *New England Journal of Medicine* 379: 904–5.

Griffith, Kati L. 2009. "U.S. Migrant Worker Law: The Interstices of Immigration Law and Labor and Employment Law." *Comparative Labor Lab & Policy Journal* 31: 125.

Griffith, Kati L., and Shannon Gleeson. 2019. "Trump's 'Immployment' Law Agenda: Intensifying Employment-Based Enforcement and Un-Authorizing the Authorized." *Southwestern Law Review* 48: 475.

Grissom, Brandi. 2015. "Dallas Sheriff Responds to Texas Governor: All ICE Detainers Honored This Year." *Dallas Morning News*, October 26.

Gulasekaram, Pratheepan, and Rose Cuison Villazor. 2009. "Sanctuary Policies & Immigration Federalism: A Dialectic Analysis." *Wayne Law Review* 55: 1683.

Gustafson, Kaaryn S. 2011. *Cheating Welfare: Public Assistance and the Criminalization of Poverty*. New York: NYU Press.

Hagan, Jacqueline. 1994. *Deciding to Be Legal: A Maya Community in Houston*. Philadelphia: Temple University Press.

———. 1998. "Social Networks, Gender, and Immigrant Incorporation: Resources and Constraints." *American Sociological Review*: 55–67.

Hagan, Jacqueline, Nichola Lowe, and Christian Quingla. 2011. "Skills on the Move: Rethinking the Relationship between Human Capital and Immigrant Economic Mobility." *Work and Occupations* 38: 149–78.

Hagan, Jacqueline, Nestor Rodriguez, Randy Capps, and Nika Kabiri. 2003. "The Effects of Recent Welfare and Immigration Reforms on Immigrants' Access to Health Care." *International Migration Review* 37: 444–63.

Haggerty, Kevin D., and Richard V. Ericson. 2000. "The Surveillant Assemblage." *The British Journal of Sociology* 51: 605–22.

Hainmueller, Jens, Duncan Lawrence, Justin Gest, Michael Hotard, Rey Koslowski, and David D. Laitin. 2018. "A Randomized Controlled Design Reveals Barriers to Citizenship for Low-Income Immigrants." *Proceedings of the National Academy of Sciences* 115: 939–44.

Hall, Matthew, and Emily Greenman. 2015. "The Occupational Cost of Being Illegal in the United States: Legal Status, Job Hazards, and Compensating Differentials." *International Migration Review* 49: 406–42.

Hall, Matthew, Emily Greenman, and George Farkas. 2010. "Legal Status and Wage Disparities for Mexican Immigrants." *Social Forces* 89: 491–513.

Hall, Matthew, Emily Greenman, and Youngmin Yi. 2019. "Job Mobility among Unauthorized Immigrant Workers." *Social Forces* 97: 999–1028.

Hall, Matthew, Kelly Musick, and Youngmin Yi. 2019. "Living Arrangements and Household Complexity among Undocumented Immigrants." *Population and Development Review*: 81–101.

Hallett, Miranda Cady. 2014. "Temporary Protection, Enduring Contradiction: The Contested and Contradictory Meanings of Temporary Immigration Status." *Law & Social Inquiry* 39: 621–42.

Hamermesh, Daniel S., Harley Frazis, and Jay Stewart. 2005. "Data Watch: The American Time Use Survey." *Journal of Economic Perspectives* 19: 221–32.

Hamermesh, Daniel S., and Stephen J. Trejo. 2013. "How Do Immigrants Spend Their Time? The Process of Assimilation." *Journal of Population Economics* 26: 507–30.

Hamilton, Erin R., Jo Mhairi Hale, and Robin Savinar. 2019. "Immigrant Legal Status and Health: Legal Status Disparities in Chronic Conditions and Musculoskeletal Pain among Mexican-Born Farm Workers in the United States." *Demography* 56: 1–24.

Hamilton, Erin R., Caitlin C. Patler, and Jo Mhairi Hale. 2019. "Growing Up without Status: The Integration of Children in Mixed-Status Families." *Sociology Compass* 13.

Hancock, Black Hawk, Bryan L. Sykes, and Anjuli Verma. 2018. "The Problem of 'Cameo Appearances' in Mixed-Methods Research: Implications for Twenty-First-Century Ethnography." *Sociological Perspectives* 61: 314–34.

Hanna, Mary, and Jeanne Batalova. 2021. "Immigrants from Asia in the United States." In *Migration Information Sources*. Migration Policy Institute, Washington D.C.

Hanson, Gordon H. 2006. "Illegal Migration from Mexico to the United States." *Journal of Economic Literature* 44: 869–924.

Harris, John R., and Michael P. Todaro. 1970. "Migration, Unemployment and Development: A Two-Sector Analysis." *American Economic Review* 60: 126–42.

Harvey, Hope. 2022. "When Mothers Can't 'Pay the Cost to Be the Boss': Roles and Identity within Doubled-Up Households." *Social Problems* 69: 261–81.

Harvey, Hope, Kelley Fong, Kathryn Edin, and Stefanie DeLuca. 2020. "Forever Homes and Temporary Stops: Housing Search Logics and Residential Selection." *Social Forces* 98: 1498–1523.

Haskins, Anna R., and Wade C. Jacobsen. 2017. "Schools as Surveilling Institutions? Paternal Incarceration, System Avoidance, and Parental Involvement in Schooling." *American Sociological Review* 82: 657–84.

Hausman, David K. 2020. "Sanctuary Policies Reduce Deportations without Increasing Crime." *Proceedings of the National Academy of Sciences* 117: 27262–67.

———. 2022. "The Unexamined Law of Deportation." *Georgetown Law Journal*.

Headworth, Spencer. 2020. "The Power of Second-Order Legal Consciousness: Authorities' Perceptions of 'Street Policy' and Welfare Fraud Enforcement." *Law & Society Review* 54: 320–53.

———. 2021. *Policing Welfare: Punitive Adversarialism in Public Assistance*. Chicago: University of Chicago Press.

Heinrich, Carolyn J. 2018. "Presidential Address: 'A Thousand Petty Fortresses': Administrative Burden in U.S. Immigration Policies and Its Consequences." *Journal of Policy Analysis and Management* 37: 211–39.

Herd, Pamela, and Donald P. Moynihan. 2019. *Administrative Burden: Policymaking by Other Means*. New York: Russell Sage Foundation.

Hernández, Kelly Lytle. 2010. *Migra!: A History of the U.S. Border Patrol*. Oakland: University of California Press.

Hernández León, Rubén, ed. 1999. *A La Aventura!: Jòvenes, Pandillas y Migración en La Conexión Monterrey-Houston*. Zamora, Mexico: El Colegio de Michoacán.

Hester, Torrie. 2015. "Deportability and the Carceral State." *The Journal of American History* 102: 141–51.

Hirota, Hidetaka. 2016. *Expelling the Poor: Atlantic Seaboard States and the Nineteenth-Century Origins of American Immigration Policy*. Oxford: Oxford University Press.

Hofferth, Sandra L., Sarah M. Flood, Matthew Sobek, and Daniel Backman. 2020. "American Time Use Survey Data Extract Builder: Version 2.8 [dataset]." College Park: University of Maryland.

Holmes, Seth M. 2006. "An Ethnographic Study of the Social Context of Migrant Health in the United States." *PLoS Med* 3.

———. 2013. *Fresh Fruit, Broken Bodies: Migrant Farmworkers in the United States.* Oakland: University of California Press.

Hondagneu-Sotelo, Pierrette. 2007. *Doméstica: Immigrant Workers Cleaning and Caring in the Shadows of Affluence.* Oakland: University of California Press.

Hong, Kari E., and Philip Torrey. 2019. "What Matter of Soram Got Wrong: 'Child Abuse' Crimes That May Trigger Deportation Are Constantly Evolving and Even Target Good Parents." *Amicus Harvard Civil Rights-Civil Liberties Law Review (CR-CL).*

Horton, Sarah B. 2016. "From 'Deportability' to 'Denounce-ability': New Forms of Labor Subordination in an Era of Governing Immigration through Crime." *PoLAR: Political and Legal Anthropology Review* 39: 312–26.

Horton, Sarah B., and Josiah Heyman. 2020. *Paper Trails: Migrants, Documents, and Legal Insecurity.* Durham, NC: Duke University Press.

Huang, Xiaoning, Neeraj Kaushal, and Julia Shu-Huah Wang. 2020. "What Explains the Gap in Welfare Use among Immigrants and Natives?" *Population Research and Policy Review* 40: 1–42.

Hudson, Kenneth. 2007. "The New Labor Market Segmentation: Labor Market Dualism in the New Economy." *Social Science Research* 36: 286–312.

Hughes, Cayce C. 2019. "From the Long Arm of the State to Eyes on the Street: How Poor African American Mothers Navigate Surveillance in the Social Safety Net." *Journal of Contemporary Ethnography* 48: 339–76.

———. 2021. "A House but Not a Home: How Surveillance in Subsidized Housing Exacerbates Poverty and Reinforces Marginalization." *Social Forces* 100: 293–315.

Hughes, Everett Cherrington. 1945. "Dilemmas and Contradictions of Status." *American Journal of Sociology* 50: 353–59.

———. 1956. "Social Role and the Division of Labor." *The Midwest Sociologist* 18 (2): 3–7.

Hull, Elizabeth. 1985. *Without Justice for All: The Constitutional Rights of Aliens.* Westport, CT: Greenwood.

Hull, Matthew S. 2012. "Documents and Bureaucracy." *Annual Review of Anthropology* 41: 251–67.

Human Rights Watch. 2009. "Forced Apart (by the Numbers): Non-Citizens Deported Mostly for Nonviolent Offenses."

Iceland, John. 2021. "Hardship among Immigrants and the Native-Born in the United States." *Demography* 58: 655–84.

Immigrant Defense Project. 2021. "Defending Immigrants Partnership." Accessed August 11, 2022. https://www.immigrantdefenseproject.org/defending-immigrants-partnership/.

Immigrant Legal Resource Center. 2012. "Understanding the Criminal Bars to the Deferred Action for Childhood Arrivals." Accessed July 4. https://www.ilrc.org/sites/default/files/documents/ilrc-2012-daca_chart.pdf.

———. 2018. "Non-LPR Cancellation of Removal: An Overview of Eligibility."

Immigrant Legal Resource Center. 2019. "Ending 287(g) in Texas."

——. 2020a. "Immigration Consequences of Texas Assault."

——. 2020b. "Update on Cancellation of Removal for Lawful Permanent Residents, INA § 240A(a)."

Internal Revenue Service. 2014. "Immigration and Taxation." *IRSNationwide.*

——. 2021. "Individual Taxpayer Identification Number (ITIN) Reminders for Tax Professionals." Accessed October 1. https://www.irs.gov/individuals/international -taxpayers/individual-taxpayer-identification-number-itin-reminders-for-tax -professionals.

IPUMS. https://www.ipums.org/.

Jacome, Elisa. 2018. "The Effect of Immigration Enforcement on Crime Reporting: Evidence from the Priority Enforcement Program." Princeton University, Department of Economics.

Jain, Eisha. 2015. "Prosecuting Collateral Consequences." *Georgetown Law Journal* 104: 1197.

——. 2019. "The Interior Structure of Immigratoin Enforcement." *University of Pennsylvania Law Review* 167: 1–50.

Jasso, Guillermina, and Mark R. Rosenzweig. 1986. "Family Reunification and the Immigration Multiplier: U.S. Immigration Law, Origin-Country Conditions, and the Reproduction of Immigrants." *Demography* 23: 291–311.

Jiménez, Tomás R, Deborah J. Schildkraut, Yuen J. Huo, and John F. Dovidio. 2021. *States of Belonging: Immigration Policies, Attitudes, and Inclusion.* New York: Russell Sage Foundation.

Jones-Correa, Michael. 2005. "Bringing Outsiders In: Questions of Immigrant Incorporation." In *The Politics of Democratic Inclusion*, edited by Christina Wolbrecht and Rodney E. Hero, 75–102. Philadelphia: Temple University Press.

Jones-Correa, Michael, and Els de Graauw. 2013. "The Illegality Trap: The Politics of Immigration & the Lens of Illegality." *Daedalus* 142: 185–98.

Jordan, Miriam. 2011. "'Silent Raids' Squeeze Illegal Workers." *Wall Street Journal.* https://www.wsj.com/articles/SB10001424052748704355304576214443126694256.

——. 2020. "Farmworkers, Mostly Undocumented, Become 'Essential'during Pandemic." *New York Times*, April 10. https://www.nytimes.com/2020/04/02/us /coronavirus-undocumented-immigrant-farmworkers-agriculture.html.

——. 2021. "Judge Rules DACA Is Unlawful and Suspends Applications." *New York Times*, September 27. https://www.nytimes.com/2021/07/16/us/court-daca -dreamers.html.

Joseph, Tiffany D. 2018. "The Growing Citizen-Noncitizen Divide: Life along the Documentation Status Continuum." Working Paper. Northeastern University.

Kaba, Mariame. 2021. *We Do This 'til We Free Us: Abolitionist Organizing and Transforming Justice.* Chicago: Haymarket Books.

Kalhan, Anil. 2014. "Immigration Surveillance." *Maryland Law Review* 74.

Kalleberg, Arne L., and Aage B. Sorensen. 1979. "The Sociology of Labor Markets." *Annual Review of Sociology* 5: 351–79.

Kamarck, Elaine. 2021. "Can Biden Pass Immigration Reform? History Says It Will Be Tough." The Brookings Institution.

Kandel, William A. 2018. "Permanent Legal Immigration to the United States: Policy Overview." Congressional Research Service.

Kanstroom, Daniel. 2007. *Deportation Nation: Outsiders in American History*. Cambridge, MA: Harvard University Press.

Kaushal, Neeraj, and Robert Kaestner. 2005. "Welfare Reform and Health Insurance of Immigrants." *Health Services Research* 40: 697–722.

Keith, Linda Camp, Jennifer S. Holmes, and Banks P. Miller. 2013. "Explaining the Divergence in Asylum Grant Rates among Immigration Judges: An Attitudinal and Cognitive Approach." *Law & Policy* 35 (4): 261–89.

Kenney, Liz, Karen Berberich, Corey Lazar, Michael Corradini, and Tania Sawczuk. 2021. "Advancing Universal Representation: A Toolkit." Vera Institute of Justice. https://www.vera.org/advancing-universal-representation-toolkit.

Kerwin, Donald, and Robert Warren. 2019. "Fixing What's Most Broken in the U.S. Immigration System: A Profile of the Family Members of U.S. Citizens and Lawful Permanent Residents Mired in Multiyear Backlogs." *Journal on Migration and Human Security* 7: 36–41.

———. 2020. "U.S. Foreign-Born Workers in the Global Pandemic: Essential and Marginalized." *Journal on Migration and Human Security* 8: 282–300.

Kim, Catherine Y. 2018. "The President's Immigration Courts." *Immigration & Nationality Law Review* 39: 315.

Kim, Jaeeun. 2018. "Migration-Facilitating Capital: A Bourdieusian Theory of International Migration." *Sociological Theory* 36 (3): 262–88.

———. 2019. "Ethnic Capital, Migration, and Citizenship: A Bourdieusian Perspective." *Ethnic and Racial Studies* 42 (3): 357–85.

———. 2022. "Between Sacred Gift and Profane Exchange: Identity Craft and Relational Work in Asylum Claims-Making on Religious Grounds." *Theory and Society* 51 (2): 303–33.

Kim, Soo Mee, and Aggie J. Yellow Horse. 2018. "Undocumented Asians, Left in the Shadows." *Contexts* 17: 70–71.

Kirk, David S., and Mauri Matsuda. 2011. "Legal Cynicism, Collective Efficacy, and the Ecology of Arrest." *Criminology* 49: 443–72.

Kirksey, J. Jacob, and Carolyn Sattin-Bajaj. 2021. "Immigration Arrests and Educational Impacts: Linking ICE Arrests to Declines in Achievement, Attendance, and School Climate and Safety in California." *AERA Open* 7.

Koball, Heather, Joseph Stinson, and Susi Martinez. 2021. "State Immigration Database." National Center for Children in Poverty.

Kocher, Austin. 2019. "Immigration Courts, Judicial Acceleration, and the Intensification of Immigration Enforcement in the First Year of the Trump Administration." In *Reading Donald Trump*, edited by Jeremy Kowalski, 83–101. New York: Springer.

Koh, Jennifer Lee. 2021. "Downsizing the Deportation State." *Harvard Law & Policy Review*.

Kossoudji, Sherrie A, and Deborah A. Cobb-Clark. 2002. "Coming out of the Shadows: Learning about Legal Status and Wages from the Legalized Population. *Journal of Labor Economics* 20: 598–628.

Kreisberg, A, Nicole. 2022. "Nativity Penalty, Legal Status Paradox: The Effects of Nativity and Legal Status Signals in the U.S. Labor Market." *Social Forces*, forthcoming.

Kwon, Andreas Dae Keun. 2016. "Defending Criminal(ized) 'Aliens' after *Padilla*: Toward a More Holistic Public Immigration Defense in the Era of Crimmigration." *UCLA Law Review* 63: 1034–1108.

Lageson, Sarah Esther. 2020. *Digital Punishment: Privacy, Stigma, and the Harms of Data-Driven Criminal Justice*. Oxford: Oxford University Press.

Lakhani, Sarah Morando. 2013. "Producing Immigrant Victims' 'Right' to Legal Status and the Management of Legal Uncertainty." *Law & Social Inquiry* 38: 442–73.

Lamont, Michèle. 1992. *Money, Morals, and Manners: The Culture of the French and the American Upper-Middle Class*. Chicago: University of Chicago Press.

Lamont, Michèle, Bo Yun Park, and Elena Ayala-Hurtado. 2017. "Trump's Electoral Speeches and His Appeal to the American White Working Class." *British Journal of Sociology* 68: S153–S80.

Lamont, Michèle, and Ann Swidler. 2014. "Methodological Pluralism and the Possibilities and Limits of Interviewing." *Qualitative Sociology* 37: 153–71.

Lanuza, Yader R., and Kristin Turney. 2020. "The Long Reach of Parental Incarceration: The Case of Institutional Engagement." *Social Science Research* 92: 102485.

Lapp, Kevin. 2012. "Reforming the Good Moral Character Requirement for U.S. Citizenship." *Indiana Law Journal* 87: 1571.

Lara-García, Francisco. 2021. "Components of Context: Respecifying the Role of Context in Migration Research." *International Migration Review*: 01979183211061506.

Lara-Millán, Armando. 2014. "Public Emergency Room Overcrowding in the Era of Mass Imprisonment." *American Sociological Review* 79: 866–87.

Lareau, Annette. 2021. *Listening to People: A Practical Guide to Interviewing, Participant Observation, Data Analysis, and Writing It All Up*. Chicago: University of Chicago Press.

Lareau, Annette, and Aliya Hamid Rao. 2016. "It's about the Depth of Your Data." *contexts*. https://contexts.org/blog/its-about-the-depth-of-your-data/.

Lasch, Christopher N. 2013. "Redress in State Postconviction Proceedings for Ineffective Crimmigration Counsel." *DePaul Law Review* 63: 959.

———. "Crimmigration and the Right to Counsel at the Border between Civil and Criminal Proceedings." *Immigration & Nationality Law Review* 35: 491.

Lasch, Christopher N., R. Linus Chan, Ingrid V. Eagly, Dina Francesca Haynes, Annie Lai, Elizabeth M. McCormick, and Juliet P. Stumpf. 2018. "Understanding Sanctuary Cities." *Boston College Law Review* 59: 1705–1773.

Le, Thai V., and Manuel Pastor. 2022. "Family Matters: Modeling Naturalization Propensities in the United States." *International Migration Review*: 01979183221112898.

Lee, Jennifer J. 2018. "Redefining the Legality of Undocumented Work." *California Law Review* 106 (5): 1617–56.

Lee, Tina. 2016. *Catching a Case: Inequality and Fear in New York City's Child Welfare System*. Rutgers University Press.

Lederman, Josh, and Julia Ainsley. 2022. "Biden White House preparing to take executive action to protect DACA 'Dreamers.'" NBC News, September 29. https://www.nbcnews.com/politics/immigration/biden-white-house-preparing-take-executive-action-protect-daca-dreamer-rcna49864.

Legomsky, Stephen H. 2006. "Deportation and the War on Independence." *Cornell Law Review* 91: 369–409.

Lemert, Edwin. 1967. *Human Deviance, Social Problems and Social Control*. Englewood Cliffs, NJ: Prentice-Hall.

Levesque, Christopher, Jack DeWaard, Linus Chan, Michele Garnett McKenzie, Kazumi Tsuchiya, Olivia Toles, Amy Lange, Kim Horner, Eric Ryu, and Elizabeth Heger Boyle. 2022. "Crimmigrating Narratives: Examining Third-Party Observations of U.S. Detained Immigration Court." *Law & Social Inquiry*: 1–30.

Lewis, Paul G., and S. Karthick Ramakrishnan. 2007. "Police Practices in Immigrant-Destination Cities: Political Control or Bureaucratic Professionalism?" *Urban Affairs Review* 42: 874–900.

Lichter, Daniel T., and Rukamalie Jayakody. 2002. "Welfare Reform: How Do We Measure Success?" *Annual Review of Sociology* 28: 117–41.

Lieberson, Stanley, and Freda B. Lynn. 2002. "Barking Up the Wrong Branch: Scientific Alternatives to the Current Model of Sociological Science." *Annual Review of Sociology* 28: 1–19.

Lind, Dara. 2018. "Denaturalization, Explained: How Trump Can Strip Immigrants of Their Citizenship." *Vox*. https://www.vox.com/2018/7/18/17561538/denaturalization-citizenship-task-force-janus.

Lipsky, Michael. 2010 [1980]. *Street-Level Bureaucracy: Dilemmas of the Individual in Public Service*. New York: Russell Sage Foundation.

Liptak, Adam, and Michael D. Shear. 2020. "Trump Can't Immediately End DACA, Supreme Court Rules." *New York Times*, June 18. https://www.nytimes.com/2020/06/18/us/trump-daca-supreme-court.html.

Lockhart III, James B. 2006. "Statement of James B. Lockhart III Before the House Committee on Ways and Means Subcommittee on Social Security Subcommittee on Oversight Hearing on Strengthening Employer Wage Reporting." House Committee On Ways And Means. Social Security Administration.

Logan, John R., and Richard D. Alba. 1993. "Locational Returns to Human Capital: Minority Access to Suburban Community Resources." *Demography* 30: 243–68.

Long, J. Scott, and Sarah A. Mustillo. 2018. "Using Predictions and Marginal Effects to Compare Groups in Regression Models for Binary Outcomes." *Sociological Methods & Research* 50: 1284–1320.

López, Jane Lilly. 2015. "'Impossible Families': Mixed-Citizenship Status Couples and the Law." *Law & Policy* 37: 93–118.

Lopez, William D. 2019. *Separated: Family and Community in the Aftermath of an Immigration Raid*. Baltimore, MD: John Hopkins University Press.

Lopez, William D., Daniel J. Kruger, Jorge Delva, Mikel Llanes, Charo Ledón, Adreanne Waller, Melanie Harner, Ramiro Martinez, Laura Sanders, and Margaret Harner. 2017. "Health Implications of an Immigration Raid: Findings from a Latino Community in the Midwestern United States." *Journal of Immigrant and Minority Health* 19: 702–08.

Low, Jacqueline. 2019. "A Pragmatic Definition of the Concept of Theoretical Saturation." *Sociological Focus* 52: 131–39.

Luker, Kristin. 2009. *Salsa Dancing into the Social Sciences*. Cambridge, MA: Harvard University Press.

Lynch, Laura, and Kate Voigt. 2020. "Restoring Integrity and Independence to America's Immigration Courts." American Immigration Lawyers Association.

Lyon, David. 2003. *Surveillance after September 11*. Malden, MA: Polity.

———. 2007. *Surveillance Studies: An Overview*. Malden, MA: Polity.

Macías-Rojas, Patrisia. 2016. *From Deportation to Prison*. New York: NYU Press.

Maggio, Christopher. 2021. "State-Level Immigration Legislation and Social Life: The Impact of the 'Show Me Your Papers' Laws." *Social Science Quarterly* 102: 1654–85.

Marienbach, Camille, and Andrew Wroe. 2017. "Continuity and Change: Immigration Worksite Enforcement in the Bush and Obama Administrations." In *The Obama Presidency and the Politics of Change*, edited by Edward Ashbee and John Dumbrell, 99–121. New York: Springer.

Markowitz, Peter L. 2010. "Deportation Is Different." *University of Pennsylvania Journal of Constitutional Law* 13: 1299–1361.

Marks, Dana Leigh. 2012. "Still a Legal Cinderella? Why the Immigration Courts Remain an Ill-Treated Stepchild Today." *Federal Lawyer* 59: 25–29.

Marrow, Helen B. 2009. "Immigrant Bureaucratic Incorporation: The Dual Roles of Professional Missions and Government Policies." *American Sociological Review* 74: 756–76.

———. 2011. *New Destination Dreaming: Immigration, Race, and Legal Status in the Rural American South*. Redwood City, CA: Stanford University Press.

———. 2012. "Deserving to a Point: Unauthorized Immigrants in San Francisco's Universal Access Healthcare Model." *Social Science & Medicine* 74: 846–54.

Marrow, Helen B., and Tiffany D. Joseph. 2015. "Excluded and Frozen Out: Unauthorised Immigrants' (Non)Access to Care after U.S. Health Care Reform." *Journal of Ethnic and Migration Studies* 41: 2253–73.

Martinez-Aranda, Mirian G. 2020. "Extended Punishment: Criminalising Immigrants through Surveillance Technology." *Journal of Ethnic and Migration Studies* 48: 74–91.

Martínez, Daniel E., Robin C. Reineke, Raquel Rubio-Goldsmith, and Bruce O. Parks. 2014. "Structural Violence and Migrant Deaths in Southern Arizona: Data from the Pima County Office of the Medical Examiner, 1990–2013." *Journal on Migration and Human Security* 2: 257–86.

Martínez, Daniel E., Jeremy Slack, and Ricardo Martínez-Schuldt. 2018. "The Rise of Mass Deportation in the United States." *The Handbook of Race, Ethnicity, Crime, and Justice*, edited by Ramiro Martínez Jr., Meghan E. Hollis, Jacob I. Stowell, 173–201.

Martínez Domínguez, Marlene. 2018. "Acceso y Uso de Tecnologías de la Información y Comunicación en México: Factores Determinantes." *PAAKAT: Revista de Tecnología y Sociedad* 8.

Martínez-Schuldt, Ricardo D., and Daniel E. Martínez. 2019. "Sanctuary Policies and City-Level Incidents of Violence, 1990 to 2010." *Justice Quarterly* 36: 567–93.

———. 2021. "Immigrant Sanctuary Policies and Crime-Reporting Behavior: A Multilevel Analysis of Reports of Crime Victimization to Law Enforcement, 1980 to 2004." *American Sociological Review* 86: 154–85.

Masferrer, Claudia, Erin R. Hamilton, and Nicole Denier. 2019. "Immigrants in Their Parental Homeland: Half a Million U.S.-Born Minors Settle throughout Mexico." *Demography* 56: 1453–61.

Massey, Douglas S. 1988. "Economic Development and International Migration in Comparative Perspective." *Population and Development Review* 14: 383–413.

——. 1990. "Social Structure, Household Strategies, and the Cumulative Causation of Migration." *Population Index* 56: 3–26.

——. 2007. *Categorically Unequal: The American Stratification System*. New York: Russell Sage Foundation.

Massey, Douglas S., Rafael Alarcón, Jorge Durand, and Humberto Gonzalez. 1990. *Return to Aztlan: The Social Process of International Migration from Western Mexico*. Oakland: University of California Press.

Massey, Douglas S., Joaquin Arango, Graeme Hugo, Ali Kouaouci, Adela Pellegrino, and J. Edward Taylor. 1993. "Theories of International Migration: A Review and Appraisal." *Population and Development Review* 19: 431–66.

Massey, Douglas S., and Katherine Bartley. 2005. "The Changing Legal Status Distribution of Immigrants: A Caution." *International Migration Review* 39: 469–84.

Massey, Douglas S., and Nancy Denton. 1993. *American Apartheid: Segregation and the Making of the Underclass*. Cambridge, MA: Harvard University Press.

Massey, Douglas S., and Nancy A. Denton. 1985. "Spatial Assimilation as a Socioeconomic Outcome." *American Sociological Review* 50: 94–106.

Massey, Douglas S., Jorge Durand, and Nolan J. Malone. 2002. *Beyond Smoke and Mirrors: Mexican Immigration in an Era of Economic Integration*. New York: Russell Sage Foundation.

Massey, Douglas S., Jorge Durand, and Karen A. Pren. 2014. "Border Enforcement and Return Migration by Documented and Undocumented Mexicans." *Journal of Ethnic and Migration Studies*: 1–26.

——. 2016. "Why Border Enforcement Backfired." *American Journal of Sociology* 121: 1557–1600.

Massey, Douglas S., and Kristin E. Espinosa. 1997. "What's Driving Mexico-U.S. Migration? A Theoretical, Empirical, and Policy Analysis." *American Journal of Sociology* 102: 939–99.

Massey, Douglas S., and Nolan Malone. 2002. "Pathways to Legal Immigration." *Population Research and Policy Review* 21: 473–504.

Massey, Douglas S., and Brendan P. Mullan. 1984. "Processes of Hispanic and Black Spatial Assimilation." *American Journal of Sociology* 89: 836–73.

Massey, Douglas S., and Karen A. Pren. 2012. "Unintended Consequences of U.S. Immigration Policy: Explaining the Post-1965 Surge from Latin America." *Population and Development Review* 38: 1–29.

Massey, Douglas S., and Fernando Riosmena. 2010. "Undocumented Migration from Latin America in an Era of Rising U.S. Enforcement." *The Annals of the American Academy of Political and Social Science* 630: 294–321.

Massey, Douglas S., and Rene M. Zenteno. 1999. "The Dynamics of Mass Migration." *Proceedings of the National Academy of Sciences* 96: 5328–35.

Mathema, Silva. 2017. "Keeping Families Together: Why All Americans Should Care about What Happens to Unauthorized Immigrants." Center for American Progress.

May, Reuben A. Buford, and Mary Pattillo-McCoy. 2000. "Do You See What I See? Examining a Collaborative Ethnography." *Qualitative Inquiry* 6: 65–87.

Mayorkas, Alejandro N. 2021. "Worksite Enforcement: The Strategy to Protect the American Labor Market, the Conditions of the American Worksite, and the Dignity of the Individual." Department of Homeland Security.

McCann, James A., and Michael Jones-Correa. 2020. *Holding Fast: Resilience and Civic Engagement among Latino Immigrants*. New York: Russell Sage Foundation.

McKenzie, David, and Hillel Rapoport. 2010. "Self-Selection Patterns in Mexico-U.S. Migration: The Role of Migration Networks." *Review of Economics and Statistics* 92: 811–21.

Mead, George Herbert. 1934. *Mind, Self and Society*. Chicago: University of Chicago Press.

Meissner, Doris, Donald M. Kerwin, Muzaffar Chishti, and Claire Bergeron. 2013. "Immigration Enforcement in the United States: The Rise of a Formidable Machinery." Migration Policy Institute.

Menjívar, Cecilia. 2006. "Liminal Legality: Salvadoran and Guatemalan Immigrants' Lives in the United States." *American Journal of Sociology* 111: 999–1037.

———. 2011. "The Power of the Law: Central Americans' Legality and Everyday Life in Phoenix, Arizona." *Latino Studies* 9: 377–95.

———. 2020. "Document Overseers, Enhanced Enforcement, and Racialized Contexts: Experiences of Latino/a Immigrants in Phoenix, Arizona." In *Paper Trails: Migrants, Documents, and Legal Insecurity*, edited by Sarah B. Horton and Josiah Heyman. Durham, NC: Duke University Press, 153–79.

Menjívar, Cecilia, and Leisy Abrego. 2012. "Legal Violence: Immigration Law and the Lives of Central American Immigrants." *American Journal of Sociology* 117: 1380–1421.

Menjívar, Cecilia, Leisy J. Abrego, and Leah C. Schmalzbauer. 2016. *Immigrant Families*. Malden, MA: Polity.

Menjívar, Cecilia, Andrea Gómez Cervantes, and Daniel Alvord. 2018. "The Expansion of 'Crimmigration,' Mass Detention, and Deportation." *Sociology Compass* 12.

Menjívar, Cecilia, and Daniel Kanstroom. 2013. *Constructing Immigrant 'Illegality': Critiques, Experiences, and Responses*. Cambridge, UK: Cambridge University Press.

Menjívar, Cecilia, and Sarah M. Lakhani. 2016. "Transformative Effects of Immigration Law: Immigrants' Personal and Social Metamorphoses through Regularization 1." *American Journal of Sociology* 121: 1818–55.

Menjívar, Cecilia, William Paul Simmons, Daniel Alvord, and Elizabeth Salerno Valdez. 2018. "Immigration Enforcement, the Racialization of Legal Status, and Perceptions of the Police: Latinos in Chicago, Los Angeles, Houston, and Phoenix in Comparative Perspective." *Du Bois Review: Social Science Research on Race* 15: 107–28.

Merton, Robert K. 1957. "Social Structure and Anomie." *American Sociological Review* 3: 672–82.

Michaud, Nicholas D. 2010. "From 287 (g) to SB1070: The Decline of the Federal Immigration Partnership and the Rise of State-Level Immigration Enforcement." *Arizona Law Review* 52: 1083.

Migration Policy Institute. 2018. "Profile of the Unauthorized Population: United States."

Miles, Matthew B., and A. Michael Huberman. 1994. *Qualitative Data Analysis: An Expanded Sourcebook*. Washington D.C.: Sage Publishing.

Milovanovic, Dragan. 1988. "Jailhouse Lawyers and Jailhouse Lawyering." *International Journal of the Sociology of Law* 16: 455–75.

Minian, Ana Raquel. 2018. *Undocumented Lives: The Untold Story of Mexican Migration*. Cambridge, MA: Harvard University Press.

Moinester, Margot. 2018. "Beyond the Border and into the Heartland: Spatial Pattern-ing of U.S. Immigration Detention." *Demography* 55: 1–47.

———. 2019. "A Look to the Interior: Trends in U.S. Immigration Removals by Criminal Conviction Type, Gender, and Region of Origin, Fiscal Years 2003–2015." *American Behavioral Scientist* 63: 1276–98.

Molina, Natalia. 2006. *Fit to Be Citizens?* Oakland: University of California Press.

Morawetz, Nancy. 2000. "Understanding the Impact of the 1996 Deportation Laws and the Limited Scope of Proposed Reforms." *Harvard Law Review* 113: 1936–62.

Morton, John. 2011. "Enforcement Actions at or Focused on Sensitive Locations." Department of Homeland Security.

Nagin, Daniel S., and Cody W. Telep. 2017. "Procedural Justice and Legal Compliance." *Annual Review of Law and Social Science* 13: 5–28.

National Conference of State Legislatures. 2015. "State E-Verify Action." Accessed October 1. https://www.ncsl.org/research/immigration/state-e-verify-action.aspx.

National Immigrant Justice Center. 2017. "Statement for the Record of the American-Arab Anti-Discrimination Committee, American Immigration Council, American Immigration Lawyers Association, HIAS, Human Rights First, Kids in Need of Defense (KIND), Lutheran Immigration and Refugee Service (LIRS), the National Immigrant Justice Center (NIJC), the National Immigration Law Center, North-ern Illinois Justice for Our Neighbors, Tahirih Justice Center, USC International Human Rights Clinic, U.S. Committee for Refugees and Immigrants (USCRI), Women's Refugee Commission." Chicago, IL.

National Immigration Law Center. 2020. "Worksite Immigration Raids." https://www.nilc.org/issues/workersrights/worksite-raids/.

Newell, Bryce Clayton, Ricardo Gomez, and Verónica Guajardo. 2017. "Sensors, Cam-eras, and the New 'Normal' in Clandestine Migration: How Undocumented Migrants Experience Surveillance at the U.S.-Mexico border." *Surveillance & Society* 15: 21–41.

Newton, Lina. 2018. "Immigration Politics by Proxy: State Agency in an Era of National Reluctance." *Journal of Ethnic and Migration Studies* 44 (12): 2086–2105.

Ngai, Mae M. 2004. *Impossible Subjects: Illegal Aliens and the Making of Modern America*. Princeton, NJ: Princeton University Press.

Nguyen, Mai Thi, and Hannah Gill. 2016. "Interior Immigration Enforcement: The Impacts of Expanding Local Law Enforcement Authority." *Urban Studies* 53: 302–23.

Núñez, Guillermina, and Josiah Heyman. 2007. "Entrapment Processes and Immigrant Communities in a Time of Heightened Border Vigilance." *Human Organization* 66: 354–65.

Obama, Barack. 2014. "Remarks by the President in Address to the Nation on Immi-gration." The White House. https://obamawhitehouse.archives.gov/the-press-office/2014/11/20/remarks-President-address-nation-immigration.

Obinna, Denise N. 2020. "Wait-Times, Visa Queues and Uncertainty: The Barriers to American Legal Migration." *Migration and Development* 9: 390–410.

Ogan, Christine, Rosemary Pennington, Olesya Venger, and Daniel Metz. 2018. "Who Drove the Discourse? News Coverage and Policy Framing of Immigrants and Refu-gees in the 2016 U.S. Presidential Election." *Communications* 43: 357–78.

Ordoñez, Franco. 2021. "As Biden Shifts on Immigration, Some Advocates See Him Giving Up Without a Fight." NPR, May 7.

Orrenius, Pia M., and Madeline Zavodny. 2005. "Self-Selection among Undocumented Immigrants from Mexico." *Journal of Development Economics* 78: 215–40.

———. 2009. "Do Immigrants Work in Riskier Jobs?" *Demography* 46: 535–51.

Ortiz, Robin, Dylan Farrell-Bryan, Gabriel Gutierrez, Courtney Boen, Vicky Tam, Katherine Yun, Atheendar S. Venkataramani, and Diana Montoya-Williams. 2021. "A Content Analysis of U.S. Sanctuary Immigration Policies: Implications for Research in Social Determinants of Health: Study Examines U.S. Sanctuary Immigration Policies and Implications for Social Determinants of Health Research." *Health Affairs* 40: 1145–53.

O'Leary, Brian M. 2012. "Operating Policies and Procedures Memorandum 12–01: Procedures on Handling Applications for Suspension/Cancellation in Nondetained Cases Once Numbers Are No Longer Available in a Fiscal Year." U.S. Department of Justice, Executive Office for Immigration Review.

Pager, Devah. 2008. *Marked: Race, Crime, and Finding Work in an Era of Mass Incarceration*. Chicago: University of Chicago Press.

Palloni, Alberto, Douglas S. Massey, Miguel Ceballos, Kristin Espinosa, and Michael Spittel. 2001. "Social Capital and International Migration: A Test Using Information on Family Networks." *American Journal of Sociology* 106: 1262–98.

Parreñas, Rhacel Salazar. 2021. "Discipline and Empower: The State Governance of Migrant Domestic Workers." *American Sociological Review* 86 (6): 1043–65.

Passel, Jeffrey S., and D'Vera Cohn. 2011. "Unauthorized Immigrant Population: National and State Trends, 2010." Pew Research Center.

———. 2014. "Unauthorized Immigrant Totals Rise in 7 States, Fall in 14: Decline in Those from Mexico Fuels Most State Decreases." Pew Research Center.

———. 2016. "Size of U.S. Unauthorized Immigrant Workforce Stable after the Great Recession." Pew Research Center.

———. 2019. "Mexicans Decline to Less Than Half the U.S. Unauthorized Immigrant Population for the First Time." Pew Research Center.

Patler, Caitlin, and Gabriela Gonzalez. 2020. "Compounded Vulnerability: The Consequences of Immigration Detention for Institutional Attachment and System Avoidance in Mixed-Immigration-Status Families." *Social Problems* 68: 886–902.

Patler, Caitlin, Erin Hamilton, Kelsey Meagher, and Robin Savinar. 2019. "Uncertainty about DACA May Undermine Its Positive Impact on Health for Recipients and Their Children." *Health Affairs* 38: 738–45.

Patler, Caitlin, and Whitney Laster Pirtle. 2018. "From Undocumented to Lawfully Present: Do Changes to Legal Status Impact Psychological Wellbeing among Latino Immigrant Young Adults?" *Social Science & Medicine* 199: 39–48.

Pedroza, Juan. 2019. "Where Immigration Enforcement Agreements Stalled: The Location of Local 287(g) Program Applications and Inquiries (2005–2012)." *SocArXiv*. January, 4.

Pedroza, Juan Manuel. 2022. "Making Noncitizens' Rights Real: Evidence from Immigration Scam Complaints." *Law & Policy* 44: 44–69.

Perreira, Krista M., and Juan M. Pedroza. 2019. "Policies of Exclusion: Implications for the Health of Immigrants and Their Children." *Annual Review of Public Health* 40: 147–66.

Pettigrew, Thomas F. 2015. "Samuel Stouffer and Relative Deprivation." *Social Psychology Quarterly* 78: 7–24.

Pew Research Center. 2021. "Most Americans Are Critical of Government's Handling of Aituation at U.S.-Mexico Border." Accessed August 11, 2022. https://www.pewresearch.org/politics/2021/05/03/most-americans-are-critical-of-governments-handling-of-situation-at-u-s-mexico-border/.

Pickett, Justin T. 2016. "On the Social Foundations for Crimmigration: Latino Threat and Support for Expanded Police Powers." *Journal of Quantitative Criminology* 32: 103–32.

Pierce, Sarah, and Jessica Bolter. 2020. "Dismantling and Reconstructing the U.S. Ommigration System." Migration Policy Institute. https://www.migrationpolicy.org/research/us-immigration-system-changes-trump-presidency.

Pindus, Nancy M., Randy Capps, Jerome Gallagher, Linda Giannarelli, Milda Saunders, and Robin Smith. 1998. "Income Support and Social Services for Low-Income People in Texas: Highlights from State Reports." Urban Institute. https://www.urban.org/sites/default/files/publication/66726/310173-Income-Support-and-Social-Services-for-Low-Income-People-in-Texas-Highlights-from-State-Reports.PDF.

Piore, Michael J. 1980. *Birds of Passage*. Cambridge, UK: Cambridge University Press.

Preston, Julia. 2010. "Illegal Workers Swept from Jobs in 'Silent Raids.' " *New York Times*. https://www.nytimes.com/2010/07/10/us/10enforce.html.

Prieto, Greg. 2018. *Immigrants under Threat: Risk and Resistance in Deportation Nation*. New York: NYU Press.

Provine, Doris Marie, Monica W. Varsanyi, Paul G. Lewis, and Scott H. Decker. 2016. *Policing Immigrants: Local Law Enforcement on the Front Lines*. Chicago: University of Chicago Press.

Pugh, J. Allison. 2013. "What Good Are Interviews for Thinking about Culture? Demystifying Interpretive Analysis." *American Journal of Cultural Sociology* 1: 42–68.

Ramji-Nogales, Jaya, Andrew I. Schoenholtz, and Philip G. Schrag. 2011. *Refugee Roulette: Disparities in Asylum Adjudication and Proposals for Reform*. New York: NYU Press.

Rathod, Jayesh M. 2013. "Distilling Americans: The Legacy of Prohibition on U.S. Immigration Law." *Houston Law Review* 51.

Ray, Shalini Bhargava. 2022. "Immigration Enforcement Priorities and Presidential Duty." *Lawfare*. https://www.lawfareblog.com/immigration-enforcement-priorities-and-presidential-duty.

Ray, Victor, Pamela Herd, and Donald Moynihan. 2020. "Racialized Burdens: Applying Racialized Organization Theory to the Administrative State." *Journal of Public Administration Research and Theory*.

Reed, Isaac Ariail. 2010. "Epistemology Contextualized: Social-Scientific Knowledge in a Postpositivist Era." *Sociological Theory* 28: 20–39.

Reich, Jennifer A. 2012. *Fixing Families: Parents, Power, and the Child Welfare System*. Routledge.

Reyes, Victoria. 2020. "Ethnographic Toolkit: Strategic Positionality and Researchers' Visible and Invisible Tools in Field Research." *Ethnography* 21: 220–40.

Rissing, Ben A., and Emilio J. Castilla. 2014. "House of Green Cards Statistical or Preference-Based Inequality in the Employment of Foreign Nationals." *American Sociological Review* 79: 1226–55.

Ro, Annie, Tim A. Bruckner, and Lauren Duquette-Rury. 2020. "Immigrant Apprehensions and Birth Outcomes: Evidence from California Birth Records 2008-2015." *Social Science & Medicine* 249.

Roberts, Dorothy. 2009. *Shattered Bonds: The Color of Child Welfare.* Hachette UK.

Robillard, Kevin, and Daniel Marans. 2018. "Abolishing ICE Isn't Very Popular (Yet)." *Huffington Post.* https://www.huffpost.com/entry/abolishing-ice-not-popular-yet_n_5b3a3916e4b08c3a8f6c803d.

Rodriguez, Cassaundra. 2016. "Experiencing 'Illegality' as a Family? Immigration Enforcement, Social Policies, and Discourses Targeting Mexican Mixed-Status Families." *Sociology Compass* 10: 706–17.

Rodriguez, Nestor, and Jacqueline Maria Hagan. 2004. "Fractured Families and Communities: Effects of Immigration Reform in Texas, Mexico, and El Salvador." *Latino Studies* 2: 328–51.

Rogerson, Richard, Robert Shimer, and Randall Wright. 2005. "Search-Theoretic Models of the Labor Market: A Survey." *Journal of Economic Literature* 43: 959–88.

Romero, Mary. 2008. "The Inclusion of Citizenship Status in Intersectionality: What Immigration Raids Tell Us about Mixed-Status Families, the State and Assimilation." *International Journal of Sociology of the Family*: 131–52.

Rosales, Rocío. 2020. *Fruteros: Street Vending, Illegality, and Ethnic Community in Los Angeles.* Oakland: University of California Press.

Rose, Nikolas, Pat O'Malley, and Mariana Valverde. 2006. "Governmentality." *Annual Review of Law and Social Science* 2: 83–104.

Rosen, Eva. 2017. "Horizontal Immobility: How Narratives of Neighborhood Violence Shape Housing Decisions." *American Sociological Review* 82: 270–96.

Rottman, Andy J., Christopher J. Fariss, and Steven C. Poe. 2009. "The Path to Asylum in the U.S. and the Determinants for Who Gets in and Why." *International Migration Review* 43 (1): 3–34.

Runciman, Walter Garrison. 1966. *Relative Deprivation and Social Justice: A Study of Attitudes to Social Inequality in Twentieth-Century England.* Berkeley: University of California Press Berkeley.

Ruszczyk, Stephen P. 2021. "Moral Career of Migrant Il/legality: Undocumented Male Youths in New York City and Paris Negotiating Deportability and Regularizability." *Law & Society Review* 55: 496–519.

Ryo, Emily. 2013. "Deciding to Cross Norms and Economics of Unauthorized Migration." *American Sociological Review* 78: 574–603.

———. 2015. "Less Enforcement, More Compliance." *UCLA Law Review.*

———. 2016. "Detained: A Study of Immigration Bond Hearings." *Law & Society Review* 50: 117–53.

———. 2018a. "Predicting Danger in Immigration Courts. *Law & Social Inquiry.*

———. 2018b. "Representing Immigrants: The Role of Lawyers in Immigration Bond Hearings." *Law & Society Review* 52: 503–31.

———. 2021. "The Unintended Consequences of U.S. Immigration Enforcement Policies." *Proceedings of the National Academy of Sciences* 118.

Ryo, Emily, and Ian Peacock. 2019. "Denying Citizenship: Immigration Enforcement and Citizenship Rights in the United States." *Studies in Law, Politics, and Society.*

Samari, Goleen, Ralph Catalano, Héctor E. Alcalá, and Alison Gemmill. 2020. "The Muslim Ban and Preterm Birth: Analysis of U.S. Vital Statistics Data from 2009 to 2018." *Social Science & Medicine* 265: 113544.

Sampson, Robert J., and Dawn Jeglum Bartusch. 1998. "Legal Cynicism and (Subcultural?) Tolerance of Deviance: The Neighborhood Context of Racial Differences." *Law and Society Review* 32: 777–804.

Sanchez, Amairini, Michele Cadigan, Dayo Abels-Sullivan, and Bryan L. Sykes. 2022. "Punishing Immigrants: The Consequences of Monetary Sanctions in the Crimmigration System." *RSF: The Russell Sage Foundation Journal of the Social Sciences* 8: 76–97.

Santellano, Karina. 2022. "Fieldwork during a Pandemic: Navigating Personal Grief and Practicing Researcher Flexibility." *Latino Studies*: 1–7.

Santos, Carlos E., Cecilia Menjívar, Rachel A. VanDaalen, Olga Kornienko, Kimberly A. Updegraff, and Samantha Cruz. 2017. "Awareness of Arizona's Immigration Law SB1070 Predicts Classroom Behavioural Problems among Latino Youths during Early Adolescence." *Ethnic and Racial Studies*: 1–19.

Sassen, Saskia. 1988. *The Mobility of Capital and Labor*. Cambridge, UK: Cambridge University Press.

———. 2013. *The Global City*. Princeton, NJ: Princeton University Press.

Schewel, Kerilyn. 2020. "Understanding Immobility: Moving beyond the Mobility Bias in Migration Studies." *International Migration Review* 54: 328–55.

Schmalzbauer, Leah. 2014. *The Last Best Place: Gender, Family, and Migration in the New West*. Redwood City, CA: Stanford University Press.

Scott, James C. 2008. *Seeing Like a State*. New Haven, CT: Yale University Press.

Sen, Amartya. 1983. "Poor, Relatively Speaking." *Oxford Economic Papers* 35: 153–69.

———. 1999. "Commodities and Capabilities." Oxford: Oxford University Press.

Shear, Michael D., and Julie Hirschfeld Davis. 2017. "Trump Moves to End DACA and Calls on Congress to Act." *New York Times*, September 5. https://www.nytimes.com/2017/09/05/us/politics/trump-daca-dreamers-immigration.html.

Shelley, Kristina J. 2005. "Developing the American Time Use Survey Activity Classification System." *Monthly Labor Review* 128: 3.

Singer, Audrey. 2004. "Welfare Reform and Immigrants." In *Immigrants, Welfare Reform, and the Poverty of Policy*, edited by Philip Kretsedemas and Ana Aparicio, 21–34.

Sjaastad, Larry A. 1962. "The Costs and Returns of Human Migration." *Journal of Political Economy* 70: 80–93.

Small, Deborah. 2014. "Cause for Trepidation: Libertarians' Newfound Concern for Prison Reform." *Salon*, January 26. https://www.salon.com/2014/03/22/cause_for_trepidation_libertarians_newfound_concern_for_prison_reform/.

Small, Mario Luis. 2009. "'How Many Cases Do I Need?': On Science and the Logic of Case Selection in Field-Based Research." *Ethnography* 10: 5–38.

———. 2011. "How to Conduct a Mixed Methods Study: Recent Trends in a Rapidly Growing Literature." *Annual Review of Sociology* 37: 57–86.

———. 2013. "Causal Thinking and Ethnographic Research." *American Journal of Sociology* 119: 597–601.

Small, Mario Luis, and Jessica McCrory Calarco. 2022. *Qualitative Literacy: A Guide to Evaluating Ethnographic and Field Research*. Oakland: University of California Press.

Somashekhar, Mahesh. 2022. "The Business Ownership Patterns of Undocumented Immigrants in the United States: An Exploratory Study." *Social Currents*: 1–24.

Song, Sarah, and Irene Bloemraad. 2022. "Immigrant Legalization: A Dilemma between Justice and the Rule of Law." *Migration Studies* 10(3): 484–509.

Soss, Joe. 2005. "Making Clients and Citizens: Welfare Policy as a Source of Status, Belief, and Action." In *Deserving and Entitled: Social Constructions and Public Policy*, edited by Anne L. Schneider and Helen M. Ingram, 291–328.

Soss, Joe, Richard C. Fording, Sanford F. Schram, and Sanford Schram. 2011. *Disciplining the Poor: Neoliberal Paternalism and the Persistent Power of Race*. Chicago: University of Chicago Press.

Soto, Gabriella, and Daniel E. Martínez. 2018. "The Geography of Migrant Death: Implications for Policy and Forensic Science." In *Sociopolitics of migrant death and repatriation: Perspectives from Forensic Science*, edited by Krista E. Latham and Alyson J. O'Daniel, 67–82. New York: Springer.

Spence, Cody, James D. Bachmeier, Claire E. Altman, and Christal Hamilton. 2020. "The Association between Legal Status and Poverty among Immigrants: A Methodological Caution." *Demography* 57.

Spring, Amy, Elizabeth Ackert, Kyle Crowder, and Scott J. South. 2017. "Influence of Proximity to Kin on Residential Mobility and Destination Choice: Examining Local Movers in Metropolitan Areas." *Demography* 54: 1277–304.

Stark, Oded, and David E. Bloom. 1985. "The New Economics of Labor Migration." *American Economic Review* 75: 173–78.

Stark, Oded, and David Levhari. 1982. "On Migration and Risk in LDCs." *Economic Development and Cultural Change* 31: 191–96.

Stark, Oded, and J. Edward Taylor. 1991. "Migration Incentives, Migration Types: The Role of Relative Deprivation." *Economic Journal* 101: 1163–78.

Stark, Oded, J. Edward Taylor, and Shlomo Yitzhaki. 1988. "Migration, Remittances and Inequality: A Sensitivity Analysis Using the Extended Gini Index." *Journal of Development Economics* 28: 309–22.

Steinberg, Robin. 2013. "Heeding Gideon's Call in the Twenty-First Century: Holistic Defense and the New Public Defense Paradigm." *Washington & Lee Law Review* 70: 961–1018.

Stevens, Jacqueline. 2011. "U.S. Government Unlawfully Detaining and Deporting U.S. Citizens as Aliens." *Virginia Journal of Social Policy and the Law* 18: 606–720.

Stewart, Eric A., Eric P. Baumer, Rod K. Brunson, and Ronald L. Simons. 2009. "Neighborhood Racial Context and Perceptions of Police-Based Racial Discrimination among Black Youth." *Criminology* 47: 847–87.

Stouffer, Samuel A., Edward A. Suchman, Leland C. DeVinney, Shirley A. Star, and Robin M. Williams Jr. 1949. *The American Soldier: Adjustment during Army Life*. Princeton, NJ: Princeton University Press.

Street, Alex, Michael Jones-Correa, and Chris Zepeda-Millán. 2017. "Political Effects of Having Undocumented Parents." *Political Research Quarterly* 70: 818–32.

Stryker, Sheldon. 2008. "From Mead to a Structural Symbolic Interactionism and Beyond." *Annual Review of Sociology* 34 (1): 15–31.

Stryker, Sheldon, and Anne Statham Macke. 1978. "Status Inconsistency and Role Conflict." *Annual Review of Sociology* 4: 57–90.

Stuart, Forrest D. 2016. *Down, Out, and Under Arrest: Policing and Everyday Life in Skid Row*. Chicago: University of Chicago Press.

Stumpf, Juliet P. 2006. "The Crimmigration Crisis: Immigrants, Crime, and Sovereign Power." *American University Law Review*, 56: 367–419.

Talukdar, Debabrata, and Dinesh K. Gauri. 2011. "Home Internet Access and Usage in the USA: Trends in the Socio-Economic Digital Divide." *Communications of the Association for Information Systems*, 28.

Taylor, J. Edward. 1987. "Undocumented Mexico—U.S. Migration and the Returns to Households in Rural Mexico." *American Journal of Agricultural Economics* 69: 626–38.

Theodore, Nik, and Robert Habans. 2016. "Policing Immigrant Communities: Latino Perceptions of Police Involvement in Immigration Enforcement." *Journal of Ethnic and Migration Studies* 42: 970–88.

Tilly, Charles. 1992. *Coercion, Capital, and European States, AD 990–1992*. Hoboken, NJ: Wiley-Blackwell.

———. 1999. *Durable Inequality*. Oakland: University of California Press.

———. 2003. "Changing Forms of Inequality." *Sociological Theory* 21: 31–36.

Torche, Florencia, and Catherine Sirois. 2018. "Exposure to Restrictive Immigration Law in Arizona Reduces Birth Weight of Latina Immigrant Women." *American Journal of Epidemiology* 188: 24–33.

Townsend, Peter. 1979. *Poverty in the United Kingdom: A Survey of Household Resources and Standards of Living*. Oakland: University of California Press.

———. 1985. "A Sociological Approach to the Measurement of Poverty—A Rejoinder to Professor Amartya Sen. *Oxford Economic Papers* 37: 659–68.

TRAC Immigration. 2021. "Immigration Court Backlog Tool, Pending Cases and Length of Wait in Immigration Courts." Syracuse University. Accessed December 4. https:// trac.syr.edu/phptools/immigration/court_backlog/court_proctime_outcome.php.

Trump, Donald J. 2015. "Donald Trump's Presidential Announcement Speech." In *Time Magazine*. https://time.com/3923128/donald-trump-announcement-speech/.

Tyler, Tom. 2017. "Procedural Justice and Policing: A Rush to Judgment?" *Annual Review of Law and Social Science* 13: 29–53.

———. 2021. *Why People Obey the Law*. Princeton, NJ: Princeton University Press.

Tyler, Tom R., and Yuen J Huo. 2002. *Trust in the Law: Encouraging Public Cooperation with the Police and Courts*. New York: Russell Sage Foundation.

U.S. Citizenship and Immigration Services. 2011. "Revised Guidance for the Referral of Cases and Issuance of Notices to Appear (NTAs) in Cases Involving Inadmissible and Removable Aliens." U.S. Department of Homeland Security.

———. 2019. "Interviewing: Introduction to the Non-Adversarial Interview." U.S. Department of Homeland Security. Refugee, Asylum, and International Operations Directorate.

———. 2021. "Instructions for Consideration of Deferred Action for Childhood Arrivals." U.S. Department of Homeland Security. Accessed December 4. https://www .uscis.gov/sites/default/files/document/forms/i-821dinstr.pdf.

———. n.d. "6.1 Lawful Permanent Residents (LPR)." U.S. Department of Homeland Security. Accessed December 4. https://www.uscis.gov/i-9-central/form-i-9 -resources/handbook-for-employers-m-274/60-evidence-of-status-for-certain -categories/61-lawful-permanent-residents-lpr.

———. n.d. "Explore My Options." U.S. Department of Homeland Security. Accessed December 4. https://www.uscis.gov/forms/explore-my-options.

U.S. Customs and Border Protection. 2019. "Southwest Border Deaths by Fiscal Year." United States Border Patrol, U.S. Customs and Border Protection.

U.S. Department of Health and Human Services. 2015. "Annual Update of the HHS Poverty Guidelines." 2015. *Federal Register* 80: 3236–37.

U.S. Department of Homeland Security. 2020. "Yearbook of Immigration Statistics: Table 39."

U.S. Department of State. n.d. "Immigrant Visa Process." Accessed July 4, 2022. https:// travel.state.gov/content/travel/en/us-visas/immigrate/the-immigrant-visa-process /step-1-submit-a-petition.html.

———. 2020. "Annual Report of Immigrant Visa Applicants in the Family-Sponsored and Employment-Based preferences Registered at the National Visa Center as of November 1, 2020."

———. 2021a. "Employment-Based Immigrant Visas."

———. 2021b. "USEmbassy.gov."

———. 2021c. "Visa Appointment Wait Times."

U.S. Immigration and Customs Enforcement. 2018. "ICE Worksite Enforcement Investigations in FY2018 Surge." https://www.ice.gov/features/worksite-enforcement.

———. 2020. "Fiscal Year 2020 ICE Enforcement and Removal Operations Report."

———. n.d. "ICE FOIA Tasking for 2017-ICFO-33429." U.S. Department of Homeland Security.

U.S. Office of General Accountability. 2020. "Employment-related Identity Fraud: Improved Collaboration and Other Actions Would Help IRS and SSA Address Risks." In *Report to the Committee on Finance, U.S. Senate*, U.S. General Accountability Office.

Valdez, Zulema, and Tanya Golash-Boza. 2018. "Master Status or Intersectional Identity? Undocumented Students' Sense of Belonging on a College Campus." *Identities* 27: 1–19.

Valverde, Miriam. 2019. "Biden Says Obama Ended Workplace Raids of Immigrants. That's Half True." Poynter Institute, Accessed October 1. https://www.politifact .com/factchecks/2019/sep/18/joe-biden/biden-says-obama-ended-workplace -raids-immigrants/.

Van Hook, Jennifer. 2003. "Welfare Reform's Chilling Effects on Noncitizens: Changes in Noncitizen Welfare Recipiency or Shifts in Citizenship Status?" *Social Science Quarterly* 84: 613–31.

Van Hook, Jennifer, James D. Bachmeier, Donna L. Coffman, and Ofer Harel. 2015. "Can We Spin Straw into Gold? An Evaluation of Immigrant Legal Status Imputation Approaches." *Demography* 52: 329–54.

Van Hook, Jennifer, and Kelly Stamper Balistreri. 2006. "Ineligible Parents, Eligible Children: Food Stamps Receipt, Allotments, and Food Insecurity among Children of Immigrants." *Social Science Research* 35: 228–51.

Van Hook, Jennifer, Jennifer E. Glick, and Frank D. Bean. 1999. "Public Assistance Receipt among Immigrants and Natives: How the Unit of Analysis Affects Research Findings." *Demography* 36: 111–20.

Van Natta, Meredith. 2019. "First Do No Harm: Medical Legal Violence and Immigrant Health in Coral County, USA." *Social Science & Medicine* 235.

Vargas, Edward D. 2015. "Immigration Enforcement and Mixed-Status Families: The Effects of Risk of Deportation on Medicaid Use." *Children and Youth Services Review* 57: 83–89.

Vargas, Edward D., and Maureen A. Pirog. 2016. "Mixed-Status Families and WIC Uptake: The Effects of Risk of Deportation on Program Use." *Social Science Quarterly* 97: 555–72.

Varsanyi, Monica W. 2007. "Documenting Undocumented Migrants: The Matriculas Consulares as Neoliberal Local Membership." *Geopolitics* 12: 299–319.

Varsanyi, Monica W., Paul G. Lewis, Doris Marie Provine, and Scott Decker. 2012. "A Multilayered Jurisdictional Patchwork: Immigration Federalism in the United States." *Law & Policy* 34: 138–58.

Vasquez-Tokos, Jessica. 2017. "'If I Can Offer You Some Advice': Rapport and Data Collection in Interviews between Adults of Different Ages." *Symbolic Interaction* 40: 463–82.

Vernice, Nicholas A., Nicola M. Pereira, Anson Wang, Michelle Demetres, and Lisa V. Adams. 2020. "The Adverse Health Effects of Punitive Immigrant Policies in the United States: A Systematic Review. *PloS One* 15.

Viladrich, Anahí. 2012. "Beyond Welfare Reform: Reframing Undocumented Immigrants' Entitlement to Health Care in the United States, a Critical Review." *Social Science & Medicine* 74: 822–29.

Villarreal, Andrés. 2014. "Explaining the Decline in Mexico-U.S. Migration: The Effect of the Great Recession." *Demography* 51: 2203–28.

Warren, Robert, and Donald Kerwin. 2015. "The U.S. Eligible-to-Naturalize Population: Detailed Social and Economic Characteristics." *Journal on Migration & Human Security* 3: 306.

———. 2017. "The 2,000 Mile Wall in Search of a Purpose: Since 2007 Visa Overstays Have Outnumbered Undocumented Border Crossers by a Half Million." *Journal on Migration and Human Security* 5: 124–36.

Wasem, Ruth Ellen. 2020. "Welcoming Communities: Immigrant Incorporation in Dallas, Texas." Policy Research Project 219. Lyndon B. Johnson School of Public Affairs at the University of Texas at Austin.

Waters, Mary C., and Philip Kasinitz. 2015. "The War on Crime and the War on Immigrants: Racial and Legal Exclusion in the Twenty-First-Century United States." In *Fear, Anxiety, and National Identity: Immigration and Belonging in North America and Western Europe*, edited by Nancy Foner and Patrick Simon. New York: Russell Sage Foundation.

Watkins-Hayes, Celeste. 2009. *The New Welfare Bureaucrats: Entanglements of Race, Class, and Policy Reform*. Chicago: University of Chicago Press.

Watson, Tara. 2010. "Inside the Refrigerator: Immigration Enforcement and Chilling Effects in Medicaid Participation." National Bureau of Economic Research.

Weil, Patrick. 2012. *The Sovereign Citizen: Denaturalization and the Origins of the American Republic*. Philadelphia: University of Pennsylvania Press.

Weiss, Robert S. 1995. *Learning from Strangers: The Art and Method of Qualitative Interview Studies*. New York: Simon and Schuster.

Welcoming America. 2021. "Welcoming America." Accessed August 26. https://welcomingamerica.org/about/.

White, Ariel. 2014. "When Threat Mobilizes: Immigration Enforcement and Latino Voter Turnout." *Political Behavior* 38: 355–82.

White House. 2015. "Modernizing & Streamlining Our Legal Immigration System for the 21st Century." https://web.archive.org/web/20150906123446/https://www.whitehouse.gov/sites/default/files/docs/final_visa_modernization_report1.pdf.

———. 2021. "President Biden Sends Immigration Bill to Congress as Part of His Commitment to Modernize our Immigration System." Press Release. January 20.

Wildeman, Christopher, Frank R. Edwards, and Sara Wakefield. 2020. "The Cumulative Prevalence of Termination of Parental Rights for U.S. Children, 2000–2016." *Child Maltreatment* 25 (1): 32–42.

Williamson, Abigail Fisher. 2018. *Welcoming New Americans?: Local Governments and Immigrant Incorporation.* Chicago: University of Chicago Press.

Williamson, Vanessa S. 2017. *Read My Lips: Why Americans Are Proud to Pay Taxes.* Princeton, NJ: Princeton University Press.

Wilmers, Nathan, and William Kimball. 2021. "How Internal Hiring Affects Occupational Stratification." *Social Forces* 101: 111–49.

Winders, Jamie. 2016. "Immigration and the 2016 Election." *Southeastern Geographer* 56: 291–96.

Wishnie, Michael J. 2007. "Prohibiting the Employment of Unauthorized Immigrants: The Experiment Fails." *University of Chicago Legal Forum* 2007: 193–217.

Wolff, Jonathan. 2017. "Forms of Differential Social Inclusion." *Social Philosophy and Policy* 34: 164–85.

Wong, Tom K., S. Deborah Kang, Carolina Valdivia, Josefina Espino, Michelle Gonzalez, and Elia Peralta. 2021. "How Interior Immigration Enforcement Affects Trust in Law Enforcement." *Perspectives on Politics* 19: 357–70.

Wong, Tom K., Karina Shklyan, Anna Isorena, and Stephanie Peng. 2019. "The Impact of Interior Immigration Enforcement on the Day-to-Day Behaviors of Undocumented Immigrants." U.S. Immigration Policy Center: 1–27.

Wong, Tom K., Karina Shklyan, and Andrea Silva. 2021. "The Effect of Intergovernmental Policy Conflict on Immigrants' Behavior: Insights from a Survey Experiment in California." *Publius: The Journal of Federalism* 52: 107–32.

Yoshikawa, Hirokazu. 2011. *Immigrants Raising Citizens: Undocumented Parents and Their Young Children.* New York: Russell Sage Foundation.

Yoshikawa, Hirokazu, Christina Weiland, Kjersti Ulvestad, Krista M. Perreira, and Robert Crosnoe. 2014. "Improving Access of Low-Income Immigrant Families to Health and Human Services." Urban Institute.

Znaniecki, Florian. 1965. *Social Relations and Social Roles: The Unfinished Systematic Sociology.* Ardent Media.

Zong, Jie, Ariel G. Ruiz Soto, Jeanne Batalova, Julia Gelatt, and Randy Capps. 2017. "A Profile of Current DACA Recipients by Education, Industry, and Occupation." Migration Policy Institute.

Page numbers followed by t or f indicate a table or figure.

A NOTE ON THE TYPE

———◆———

THIS BOOK has been composed in Miller, a Scotch Roman typeface designed by Matthew Carter and first released by Font Bureau in 1997. It resembles Monticello, the typeface developed for The Papers of Thomas Jefferson in the 1940s by C. H. Griffith and P. J. Conkwright and reinterpreted in digital form by Carter in 2003.

Pleasant Jefferson ("P. J.") Conkwright (1905–1986) was Typographer at Princeton University Press from 1939 to 1970. He was an acclaimed book designer and AIGA Medalist.